Franck BERGEROT

JAZZ

Franck BERGEROT

JAZZ

CHAMBERS

Translator
Richard Elliott

Editor
Stuart Fortey

Consultant
Kenny Mathieson

Series editor
Camilla Rockwood

Publishing manager
Patrick White

Prepress
David Reid

Proofreader
Ian Howe

Originally published by Larousse as *Le Jazz dans tous ses états* by Franck Bergerot

© Larousse 2005

English-language edition
© Chambers Harrap Publishers Ltd 2006

ISBN-10 0550 10271 X
ISBN-13 978 0550 10271 3

Cover image: John Coltrane © Rue des Archives

Typeset by Chambers Harrap Publishers Ltd, Edinburgh
Printed by Mame, France

CONTENTS

SWING: THE FIRST CLASSIC JAZZ (1930-1939)

BEBOP: THE FIRST AVANT-GARDE (1940-1948)

COOL: WHITE JAZZ TAKES THE INITIATIVE

HARD BOP: BLACK JAZZ FIGHTS BACK (1954-1959)

FREE JAZZ: THE TASTE OF FREEDOM (1960-1968)

EXPLOSION AND FUSION (1968-1979)

END OF THE CENTURY (1980-2000)

INTRODUCTION

J azz has come to be seen as the defining music of the 20th century –
the century in which it was born and developed. Its development
is not unlike that of classical music. However, whereas classical
music has taken half a millennium to get to where it is now, jazz has
developed with remarkable speed. In the 1980s, the pace of this
development started to slow down, but not before it had given rise to a
contemporary scene that is now richer and more diverse than ever. Some
of the more recent figures in a line of pioneers extending from Jelly Roll
Morton to Albert Ayler have stopped describing their music as jazz
altogether, and the tradition of fusion – from Duke Ellington to Weather
Report – has reached the point where jazz is now only progressing
sideways, combining different strands from its own history with external
styles and influences. While it may be disconcerting to see musicians
throughout the world appropriating what was initially the property of the
black American community, the creators of the genre can, at the
beginning of the 21st century, claim to have founded an important lineage
among the artistic elite. Their inheritance continues to give meaning to a
range of musical forms that are still grouped together – on the shelves of
record shops, on the stages of major festivals and in the press – under the
label 'jazz'.

Written during a period of important questions for jazz, this book makes
no attempt to establish a fixed definition of jazz in the way that fossilized
folk forms can be defined. Nor does it attempt to say what jazz should be.
Instead it seeks to establish its genealogy, to show what it has bequeathed
to the contemporary scene and to trace its development from the founding
fathers to the dissidents of the late 20th century, as well as from its country
of birth to its countries of adoption.

This book contains:

• A history of jazz

It traces the origins of jazz back to the transportation of slaves from Africa
to America and systematically relates the music to the society that
produced it: each chapter opens with an introductory section on the
historical context. In addition to describing social events and occurrences
either directly related to jazz or which shaped contemporary thinking in a
wider sense, these chapter introductions also describe innovations within
the music industry – performance, publishing, recording, instrument
making and so on. They also chart important developments in related
musical forms such as blues, gospel and other genres with their roots in the
African-American diaspora.

One practical feature of the book is the way it divides the chronology of
jazz into decades: pre-1900 (the roots), 1900–19 (New Orleans), 1920–9
(the birth of Chicago jazz), 1930–9 (swing), 1940–9 (bebop); although
beyond this point the divisions blur as developments speed up and new

styles proliferate. Even during the early decades things are not that straightforward.

We have therefore taken the liberty of adapting this chronological division to suit our own purposes, attempting to combine accuracy and flexibility while bearing in mind the arbitrary character of such a division. The approach we have adopted takes account of the lack of clear-cut borders between styles and the fact that the appearance of one style is not necessarily accompanied by the disappearance of another. After describing new trends, each chapter therefore looks at the veterans who remained active – whether influenced by the new developments or not – and at older trends that were revived or revitalized upon coming into contact with new impulses.

As a rule, historians lack the sense of perspective required to examine the most recent period, and we are no exception. While we may be able to offer a perspective on the years 1960–70 that was not available to earlier authors (those from whom we learned the history of jazz), the chapter on the period 1980–90 should be regarded as a sketch, a provisional assessment designed to help readers understand what is going on in the current scene.

• An examination of jazz developments throughout the world

Born in the United States, jazz immediately spread to other countries, spawning imitators and genuinely creative musicians, and even influencing or being influenced by indigenous musical forms. We have tried to show, chapter by chapter, how jazz gradually set the world on fire and how it reflected the various tensions and aspirations of the 20th century. Each of the first eight chapters concludes with an appraisal of jazz's place in the world; for historical reasons this concern lies at the very heart of the final two chapters.

• Special pages on outstanding figures

This book is neither a dictionary nor an exhaustive chronology. Instead of providing lists of faceless names and unexplained facts for each new style and period, we have chosen to comment on the individuals and events that we believe to be most representative. We have focused on a number of outstanding artists – painting a portrait of the individual and providing a discography, a listening guide or an account of life in the recording studios of the time – with the object of shedding light on a certain style or period. Readers may occasionally be surprised, especially in the final chapter, not to see the name of a popular jazzman or one who happens to be a particular favourite of theirs. They should not take this as a sign of ill-will towards these musicians; indeed, in order to keep the book concise the author himself has had to leave out a number of his own favourite artists where he considers them insufficiently important from a historical point of view.

•Theory

Understanding jazz involves being able to distinguish different styles. This is done by getting used to listening to jazz, feeling at home with the different styles and following what the musicians are doing. We have therefore added a number of short sections on music theory to the text. Our aim is not to turn the reader into a musicologist, but to satisfy the needs of those wanting to learn more about the technical details of the music, enable those who wish to do so to get a handle on or visualize the concrete realities of the jazz musician at work, and point out certain tangible facts by means of diagrams and timed listening based on compact disc times. In doing so we have taken a few short cuts for which we hope our more knowledgeable readers will excuse us. The 'theory lessons' are based primarily on the principles of classic jazz. Having digested these, and without penetrating too far into the sophisticated logic of modern jazz, readers will gain an understanding of the developments and reinterpretations that have gradually led jazz away from its classic form. Anyone put off by this kind of approach can simply skip the theory pages without interrupting the flow of their reading or return to them later should they wish to do so.

•An index

A single alphabetical listing contains a wide selection of the proper names mentioned in the book as well as stylistic and technical jazz terms. Readers can look up the latter to find the pages on which they are explained.

•Listening guide

Throughout the book, references to recordings are given in the margin next to the relevant section of text. The recommended recordings do not claim to be the best in the history of jazz. The selection provided is simply designed to illustrate the ideas discussed in the text. In some cases, therefore, we have chosen early works rather than undisputed masterpieces because of what they tell us about the birth of a genre. Some of the examples chosen are primarily of historical value. Readers will be able to find the relevant recordings in a multimedia library or may wish to enrich their own record collections by buying them.

Discography: instructions for use

For the period dominated by the 78rpm record, we have identified works by the name of the musician to whom the reader is being invited to listen, the title of the track (in italics), the bandleader (if different from the musician), the original record company and the date of the recording (in brackets).

We also give the name of a recommended compilation or reissue (in inverted commas) on which the track can be found. Prior to the mid-1950s, recorded works were released two at a time on discs containing a single track per side. With the appearance of the LP and later the compact disc, pieces originally recorded on 78s were grouped together or split up and released on collections with varying and often quirky titles and contents which can drive the music lover to distraction. The releases we recommend have been selected on the basis of the quality of the editing (choice of tracks, quality of liner notes, quality of sound transfer), their availability and various practical considerations (we have favoured releases that bring together a number of the recommended pieces). If readers prefer a different release, they can take the details we have provided (name of bandleader, track title, original label and recording date) to a good record shop or use them to find a suitable disc on the Internet.

In the case of works originally released on LP, we give the name of the bandleader or group, the names of any other musicians we wish to highlight (in brackets) and the album title (in inverted commas). Occasionally we also draw attention to a particular track (in italics). Since the labels on which recordings are reissued are liable to change, we generally give the original record label. In the case of a 'must hear' album, we also sometimes mention the most recent label on which the album has been rereleased. In addition, we also recommend a number of good-quality compilations and anthologies, particularly on the 'Context' pages at the beginning of each chapter.

Finally, we also sometimes draw attention to specific passages of a recording by referring to the time elapsed (for example 1:43–2:03) as shown on the compact disc player's time display. The timing can vary from one release to another but will be correct for the version we have recommended.

Context

SOCIETY. From the earliest days, the colonization of the New World depended on a source of cheap labour. Initially this labour was recruited from among the indigenous population. In 1515, however, a priest named Bartolomé de Las Casas was moved by the plight of the native people and intervened on their behalf with the Spanish authorities. Following his ill-considered advice, Europe turned to Africa, which furnished a workforce all the more submissive for having been transported to a foreign country. The lure of tropical produce encouraged European merchants to invest in a triangular exchange of commodities in the name of civilization and free trade. Manufactured goods were exported to the coast of West Africa, where they were traded with the local rulers for 'ebony wood' (shipments of slaves). This 'cargo' was in turn exchanged in the Americas for goods such as coffee, tobacco, sugar, rice, cotton and indigo. Captured further and further inland by Arab or African slavers, the slaves were branded and crammed like cattle into ships which were fitted out so as to deliver

maximum returns. Such large numbers were needed in each shipment to offset the high mortality rate during the crossing. After being held in quarantine off the American coast, the slaves were exhibited, sold and taken to the plantations of their new owners. A lucky few were made domestic servants. The rest were put to work in the fields, where they had to endure long hours and a work-rate that would not even be expected of farm animals. In 1619, 20 black servants were brought ashore at Jamestown (Virginia), the first permanent English settlement in the New World (founded in 1607). Others were soon being shipped to New Amsterdam (New York) and Boston. The first few were given contracts but it is known that slavery was established in the English

A slave market

colonies of North America as early as 1640. In 1661, Virginia's first 'black code' – an early attempt to regulate slavery through the law – came into force. At the Declaration of Independence (1776), the black population of the newly founded United States was 750,000. This figure rose to two million in 1830 and nearly four million in 1860. Slavery was challenged by the Quakers as early as 1688 and abolitionism gradually gained momentum throughout the 18th century. In France, the National Convention abolished slavery in the French colonies in 1794 (although it was restored by Napoleon in 1802). In 1807, the British parliament voted for the abolition of the slave trade (although those in slavery at the time were not emancipated until the passing of the Slavery Abolition Act in 1833). The European powers condemned the slave trade at the Congress of Vienna in 1815 and slave traders were outlawed. In the southern United States a system of slavery based on transportation was replaced by one based on breeding (selection and forced reproduction).

During the 19th century, although slavery was out of step with the economic realities of both the Old World and the northern United States, the invention of the cotton gin (1793) and the demand for cotton from the rapidly expanding European textile industry triggered an economic upswing that depended on a captive black workforce. A number of factors led to growing tension between the north and the south: economic disagreements between the protectionist northern states and the free-market southern states, an increase in abolitionist sentiment in the north (Harriet Beecher Stowe's *Uncle Tom's Cabin* was published in 1852), the development of the Underground Railroad (an association of freed slaves and whites that helped slaves escape northwards) and an increasing number of slave revolts which led to a tightening of the 'black codes' and a movement towards segregation (New Orleans passed the first laws on segregation in public places in 1816). In 1861, Abraham Lincoln became president after campaigning against slavery at a time when the governing Democratic Party was divided on the issue. The southern states seceded and lost the war against the north in 1865. The abolition of slavery was written into the constitution.

THE MUSIC INDUSTRY. During the 19th century, the manufacture of musical instruments in Europe underwent changes that would exert a profound influence on black American music. The valve was introduced across the range of brass instruments (trumpet, cornet, tuba, etc). Theobald Böhm, a German, improved the key mechanism of the flute, clarinet and oboe. Böhm's work also inspired the Belgian Adolphe Sax to invent the saxophone, which he unveiled in 1841. The various patents relating to the upright piano (notably that taken out by the American John Isaac Hawkins in 1800) laid the foundations for the instrument's subsequent conquest of the West. Another invention that would contribute to the democratization of the piano was the mechanical or player piano developed by Claude Félix Seytre of Lyons in 1842. The first bass-drum pedal was designed by Cornelius Ward in 1840. The main instrument in rural America was the (often home-made) violin. In 1833, the stringed-instrument maker Christian Friedrich Martin, the father of the American guitar, opened his first shop in New York. On the plantations, African Americans made *banias* or *banjars* (banjos) with three or four strings and a high drone-string attached halfway along the neck. Popularized by white minstrels, the five-string banjo went into production in 1840.

RELATED MUSICAL GENRES. The New Orleans concert pianist Louis Moreau Gottschalk was the self-styled ambassador in the United States of the virtuoso European Romantic piano style, but also took his inspiration from the music of the African Americans. He anticipated ragtime by imitating the banjo style on the piano ('The Banjo', 1854).

Having originally appeared in Switzerland in the 15th century, the basic repertoire of beats played on the military side drum gradually developed in Europe into the drum roll in the 18th century. This repertoire was adopted by the American armies, in which the fife was gradually replaced by brass instruments.

African origins

Upon arrival in the United States, each new slave was renamed and members of the same tribe or even the same family were split up at the slave markets. Neither their languages nor their beliefs survived this upheaval. Some states even prohibited African musical instruments, particularly drums, which could have been used to incite slaves to revolt. It could thus be argued that the African-American people were born of cultural genocide; in which case it is admirable that, having started with nothing, they succeeded in inventing a culture for themselves, appropriating and adapting the foreign musical forms that were imposed on them. One important difference between the black populations in the north and the Africans transported to the Caribbean or Latin America is that the latter were able to preserve their African rituals and retain their rhythms and instruments.

However, the reality was more complex. During the colonial period, numerous witnesses in the northern states described African dances accompanied by drums and body percussion being performed on religious holidays such as Pentecost, which the African Americans adopted as their own special festival (Pinkster Day). For a long time after this festival disappeared, up to the end of the 19th century, the custom continued of dancing to drums in Congo Square (now Beauregard Square) in New Orleans on Sundays and feast days. Eighteenth- and nineteenth-century travel journals provide numerous accounts of a singing tradition peculiar to the plantations. Observers express surprise at the remarkable melodic and rhythmic qualities of the music, at the timbre of the voices and at the involvement of the body in the music. The banjo, which originated in Africa, seems to have escaped the various prohibitions. In the 1820s, curiosity led white Americans to visit the African Grove, New York's black theatre, not only to see black productions of Shakespeare but also to listen to the songs performed by popular demand before and after the play, during the intervals and even during the piece itself.

Black American music was thus the

Black celebration as seen in an American print

fruit of both memory and forgetting. In Cuba, members of the various African nationalities grouped together in mutual aid societies (the *cabildos*) that preserved their ethnic religions and musical customs, but in the United States the intermixing of the tribes and their dispersal across a vast continent led to a kind of pan-Africanism that became cut off from its roots when the slave trade ceased.

With growing urbanization and relative integration, other forms of music would develop as a result of the corruption of European musical genres by a residual African tradition that was reimagined from generation to generation.

Secular songs

After the Civil War, numerous eyewitnesses wrote accounts of, and even collected, the music of black Americans (for example, *The Slave Songs of the United States*, published in 1867). These accounts provide basic descriptions of the dances, instruments and physical exertions of the performers and sometimes reproduce the words of the songs. But they often also admit the difficulty of transcribing the musical forms, melodies, rhythms and range of colours with any degree of precision.

Slaves sang to keep their spirits up while working or to maintain the rhythm of a repetitive movement. Rowers, road makers, railroad layers, stevedores, corn huskers, reapers and woodcutters all had their own songs. These work songs involved the singing of collective responses to the cries of a leader. 'Field hollers', on the other hand, were sung by solitary workers as a way of calling for help or drawing attention to their presence or simply in order to express the sheer effort required by their work. Somewhere between a song and a shout, field hollers were not dissimilar to the calls of herdsmen or auctioneers. Black Americans also sang in the evening after work in their family groups. Their cradle songs and satirical or narrative songs have been linked by certain authors to the *griot* tradition of West Africa.

In the north as well as in New Orleans (where there was a strong Catholic, and therefore more liberal, tradition), numerous songs for dancing to could also be observed. Eyewitness accounts describe a number of consistent features that are strongly evocative of the musicians' ancestral Africa and that foreshadow certain characteristics of blues or jazz. In addition to the performers' considerable physical investment in their music, observers were greatly struck by their improvisational skills. The singers constantly reinvented their tone colour, using head voices, yodelling effects and vocal distortions resembling growls and groans (*moanin'*). They also demonstrated a very free approach towards the words, choice of notes and rhythmic structure – even in what was fundamentally a unison song. This gave rise to a permanent dialogue between the individual and the chorus – a dialogue that would later be found between the bluesman and his guitar or the soloist and his band.

The rhythmic regularity impressed and perplexed observers all the more as it struggled to hold its own against the effects of syncopation, the performers picking out the offbeat with their hands in opposition to the main beat drummed out by their feet. This effect is similar to the distribution of accents

Cotton picking in the southern United States

between different drums in African polyrhythmic music, the rhythmic distribution of beats in jazz drumming and the backbeat played on the hi-hat (foot-operated double cymbal).

Whether listening to rousing pieces or ballads, observers were disconcerted by the sad, melancholic tonality of this music based on the major (often pentatonic) scale, as the major scale in the Western musical tradition was associated with positive sentiments. Noting the instability of the melodic pitch, the commentators expressed reservations about the music. They were probably already experiencing the 'blue note'.

From Protestant hymns to spirituals

Since black Americans lacked civil rights, they took charge of their own destiny through the church. It was here that their first leaders came to the fore.

It was also within the church that an original African-American music began to take shape. The first known baptism of a black American dates from 1641 and white ministers were the first to take an interest in the education of slaves. Black congregations were taught to sing the psalms by means of the 'lining out' technique: the celebrant would sing a verse and the congregation would repeat it, a process adopted readily by black Americans as it recalled the responses sung by African choruses.

Soon after 1730, this evangelization reached a turning point with the Awakening in England and the Great Awakening in America, which shook up the nonconformist Protestant sects. Keen to rouse the faith of their congregations, the new preachers met with considerable success among the labouring classes and the destitute. Responsive to the fervour of the sermons and the new hymns taken from the collections of Dr Isaac Watts and the Wesley brothers, the black population in particular was seduced by a

Modes

Natural acoustic laws determine whether certain notes are consonant or dissonant when sounded together. Consonant notes produce a feeling of comfort, order and completion. Dissonant notes inspire uneasiness, disorder and instability. In developing music, mankind took these physical realities into account and devised the octave (the interval between, for example, a low and a high C). Scales were also devised that corresponded to different 'modes'. The mode determines the number of degrees in the scale: pentatonic scales have five degrees, hexatonic scales have six, and heptatonic scales have seven. The mode also determines the position of the degrees as measured by the interval separating them from the first degree (tonic): minor, major or augmented second, minor or major third, perfect or augmented fourth, perfect, augmented or diminished fifth, minor or major sixth and minor or major seventh. Throughout the world there are many different modes with very different profiles:

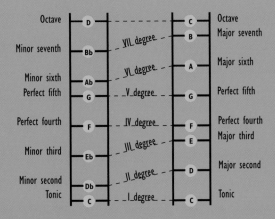

Two heptatonic scales (or modes).
Left: an Indian mode, the Bhairavi mode. Right: the European major mode.

Key

Following a complex process of development, Western classical music has ultimately confined itself to the use of a single mode – the major scale (and, without going into detail here, its relative minor) – across most of its repertoire. European composers have nevertheless learned over the course of the centuries to enrich their work by transposing this scale to different pitches within the same piece (key changes, also known as modulation). Thus, the music can move from a major scale whose first degree is situated on a certain note (C, for example) to an identical scale starting on some other note of the original scale (for example E). The names of the notes that make up the new scale have changed, but the intervals between the degrees of the scale remain identical to those of the original C major scale: E (tone) F# (tone) G# (semitone) A (tone) B (tone) C# (tone) D# (semitone) E.

Transposing the major scale from degree to degree, Western music ended up with twelve keys of different pitches based on the same model. In order for the same keyboard to provide access to all the keys with twelve piano keys per octave, a little cheating was done with the positioning of the degrees of the scale. The end result of a gradual adjustment of the tuning system (which took place over several centuries) was a division of the octave into twelve equal semitones. Known as 'equal temperament', this system was exported with keyboard instruments and spread rapidly to the colonized world.

Blue notes

Traditional musical forms do not generally use modulation within the same piece, but may use a multitude of different modes from piece to piece. In certain African tribes in which it is customary to sing in fourths, the top voice may even use a different scale to the bottom one in order to preserve the perfect fourth interval over all the degrees of the scale. It can be imagined, therefore, that Africans transported to the United States would have wanted to change the pitch of certain degrees of the Western major scale (the movement towards equal temperament having already started) in order to correct pitches that sounded wrong to their ears. Why did these 'corrections' focus on the third and seventh degrees? And why did this phenomenon not affect the African diaspora in places other than the United States? Many different hypotheses have been put forward – some serious, some rather eccentric.

These unstable notes that fluctuated between major and minor were named blue notes. They are a characteristic of the pentatonic mode that seems to have become dominant within the African-American community very early on, eventually developing in the 20th century into the 'blues scale'. This scale contains an unstable third, an essentially minor seventh and a less common third blue note: a transitional note between a fourth and a fifth which acquired considerable importance in jazz and became known as the 'flat fifth'.

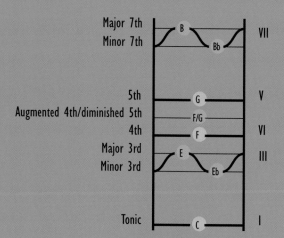

Pentatonic mode on which the blues scale is based.
(Example assumes a scale starting on C)

spontaneous form of service that invited them to experience God through song and a trance-like state. To the determinist theology which held that the soul is predestined to salvation or damnation, John Wesley, in Great Britain, had opposed a theology of hope in which individuals are responsible for earning their own salvation. Imported into the United States by the Methodists, this concept of salvation offered a long-awaited answer to the despair of black Americans, who were also drawn to the Baptist church. Following the founding of the African Baptist Church in Savannah, Georgia, in around 1780, independent black churches started to proliferate in the north. The year 1801 saw the publication of *A Collection of Hymns and Spiritual Songs from Various Authors*, which brought together the favourite

Sermon at a camp meeting

Protestant hymns of black congregations. These congregations took greater and greater liberties with the hymns and the practice of lining out. They adopted livelier tunes that were easier to remember and added choruses that related to their everyday lives through a system of double meanings (for example, the River Jordan referred to the Mississippi and the Promised Land to the northern states, while Jerusalem and Jericho became code names for the route to be followed by escapers). Although the harmonic structure of Protestant hymnody lingered on, it was transformed by the musical habits of black Americans: alterations in voice timbre, body movements, hand-clapping, spontaneous initiatives by individual chorus singers, a strong beat, complex syncopation and the addition of minor intervals or blue notes. After holding forth in a vehement sermon, the celebrant would improvise refrains that would be interspersed with interjections from the fired-up congregation.

This phenomenon became widespread with the success of the Second Great Awakening (1800–30) and the 'camp meetings' at which white and black Americans came together in forest clearings to pray for several days at a time. It was at these meetings that the new type of religious song known as the 'spiritual' took shape. There were white spirituals as well as Negro spirituals, and the precise ways in which they influenced each other are the subject of endless debate. What is known for certain is that the white participants at these meetings were fascinated by the fervour of the singing they heard coming, well into the night, from the tents reserved for the black Americans. The spectacle that most astounded them, however, was the 'ring shout' (thought to have originated in an African ceremony), in which the black participants paraded in a circle in a trance-like state. Their shuffling gait ('shuffle step') produced a loud noise that provided the rhythm for their singing, which gathered pace over the course of several hours.

Black philharmonics and white minstrels

Since slave owners were excluded by their Puritanism from any personal artistic involvement, they entrusted their slaves (whose musical gifts they had noted) with the musical organization of their festivities. As early as the 17th century, the press contained many small notices concerning musically accomplished slaves under headings such as 'For Sale' or 'Escaped Slave Sought'. Most of these musicians were violinists, but successive wars found them playing fifes, bugles and drums in military bands. The first black brass bands appeared at the beginning of the 19th century and dance bands began to get bigger: a clarinet or maybe a cornet, two or three violins, a cello, a triangle, a tambourine and a bass drum. In the poor New York district of Five Points in the mid-19th century, the effect on the visitor of the black music played in the neighbourhood's cheap bars anticipated that produced by the first jazz bands. But the African Americans also had their classical singers (Elizabeth Taylor Greenfield, nicknamed 'The Black Swan'), their teachers (Newport Gardner), their virtuosi (the multi-instrumentalist Frank Johnson), a theatre in New York (the African Grove) and a black philharmonic society in New Orleans. However, such ambitions to master Western music were not to the taste of all white Americans, many of whom preferred to hear blacks playing their own music – the main attraction of an American musical scene that was still very much tagging along behind Europe.

White America was so fascinated by its black community that from 1810 onwards white actors known as 'minstrels' blacked up to perform the music of the plantations. Small itinerant troupes (minstrel shows) sprang up across the whole country. They performed sketches and songs that ridiculed the blacks, who were represented with stereotypical physical and psychological traits (exaggerated lips, clumsy behaviour and an easy-going naivety). Two characters topped the bill: the ragged, lame stable boy Jim Crow – whose name came to stand for the segregation laws introduced at the end of the 19th century – and the black urban dandy Zip Coon. The minstrels' favourite instrument was the five-string banjo that had originated in Africa. As well as becoming the preferred instrument of the white farming communities of the Appalachians, the banjo would eventually spread as far as the drawing rooms of Victorian England.

LISTENING
GUIDE
Ed Young: 'Jim and John' (Alan Lomax, 1959)[1]. Sid Hemphill: 'Emmaline, Take Your Time', 'Old Devil's Dream' (Alan Lomax, 1959)[1]. Leroy Gary: 'Mama Lucy' (Alan Lomax, 1959)[1]. Dock & Henry Reed, Vera Hall: 'Trouble So Hard' (John A Lomax, 1936)[2]. Ed Lewis: 'Stewball' (Alan Lomax, 1959)[1]. Joe Washington Brown, Austin Coleman: 'Run, Old Jeremiah' (John A Lomax, 1934)[2]. Katherine and Christine Shipp: 'Sea Lion Woman' (Herbert Halpert, 1940)[3]. Sidney Carter: 'Didn't Leave Nobody but the Baby' (Alan Lomax, 1959)[1].

CD GUIDE
1. *Southern Journey, Vol 3*, Rounder.
2. *Afro-American Spirituals, Work Songs and Ballads*, Rounder.
3. *Afro-American Blues and Game Songs*, Rounder.

JIM CROW.
NEW YORK.
Published by Firth & Hall, No 1 Franklin Sq

THE LOMAX COLLECTIONS

Although there are no recordings marking the actual genesis of black American music, a good idea of what it was like in the early days can be gained from various recordings made for the Library of Congress — notably those collected by John A Lomax and his son Alan between 1933 and 1942. In 1959, Alan set off for the southern states again, armed this time with stereophonic recording equipment. He travelled deep into the rural South, which had remained largely untouched by modern life.

These recordings (see discography on opposite page) reveal forgotten aspects of black American culture, such as Ed Young playing the fife accompanied by hand-held drums ('Jim and John'), Sid Hemphill's pan-pipes accompanied by a five-string banjo descended from the *banjar* of the plantations ('Emmaline, Take Your Time') and a military drum played in a very African-sounding way ('Old Devil's Dream'). Many of these pieces evoke the hollers and moans that anticipated the blues; it was their unstable notes that disconcerted white listeners. Of the other recordings, 'Mama Lucy' and the spiritual 'Trouble So Hard' are sung in pentatonic mode with a mainly minor though occasionally major third and a fifth that veers between the perfect and the diminished. Among the numerous work songs recorded in state penitentiaries, 'Stewball', borrowed from Irish folk music (and rendered barely recognizable), is among the most notable. Also to be heard are a ring shout ('Run, Old Jeremiah'), which was a survivor from the camp meetings, a series of nursery rhymes ('Pullin' the Skiff', 'Old Uncle Rabbit', 'Sea Lion Woman') and a haunting lullaby ('Didn't Leave Nobody but the Baby') — all of which display some of the rhythmic qualities inherited from African culture.

Did these pieces remain untouched by the evolution that blues and gospel music had undergone by the time these recordings were made? Whatever the case, looking through these windows on black American history calls up strong emotions — emotions that help one to understand jazz properly, even jazz in its most modern forms.

Context

SOCIETY. In the southern states, the Civil War was followed by Reconstruction (1867–77), which took place in a climate of violent resentment on the part of the white population. Deprived of education, the black community had its first taste of freedom and ownership in a context of utter economic destitution and a complete absence of civil rights. As a result it became an easy scapegoat. The large plantations were divided up

but the redistribution promised by the northern politicians (40 acres and a mule for every slave) never happened. Black Americans found themselves sharecroppers in the service of white landowners. Their smallholdings were soon ravaged by boll weevil, which became the main cause of southern dissatisfaction and a favourite subject for the blues. Unprepared for the responsibilities and isolation of running a family business, black farmers were plunged into poverty. In 1877, the

Lynching scene from the film *Birth of a Nation* by D W Griffith, 1915

withdrawal of Federal troops left the way clear for the 'Jim Crow' laws. Recognized by the Supreme Court in 1896, these laws imposed strict segregation and deprived the black population of some of its newly acquired civil rights. Secret societies such as the Ku Klux Klan (formed in 1866) perpetrated frequent acts of violence against blacks (2,500 lynchings were reported between 1884 and 1900). Many families fled the rural areas and moved to the cities – first of all the southern and later the northern cities. There they discovered an alien way of life (unemployment, urban insalubrity and crime) and encountered more racism. The white populations of the north were not willing to tolerate either overcrowding or job competition from a new workforce excluded from the trade union movement. They rallied to the racism imported by white migrants from the south, who had also been attracted to the economically successful northern cities. The lynchings that were common in rural areas were replaced by urban riots that exploded at the beginning of the 20th century. Huge ghettos emerged, such as South Side in Chicago and Harlem in New York City. Gradually, new elites developed at the black universities founded during Reconstruction, the first of which was Fisk University in Nashville (1866). The most important leader to come to the fore after the Civil War was Booker T Washington. Non-political, Washington preached patience in the face of adversity and integration through merit and hard work. He gave concrete expression to this doctrine by founding an institute of vocational education in Tuskegee in Alabama.

In the early years of the 20th century, W E B Du Bois, who had studied at the universities of Harvard and Berlin, opposed Washington's cautious approach and founded the Niagara movement. In 1909, Niagara joined forces with a white group to form the NAACP (National Association for the Advancement of Colored People), which defended the rights of black

Americans in the courts and promoted black artists. In 1911, black and white Americans again came together to fight discrimination at work and help tackle the social problems resulting from the influx of black citizens into the northern cities. The organization they founded was called the National Urban League.

However, the main institutions within the black community continued to be the churches. Developing out of the mother churches (Baptist and Methodist) or nonconformist churches (Pentecostal and Sanctified), their numbers increased. They became a significant economic force and played an active role in the life of the city – in terms of housing, politics, charitable works and community associations.

THE MUSIC INDUSTRY. At the turn of the century, American stringed-instrument making (notably Martin, Gretsch and Gibson) exploded with the production of many different models (guitar, mandolin, ukulele and the five-, seven-, four- or six-stringed banjo). Adopted by the white farming communities of the Appalachians and much appreciated by middle-class women in particular, the five-stringed banjo was soon abandoned by black musicians. In the 1880s, there was an increase in the number of drum-kit patents applied for (such as snare-drum tripod, bass-drum pedal and cymbal stand). Thaddeus Cahill's Dynamophone (or Telharmonium), first tested in 1895, enabled concerts to be broadcast by telephone a century before the invention of the MIDI standard or MP3 player. Between 1900 and 1931, more than 2,500,000 player pianos were sold. The instrument had been equipped with a full 88-note keyboard in 1901. In 1877, the simultaneous invention by Charles Cros in France and Thomas Edison in the United States of a machine to record and reproduce sound led to a patent war (covering engraving procedure, recording media, duplication and playback equipment) that was won at the beginning of the 20th century by the American Gramophone Company, the Columbia Phonograph Company and the Victor Talking Machine Company. Only the last of these paid any serious attention to new black music.

RELATED MUSICAL GENRES. Led by New York's Broadway and the music publishing industry based in Tin Pan Alley, the American theatre circuit impressively combined European theatrical and musical traditions with the rhythms and melodies of the black community as popularized by the minstrels. Extravaganzas, vaudevilles, follies and revues of all kinds preceded the advent of the musical.

Director of the National Conservatory of Music in New York from 1892 to 1895, Antonín Dvořák encouraged young American composers to break away from the influence of Germanic music and turn their attention instead towards America's own rich popular (and mainly black) heritage. Among his students were the black singer Harry T Burleigh, who composed a number of chamber music works inspired by the black American folk tradition, and the black conductor Will Marion Cook. Head of the United States Marine Band from 1880, the white composer John Philip Sousa gave a new impetus to the vogue for brass bands, and towards the end of the century his successor, the trombonist Arthur Pryor, added the cakewalk to their repertoire.

The various forms of black American music joined the list of traditional musics that were finding their way into urban culture throughout the world, giving birth to new genres such as the tango, the paso doble, the musette, the beguine, the Cuban sound and klezmer music.

Jubilee and gospel

From the emancipation of the slaves to the first jazz recording in 1917, the predominant American musical forms gradually took shape in the melting pot that was the United States. Jazz was still waiting to be born out of a black American music carrying three offspring: the secular popular song that would develop into the blues, religious music in the process of transformation, and syncopated instrumental music. This latter would become jazz in the true sense.

The jubilee style and the concert tradition

LISTENING GUIDE
Fisk University Jubilee Singers: 'There Is a Balm in Gilead' (Victor, 9 December 1909)[1].
Tuskegee Institute Singers: 'Live A-Humble' (Victor, 31 August 1914)[1].
The Dinwiddie Colored Quartet: 'Gabriel's Trumpet' (Victor, 31 October 1902)[2].

CD GUIDE
1. *Negro Spirituals, the Concert Tradition, 1909–48*, Frémeaux.
2. *La Grande Époque du Gospel, 1902–44*, Best of Gospel. Despite the relatively late recording dates, many of the tracks on 3. *Negro Spirituals/ Gospel Songs, 1926–42* (Frémeaux) also convey a vivid impression of this transitional period.

Soon after the founding of Fisk University in Nashville, a group of students assembled a repertoire of classical choral songs and Negro spirituals in classical arrangements that followed the principles of European harmony. Their choir – the Fisk Jubilee Singers – gave several concerts in aid of the university. Their name came from the Old Testament – after every 50th Pentecost, there was a 'year of jubilee', when all slaves were to be freed. Soon the Fisk Jubilee Singers were so successful that they were touring as far afield as Europe. They created a new genre, the 'jubilee song', which was taken up by many other choirs, including the Tuskegee Institute Singers. Black solo singers such as Harry T Burleigh, who studied composition under Dvořák and performed sentimental ballads, also took up the style. In 1916, Burleigh published a collection of Negro spirituals with piano accompaniment entitled *Jubilee Songs of the United States of America*. Originally, however, jubilee songs were performed by quartets, representing a reduction of choral singing to the bare essentials: bass, baritone, tenor and soprano (or low tenor and lead tenor in the case of all-male groups). A degree of doubling up was also permitted, with the result that the 'quartets' could sometimes contain five or more members. These quartets followed a path somewhere between the strict tradition established by the Fisk Jubilee Singers and the more spontaneous forms (influenced by popular vocal groups such as barbershop quartets and glee clubs) that heralded modern gospel.

From spirituals to gospel

While the black middle classes welcomed the success of the jubilee style, they regularly protested (via the Baptist and more importantly the Methodist church authorities) against the overly physical style of prayer inherited from the camp meetings, the use of musical instruments in church and the corruption of religious song by the secular genres. The poor populations of the south, on the other hand, longed for a more spontaneous form of liturgy, and under the banner of Pentecostalism a host of nonconformist, so-called 'Sanctified' churches were founded around the turn of the century. These churches put into practice the words of David in Psalm 150: 'Praise God with the sounding of the trumpet, praise him with the harp and lyre, praise him with tambourine and dancing, praise him with the strings and flute, praise him with the clash of cymbals, praise him with resounding cymbals.' Musical instruments thus suddenly appeared in church, which was regarded as a place dedicated to the manifestation of the Holy Spirit. Impassioned sermons, improvised responses, dancing and trances were all encouraged. Everyday urban life crept into the words of songs and the influence of the secular genres increased. In the New Testament congregations discovered a God of mercy, incarnate in Jesus, who was more attentive to real-life preoccupations. The spiritual gradually gave way to the gospel hymn.

The first of the National Baptist Conventions, which over the years provided a showcase for young composers, was organized in 1886. Representing the transition between the gospel hymn and the gospel song commercialized in the 1930s, Lucie Campbell-Williams ('Jesus Gave Me Water', 'In the Upper Room') made a name for herself at the 1916 convention. In the same year, Charles A Tindley published his *New Songs of Paradise*, which was reissued at regular intervals until the 1940s. This collection contained standards such as 'I'll Overcome Some Day' (the hymn adopted by civil rights marchers in the 1960s under the title 'We Shall Overcome'). Unfortunately, no recordings have survived that chart the birth of gospel other than a few by the Dinwiddie Colored Quartet.

The blues

Bluesman Wilson Jones ('Stavin' Chain') photographed by Alan Lomax in Lafayette (Louisiana) in 1934.

After all the hope offered by the abolition of slavery, black Americans had a rude awakening. The circumstances of their emancipation were far from ideal. Dispersed as sharecroppers on small plots, they expressed their collective depression in an individual, intimate way. The word 'blues' referred simultaneously to a feeling, a range of song forms, a verse form and an instrumental form. It is thought to have derived from the old English expression, 'the blue devils' (those that take possession of the spirits of the depressed). During the 19th century, the expression 'I got the blues' gradually gained currency in the United States. The term was appropriated by black Americans, who also used it to designate the unstable notes (blue notes) whose ambiguity was systematized by the bluesmen.

The message of the blues

The blues has deep roots. Hollers and plantation

songs anticipated both the emotional and melodic content of the genre and links have even been established with Africa. In the form it took after emancipation, the blues expressed a feeling of resigned despair that only increased in intensity when blues singers arrived in the city. For although the blues originated in rural areas, it was common for bluesmen to pick up their bundle of belongings and their guitar (their one true companion) and walk away from their lives as poor black southern farmers. Blues singers were dropouts and misfits, and they often suffered from some kind of disability (many of them bore the epithet 'Blind'). Unemployed vagabonds, fare-dodgers (the train occupied an important place in their everyday lives), liars, show-offs, womanizers, drinkers, fighters and occasionally serious criminals, they discovered that the city was a jungle where they sometimes had to use force to carve out a niche for themselves. When the blues singer took up his guitar, he confided to it the troubles of his existence.

Hard-up and taking comfort from the hypnotic rhythm of his guitar, the bluesman sang of poverty ('No Shoes'), emotional or sexual misery (Empty Bed Blues), alcoholism ('One Scotch, One Bourbon, One Beer'), sickness ('TB Blues'), prison ('Penitentiary Blues') and wandering ('Homeless Blues'). He even personified the blues itself ('The First Time I Met the Blues'). There are, of course, more cheerful blues full of (often salacious) humour, although their tone is nevertheless bitter and sarcastic. Occasionally the bluesman might feel touched by the Holy Spirit and join the ranks of itinerant preachers who took up positions on street corners, drawing crowds with the sound of their guitar and their praising of the Lord. However, the bluesman's repentance would rarely last long.

Birth of the blues

There is a general consensus that the blues originated at the end of the 19th century as a result of the contact between African traditions and the European folk ballad in the region known as the Delta (in the north-west of the state of Mississippi between Vicksburg and Memphis). Delta blues remained an unpolished musical form. It consisted of the haunting rhythm of the guitar (often played as slide guitar by moving the neck of a bottle or a knife blade up and down the strings), a harsh, strained singing style with frequent use of head voice and a poetry rich in innuendo that featured metaphors strung together without any apparent logic. Originally, the blues was free-form. The performer would sing (barely more than speak) essentially improvised words without worrying about keeping strict time. All that mattered was the beat. A poetic form that may have had African origins became the norm. This was based on a tercet with a repeated first line. By virtue of three lines of roughly four bars each, a basic twelve-bar structure was arrived at.

When the black bandleader W C Handy discovered the blues while on tour in the south, he noted the success this music enjoyed among the local population and lost no time in writing his own blues tunes. In 1912, he published 'The Memphis Blues', which was based on a hybrid structure combining a couplet of 20 bars with a twelve-bar blues. The trend was set: to satisfy the needs of music publishing and band performance, the blues adopted a fixed twelve-bar structure that was subsequently used throughout the world.

From regional to urban styles

While enjoying success on the jazz stage, the blues continued to lead a double life, remaining faithful to its popular rural roots. Because of the individuality of its performers, who were in revolt against any form of academicism, it is difficult for the uninitiated to distinguish between different regional styles. Bordering the Delta, Texas produced a singing style that was just as unpolished, but with a more logical, narrative poetry and a guitar style whose nimbler ornamentation hints at a Spanish influence from neighbouring Mexico. When it reached the East Coast, where racial tension was less acute, the blues seemed to gain a degree of refinement, particularly as a result of coming into contact with ragtime, whose alternating bass and transparent structure was adopted by the blues guitar. The twelve-bar structure thus became the norm here just as it did in the cities, where the blues assumed a more orchestral form prior to the electrification of music in the 1940s. In the 1930s, Texas and the Delta supplied the cities to the north, from Memphis to Kansas City, Saint Louis and Chicago, as well as the east and Los Angeles, with successive waves of migration. The stylistic distinctions between these cities often arose less as a consequence of geography than as a result of the local conditions of production.

The earliest recordings of rural blues date from the second half of the 1920s and feature the work of artists born mostly after 1900. These recordings nevertheless give us an idea of the main regional styles – Delta: Bukka White, Skip James, Tommy Johnson, Charlie Patton, Son House and Big Joe Williams; Texas: Texas Alexander, Blind Lemon Jefferson and Leadbelly; East Coast: Blind Blake, Reverend Gary Davis, Blind Willie McTell and Josh White.

LISTENING GUIDE
Charlie Patton: 'Revenue Man Blues' (Vocalion, 31 January 1934).
Blind Lemon Jefferson: 'Lonesome House Blues' (Paramount, October 1927).
Josh White: 'Blood Red River' (Or, 15 August 1933).

CD GUIDE
Blues, 36 Masterpieces of Blues Music, 1927–42, Frémeaux

Traditional forms of modal music develop in a linear, horizontal manner, the melodic line unfolding in time with reference to a root note often held continuously (drone). Western music, on the other hand, restricts itself to a single mode, the all-powerful major mode (and its relative minor), and diversifies its musical material by adding substance in the form of harmony. Through contact with this additional substance in the form of guitar accompaniments borrowed from white folk music, the black American pentatonic mode (see p.18) eventually gave rise to the blues.

Harmony: chords and their function

Through their exploration of polyphony and in superimposing melodic lines in thirds, Western composers became accustomed to thinking in terms of vertical groups of notes produced simultaneously by different voices – in other words, chords. They discovered that by piling up intervals of a third above each degree of the scale, they could obtain in each case a résumé of the major scale, which would be presented from a different angle each time and given a different coloration.

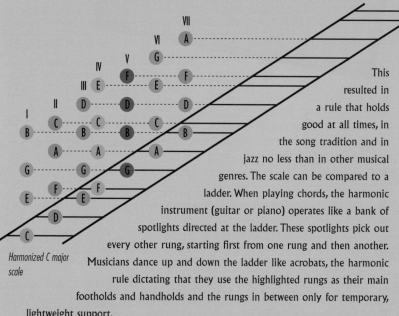

Harmonized C major scale

This resulted in a rule that holds good at all times, in the song tradition and in jazz no less than in other musical genres. The scale can be compared to a ladder. When playing chords, the harmonic instrument (guitar or piano) operates like a bank of spotlights directed at the ladder. These spotlights pick out every other rung, starting first from one rung and then another. Musicians dance up and down the ladder like acrobats, the harmonic rule dictating that they use the highlighted rungs as their main footholds and handholds and the rungs in between only for temporary, lightweight support.

The chords have different characters (major or minor) depending on the positioning of the major and minor thirds. The acrobat-musicians need to constantly adjust their holds on the ladder, whose appearance changes with each new chord. The functions of these chords vary according to the degree of the scale on which they are built. There are three main functions. The chord built on the first degree of the scale (I) is called the 'tonic chord'. The acrobat-musician remains in contact with the ground and the spectator-listener experiences a feeling of stability. On the fourth degree (IV) or 'subdominant chord', the acrobat-musician loses contact with the ground and is able to move around as if weightlessly.

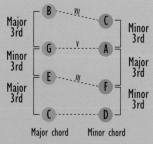

Two chords with different characters

The chord constructed on the fifth degree or 'dominant' has a special character which has also earned it the name dominant seventh (V7) as its third is major and its seventh minor. The interval between the third and seventh degrees is therefore dissonant in this chord and has a tendency to throw the acrobat-musician off balance. This may be an opportunity for virtuosity but the tension that ensues calls for repose and a return to the stability of the first degree in order for the acrobat-musicians to regain their balance. Called the tritone or diminished fifth, this dissonant chord has, throughout the history of Western music, been the cause of conflict between musical fundamentalists who have wanted to banish it and those who have wanted to use it to invent new figures.

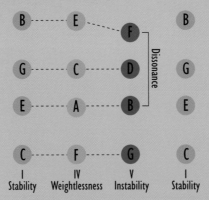

The three main functions of functional harmony. On I and IV the major seventh is often passed over in silence, but jazzmen have made great use of it.

Functional harmony corrupted by the blue notes

During the period of history under consideration, the melodies of American folk music and spirituals were based around I, IV and V7 chords. What distinguished the blues was the corruption of these chords by blue notes in the black American pentatonic scale. Under their influence, I and IV chords became seventh chords destabilized by the dissonant tritone interval:

In the blues, the seventh acquires a different status, independent of the dominant to which it was previously attached. Jazz musicians were to make the most of the instability affecting the other degrees of the scale. The black American pentatonic scale was in turn corrupted by European harmony, eventually becoming the blues scale (see diagram on the following page):

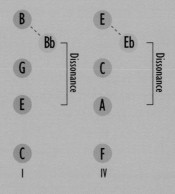

The alteration of I and IV chords by blue notes

Jazz musicians would also make ample use of these enrichments.

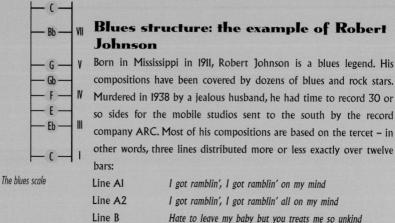

The blues scale

Blues structure: the example of Robert Johnson

Born in Mississippi in 1911, Robert Johnson is a blues legend. His compositions have been covered by dozens of blues and rock stars. Murdered in 1938 by a jealous husband, he had time to record 30 or so sides for the mobile studios sent to the south by the record company ARC. Most of his compositions are based on the tercet – in other words, three lines distributed more or less exactly over twelve bars:

Line A1	*I got ramblin', I got ramblin' on my mind*
Line A2	*I got ramblin', I got ramblin' all on my mind*
Line B	*Hate to leave my baby but you treats me so unkind*

Each line evokes a response from the guitar in the form of a melodic variation. This can also be played on other instruments such as the harmonica. In terms of harmonic structure, the first call-response (A1) is based on the tonic (I) chord (in this case F). The second sung call (A2) is based on the subdominant (IV) chord (Bb) with the guitar replying on chord I (F). The third call is based on chord V7 (C7), the guitar replying and concluding on chord I (F).

I	(IV)	I	I	IV	IV	I	I
sung call (A1)		guitar response		sung call (A2)		guitar response	

V	(IV)	I	I
sung call (B)		guitar response	

Common variants in brackets. In bar ten, Robert Johnson generally used the variant indicated.

LISTENING GUIDE
Robert Johnson:
'Ramblin' on My Mind'
(Vocalion, 23 November 1936)[1].
John Lee Hooker:
'Boogie Chillen'
(Modern, 3 November 1948)[2].

CD GUIDE
1. Robert Johnson, *The Complete Recordings*, Columbia.
2. John Lee Hooker, *The Legendary Modern Recordings, 1948–54*, Ace.

Attentive listeners will notice that Johnson also bends the rules to a certain extent, particularly in the first guitar response to each of the couplets of 'Ramblin' on My Mind'. In his first take of this song he adds three beats to the first couplet and in his second take a full bar. A pure product of rural Mississippi, Johnson takes rhythmic liberties that would have been difficult to imagine on the jazz or music-hall stage at a time when twelve-bar blues had become a standard form. And listening to the recordings made by the veteran bluesmen of the south during the preceding decade, it is difficult to find anything other than a very approximate version of the structure shown in the diagram above. Even among more modern singers, notably John Lee Hooker, who made the 'talking blues' his speciality, there are many examples of the use of free time signatures.

Syncopated music

Alongside religious music, which at the turn of the century could only be enjoyed in the concert hall in its most refined forms, and blues, which until around 1910 remained a rural genre, black musicians also enjoyed growing success in the field of public entertainment. They played for and introduced their rhythmic ideas into philharmonic societies and brass bands, ballrooms, permanent and travelling theatres, operetta companies and minstrel shows. White America succumbed to the charms of syncopation.

Black minstrels and the Cakewalk

Now participating at every level of America's new musical scene, black musicians started to claw back from the white minstrels what was rightfully theirs. Troupes of black minstrels began to proliferate in the 1860s. They wore heavy black make-up just like their white counterparts, parodied the so-called 'Ethiopian' music of the plantations and at the same time (like mirrors endlessly reflecting each other) caricatured the refined manners and clothes of the white population. The success of this exercise in competitive grotesquery – half giving in to popular clichés and half engaging in subversive satire – would be a permanent temptation for black jazzmen. Made up originally of a few artists who could act, dance and sing while accompanying themselves on the banjo or sometimes the guitar, minstrel troupes gradually increased in size. Before long they included musicians capable of playing in the concert hall or marquee (violin, cello, clarinet, oboe, banjo, mandolin, double bass and percussion) and in parades which publicized the show (wind, drums and cymbals).

In addition to performing dances of the period (quadrilles, marches and polkas) as reinvented by the slaves, the minstrels popularized the Cakewalk. The Cakewalk had originated in the plantations and took its name from a competition in which the winners (the best dancers) would be given a piece of cake by the plantation owner. The Cakewalk introduced the syncopation common in black American music into the ballrooms and drawing rooms of white society and corrupted the songs and dances that had previously held sway there. From the still rather stilted two-step (1890s) to the frenetic Charleston (around 1920), the Cakewalk gradually led dancers away from the military stiffness of the march, the athletic vigour of the polka and the corseted exhilaration of the waltz.

Ragtime

Ragtime is thought to have developed from the adaptation of the Cakewalk for the piano by black pianists who had either been professionally taught or had learned to play on the living-room piano (which had been relatively widespread since the end of the 19th century). The most common explanation of the name 'ragtime' is that it described the music's syncopation – its jagged, disjointed beat ('ragged time'). Scott Joplin's first published piece was called 'Original Rags' and bore the subtitle 'Picked by Scott Joplin' as if he had simply pulled out fragments of melody here and there from the repertoire of the plantations.

Joplin, the best known of ragtime composers, was born in 1868. His parents were former slaves. He took lessons in classical piano from a German piano

teacher before leaving his home town and offering his services as a pianist to theatres, nightclubs and brothels, pitting himself against his local rivals in merciless musical duels. During the 1893 Chicago World Fair, he led a small group in which he played piano and cornet, although he was based in Missouri – at St Louis and later Sedalia. It was in Sedalia that he composed his first rags and there too that he published 'Maple Leaf Rag' (1899), which became his first success (selling 75,000 copies in six months). Full of syncopation and polyrhythmic effects, ragtime is based on a left hand that switches between a robust walking bass and a brisk, light style (alternating bass, in which a bottom note is played on the main beat and a higher chord on the unaccented beat, producing a 'poum chick, poum chick' effect). Ragtime is based around a virtuoso style inherited from Romantic piano music. Its basic structure, inspired by salon music, is a series of four 16-bar 'strains', the third of which (the 'trio') departs from the original key. While Scott Joplin's success has led historians to focus on his Missouri rivals (Louis Chauvin and Tom Turpin) and pupils (James Scott and the white composer Joseph Lamb), a large number of composers, both black and white, had already adopted ragtime before the publication of 'Maple Leaf Rag'. The genre developed simultaneously in Baltimore, Philadelphia, Boston, Memphis, New Orleans and even New York, where Ben Harney played ragtime in Tony Pastor's Music Hall as early as 1896.

Scott Joplin was an ambitious composer (he also wrote an opera entitled *Treemonisha*) and did not appreciate the excesses of the vogue for ragtime. In 1908, he published a manual called *School of Ragtime, 6 Exercises for Piano*, designed to rein in pianists tempted by excessively spirited tempi or overly free interpretations. What did he make, then, of the contests between rival pianists? It was inevitable that liberties would be taken with the form and that the bordellos would not reverberate with the sound of classic ragtime alone. It is thought that at the same period, amid all the hubbub of the barrelhouses, honky tonks and juke-joints, a vigorous style of music known as boogie-woogie (impregnated with the blues and the sound of African drums) was already being played on clapped-out bar-room pianos.

LISTENING GUIDE

The Victor Minstrels: 'The Cake Walk' (Victor, 13 December 1902)[1].
Scott Joplin: 'Maple Leaf Rag', 'Original Rags', 'Cascades'[2].

CD GUIDE
1. *From Cake-Walk to Ragtime, 1898–1916*, Frémeaux.
2. Scott Joplin, *King of Ragtime Writers, from Classic Piano Rolls*, Biograph.

SYNCOPATION AND RAGTIME

In Europe, rhythmic clarity is preferred and the beat is accentuated in the most basic way. Marching in step, soldiers count: 1-2, 1-2 (LEFT-right, LEFT-right). Polka dancers think in terms of: 1-2-3-4. The odd beat is strong and the even beat is weak. Each beat can in turn be subdivided into quavers and semiquavers accentuated in a similar fashion. The main notes of a melody are played on the strong beats and it is important to avoid playing notes that are alien to the main harmony on these beats. As they are accentuated, there would be a danger of them clashing with the chord or harmony. They can, however, be played on the weak beats without any problem.

Syncopation

Africa prefers the ambiguity of cross rhythms and does not share this hierarchical concept of the bar. Within a group of drummers a variety of rhythms will be heard. A drummer will play a different rhythm to his neighbour. The result is an accentuation of the weak beats, which – to the Western ear – are without solid rhythmic foundation. Americans were astonished to hear black singers clapping on the offbeat or weak beat, yet they adopted the habit. Indeed, American audiences habitually clap on the offbeat, giving their hand-clapping an irresistible lightness that contrasts strongly with the heavy on-the-beat clapping of European audiences. This rhythmic lightness also entered American folk music by way of the five-string banjo and the outmoded 'frailin' style' (also known as stroke style or rapping style). This style of playing is still used by the white farmers of the Appalachians, but was actually inherited from the ancient *banjar* of the plantations (listen to 'Emmaline, Take Your Time'). Its main technique involves plucking the string on the main beat with the right hand and playing the notes of the melody on the offbeats by bringing the fingers of the left hand down onto the string in a percussive manner ('hammering on'). More importantly, as if he were adding a drum to a polyrhythmic ensemble, the banjo player strikes the 'fifth string' of the instrument with his thumb on the final semiquaver of the beat, producing a sustained note (drone or pedal note) struck ahead of the following beat. This effect, which involves displacing the playing of the notes relative to the rhythmic framework, is called syncopation. It can be heard clearly in the opening bars of 'Maple Leaf Rag'.

LISTENING GUIDE
Sid Hemphill, Lucius Smith: 'Emmaline, Take Your Time', 'Old Devil's Dream' (Alan Lomax, 1959)[1].
Scott Joplin: 'Maple Leaf Rag'[2]; 'Cascades'[2].

CD GUIDE
1. *Southern Journey, Vol 3*, Rounder.
2. Scott Joplin, *King of Ragtime Writers*, from *Classic Piano Rolls*, Biograph.

Opening bars of 'Maple Leaf Rag'

Many accounts claim that ragtime piano was born of the desire to transpose the unusual rolling rhythm of the five-string banjo to the piano. Making systematic use of syncopation, ragtime at first astonished and then delighted Europeans. They were used to marching stiffly in step and sticking strictly to the beat, but syncopation encouraged them to give in gradually to the body's natural swaying motion between each step.

The polyrhythmic illusion

Although the 2/4 time signature leads one to expect the tune to be divided into two groups of four even semiquavers, bars 3 and 4 of the trio of 'Maple Leaf Rag' (1:33–1:34) feature a rhythmic motif of three repeated semiquavers. The last note of the motif (the F highlighted in red in the musical excerpt reproduced below) is thus repeated insistently three times despite occurring in a different position in the bar on each occasion. The composer therefore creates the illusion in the right hand of superimposing duple time (2/4) over a triple (6/8) beat. This metrical displacement and superimposition delighted the public and was later much used by all types of jazzmen from drummers to composers (notably in the first few bars of Glenn Miller's 'In the Mood').

Bars 3 and 4 of the trio of 'Maple Leaf Rag'

The structure of ragtime

In terms of structure, 'Maple Leaf Rag' consists of four 16-bar strains: A, B, C and D. Strains A, B, and D are in A♭, while strain C, the trio, which constitutes a kind of central interlude, is in D♭. They are arranged as follows:

A (0:00–0:18) A (0:19–0:37)

B (0:37–0:54) B (0:55–1:12)

A (1:13–1:30)

C (1:30–1:47) C (1:47–2:03)

D (2:04–2:20) D (2:20–2:37)

There are also variations on this pattern. For example, in 'Cascades' (also by Joplin) there is no return to strain A before strain C. The transition is achieved by means of a brief modulating passage that moves from C to B♭. The fourth and final section introduces a further modulation, this time taking the key to E♭.

Introduction (0:00–0:05)

A (0:05–0:25) A (0:26–0:46)

B (0:46–1:06) B (1:06–1:25)

Modulating passage (1:26–1:30)

C (1:31–1:50) C (1:50–2:08)

D (2:09–2:27) D (2:28–2:46)

Vaudeville and musicals

Originally staged in Massachusetts before being presented in New York in 1894, *The Creole Show* featured a number of attractive young black girls alongside Sam Lucas, the main star of the black minstrel shows. In 1896, *Oriental America* presented an entirely black cast on Broadway for the first time ever, and from 1898 a coterie of composers (Will Marion Cook, Robert Cole, J Rosamond Johnson), authors (James Weldon Johnson, Paul Lawrence Dunbar) and variety artists (Bert Williams and George Walker) brought to the attention of the public a black musical style which subsequently (from 1910) found a home in Harlem's theatres (the Lafayette and the Lincoln). This was a time when black theatres were springing up across the whole country, opening their doors to black vaudeville troupes whose shows consisted of numbers inspired by the minstrels and European operetta. Abandoned by James Bland during a trip to Europe in the 1880s, Negro-style make-up gradually disappeared and by 1920 black performers had all but turned their backs on the themes of slavery and the plantation. Now it was urban life and Africa that provided them with inspiration (for example, *In Dahomey* by Will Marion Cook), subjects they portrayed in a manner that caused a sensation among the white public (Florenz Ziegfeld bought the rights to numbers from *Darktown Follies*, staged in Harlem in 1913, for his own *Follies*).

Orchestral ragtime and the drum kit

Between 1910 and 1920, ragtime conquered white America – even rural white America, where it was adopted by the local string bands (violin, guitar, mandolin and the newly adopted five-string banjo). Contact between the black and white communities, moreover, was so abundant that the stylistic distinction between the music of the two, particularly between the white string band and the black 'spasm band' or 'jug band' was not always clear-cut. The jug band, which would later become extremely popular in Memphis in the 1920s, often featured improvised instruments and objects intended for other uses: comb and paper, a jug transformed into a double bass, or washboard percussion. The black bands, however, abandoned the five-string banjo as it had become rather suspect in the hands of the minstrels. Instead they took up either the guitar or the guitar-like four- or six-string banjo. It was on this type of banjo that Fred Van Eps and Vess Ossman, the white virtuosi of ragtime, made a name for themselves. The white as well as the black brass bands that proliferated at this time and the orchestras that accompanied variety shows were also influenced by syncopation. The new syncopated music was often syncopated in name only, but it featured a new instrument that thrilled the crowds: the drum kit. The drum kit brought together all the different percussion instruments of the brass band (bass drum, snare drum, cymbals and various accessories), placing them within reach of a single instrumentalist. The white drummer James Irving Lent was one of the main attractions of Will Marion Cook's musical *In Dahomey*, first staged in 1902, and in 1905 the black drummer Buddy Gilmore (who later joined James Europe's Society Orchestra) could be seen playing with the Nashville Students. At this time the drummer was seen as a kind of acoustic 'props man', emphasizing the melody using military-style drumming techniques accompanied by a kind of rhythmic

LISTENING GUIDE

Sousa's Band: 'Trombone Sneeze' (Victor, 30 January 1902)[1].

Victor Dance Orchestra: 'Cake-Walk in the Sky' (Victor, 10 April 1905)[2].

Vess L Ossman: 'Saint Louis Tickle' (Victor, 24 January 1906)[2].

Fred Van Eps: 'Notoriety Rag' (Victor, 19 March 1914)[2].

The Six Brown Brothers: 'That Moaning Saxophone Rag' (Victor, 20 November 1914)[2].

The Versatile Four: 'Down Home Rag' (His Master's Voice, 3 February 1916)[3].

Europe's Society Orchestra: 'Too Much Mustard' (Victor, 29 December 1913)[1], 'Castle House Rag' (Victor, 10 February 1914)[3], 'Castle Walk' (Victor, 10 February 1914)[2].

James I Lent: 'The Ragtime Drummer' (Edison Bell, 1904)[3].

CD GUIDE
1. *Ragtime, Vol 1, 1897–1919*, Jazz Archives.
2. *From Cake-Walk to Ragtime, 1898–1916*, Frémeaux.
3. *Anthology of Jazz Drumming, Vol 1, 1904–28*, Masters of Jazz.

James Europe and his
band in 1914

gesticulation during sustained notes and silences.

In 1910, James Europe founded a black musicians' guild called the Clef Club and in May 1912 gave a concert in Carnegie Hall with a 125-strong orchestra consisting of mandolins, guitars, banjos, violins, cellos, saxophones, brass, percussion … and ten pianos. While the precursors of New York jazz were emerging in connection with the activities of the Clef Club and later the Tempo Club (the cornetist Crickett Smith, the pianist Willie 'the Lion' Smith and the drummer Louis A Mitchell), James Europe, at the head of a smaller band, was providing the white dancers Vernon and Irene Castle with rhythms for which America would go crazy: the Turkey Trot, the foxtrot, the Castle Walk, the Fish Walk and other manifestations of the one-step. Europe did not yet know that success awaited him on the continent whose name he bore, and where at the same time war would break out.

New Orleans

Since the end of the 20th century, music historians have been putting the importance of New Orleans into perspective and stripping it of many exaggerations and legends. At the beginning of that century, the 'Crescent City' did not have a monopoly on syncopated music or black bands with drums. Nevertheless, something very special did occur there.

African Americans and Creoles

In the 19th century, New Orleans was Catholic, Latin, open to the Caribbean, and the only city in North America to celebrate Carnival. It was founded by the French in 1718, became the capital of Louisiana in 1722, was ceded to Spain in 1762, restored to France in 1800 and sold to the United States in 1803. While the first segregationist laws were passed there in 1816, they were applied relatively flexibly during the 19th century. French aristocrats kept black or mixed-race (Creole) mistresses fairly openly and a large mixed-race population existed alongside the white one. Neither dance nor theatre was subjected to Puritan prejudices, and up to the time of the Civil War New Orleans had a flourishing musical scene. Having benefited from European-style musical training, the Creoles occupied an important place in this scene. It was not unusual for them to be seen playing alongside white musicians or standing in for colleagues in the Negro Philharmonic Society. African drumming was tolerated, and accompanied the Sunday dancing on Congo Square up to the end of the 19th century.

In 1894, the city voted for strict segregation. The Creole population had to leave downtown New Orleans and its French Quarter and join the African Americans in the outlying districts set aside for them. This led to intense competition between two communities equally proud of their respective traditions: on the one hand, the sophistication of the Creole musicians, who could read music and were well versed in the harmonic and orchestral refinements of the European tradition and the repertoire of the concert halls and ballrooms, and who were proud of their light skin, their French-style education and their refined manners; on the other hand, American polyrhythmic pan-Africanism, the religious tradition of the camp meetings, the nascent blues (still influenced by the repertoire of musical forms that had developed under slavery – work songs, hollers and laments), inflected blue notes, individual inventiveness in collective music-making, and the use of the body. The influence of the nearby Caribbean should also not be overlooked. Cuban and Mexican bands are known to have performed in the city, and residual traces of their influence can be heard in all kinds of music from Jelly Roll Morton to the local rhythm and blues.

Outdoor music

Another feature of New Orleans was the existence of benevolent societies and clubs which guaranteed their members various benefits including a decent funeral. The famous funeral processions – led by bands playing slow tunes on their way to the cemetery and happy tunes as they made their way back down to the city, followed by onlookers (the 'second line') who would contribute improvised dancing or percussion – are known to have existed from the beginning of the 19th century. Bands were also hired to announce and accompany other events organized by these clubs (such as fashionable picnics by the shore of Lake Ponchartrain, sports events, balls and carnival events). Depending on the circumstances (private party or public ball, indoor or outdoor event), these bands were either brass-based (trumpet, or more commonly cornet, valve trombone, replaced by the slide trombone after 1905, and tuba) or wind- and-strings-based (saxophone, visible on photographs from around 1910, clarinet, mandolin, guitar, banjo, violin, cello and double bass). The use of brass-band percussion became widespread around this time. The language of the snare drum was borrowed from the military side drum that originated in Europe: a repertoire of drum rolls precisely classified according to the number of strokes on the drum head. New Orleans percussionists, however, favoured the 'press roll' (featuring an indeterminate number of strokes) that had emerged in popular music at the end of the 19th century. They began to alternate strokes of the bass drum on the main beat with snare-drum press rolls on the offbeat. As New Orleans was a sunny southern town, music was frequently performed outdoors. Marching bands would cross the path of 'wagon bands' riding on the backs of horse-drawn removal wagons. Sitting with their legs hanging over the edge of the wagon (with the tailgate down) in order to give their instrument the space it needed, trombonists would indulge in vigorous slide effects that delighted the public and gave rise to what became known as the 'tailgate style'. An encounter between two bands would be an occasion for relentless musical jousting. The black musicians would give free rein to their imaginations, thereby compensating for their lack of formal musical training compared to the Creoles. They gradually took greater and greater liberties with melody, as the singers of spirituals and work songs had already started to do. In this way the New Orleans 'Holy Trinity' style developed, based on a form of spontaneous collective counterpoint: the cornet played the melody and variations, the clarinet, playing above the cornet, embroidered the melody with considerable virtuosity and the trombone underpinned the whole with a vigorous counterpoint. It is said that around 1905 the trumpeter Buddy Bolden, playing in Lincoln Park, turned his cornet in the direction of nearby Johnson Park, where John Robichaux was playing, and stole the Creole's audience – evidence of how rapidly the public of the time could be seduced by music that was less refined but also less mannered and more exciting.

The revival of indoor music

The defeat of the southern states in the Civil War and the economic decline that followed led to the collapse of cultural life in New Orleans. The historian Ronald L Morris attributes the renaissance of the 1880s to the influx of Italian immigrants into a French Quarter that was in a state of rapid decline. It would even appear that throughout the history of jazz, in an effort to assert themselves in the face of the Anglo-Saxon Protestant majority, Italian and Jewish immigrants from central Europe connived with black Americans against Irish immigrants – hence the large number of white jazzmen of Jewish and Italian origin.

Thus, it was only natural that the Sicilian Mafia in New Orleans should turn to the black populace for help in reviving the entertainment market in the drinking establishments over which it was fighting with the Irish for control. The black bands did not, as has been claimed, play in the bordellos of the red-light district of Storyville (which only employed pianists, in particular ragtime specialists such as Tony Jackson and Jelly Roll Morton). Musicians looking for work used to meet in the barbershops on the edge of Storyville, in what was known as 'Black Storyville'. And in the evening, groups such as Buddy Bolden's could be heard in the ballrooms (Funky Butt Hall or the Odd Fellows and Masonic Hall) and nightclubs (including various clubs belonging to Tom Anderson, Johnny Lala's Big 25, Pete's Lala and the Red Onion) around Rampart Street and Perdido Street.

Thanks to the 'double drumming' technique (whereby the drummer uses the same stick to strike the bass drum and snare drum alternately) and later the bass-drum pedal, which at around the turn of the century left the drummer's hands free to play the snare drum and various accessories, the custom developed of uniting snare drum, bass drum and cymbals in the hands of one man. At this time the double bass was still played with the bow. Pizzicato did not become widespread until after 1910 with Bill Johnson, Wellman Braud and Pops Foster. The minstrels' five-string banjo was replaced by the guitar, but – also in the 1910s – guitarists such as Bud Scott

Buddy Bolden (back row, second from right) and his band

and Johnny Saint-Cyr began to favour the plectrum banjo (six-stringed or more commonly four-stringed), whose greater sonority could hold its own against the brass and percussion.

Some players ...

The prehistory of New Orleans jazz is shrouded in legend. Its principal characters are known to us from accounts that are variously contradictory and fanciful. The trumpeter Buddy Bolden (active from 1897), the first star of 'prehistoric' jazz, is one such legendary figure. His biographical details may be uncertain but his powerful playing ensured that his name was remembered. In his wake, the cornet was dominated by black players including Bunk Johnson, Mutt Carey, King Oliver and his young pupil Louis Armstrong.

While the Creoles boasted a number of important cornetists (Freddie Keppard, Buddy Petit and Manuel Perez), they mainly stood out as players of string and woodwind instruments in dance orchestras (Armand Piron and the multi-instrumentalist John Robichaux on the violin; and Alphonse Picou, Lorenzo Tio Sr and their successors Lorenzo Tio Jr, George Baquet, Sidney Bechet, Jimmie Noone, Barney Bigard, Albert Nicholas and Omer Simeon on the clarinet). As always, the exceptions prove the rule: the famous clarinetist Johnny Dodds was black and the trombonist Kid Ory was a Creole.

The first great New Orleans percussionists played bass drum with brass bands such as the Excelsior, the Onward and the Columbia. The names of many of those renowned for the quality of their beat have lived on – 'Black Benny' Williams and Ernest Trepagnier, to name but two. The first to adopt the bass-drum pedal in order to combine a strong beat with virtuoso drumming was Dee Dee Chandler, while Red Happy Bolton, who played in John Robichaux's band, is credited with the first drum solos. Louis Cottrell is thought to have been the first to use the press roll, subsequently teaching it to Baby Dodds (see the next chapter). Among the first bass-drum players to adopt the double-drumming technique was the white drummer Papa Jack Laine. This shows that white musicians also took an early interest in jazz.

The diaspora

The drift of New Orleans musicians towards the northern cities was for a long time attributed to the closure of the Storyville brothels in 1917. This explanation, however, overlooked the role played by segregation, which had been prompting black Americans to move north ever since the beginning of the 20th century. And in a wider sense there was a desire among the population as a whole to flee a damaged economy. With its role as an important shipping centre threatened by the development of the railways, New Orleans had been in rapid decline since the end of the 19th century.

From 1909 – the year that the bassist Bill Johnson emigrated to California – countless musicians left the city to try their luck elsewhere. Jelly Roll Morton had already been on the road since 1907. In 1914, Freddie Keppard joined Bill Johnson in Los Angeles, where they founded the Original Creole Orchestra. That same year, Sidney Bechet landed in a Texan jail after giving Clarence Williams the slip while on tour. Employed to play on paddle steamers, New Orleans musicians spread the word northwards along the banks of the Mississippi, and in 1915 Chicago emerged as their favourite destination. There, their music became known as 'jass', a word whose origin has given rise to many different explanations, not a few of them far-fetched. A number of African (by way of black American slang) and even French etymologies have been proposed. The late 19th-century American slang term 'jasm' (meaning 'semen' and, by association, vitality) has been suggested as one possible derivation; and it is known that the verb to 'jass' or 'jazz' was used at the beginning of the 20th century to denote both sexual intercourse and sporting or musical energy. In 1915, during a concert given in Chicago by Tom Brown's band, a member of the audience is supposed to have called out 'Jass it up!', an expression thought to have been inspired by the aphrodisiac properties of New Orleans music. Up to this point no one had known what to call it; but now the word 'jass' helped the music to attract a particularly exuberant audience.

THE NEW ORLEANS SOUND

Jealous of his art to the point of concealing his fingers beneath a handkerchief, the black cornetist Freddie Keppard apparently refused to make a recording in 1916, and so the honour of making the first jazz record fell to a white ensemble, the Original Dixieland Jazz Band, in 1917. Another five years passed before black New Orleans music could be heard on disc. What, then, did it sound like in the years 1910–20?

Late recordings

It is tempting to turn to Freddie Keppard's Jazz Cardinals for the answer, but by the time he led his band into the studio, he had been playing with various groups in Chicago for four years and may well have acquired new habits from them. In 1926, he nevertheless made a lively recording with Johnny Dodds, one of the south's most famous clarinetists, but even this is perhaps already too careful and precise to be taken into consideration.

Recordings made by the trombonist Kid Ory with Spike's Seven Pods of Pepper Orchestra (or Ory's Sunshine Orchestra) in 1922 are perhaps more authoritative, despite being made in Los Angeles. They also feature a cornet player of indisputable maturity and elegance who would go on to lead well-balanced bands of his own: Mutt Carey.

Clarence Williams (back left) with Armand Piron's orchestra

'Ory's Creole Trombone' gives us an opportunity to hear the vigorous slide effects of the tailgate style but overall the playing is fairly stiff. It should be remembered, however, that the studio could be an extremely inhibiting place for those entering it for the first time, especially when the sound engineer imposed all kinds of restrictions on the drummer. An interesting comparison can be made with recordings of the Original Dixieland Jazz Band (see the beginning of the next chapter) made as early as 1917–18 which reveal a drummer on brilliant and energetic form.

From the relatively late recordings made by Sam Morgan's Jazz Band via the band of the Creole bandleader Armand Piron to the sides recorded by the California Poppies (led convincingly by the cornetist Ernest B Coyault), the 1920s provide us with a number of examples of what the music of New Orleans must have been like in the 1910s. Solos are rare; where they do occur they tend to be breaks (the band suddenly falls silent for one or two bars, allowing an instrumentalist to demonstrate his virtuosity). As early as 1923, however, the cornetist Tommy Ladnier and the clarinetist Jimmie Noone seemed very much at home with solo playing on 'Play That Thing' with Ollie Power's Harmony Syncopators. While saxophones still only played a secondary role, they nevertheless appear on many photographs dating from just before 1920.

Sadly, there are no recordings of New Orleans brass bands prior to those made in 1951 by the Eureka Brass Band led by Percy Humphrey (the son of James Humphrey, who formed the Eclipse Brass Band in 1881). In 1945, however, the New Orleans veteran trumpeter Bunk Johnson re-formed a brass band specifically in order to record with a group of older musicians including the drummer Baby Dodds.

Jelly Roll Morton

Although the piano was not a permanent fixture of the earliest New Orleans line-ups, the city could boast a school of ragtime piano presided over by Tony Jackson, whose heir apparent was Jelly Roll Morton. A comparison inevitably suggests itself between the first recordings made by Jelly Roll Morton on disc or paper roll and those of Scott Joplin, particularly as some of the New Orleans pianist's compositions date from before 1910.

Indeed, there is a story that around this time Scott Joplin returned the score of 'King Porter Stomp' (which the younger pianist had sent him) without any critical comments at all. However, according to the pianist James P Johnson, who heard his New Orleans colleague play 'The Jelly Roll Blues' in New York sometime after 1910, Morton was no ordinary pianist who stuck to classical music theory. Especially striking are the formal liberties taken

by Jelly Roll Morton when using the twelve-bar blues structure, alternating for example 16-, 32- and even 14-bar sections ('Shreveport Stomp', 1:20–1:36, 1:37–1:51). In 'The Pearls', the two silent bars (1:27, 1:53, 2:18, 2:43) in the 32-bar trio and the delayed start of the melody have a disorientating effect on the listener and anticipate the rule-breaking indulged in by Miles Davis and his nonet. Jelly Roll Morton was not alone in taking structural liberties of this kind. Before the standardization of the 1930s, they were relatively common in jazz. Kid Ory includes a twelve-bar structure within a ragtime form (1:48–2:01) in 'Ory's Creole Trombone' and Freddie Keppard uses a ten-bar line (0:00–0:11, 0:20–0:31) in the first section of 'Stock Yards Strut'.

However, Jelly Roll Morton went further. This is evident in the introduction of his 'Jelly Roll Blues', which starts in F sharp and ends up in the diametrically opposed key of B flat. And in 'Shreveport Stomp' (1:20–1:36, 1:37–1:51), he performs breathtaking harmonic acrobatics with similar ease.

Was Jelly Roll Morton already improvising when he composed these pieces? All the indications are that he was. On his recordings of 1923 and 1924 he constantly changes his approach in the course of each piece, whereas Scott Joplin's work suffers from the repetition of the same thematic material. The diversity of the treatment of the blues in each of the choruses of 'Jelly Roll Blues' is nothing short of astounding, and in the sixth chorus of 'New Orleans Joys' (1:56–2:17) Morton affects to ignore the tempo — while never losing sight of it — by playing unconventional rhythmic values. It is not only his right hand that operates in such an imaginative way. The simultaneous independence and interaction of his two hands is remarkable, the left hand either joining with the right or allowing it the freedom to play extremely fast breaks that interrupt the repeated sequences of the alternating bass. It is interesting to note the use of phrasing borrowed from the Spanish Caribbean (geographically close to New Orleans) of which Jelly Roll was very proud: after the modulation to E in 'Jelly Roll Blues', 2:06; the last part of 'Shreveport Stomp', 3:39–3:43 and 3:48–3:51; and the entire opening of 'New Orleans Joys', a number of passages of which also borrow from boogie-woogie, 0:53–1:00 and 1:15–1:20.

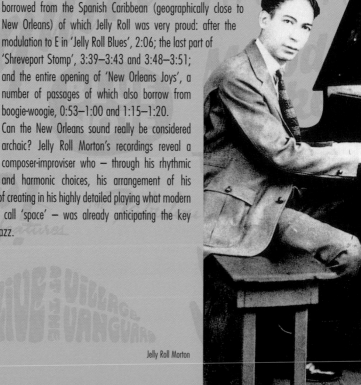

Jelly Roll Morton

Can the New Orleans sound really be considered archaic? Jelly Roll Morton's recordings reveal a composer-improviser who — through his rhythmic and harmonic choices, his arrangement of his material and his way of creating in his highly detailed playing what modern jazzmen would later call 'space' — was already anticipating the key elements of modern jazz.

Europe takes to the Cakewalk

The musical gifts of the black population and the existence of the banjo started to feature in Europeans' accounts of their travels to the New World in the 18th century. In 1782, a 'Negro Jig' was included in a collection of Scottish dances. In the 1820s, it was common for travellers to visit the African Grove theatre while in New York, and two decades later Charles Dickens wrote about the black taverns of the Five Points neighbourhood in Manhattan. In New Orleans, travellers visited Congo Square for the dancing. In 1838, Europe welcomed Frank Johnson's brass band, which even performed at Buckingham Palace. In 1844, the appearance in Dublin of the white minstrel Joel W Sweeny may have been the reason for the adoption of the banjo by Irish folk musicians, and the vogue for the instrument was reflected in the drawing rooms of Victorian Britain. During the second half of the century, minstrel shows and spirituals singers acquired a following in South Africa.

In 1873, the Fisk Jubilee Singers performed in Liverpool and collections of Negro spirituals were published all over the world.

In the 1880s, the black minstrel James Bland became the idol of the European music hall. In 1893, at the World's Columbian Exposition in Chicago, visitors from all corners of the globe saw the *Creole Show* and discovered the Cakewalk and ragtime, both of which John Philip Sousa subsequently took across the Atlantic to the Paris World Fair in 1900. Three years later, the percussionist James Irving Lent, performing in the black musical *In Dahomey* at the Shaftesbury Theatre in London, was announced as 'America's Best Orchestral Drummer'. Claude Debussy included a cakewalk ('Golliwog's Cakewalk') in his *Children's Corner* suite (1906–8). The band of the French Republican Guard recorded 'Le Vrai Cakewalk' as early as 1906, and after 1910 many recordings – by the xylophonist William Ditcham, the Empire Military Band and the Orchestre Tzigane du Volney, among others – were made in London and Paris. The black composer J Rosamond Johnson was musical director of the Hammerstein Opera House in London from 1912 to 1913, and the cornetist Julien Poret found himself playing ragtime pieces when he took up employment at the Luna Park amusement park in Paris in 1913. He also composed them himself from 1914. After joining the French Army Band, he was sent to America in 1915 as part of a mission to entice the United States into the war and heard groups of black musicians in Chicago, to which he referred in his memoirs as jazz bands. In London, members of the New York Clef Club took up a residency at Ciro's Club.

LISTENING GUIDE
Band of the Republican Guard: 'Le Vrai Ragtime' (G & T, 1906)[1].
William Ditcham: 'Alabama Skedaddle' (Bell Disc, October 1910)[1].
Orchestre Tzigane du Volney: 'Oh! That Yankianna Rag' (Gramophone, September 1912)[1].
The Ciro's Club Coon Orchestra: 'Saint Louis Blues' (Columbia, September 1917)[2].

CD GUIDE
1. *From Cakewalk to Ragtime*, Frémeaux.
2. *Américains en Europe (1917–39)*, Swing / EMI.

43

Context

SOCIETY. On 2 April 1917, the United States declared war on Germany. A few months later, American troops disembarked in France, arriving at the front in Spring 1918. Industry in the USA's northern cities, driven by the war effort, accelerated the emigration of black Americans from the south, taking it to record levels. The ghettos grew in size but were ignored by the

Republicans, who had been brought to power after the European adventure by a liberal but conservative and inward-looking America.

Prohibition (1919–33) led to an enormous volume of illegal liquor trafficking. This was controlled by the Jewish and Sicilian Mafias, who opened the doors of their bars and nightclubs to black musicians. Following anti-corruption campaigns in Chicago around 1928, a decline in gangsterism led many jazz musicians to move to New York and Kansas City. Support

Protest march along New York's Fifth Avenue against the St Louis riots of July 1917

for the Russian Revolution provoked the first wave of anti-Communism (including the execution of Sacco and Vanzetti in 1927). After a period of relative calm, the Ku Klux Klan increased its activities and tension between white and black populations intensified, resulting in riots in Houston and St Louis in 1917 and in many other towns and cities across the country during the so-called Red Summer of 1919.

The black political elite toughened its stance. In 1917, *The Messenger*, a radical black magazine, advocated resistance to conscription. The Senate expressed its alarm in a report on black radicalism published in 1919. In spite of Marcus Garvey's arrest for fraud in 1923 and the failure of his 'back to Africa' movement, his separatist nationalism met with a strong, long-lasting response. The first black trade union, the Brotherhood of Sleeping Car Porters, was founded in 1925.

European composers at home and abroad embraced the sounds of the modern world (Varèse's *Amériques*, composed during 1918–22), explored the world of automatism and the subconscious (the *First Surrealist Manifesto* of 1924) and drew inspiration from the 'Negro arts' (Blaise Cendrars' *Anthologie Nègre*, 1921; Stravinsky's *Ragtime*, 1918). The 'Negro arts' were also prominently featured at the 1925 International Exhibition of Decorative Arts in Paris, providing a source of inspiration for the designers of the city's new American bars.

In New York, moonshine liquor lured the city's intellectual elite into the bars of Harlem, where they were happy to slum it with the locals in the belief that they were tapping into the energy that had helped forge the American identity. In 1925, the literary review *Survey Graphics* published a special issue entitled 'Harlem: Mecca of the New Negro'. There was great enthusiasm for the Harlem Renaissance (1924–30), a multidisciplinary artistic movement that revealed the existence of a black literature (for example, *Autobiography of an Ex-Colored Man* written by J Weldon Johnson back in 1912, and the first and only issue of a radical literary review launched by Langston Hughes in 1926 and entitled *Fire!!!*).

THE MUSIC INDUSTRY. As the main patents relating to the gramophone record began to expire, the large companies Columbia and Victor Talking Machine saw their monopolies eroded by smaller labels such as Gennett, Paramount, Okeh, Vocalion and the black firm Black Swan. The resulting lowering of prices took advantage of the economic potential of the black public, leading to the creation of 'colored catalogs' and 'race series'. Recording studios, initially concentrated in New York, started to proliferate in 1922. Record companies began to decentralize their facilities and sent talent scouts to urban and rural areas in the south in search of talented local artists.

The disc won out against the cylinder and playing systems were standardized. 'Electric' recording (using valve amplifiers and electric microphones and motors) came into general use in 1925 and a uniform playing speed of 78rpm was established. These advances gave post-1925 recordings a far higher standard of sound reproduction than the earlier 'acoustic' recordings.

The hi-hat pedal appeared in the catalogue of the drum manufacturer Ludwig around 1928.

RELATED MUSICAL GENRES. In 1924, the record companies' talent scouts started to bring authentic southern blues to people's attention. While some bluesmen were recorded locally, others – such as Big Bill Broonzy – took the road to Chicago. Similarly, after initially favouring gospel quartets such as the Norfolk Jubilee Quartet and small rural choirs such as the Holy Ghost Sanctified Singers, the record companies began to record preachers (A W Nix, J M Gates, J C Burnett), female evangelists of the Holiness Church (such as the first recorded gospel soloists Arizona Dranes and Sister Cally Fancy) and 'guitar evangelists' – itinerant preachers steeped in the archaic blues style (for example, Blind Willie Johnson), some of whom were themselves repentant bluesmen. Also recorded in the 1920s were singers of solo spirituals drawing on both European and black traditions (among them the actor Paul Robeson and the opera singer Marian Anderson). The talent scouts' quest also took them to white rural areas, where they brought to light the many influences between blues, ragtime and country. At the end of 1927, the country singer Jimmie Rodgers started a craze for the 'blue yodel'.

In New York, the string of revues known as *George White's Scandals* supplanted the *Ziegfeld Follies* on Broadway in the 1920s and brought George Gershwin to public attention. Before long, however, Gershwin left to concentrate on musicals (*Lady Be Good*, *Oh, Kay!*, *Strike Up the Band* and *Funny Face*). Other pioneers of this new genre included Irving Berlin (*Blue Skies*) and, most importantly, Jerome Kern (*Show Boat*). Inspired by the rhythms of black music, their work would later be an important source of material for jazzmen.

LISTENING GUIDE
1. *Negro Spirituals/Gospel Songs, 1926–42*, Frémeaux.
2. *Blues, 36 Masterpieces of Blues Music, 1927–42*, Frémeaux.

New Orleans in Chicago

In the 1910s, Italian and Jewish immigrants from central Europe put an end to the Irish hegemony in the Southside neighbourhood between the Chicago River and Lake Michigan. They established a good relationship with the black Americans from the south, whose ghetto continued to develop throughout the century. There, black musicians from New Orleans began to make a name for themselves in the nightclubs that flourished in the vicinity of 35th Street and State Street, earning Chicago a reputation as the capital of jazz – a reputation that lasted until New York's arrival on the scene at the end of the 1920s.

White bands steal the show

Initially, however, it was white bands that attracted most of the attention. Many of these bands moved to Chicago, bringing the syncopated music of New Orleans with them. The word 'jass' began to catch on when Stein's Band From New Orleans arrived in the city in 1916. Under the leadership of Nick La Rocca, the group changed its name to the Original Dixieland Jass Band (ODJB). The band was soon invited to play its 'jass' (written 'jazz' for reasons of modesty) at the high-class Reisenweber's restaurant in New York. After an initial failed recording session with Columbia, it recorded the 'first jazz record' ('Livery Stable Blues – Dixie Jazz Band One Step') for Victor on 26 February 1917. It was a great success.

How good is this recording? For a long time, experts regarded the white bands of New Orleans as stiff and over-reliant on the basic rhythms of the polka and military march, and considered their 'collective' ensemble style caricatured and frenzied. 'Livery Stable Blues', with its animal imitations, supports this view, but it is by no means certain that black musicians of the period played any differently. Today, with the benefit of greater hindsight, there is a better appreciation of the qualities of the white combos – the imaginative virtuosity of their rhythm sections and the elegance of their ensemble playing. Careful listening to 'Tiger Rag' (1918) by the Original Dixieland Jazz Band reveals an authentic jazz drummer (Antonio Sbarbaro, alias Tony Spargo), the only member of the band who really improvises his part. Other white line-ups, such as the Original New Orleans Jazz Band ('Ja-Da') and the Louisiana Five ('Slow and Easy'), give more fluid performances. Jumping forward to 1922 and 'Panama', recorded by the New Orleans Rhythm Kings (NORK), the variations played by the cornetist Paul Mares at the heart of the ensemble and a solo by the clarinetist Leon Roppolo seem way ahead of anything else recorded that year.

The dawning of black jazz

Up to 1923 there is no real basis on which to compare black and white bands. Before 1920, gramophone records were expensive items and record companies did not regard the black population as a lucrative market. Moreover, all the recording studios were in New York. As a result, most of the recordings of the 1910s are of the syncopated music of that one city, whether black or white. The only exceptions are recordings made by a small

LISTENING GUIDE
Original Dixieland Jazz Band: 'Livery Stable Blues' (Victor, 26 February 1917)[1], 'Tiger Rag' (Victor, 25 March 1918)[2].
Original New Orleans Jazz Band: 'Ja-Da' (Gennett, December 1918)[3].
Louisiana Five: 'Slow and Easy' (Columbia, 16 December 1919)[3].
New Orleans Rhythm Kings: 'Panama' (recorded under the name of the Friars Society Orchestra, Gennett, 30 August 1922)[3].
King Oliver's Creole Jazz Band: see the following pages.

CD GUIDE
1. Original Dixieland Jazz Band, Vol 2, First Jazz Recordings, 1917–23, Jazz Archives.
2. Jazz New Orleans, 1918–44, Frémeaux.
3. Early Jazz, 1917–23, Frémeaux

number of white New Orleans bands visiting the city.

The first record companies to venture into the field were the smaller outfits. Founded in Los Angeles, the Sunshine label recorded Kid Ory's band as early as Summer 1922. That same year, Gennett opened a studio in Richmond, Indiana (a car drive from Chicago), and Paramount set up business in the centre of Chicago itself, followed a year later by Columbia, Victor, Okeh and Brunswick. Interest in the Louisiana 'breeding ground' meant that it was not long before mobile recording units reached New Orleans, followed soon after by permanent studios. The black musician's time had come.

There is not enough space here to list all the New Orleans bands of the 1920s that made a name for themselves, whether with their recordings or by playing in the city's nightclubs or dance halls (often their reputation spread as far as New York). If we had to name only one, it would be King Oliver's Creole Jazz Band, simply because this was a band that changed the course of jazz history. The cornetist Joseph 'Joe' Oliver won his title 'King' in a 'cutting contest' (competitive playing) with Manuel Perez and Freddie Keppard, the two pretenders to Buddy Bolden's crown, in New Orleans. After moving to Chicago at the invitation of the bassist Bill Johnson in 1918, he then travelled to San Francisco three years later. Upon his return to Chicago the following year, he summoned his young disciple Louis Armstrong from New Orleans to play second cornet in his Creole Jazz Band. Recording for the first time on 5 April 1923, this band made the transition from the traditional New Orleans collective style – which King Oliver had brought to a pinnacle of perfection – to the beginnings of a more modern style in the playing of Louis Armstrong, who was soon to become its leading exponent.

King Oliver's Creole Jazz Band in 1923. From left: Honoré Dutrey (trombone), Baby Dodds (drums), King Oliver (cornet), Lil Hardin (piano), Bill Johnson (bass, playing banjo), Johnny Dodds (clarinet), Louis Armstrong (cornet, playing trombone)

IN THE STUDIO WITH KING OLIVER

On 5 April 1923, the cornetist King Oliver's Creole Jazz Band was invited to record for Gennett, a newly founded subsidiary of the Starr Piano Company, which had just installed a studio in a shed at its Richmond factory. Unfortunately, the studio was close to a railway line and the sound engineer had to juggle the recording sessions to avoid the trains. In spite of these less-than-perfect conditions, preparations were made to record what some consider to be the first true jazz record.

Recording constraints

In addition to the pianist Lil Hardin, who had studied at Fisk University, King Oliver's band included some of the biggest names in New Orleans jazz: Louis Armstrong (second cornet), Honoré Dutrey (trombone), Johnny Dodds (clarinet), Bud Scott (six-string banjo) and Baby Dodds (drums), who was forbidden to use either bass or snare drums by an engineer fearful of 'popping'. As for the bassist Bill Johnson, he was simply asked not to play. Studios at this time preferred wind basses such as the tuba and the Creole Jazz Band used a bass saxophone for its later recordings.

LISTENING GUIDE

King Oliver's Creole Jazz Band: 'Dippermouth Blues', 'Canal Street Blues', 'Froggie Moore', 'Chimes Blues', 'Mandy Lee Blues' (Gennett, 5–6 April 1923).

CD GUIDE

Louis Armstrong, *Complete Edition, Vol 1, 1923*, Masters of Jazz.

These measures were necessitated by the entirely 'acoustic' recording technology of the day. The sound was captured by an enormous horn and transferred to the engraving needle mechanically. Balance was achieved by adjusting the positions of the instruments, and the musicians were invited to approach the horn when they had a solo to play. Louis Armstrong's big sound meant he had to be set back at some distance from the leader and Lil Hardin's piano was moved around according to its role in each piece.

The maximum duration of a 12-inch 78rpm record was three minutes and Lil Hardin was responsible for rearranging the music as required. Players were naturally somewhat nervous, particularly as there was no possibility of correcting takes. Until the advent of magnetic tape in the 1950s, recordings relied on the direct engraving principle. One mistake meant starting again from the top. On 'Dippermouth Blues', Baby Dodds forgets his break and Bill Johnson is left hanging on. Seething with impatience, he cries out: 'Oh, play that thing!'. The sound engineer liked this intervention and got Johnson to repeat it on the master take, when he made it sound like a shout of joy hailing the birth of jazz.

Masterpieces of the 'collective' style

These recordings, and in particular 'Canal Street Blues', show a supreme mastery of the art of the 'collective'. The second cornet, the clarinet and the trombone weave their own distinct parts around the first cornet's statements and melodic variations, pursuing their own paths without ever getting in the way of their partners. No other band of this period managed to combine such transparency of the individual parts with such perfect complementarity. This achievement is all the more impressive as the material is completely reinvented with each new cycle as if in response to a precise, predetermined plan. 'Papa Joe' was bringing the New Orleans 'collective' style to its logical conclusion. The next phase – under Louis Armstrong – would see a shift of focus to individual improvisation.

In a sense King Oliver was passing on the baton to his young disciple. When in 'Dipper Mouth Blues' he invites Armstrong to lead the combo (1:08–1:23), he is doing no more than resting his lips in preparation for his solo – three fantastic rhythmic variations based around the root and third-degree blue note, played with irresistible conviction in the 'wah-wah' style (opening and closing the bell of a brass instrument, generally with a plunger cup). In 'Froggie Moore', however, the way Louis Armstrong once again leads the band (1:43–2:19) makes the final ensemble section, led by King Oliver (2:20–2:59), seem somewhat lacklustre by comparison. His young disciple's rhythmic and melodic initiatives already belong to a later period, anticipating the Louis Armstrong of the second half of the 1920s. The same modern quality can be heard in his first recorded solo ('Chimes Blues', 1:53–2:28) — one that was evidently carefully prepared and possibly memorized but whose architecture is nevertheless quite extraordinary.

Repertoire and standard practice

The repertoire of jazz bands of this period consisted chiefly of multiple cycles of twelve-bar blues ('Chimes Blues': 0:06–0:23, 0:24–0:41, 0:41–0:58, etc) and ragtime structures ('Froggie Moore') featuring alternating sections of 16 bars (0:05–0:24, 0:24–0:43, 0:44–1:02, etc) or 32 bars (1:43–2:19), sometimes separated by an interlude. But much more irregular structures were also adopted. In 'Mandy Lee Blues', for example, a 16-bar cycle (0:06–0:27) is followed by an 18-bar cycle (0:28–0:52), which is in turn succeeded by a hybrid section that marries a peculiar six-bar modulation (1:09–1:16) to a twelve-bar blues (0:52–1:08).

Although the instrumentalists were not yet ready for genuine improvisation, the variety of approaches offered by these episodic compositions kept repetition of the basic melodic material to a minimum. Most of the cycles were ensemble sections; solos were still very much the exception. Nevertheless, musicians would occasionally find themselves playing alone, with the band simply marking the beat with a brief exclamation. This is called 'stop time' (for example, the piano solo on 'Chimes Blues', 1:17–1:52). Most often, though, solos would be limited to a short 'break' ('Mandy Lee Blues', 1:25–1:27), in which the band would fall silent in order to allow one of the instrumentalists to play a phrase unaccompanied.

Rise and fall

In June 1923, after returning to Chicago, Oliver's band took advantage of the arrival of a team of engineers that had been sent by the New York label Okeh to record the local musicians. On 28 August, the Creole Jazz Band criss-crossed the streets of the city on the back of an advertising truck to publicize the release of their new version of 'Dipper Mouth Blues'. King Oliver returned to Richmond to record in October, and that same month Columbia, Okeh and Paramount hastened to Chicago to record him. It seems likely that they swamped the market as a result, and Oliver had to wait until 1926 before entering the recording studio again, this time with an outfit named King Oliver's Jazz Band. Louis Armstrong, however, had left two years before and it was now he who would determine the course taken by jazz. King Oliver died in 1938 in poverty and oblivion.

King Louis

At a time when there was no shortage of recording sessions and tours for the Creole Jazz Band, Louis Armstrong was encouraged to spread his wings by Lil Hardin, whom he married in February 1924. He left the band between two bookings at the Lincoln Gardens in Chicago. In September 1924, he was invited to New York to join Fletcher Henderson's band, over which he came to exert a decisive influence. Offers immediately began to pour in, and in a single year he played on more than a hundred sides, both under Henderson's leadership, with singers such as Bessie Smith ('Saint Louis Blues') and Eva Taylor ('Cakewalkin' Babies'), and with Clarence Williams's small-scale line-ups, in which he frequently crossed the path of Sidney Bechet ('Texas Moaner Blues').

After returning to Chicago in 1925, he played all the city's major venues, including the Dreamland Café (with his wife's Syncopators), the Vendome Theater (with Erskine Tate) and the Sunset Café, before becoming the star of the Savoy Ballroom. He also became the star of Columbia, which had taken over the Okeh label, and formed a studio band called the Hot Five (later temporarily expanded into a Hot Seven). It was with the Hot Five, after exchanging his cornet for a trumpet, that he cut the first great masterpieces in the history of jazz. In 1928, Lil Hardin was replaced on piano by Earl Hines, who provided Armstrong with the harmonic support he needed. The following year, after a four-month stint at Connie's Inn in Harlem with the review *Hot Chocolates*, he settled in New York.

Many more masterpieces followed, both with big bands and at the head of small groups during the New Orleans revival, as trumpeter and as singer (particularly when his lips began to cause him trouble). He may have been criticized for pandering to white America's stereotype of the good-natured, simple-souled black man, but for jazz lovers and musicians alike he remained one of the greatest trumpeters of all time, whose powerful, intense sound and profound lyricism were unrivalled. He was the first to organize his band around the soloist, the first to depart from the practice of playing simple variations on the melody (for which he substituted a conscious exploration of the chords proposed by the accompaniment), and the first to give the solo an architecture of its own. Thanks to the quality of his timing and the variety of his rhythmic ideas, he is considered the first great swingman in the history of jazz.

LISTENING GUIDE
Bessie Smith: 'Saint Louis Blues' (Columbia, 14 January 1925)[1].
Eva Taylor: 'Cakewalkin' Babies' (Okeh, 8 January 1925)[2].
Clarence Williams's Blue Five: 'Texas Moaner Blues' (Okeh, 17 October 1924)[2].
See also the following pages.

CD GUIDE
1. Louis Armstrong, *The Quintessence, 1925–40*, Frémeaux.
2. Louis Armstrong, *The Quintessence 2, 1923–46*, Frémeaux.

Louis Armstrong in 1931

LOUIS ARMSTRONG: HIGH-TEMPERATURE JAZZ

n the United States the word 'hot' had been associated with black music since the 19th century. In the 1920s, the adjective was used more specifically to distinguish between real jazz and the various syncopated forms still closely related to ragtime. Somewhat later, the term 'swing' came into use. Real jazz was hot and it swung. It is in the music of Louis Armstrong that the phenomenon of swing, whose rhythmic devices are analysed later in the chapter, can be heard most clearly.

Guide to the early masterpieces

The historic sides recorded by Louis Armstrong after leaving King Oliver's band can be classified as follows:

October 1924 — October 1925	Fletcher Henderson Orchestra	Eleven musicians (variable line-up)
November 1925 — November 1926	Hot Five	With Kid Ory (trombone), Johnny Dodds (clarinet), Lil Armstrong (piano), Johnny Saint-Cyr (banjo)
May 1927	Hot Seven	Hot Five + Peter Briggs (tuba) and Baby Dodds (drums); John Thomas replaces Kid Ory
September 1927 — December 1927	Hot Five	Hot Five + Lonnie Johnson (guitar) in December
June 1928 — December 1928	Hot Five or Savoy Ballroom Five	Variable line-up including Earl Hines (piano) and Zutty Singleton (drums)

In addition to the bands listed in this table, between 1924 and 1925 Louis Armstrong also recorded with Clarence Williams's Blue Five, Lil Armstrong's Red Onions Jazz Babies and numerous singers, including Ma Rainey, Alberta Hunter (under the name of Josephine Beatty), Clara Smith, Bessie Smith and Trixie Smith.

A hot soloist in a straight band

In 1924, Fletcher Henderson and his orchestra recorded the very sweet 'Mandy Make Up Your Mind'. The introduction is straight, faithful to the score and firmly on the beat. After a stiff, jerky Coleman Hawkins solo (0:53–1:04), a supple athlete enters the arena in the form of Louis Armstrong (1:09–1:28). While still improvising around the melody, he pulls it apart, scattering the ornamented fragments to either side of their original positions. His abundant syncopation creates surprise and melodic suspense but also harmonic tension, as in the bold looping figures with which he rushes forward between bars eight and nine of his solo (1:20–1:24). Whereas the jazz novice may only hear a slightly wild sort of elegance, a more seasoned ear will recognize the harmonic transgressions that would later become the stuff of bebop. Enlivened by an exciting vibrato, Armstrong's sonority displays an incredible richness across the whole range of his instrument. It opens out into a series of isolated or repeated notes that snap like banners in the wind, but he also phrases his playing and modulates his sound by means of a highly varied articulation. Finally, in the descending figure of the fourth bar (1:14–1:15), he makes the sequence of regular quavers swing in a highly characteristic way through his asymmetrical placing of the notes.

The Hot Five and the Hot Seven

The various elements of Louis Armstrong's art were already present in his work with Fletcher Henderson, but they lacked the right framework. This was provided by the Hot Five and the Hot Seven, in which Armstrong hooked up with colleagues from the Creole Jazz Band and reacquainted himself with some of the old Louisiana tunes ('Heebie Jeebies', 'Cornet Chop Suey', 'Potato Head Blues'). Armstrong led his new bands with a relaxed authority that makes the edgy exhilaration of the Original Dixieland Jazz Band seem positively prehistoric. These collective-style tunes that constituted the bulk of King Oliver's material now incorporated numerous solos ('Hotter Than That', 'Skid-Dat-De-Dat', 'Tight Like This').

LISTENING GUIDE

Fletcher Henderson Orchestra: 'Mandy Make Up Your Mind' (Paramount, December 1924)[2].
Louis Armstrong and His Hot Five: 'Heebie Jeebies', 'Cornet Chop Suey' (Okeh, 26 February 1926)[1], 'Skid-Dat-De-Dat', 'Big Butter and Egg Man' (Okeh, 16 November 1926)[2], 'Hotter Than That' (Okeh, 13 December 1927)[1], 'West End Blues' (28 June 1928)[1].
Louis Armstrong and His Hot Seven: 'Potato Head Blues' (Okeh, 10 May 1927)[1].
Louis Armstrong and His Savoy Ballroom Hot Five: 'Tight Like This' (12 December 1928)[1].
Louis Armstrong and Earl Hines: 'Weather Bird' (Okeh, 5 December 1928)[1].

CD GUIDE

1. Louis Armstrong, *The Quintessence, 1925–40*, Frémeaux.
2. Louis Armstrong, *The Quintessence 2, 1923–46*, Frémeaux.

While adhering to the principle of melodic variation, each of Armstrong's solos displays a strong sense of architecture (note his skilful holding back in order to build up the necessary pressure for his final explosive solo on 'West End Blues', 2:33–2:56). The superb authority and sassy independence of his stop-time playing on 'Cornet Chop Suey' (1:48–2:09) and 'Potato Head Blues' (1:55–2:40) are inspired by an acute awareness of harmonic texture. The liberties he takes on 'Big Butter and Egg Man' show why he soon tired of Lil Hardin's rudimentary harmonies and sought the enlightened support of Earl Hines in the later recordings by the Hot Five and the stunning duo 'Weather Bird'.

The story goes that while recording 'Heebie Jeebies' he dropped the words he was supposed to be singing and replaced them with onomatopoeic sounds, thereby inventing scat. He turned to this technique frequently ('Skid-Dat-De-Dat', 'Hotter Than That', 'West End Blues'). When he did, his singing was the exact vocal equivalent of his instrumental playing – or possibly the other way round, since his trumpet seems to be simply the medium of some inner musical voice. This explains the naturalness and intensity of his introductions ('Cornet Chop Suey' and the famous 'West End Blues'). It also explains the profundity of his playing, whether he is giving free and joyful rein to his happy nature ('Hotter Than That') or revealing the deep-down sadness of a heart saddened by the condition of black Americans ('Skid-Dat-De-Dat' or 'Tight Like This'). The blues – less its form than its phrasing, its laid-back character and its acceptance of the inevitable – is another essential element in the jazz created by Louis Armstrong.

Chicago's bandleaders

The bosses of Chicago's clubs went to considerable expense to emulate the sumptuousness of clubs in New York. New Orleans bands working in the city curbed their natural exuberance and took on more players. These bands were led by local musicians who had learned their trade in vaudeville: Dave Peyton (a prominent member of the local black community and author of a weekly column in *The Chicago Defender*), Charles Cooke ('Doc Cook', who had a doctorate from the American Conservatory of Chicago and who hired Jimmie Noone and Freddie Keppard), Carroll Dickerson (leader of the large Savoy orchestra from which Armstrong borrowed the personnel for his second Hot Five, later taking them to New York), Erskine Tate (leader of the Vendome Theater orchestra, of which Armstrong was the star) and Luis Russell (an adoptive citizen of New Orleans who moved first to Chicago and then, in 1927, to New York, where he headed a big band that Armstrong would take over in the 1930s).

At the Apex Club, the clarinetist Jimmie Noone, a Creole from New Orleans, developed an original band style based on subtle coloration. At the opposite end of the spectrum, the pianist Clarence Williams remained faithful to the New Orleans style. He based his Blue Five at the New York studios of the Okeh label, whose artistic director he had become after earlier experiences as a publisher in New Orleans and Chicago.

Jelly Roll Morton: the first arranger

Although he wandered far and wide after 1907, Jelly Roll Morton remained a fervent ambassador for New Orleans music. Nevertheless, he kept its spontaneity in check in his compositions, laying the groundwork for the simulated improvisation with which André Hodeir experimented in the 1950s. His recordings with the Red Hot Peppers, which earned him a reputation as one of the first arrangers in the history of jazz, were relatively late (1926–7). His 'Original Jelly Roll Blues', however, is thought to be the first jazz arrangement protected by copyright (registered with the Library of Congress on 22 September 1915). The lasting achievement of the Red Hot Peppers – numbering between seven and nine players, mostly from New Orleans – is the remarkable imagination displayed in their harmonizations, range of timbres, general organization of the pieces and rhythmic inventiveness. Jelly Roll Morton gave his musicians (especially the drummer) very precise instructions – evidence of a surprising discipline in a semi-delinquent whose bragging led to his being elbowed out of the profession in the 1930s.

The unjustly overlooked Sidney Bechet

Sidney Bechet was hardly a more stable character than Morton: he arrived in Chicago in 1917, was deported from Britain in 1921 and was imprisoned in France in 1929. Until the end of the 1930s his career was fairly chaotic, which explains why he is unjustly overlooked while Louis Armstrong is described as the first soloist in the history of jazz. After hearing him play with Will Marion Cook's Southern Syncopated Orchestra at London's Philharmonic Hall, the conductor Ernest Ansermet wrote in the Swiss music

Sidney Bechet

journal *Revue de la Suisse Romande* in October 1919: 'The Southern Syncopated Orchestra includes an extraordinary clarinetist who is, it would seem, the first of his race to have composed blues for the clarinet of any real accomplishment. … These compositions already have the makings of a distinct style; they are gripping, abrupt, jerky, and come to a sudden, merciless conclusion like Bach's second *Brandenburg Concerto*. How touching it was to meet this large black youth … who can say nothing of his art other than that he "goes his own way" – which is quite possibly the great road down which the world will rush headlong tomorrow.'

Bechet's only recordings from this period are those made between 1923 and 1925 under the direction of Clarence Williams with a number of different singers and occasionally alongside Louis Armstrong, of whom he had no reason to be envious. Whether on the clarinet or soprano saxophone, which he took up in 1919, he produced a sound of extraordinary power and ferocity, enlivened by a wide, fast vibrato that magnified the extrovert lyricism of his playing. His modern, rhythmic phrasing (note the way he tears up the background on Clarence Williams's 'Old Fashioned Love', 0:45–1:55) led the saxophonist David Liebman to declare that if the notes in Bechet's arpeggios were replaced with chromatic sequences, the result would resemble the music of John Coltrane.

Chicago's decline

On the eve of the stock market crash of 1929, the underground fraternity that ran the entertainment industry suffered great damage as a result of both the municipal campaigns against organized crime and the settling of scores. Little by little, the jazz world migrated to the new capital of jazz, New York, and to Kansas City, which was by this time in the hands of the gangsters. Earl Hines was one of the few jazzmen of any repute to stay behind in Chicago, emceeing at the newly opened Grand Terrace, which was controlled by Al Capone's cartel.

Experts agree that the 'jazz' recordings made before 1923 were not really jazz because they did not swing. They were varieties of syncopated music not dissimilar to ragtime. Nevertheless, by the time of the first recordings in 1917, 4/4 time – accentuated by the bass drum and the double bass, sometimes on every beat and sometimes on the main beats in the manner of alternating bass – was already starting to become widespread. The semiquaver phrasing of 2/4 time typical of ragtime and the march was thus in the process of mutating into a 4/4 bar divided into quavers.

Tempo

This led to a new approach to tempo that was more relaxed and measured. The breathless, edgy, jerky, staccato (each note detached) style of playing inspired by syncopation gradually gave way to freer breathing and a more supple, easy-going and legato (smooth, flowing) style. This more relaxed approach was the fruit of a 'science of tempo' that emerged at the time of the recordings of 1923.

The main way in which classical musicians bring a piece of music to life is by interpreting its regular tempo freely. In dance music – which includes early jazz – this regularity is sacrosanct. In order to eliminate any mechanical, relentless quality, a degree of suppleness has to be introduced into the phrasing. Phrasing is made up of articulation and timing. Articulation determines the degree of separation or slurring of notes, the way in which and degree to which they are sustained and accented. Timing, for the jazzman, determines the precise placing of a note within a fixed tempo. This can be seen as a supreme refinement of the art of syncopation. Syncopation consists in playing the main notes of a melody ahead of the beat, favouring the offbeats. This art of displacement was gradually refined to the point where the placing of the notes could no longer be indicated in the score and gave rise to expressions such as 'playing behind the beat' and 'phrasing on the bottom of the beat'. It presupposes an infallible awareness or internalization of the tempo. This can be heard at work in the recordings of the Creole Jazz Band and finds its full expression with Louis Armstrong, who is regarded as the father of swing.

Irregular phrasing

On a more systematic level, jazzmen more or less deliberately adopted a particular form of timing that can also be found in the traditional Irish hornpipe and is used by early music specialists playing period instruments. Where there is a sequence of regular quavers, the first note is lengthened and the second shortened. The jazz quaver can be approximately represented in terms of triplets as follows:

The jazz quaver

This form of phrasing is described as 'ternary', which is misleading. 'Ternary' suggests that musicians are thinking precisely in terms of '2 + 1'. In fact, they are not thinking at all. When playing in duple time (regular quavers in pairs) they fall into a natural asymmetry that is more or less ternary depending on the particular tempo and style. Jazz is written and conceived of in quavers, not triplets, with the melody proceeding by means of pairs of uneven notes (long–short). Quaver triplets (consisting of three equal notes) are alien to it and are exceptional, representing a disruption of the musical discourse. This is why the term 'irregular phrasing' is preferred to the term 'ternary phrasing'. Having said this, during the second half of the 20th century, there has been a noticeable tendency for rhythm sections to break irregular phrasing down into real triplets consisting of equal quavers – in blues and gospel as well as in modern jazz.

Tension and release

Some theorists emphasize the natural swing that irregular phrasing gives the melodic line. When a person walks he moves forward steadily, placing one foot in front of the other, one-two, one-two... and yet the sound of his footsteps, the beating of his shoulder bag against his side and the flapping of his clothes around him are not symmetrical because symmetry does not exist in nature. He is not a machine, but a human being made of flesh and blood, and when he walks everything impels him to dance.

Other theorists insist on the muscular quality that the rhythm of a piece of music acquires as a result of irregular phrasing in combination with the various elements of articulation – just as one can tell the difference between the click of a metronome and the beating of the heart. It is about tension and release. By accentuating the off-quaver, jazz phrasing emphasizes the elasticity of the release. A word was found in the 1930s to sum up this rhythmic philosophy: 'swing'. Duke Ellington wrote 'It Don't Mean a Thing If It Ain't Got That Swing' in 1932. But it was at the beginning of the 1920s that jazzmen first acquired that strong sense of tempo which internalizes the precision of the rhythmic bounce and transforms it into elasticity – that momentum that allows them to defy gravity and float freely above the bar lines.

Each age has its fundamentalists and progressives who disagree on the definition of swing, the former insisting on the legibility of the 'bounce', the latter on its internalization, which allows musicians to produce it naturally and play weightlessly. The word was used by Isidore Witmark in 1899 to describe the rhythmic qualities of ragtime. His mention of 'swing feeling' with reference to musical scoring relates to the irregular phrasing that was to triumph in the 1930s, but modern jazzmen now use other kinds of language when referring to the rhythmic values associated with the word 'swing'. The general public, unconcerned by such subtleties, use the term as a way of designating any kind of music with a lively rhythmic pulse that sweeps the listener along.

New York: stride piano and big bands

In New York in 1917, all eyes were on the war in Europe. The maestros of syncopation polished their instruments ready to go and boost the morale of the armed forces. Seduced by their rags and foxtrots, the 'Old World' would remain a land of plenty for these musicians after the war. New York's somewhat stiff and starchy band music was late to take note of the rhythmic revolution under way not only in Chicago but also among the pianists of Harlem.

LISTENING GUIDE
Jim Europe's 369th US Infantry Band: 'Saint Louis Blues' (Pathé, 7 March 1919)[1].
Mitchell's Jazz Kings: 'Hep!' (Pathé, 5–6 December 1921)[1].
Gorman's Novelty Syncopator: 'Barkin' Dog' (Columbia, 30 September 1919)[1].
Paul Whiteman: 'I'll Build a Stairway to Paradise' (from George White's Scandals of 1922, Victor, 1 September 1922)[2], Rhapsody in Blue (Victor, 10 June 1924)[2].
James P Johnson: 'The Harlem Strut' (Black Swan, August 1921)[3], 'Carolina Shout' (Okeh, 18 October 1921)[3].
Fats Waller: 'Handful of Keys' (Victor, 1 March 1929)[4], 'Valentine Stomp' (Victor, 2 August 1929)[4].
Willie 'The Lion' Smith: 'Echoes of Spring', 'Passionnette' (Commodore, 10 January 1939)[5].

CD GUIDE
1. Early Jazz, 1917–23, Frémeaux.
2. George Gershwin, A Century of Glory, Frémeaux.
3. James P Johnson, Harlem Stride Piano, 1921–9, Jazz Archives.
4. Fats Waller, The Quintessence, 1929–43, Frémeaux.
5. Willie 'The Lion' Smith, The Chronological, 1938–40, Classics.

Easy success

Tim Brynn with the 350th Infantry Band (the Seventy Black Devils, whose drum-major was the pianist Willie Smith), Will Vodery with the 807th, and Jim Europe with the 369th (the Hellfighters, for whom Noble Sissle played bass drum) were among those who returned from France covered in glory and with fond memories of a country in which they had been acclaimed. Countless bands went on tour to Europe from 1919 onwards. These included the drummer Louis Mitchell's Jazz Kings (the most 'jazzy' of the bands that came out of the Clef Club and Tempo Club) featuring the trumpeter Cricket Smith, and Will Marion Cook's Southern Syncopated Orchestra with Sidney Bechet, as well as white groups inspired by the London success of the Original Dixieland Jazz Band. Success that was so easy to come by did nothing for swing.

In 1921, the white bandleader Paul Whiteman, the new star of Victor Records, worked on Florenz Ziegfeld's revues. After initially following in the footsteps of the Original Dixieland Jazz Band, he formed a 'symphonic jazz' orchestra and commissioned Rhapsody in Blue from George Gershwin in 1924. Originally composed for two pianos, the piece was orchestrated for jazz band by Whiteman's arranger Ferde Grofé. The clarinetist Ross Gorman (who was already well known for his animal imitations inspired by the success of 'Livery Stable Blues') was given the opening bars to play. The city's black musicians were busy too. The pianist Eubie Blake and the singer Noble Sissle created the Broadway hit Shuffle Along (the first all-black revue to become a huge success), which heralded the Harlem Renaissance. However, it was away from orchestral music and musical theatre that Eubie Blake made his most important contribution to the rhythmic revolution that had begun to shake up the musical scene in New York.

The stride revolution

In the capital of show business, the virtuosos of ragtime piano indulged in long, merciless duels staged at Harlem 'rent parties'. These musical duels were held in private apartments – either to circumvent the rigours of prohibition or to give a helping hand to tenants who were having difficulty paying their rent. The participants would cover the entire keyboard in a single piece in an attempt to finish in a key that would cause problems for the next pianist. They would crank up the tempo, improvise complex figures based on the language of classic ragtime (notably syncopation and rhythmic displacement), enrich the harmonic progressions, inflect the melody with blue notes and punctuate their performances with repeated sequences (riffs) guaranteed to win the audience over.

This love of showing off their skill led to an extension of the interval at the heart of the alternating bass. In a breakneck to-and-fro motion, the left hand constantly sought higher top chords to answer the bass notes (which soon became tenths). Was it the brisk pace of this bass line that gave 'stride piano' its name? Either way, the left hand, carried along by its own momentum, accentuated the higher chord with the effect that ragtime's original time signature of two beats to a bar slipped to four in a bar with accents on the offbeats (second and fourth). This nimbler way of feeling the beat ushered in a lighter, more fluid and more relaxed style, and irregular phrasing (see p.55) gradually made its entrance.

Rare pre-1923 recordings suggest that stride pianists were ahead of the Chicago jazzmen with this rhythmic revolution; they might even have influenced them. One thing is certain: the piano rolls recorded by James P Johnson around 1917 are heavily influenced by ragtime, whereas his first masterpieces ('The Harlem Strut' and 'Carolina Shout'), dating from 1921, are most definitely examples of stride piano – and they certainly swing. In the orchestral versions that he recorded the same year, however, we still find the stiff, jerky rhythms of the early syncopated music. James P Johnson was the chief exponent of a genre whose possible precursors were Eubie Blake and Luckey Roberts. His main rival was Willie 'The Lion' Smith, who was steeped in the classical tradition, while his best-known pupil was the larger-than-life Fats Waller. At the head of various small groups, Waller subsequently updated the stride style for the 1930s, and modern jazz pianists from Art Tatum to Thelonious Monk and Keith Jarrett have continued to make use of it to this day.

The first big band

The affable, cultured Fletcher Henderson settled in New York as a young man in 1920, dropping his chemistry studies in order to devote himself to music. Starting off as a publisher's demonstrator (performing sheet music for the benefit of customers), he soon became musical director of Black Swan, the leading black record label. Accompanying the female blues singers who recorded for the label, Henderson worked regularly with a small circle of musicians that he formed into a band in the winter of 1923–4 for engagements at New York's Club Alabam. Before long, Henderson and his band took up a residency at the Roseland Ballroom on Broadway, one of New York's most sumptuous ballrooms. The band consisted of two trumpets, a trombone, three reeds (saxophones and clarinets), a pianist (the bandleader himself), a banjo, a tuba and a drummer. With this line-up divided into sections or desks – trumpets, trombones (the second of which was only added at the end of the 1920s), reeds and rhythm section – the big band was born.

If Fletcher Henderson lacked authority, his musicians more than made up for it. They were young, brilliant and overflowing with a creativity whose various influences included ragtime, the authenticity of the black female singers they accompanied, New Orleans polyphony, the light music of the day and Paul Whiteman's ambitious symphonic style. The advertising copy for their record 'Chattanooga – Ghost of the Blues' described their music as mysterious and savage, a blend of jazz and soothing symphony.

It was at this point that Louis Armstrong came onto the scene. Having noticed him in New Orleans in 1921, Fletcher Henderson wrote to him in Chicago inviting him to come and beef up his trumpet section (at the same time Henderson recruited the clarinetist Buster Bailey, who had recently joined King Oliver's band). The other musicians were immediately won over by the new cornetist's style, and by modelling themselves on him the band became more unified. In less than a year, the Fletcher Henderson Orchestra became the best band in New York. By the time of Armstrong's departure, the band's best players – the trombonist Charlie Green, the tenor saxophonist Coleman Hawkins and the drummer Kaiser Marshall – had learned much from him. From this point on, Henderson recruited only the best players in the land, such as Joe Smith, Rex Stewart, Tommy Ladnier (trumpets), Benny Morton, Jimmy Harrison (trombones), Benny Carter (sax) and June Cole (tuba).

The arranger

A key figure appeared in jazz bands at this time: the arranger. The arranger's job was to turn a simple melody – whether a song, a blues or a tune composed by one of the musicians – into a band score. This process involves devising and organizing a musical scenario that respects the original structure, provides it with a rhythmic framework (sometimes very different to the original one), supplements it with an introduction and conclusion or coda, melodic variations, breaks and improvised passages, and even sometimes changes the order of its sections. The arranger also has to provide a background to the original tune in the form of secondary themes and counter-melodies.

The arranger uses the band as a painter uses his palette, selecting and applying orchestral colour and timbres and bringing together instruments belonging either to the same family (each section – for example, trumpets, trombones and reeds – playing a distinct role) or to different families. The arranger superimposes these colours in harmonic layers around the chords that carry the melody.

Don Redman provided the arrangements for Fletcher Henderson from the earliest days of his band. A comparison of 'Copenhagen' (1924) or his masterpieces 'The Stampede' and 'The Henderson Stomp' (both 1926) with his earlier work, however, indicates that working alongside Louis Armstrong stimulated his creativity. He made very effective use of the members of Henderson's band, employing his fertile imagination to achieve dramatic and architectural effects, bringing musicians together into ensembles (the clarinet trio was a particular favourite of his), playing with the contrasts between the brass and reed sections, and allowing for both individual and collective improvisation.

The new ideas reach the provinces

Don Redman's departure in 1927 left a hole at the heart of the band. Fletcher Henderson turned to the technique – common at the time – of 'head arrangements', which involved the learning and performing of music

LISTENING GUIDE

Fletcher Henderson: 'Ghost of the Blues' (Emerson, spring 1924)[1], 'Copenhagen' (Vocalion, 30 October 1924)[2], 'The Stampede' (Columbia, 14 May 1926)[2], 'The Henderson Stomp' (Columbia, 3 November 1926)[2].
Bennie Moten: 'Moten Stomp' (Victor, 12 June 1927)[3].
McKinney's Cotton Pickers: 'Stop Kidding' (Victor, 12 July 1928)[4].

CD GUIDE

1. Fletcher Henderson, *The Chronological, 1924*, Classics.
2. Fletcher Henderson, *The Quintessence, 1924–36*, Frémeaux.
3. Bennie Moten, *Vol 1, 1926–9*, Jazz Archives.
4. McKinney's Cotton Pickers, *The Chronological, 1928–9*, Classics.

without the aid of written parts. Fletcher Henderson also took up the pen himself or occasionally handed it to a saxophonist who was already in great demand: Benny Carter. Creativity was also to be found outside New York in the many competing big bands that sprang up on the Fletcher Henderson model, chief of which were McKinney's Cotton Pickers, based in Detroit. Don Redman joined this band, where he worked alongside another talented arranger, John Nesbitt. From the Great Lakes to the southern states, the new black music was to be found all over the Midwest plains. Heavily influenced by the blues and the showmanship of the last minstrels, classic Missouri ragtime now adopted New York-style band-sizes along with a correspondingly more varied compositional style and New Orleans-style improvisation. Numerous bands formed after hearing this music on record and on the radio, including those of Bennie Moten (Kansas City), Alphonso Trent (Dallas), Troy Floyd (San Antonio), Zack Whyte (Cincinnati), Walter Page's Blue Devils (Oklahoma City) and Jesse Stone and his Blue Serenaders (Dallas).

Duke Ellington and Bubber Miley

For Fletcher Henderson, competition was also to be found closer to home. In Harlem, Charlie Johnson was playing at the Small Paradise Club, and the Missourians were at the Savoy Ballroom. In December 1927, the latter handed over the stage of the Cotton Club to the orchestra of Duke Ellington, a young pianist from Washington.

After starting out by playing at the various functions that were a familiar feature of the capital's social life, Ellington had arrived in New York with a number of friends in 1923. From 1924, he led the Washingtonians at the Kentucky Club on Broadway. The band really found its feet in 1926 under the influence of the trumpeter Bubber Miley. Miley was an inspired

Duke Ellington and his Cotton Club Orchestra, 1931

composer and improviser who combined a highly developed sense of melody with expressive wah-wah (mute) and 'growling' effects similar to those used by the bluesmen and black preachers. With the trombonist Charles Irvis, who was replaced before long by Joe Nanton, he specialized in extravagant sounds that fitted in perfectly with the themes, scenery and exotic dancing of the revues of the day. Duke Ellington was quick to understand the effect to which these unusual colours could be put, and he was soon collaborating with his trumpeter on pieces in a new style that acquired the name 'jungle' – a style that spawned many imitations (for example, Charlie Johnson's 'The Boy in the Boat'). While Africa was certainly not absent from the imaginative world of 'jungle' – and a large section of the black population, inspired by Marcus Garvey, dreamed of returning to that continent – it also celebrated black America: the colourful, ruthless jungle of its ghettos, the 'black beauty' that had white audiences jostling to get into the Cotton Club, the black race's pride in itself and the hope of one day seeing the black population fully integrated into a creolized society (as in 'Black and Tan Fantasy', a subject returned to by Ellington in 1943 in *Black, Brown & Beige*).

Ellington's masterpieces and performers

The first masterpieces of the new style appeared in 1926 and 1927: 'Black and Tan Fantasy', 'East Saint Louis Toodle-Oo' and 'Creole Love Call' (on which Adelaide Hall sings wordless vocals inspired by Bubber Miley's trumpet playing). Duke Ellington's band took up its residency at the Cotton Club on 4 December 1927 and Ellington became one of the club's favourite stars, benefiting from live radio broadcasts that made his music known throughout the whole of the United States. Aware of his new responsibilities, the bandleader worked flat out studying harmony and orchestration, both by himself and with the help of Will Marion Cook and especially Will Vodery, who had become principal arranger with the Ziegfeld Follies. In 1928, Ellington wrote 'Black Beauty', 'The Mooche' and 'Hot and Bothered' single-handed. The charm of each of these pieces derives from the personality of the musicians for whom the various parts were written: the sweetness of the trumpeter Arthur Whetsol in 'Black Beauty', the spellbinding sensuality of the saxophonist Johnny Hodges intensifying Bubber Miley's expressive violence in 'The Mooche' (2:00–2:23), and the Creole elegance of the clarinetist Barney Bigard. Ellington was inspired by the musicians with whom he surrounded himself and they in turn were able to give of their best when playing the Duke's music. He always wrote for specific musicians and wanted to know everything about their character – even down to the way they played cards!

Faithful to his original circle of musicians (only death parted him from Johnny Hodges and Harry Carney), Duke Ellington constantly adapted his style during his career but always remained true to the spirit of his first band. Each musician who left the band was replaced by one who would ensure continuity, even if he also contributed new stylistic elements. Thus Bubber Miley was replaced in 1929 by Cootie Williams, a player familiar with the 'jungle' style who was also young and willing to go along with the changes that occurred during the 1930s. And in 1943, when Barney Bigard left the saxophone section, he was replaced by another clarinet specialist, Jimmy Hamilton, who, despite having much in common with Benny Goodman, emphasized the 'woody' tone of the instrument. Indeed, each time Ellington increased the size of his band it was with the intention of introducing a new colour, such as the Latin hue that the trombonist Juan Tizol (the composer of 'Caravan') brought to the music.

The self-taught colourist

In terms of orchestration, Ellington was a painter with a highly personal sense of colour. This culminated in 1930 in the deployment of instruments against their natural timbre in 'Mood Indigo' (low clarinet, high trombone, and trumpet in the middle). This same sense of colour and self-taught empiricism are evident in his use of harmony. There is a disarming lightness of touch in the work of this most dandified of bandleaders, and a humorous impudence in the way he appropriated what the Impressionist composers of the turn of the century had only acquired by dint of long, hard study. But he never descends into the artifice that characterizes many of the 'modernistic' experiments of his colleagues. The chromatic aberrations of the blues, for example, were a valuable source of inspiration for his famous 'Mood Indigo', which is intimately 'bluesy' without actually being a blues number.

LISTENING GUIDE
Charlie Johnson: 'The Boy in the Boat' (Victor, 19 September 1928)[1].
Duke Ellington: 'East Saint Louis Toodle-Oo' (Vocalion, 29 November 1926)[2], 'Black and Tan Fantasy' (Brunswick, 7 April 1927)[2], 'Creole Love Call' (Victor, 26 October 1927)[2], 'The Mooche', 'Hot and Bothered' (Okeh, 1 October 1928)[2], 'Mood Indigo' (Brunswick, 17 October 1930)[2].

CD GUIDE
1. Charlie Johnson, *The Complete Sessions, 1925–9*, Jazz Archives.
2. Duke Ellington, *The Quintessence, 1926–41*, Frémeaux.

Singers and pianists in thrall to the blues

The classic blues singers

The female singers who sang the blues on the professional music circuit are known as the classic blues singers. Having grown up in vaudeville or with itinerant troupes of minstrels, they were more music-hall singers than authentic blues singers and often had vibrant personalities and tragic lives. In 1920, the enormous success of 'Crazy Blues', recorded for Okeh by Mamie Smith, inspired a host of 'colored catalogs', 'race series' and 'race records' by black singers of the same type, including Ma Rainey, Clara Smith, Edith Wilson, Alberta Hunter, Ida Cox, Ethel Waters, Sarah Martin and Bessie Smith (nicknamed the 'Empress of the Blues'). These singers were accompanied by small studio bands (such as Fletcher Henderson's Black Swan Troubadours or Clarence Williams's Blue Five). In this way, black jazzmen were able to win the confidence of producers, and black singers were able to lay the groundwork for jazz vocals.

Boogie-woogie: the poor man's ragtime

Boogie-woogie speeded up the dissemination of the blues, whose structure it adopted. Having seen the light of day on clapped-out pianos in southern bars at the end of the 19th century, it can perhaps be regarded as the poor man's ragtime. While they were inclined to turn their noses up at it in the 1910s, ragtime pianists were not above adopting the nonchalance of its left-hand part, a powerful bass line made up of irregular quavers (unlike the

LISTENING GUIDE
Mamie Smith: 'Crazy Blues' (Okeh, 10 August 1920)[1].
Bessie Smith: 'Empty Bed Blues' (Columbia, 20 March 1928)[1], 'Saint Louis Blues' (Columbia, 14 January 1925)[2].
Jimmy Blythe: 'Chicago Stomp' (Paramount, April 1924)[3].
Pinetop Smith: 'Pinetop's Boogie Woogie' (Vocalion, 29 December 1928)[3].

CD GUIDE
1. *Women in Blues, 1920–43*, Frémeaux.
2. Louis Armstrong, *The Quintessence, 1925–40*, Frémeaux.
3. *Boogie Woogie, 1924–45*, Frémeaux. For those interested in the birth of boogie-woogie, the two-volume anthology 'Boogie Woogie Story' (Milan Jazz) is also recommended.

DUKE ELLINGTON DISCOGRAPHY

Duke Ellington's recording career extended from 1924 to 1974, the year of his death. During these 50 years the bandleader remained true to himself while at the same time never ceasing to absorb jazz's new trends. Assembling a representative collection of his work presents more problems than it does for any other recording artist, particularly where his 78rpm recordings are concerned – a veritable hotchpotch of sides scattered across different catalogues as a result of the bankruptcies, mergers and takeovers that have plagued the recording industry over the years. What makes matters worse, however, is that Duke Ellington frequently used to change the name of his band in order to circumvent exclusive recording contracts (the Washingtonians, the Kentucky Club Orchestra, the Cotton Club Orchestra, the Whoopee Makers, the Harlem Footwarmers, the Jungle Band, the Ten Blackberries, the Harlem Hot Chocolates). By making many different recordings for a multitude of labels, he was also able to return to compositions and improve on any interpretations he was unhappy with. The table below gives a few reference points for the 78rpm years, 1926 to 1950.

Period	Works	Characteristics and developments
1926 1929	'East Saint Louis Toodle-oo' (Vocalion, 29 November 1926) 'Black and Tan Fantasy' (Brunswick, 7 April 1927, or Victor, 26 October 1927) 'Creole Love Call' (Victor, 26 October 1927) 'Jubilee Stomp' (Victor, 26 March 1928) 'The Mooche' (Okeh, 1 October 1928, or Brunswick, 17 October 1928)	Creation of the 'jungle' style. Line-up: Bubber Miley, Louis Metcalf (trumpets), Joe Nanton (trombone), Rudy Jackson, Otto Hardwick, Harry Carney (reeds), Duke Ellington (piano), Fred Guy (banjo), Bass Edwards (tuba), Sonny Greer (drums). In 1927–8, the trumpet section is expanded to three, Johnny Hodges and Barney Bigard replace Jackson and Hardwick, and Wellman Braud introduces the string bass.
1930 1938	'Mood Indigo' (Brunswick, 17 October 1930) *Creole Rhapsody* (Victor, 11 June 1931) 'It Don't Mean a Thing' (Brunswick, 2 February 1932) 'Sophisticated Lady' (Columbia, 15 February 1933) 'Solitude' (Victor, 10 January 1934) 'In a Sentimental Mood' (Brunswick, 30 April 1935) 'Clarinet Lament' (Brunswick, 27 February 1936) 'Caravan' (Columbia, 14 May 1937) 'Braggin' in Brass' (Brunswick, 3 March 1938)	Development of the jungle style. Trumpets: Cootie Williams replaces Miley (1929). Arrival of Rex Stewart in 1934. Trombones: arrival of Juan Tizol (1929) and Lawrence Brown (1932). Rhythm section: Fred Guy switches to guitar, Billy Taylor replaces Wellman Braud. First suite (*Creole Rhapsody*) written in 1931.Due to its length it has to be split between two sides of a 78. First European tour in 1933. From 1936, small groups from the band get together in the studio with or without Ellington to record under the direction of Johnny Hodges, Cootie Williams, Rex Stewart and Barney Bigard.

Period	Works	Characteristics and developments
1939 1942	'Solitude', 'Sophisticated Lady' (Columbia, 14 February 1940) 'Koko', 'Jack The Bear' (Victor, 6 March 1940) 'Concerto for Cootie', 'Conga Brava' (Victor, 15 March 1940) 'Cotton Tail' (Victor, 4 May 1940) 'Take the A Train' (Victor, 15 February 1941) 'The C Jam Blues' (Victor, 21 January 1942)	Start of collaboration in 1939 with pianist and composer Billy Strayhorn, who helps Ellington with his writing. 1940 sees a host of masterpieces with a band reinvigorated by the arrival of saxophonist Ben Webster and double bass player Jimmy Blanton. Duke Ellington records a series of duos with Blanton. Ray Nance replaces Cootie Williams in 1940.
1943 1949	*Black, Brown & Beige* (Prestige, 23 January 1943) 'Carnegie Blues' (V-disc, 8 September 1945) 'Happy-Go-Lucky-Local' (Musicraft, 25 November 1946) *Liberian Suite* (Columbia, 24 December 1947) *The Tattooed Bride* (World Records, 10 December 1948)	Concert at Carnegie Hall and composition of the suite *Black, Brown & Beige*. Studio strikes. Ellington's work is mainly represented by live recordings (notably at Carnegie Hall) during this time. Ellington experiments with more ambitious forms (a number of long suites) and new musicians arrive.

This table does no more than provide a few reference points and collectors will have to be prepared to pick their own way through Ellington's work from these years (during which more than 1,000 sides were recorded). His output is so vast that it is always possible to discover a lesser-known gem from a particular recording session tucked away somewhere. For those wanting a total overview of his recordings, large complete editions are available. For those new to his work, there are a number of compilations available that provide excellent introductions to Duke Ellington and his times.

In 1950, Ellington re-arranged many of his older compositions in order to take advantage of new technology – the microgroove record or LP (*Masterpieces*, Columbia). Thanks to the grouping of numbers into albums and the visual distinction of the record sleeves, it becomes easier to find one's way around his recordings from this time onwards.

Taking advantage of a period of experimentation (*Ellington Uptown*, Columbia, with the drummer Louie Bellson), Johnny Hodges left the band in 1951 to do his own thing. After his return in 1955, Duke Ellington unveiled a new line-up at the Newport Festival (*At Newport 1956*) that would allow him to fulfil his new ambitions. The new band consisted of Clark Terry, Willie Cook, Cat Anderson (trumpets), Ray Nance (trumpet, violin), Quentin Jackson, Britt Woodman, John Saunders (trombones), Jimmy Hamilton, Johnny Hodges, Russell

Procope, Paul Gonsalves and Harry Carney (reeds), Duke Ellington (piano), Jimmy Woode (double bass) and Sam Woodyard (drums).

This line-up was to undergo many changes, but it was based around a solid core of three key figures: Paul Gonsalves (of whom Ellington, when asked about avant-garde jazz, said that he had his own avant-garde in the form of Gonsalves), Sam Woodyard, who set a steady beat for the band until the end of the 1960s, and Billy Strayhorn, the Duke's alter ego, who was largely responsible for repertoire. It will be noticed that there is no longer a guitar in the line-up.

Individual pieces were superseded by albums with specific themes (*Blues in Orbit*, Columbia, 1958–9; Paris and its songs in *Midnight in Paris*, Columbia, 1962; Billy Strayhorn's grief in …*And His Mother Called Him Bill*, RCA, 1967). More commonly, they were presented in the form of suites (*Far East Suite*, RCA, 1966; *New Orleans Suite*, RCA, 1970). Some albums also gave Ellington an opportunity to revisit the classics, which he did with a fresh, imaginative approach (Tchaikovsky and Grieg in *The Nutcracker Suite* and *Peer Gynt Suite Nos 1 & 2*, Columbia, 1960, and even Shakespeare in *Such Sweet Thunder*, Columbia, 1956–7).

There are also many live recordings of concerts and galas (it is always a treat to hear Ellington playing music for dancing to), recordings of small groups of Ellington regulars (Johnny Hodges, *Everybody Knows Johnny Hodges*, Impulse, 1964), sacred concerts from the end of the 1960s, and the work for piano, which starts with the solo piano version of 'Black Beauty' (Okeh, 1 October 1928) and gradually assumes greater importance (*Piano Reflections*, trio with Wendell Marshall and Butch Ballard, Capitol, 1953; 'Money Jungle', trio with Charles Mingus and Max Roach, Blue Note, 1962; *Piano in the Foreground*, trio with Aaron Bell and Sam Woodyard, Columbia, 1961; *This One's for Blanton*, duo with Ray Brown, Pablo, 1972, and – last but not least – *Duke Ellington & John Coltrane*, quartets, Impulse, 1962).

Ma Rainey and her Georgia Jazz Band, 192[...]

LISTENING GUIDE

The New Orleans Rhythm Kings: 'Panama' (Gennett, 30 August 1922)[1].
Bix Beiderbecke: 'Singin' the Blues' (Okeh, 4 February 1927)[2], 'In a Mist' (Okeh, 9 September 1927)[2].
Red Nichols: 'That's No Bargain' (Brunswick, 16 December 1926)[3].
Eddie Condon: 'Makin' Friends' (Okeh, 30 October 1928)[4].

CD GUIDE
1. *Early Jazz, 1917–23*, Frémeaux.
2. Bix Beiderbecke, *The Quintessence, 1924–30*, Frémeaux.
3. The Red Heads, *The Complete*, Jazz Archives.
4. Eddie Condon, *His Best Recordings, 1928–46*, Best of Jazz.

even crotchets of jazz bass), to which experts have ascribed African origins. In a system of complementary cross-rhythms, the right hand in boogie-woogie plays effective, repetitive melodic figures heavily inflected by blue notes. While the pioneers of the genre were Jimmy Yancey and Cow Cow Davenport, the first boogie recording was made by Jimmy Blythe ('Chicago Stomp') in 1924. The first 'classic' was Meade 'Lux' Lewis's 'Honky Tonk Train Blues' of 1927, while Clarence 'Pinetop' Smith's 'Pinetop's Boogie Woogie' of 1928 was the first to actually bear the name 'boogie'. After a relatively short period of popularity, boogie-woogie enjoyed a revival at the end of the 1930s, bringing the names of Pete Johnson and Albert Ammons to public attention. The 'shuffling' boogie-woogie left-hand part was widely adopted by jazzmen – both pianists and drummers – in the 1930s and even provided the basis for rock and roll and post-war urban blues.

White jazz: the second generation

In 1921, young white Chicagoans from well-to-do backgrounds would go to listen to the New Orleans Rhythm Kings, an ultra-elegant white New Orleans band, at the Friar's Inn. The audience regularly included members of the Austin High School Gang, the hard core of white Chicago jazzmen. They included Jimmy Portland (cornet), Bud Freeman (tenor sax), Frank Teschemacher (alto sax and clarinet) and Dave Tough (drums). Another enthusiastic member of the audience was the cornetist Bix Beiderbecke, who had to scale the walls of Lake Forest Military Academy in order to hear his heroes play.

Before long the Austin High School Gang were venturing into the 'black-and-tan' bars of the black neighbourhood (bars open to both white and black customers). There they discovered Louis Armstrong. They attempted to imitate him, but – since they had a more delicate sensibility and had benefited from a more sophisticated education – ended up inventing something completely different. They were receptive to the blues not because they were victims of racial exclusion but because they were would-be Romantics driven to self-destruction who wanted to turn their backs on their social origins.

After his initial success with the Wolverines, Bix Beiderbecke moved away from Chicago, delivering his most beautiful solos alongside the saxophonist Frankie Trumbauer, who shared his musical discipline and in particular his knowledge of theory. Trumbauer also encouraged Bix to record, on the piano, his famous 'In a Mist', a manifesto for a youth torn between ragtime, blues and the harmonic experiments of the Impressionist composers. In return, Bix taught his friend ('Tram' for short) to shake off some of the stiffness and sentimentality of much light white music.

Playing in the bands of Paul Whiteman and the impresario Jean Goldkette, the pair reached New York, where other young white musicians such as the cornetist Red Nichols, the trombonist Miff Mole and the violinist Joe Venuti were at work. Many white Chicago jazzmen had gathered in New York and there has been a tendency for all white pre-1930 jazz to be lumped together. In reality it was a very disparate scene, ranging from the energetic jam sessions centring on the guitarist Eddie Condon to the polished jazz of Red Nichols (with whom the future stars of swing – Glenn Miller, Benny Goodman and Gene Krupa – were laying the foundations for what was to come). The term 'Dixieland' came to be used around this time to describe white jazz that had remained true to the New Orleans style.

LISTENING GUIDE

Johnny Dunn: 'You Need Some Loving' (Columbia, 13 March 1928)[1].
Joe Smith (1:28–2:00), Rex Stewart (0:00–00:15; 2:37–2:52): 'The Stampede' (with Fletcher Henderson, Columbia, 14 May 1926)[2].
Tommy Ladnier (0:18–1:14), Joe Smith (1:15–1:41): 'Snag It' (with Fletcher Henderson, Harmony, 20 January 1927)[3].
Red Nichols: 'Plenty Off Centre' (Pathé, March 1926)[3].
For Oliver, Armstrong, Beiderbecke and Miley (with Ellington), see elsewhere in this chapter.

The soloists and sidemen of hot jazz

CD GUIDE

1. Jelly Roll Morton, Complete Edition, Vol 4, 1927–8, Masters of Jazz.
2. Fletcher Henderson, The Quintessence, 1924–36, Frémeaux.
3. The Red Heads, The Complete, Jazz Archives.

No instrument escaped the influence of Louis Armstrong at the end of the 1930s. In a more general sense, however, the point of reference was the music of New Orleans (other than for the piano, which was dominated by the New York school). It was in New Orleans that the black American identity had created the most distinctive blend of all the different elements that made it original: the luminous fervour of the spiritual, the darker ambiguity of the blues, the pianistic expertise of ragtime and the imagination of the black minstrels – the whole carried by a gravelly, 'dirty' timbre borrowed from preachers and bluesmen. In hot jazz the traditional sound of Western musical instruments was subverted, personalized by each player, vocalized, subjected to throat effects (growl) or mute effects (just as in Africa the sound of the kora or Malian harp is accompanied by the vibrating of beads and the ringing of bells).

The trumpet

Alternatives, however, were already on the horizon. Would it be an exaggeration to talk of a New York school on the basis of Bubber Miley,

LISTENING
GUIDE
Kid Ory: 'Gate Mouth'
(with the New Orleans
Wanderers, Columbia,
13 July 1926)[1].
Honoré Dutrey: 'Bull
Fiddle Blues' (with
Johnny Dodds, Victor, 6
July 1928)[1].
Jimmy Harrison:
'Fidgety Feet' (with
Fletcher Henderson,
Vocalion, 19 March
1927)[2], 'Walking' That
Thing' (with Charlie
Johnson, Victor, 19
September 1928)[3].
Miff Mole: 'Alabama
Stomp' (with Red
Nichols, Pathé, 14
September 1926)[4].
Benny Morton: 'Jackass
Blues' (with Fletcher
Henderson, Columbia,
14 May 1926)[2].
Johnny Dodds: 'Clarinet
Wobble' (Brunswick, 21
April 1927)[5].
Jimmie Noone: 'Apex
Blues' (Vocalion, 23
August 1928)[6].

Johnny Dunn and Joe Smith alone? It is quite possible that New York did not wait for King Oliver before adopting wah-wah mute effects. While the expressive power of Miley cannot really be compared with the still somewhat stiff elegance of the other two, nevertheless all three possessed the technical ability demanded on the New York scene at the time. Trumpeters sought to break free from Armstrong's domination by developing a more elegant, sophisticated and delicately toned style. Following in the footsteps of white New Orleans cornetists such as Paul Mares of the New Orleans Rhythm Kings, Bix Beiderbecke succeeded in finding an alternative way forward that was adopted by many white musicians (including Red Nichols and later Bobby Hackett) right up to the emergence of cool jazz. In the 1930s, this new style also appealed to a number of black trumpeters such as Rex Stewart and Roy Eldridge. Throughout the 1920s, however, Rex Stewart had been a boisterous disciple of Louis Armstrong, and Henry 'Red' Allen and Jabbo Smith were encouraged to imitate Armstrong by their record companies (Victor and Vocalion), who wanted to compete with Okeh. Of these two, only Allen managed to emerge from Louis Armstrong's shadow in the 1930s and develop a personal style. Others, such as Tommy Ladnier (black) or Mugsy Spanier (white) went back to 'Papa Joe' (King Oliver) for their inspiration. Ladnier subsequently moved forward, whereas Spanier embodied the deep-rooted attachment to New Orleans that persisted among white Chicago jazzmen.

The trombone

The preoccupation of trombonists right up to the present has been to conquer the inherent sluggishness of the slide and escape from the instrument's functional role of providing counterpoint in the early jazz

Bix Beiderbecke and his Rhythm Jugglers, 1925

Omer Simeon: 'Black Bottom Stomp' (Victor, 15 September 1926)[1].
Barney Bigard: 'Clarinet Lament' (Brunswick, 27 February 1936)[8].
Pee Wee Russell: 'Feelin' No Pain' (with Red Nichols, Brunswick, 15 August 1927)[9].
For Charlie Green ('Empty Bed Blues' with Bessie Smith), Sam Nanton ('Black and Tan Fantasy' with Duke Ellington), Jack Teagarden ('Makin' Friends' with Eddie Condon), Sidney Bechet ('Texas Moaner Blues' with Clarence Williams), Leon Roppolo ('Panama' with the New Orleans Rhythm Kings), Buster Bailey ('Fidgety Feet' with Fletcher Henderson) and Benny Goodman ('Shim-Me-Sha-Wabble' with Red Nichols), see elsewhere in this chapter.

CD GUIDE
1. *Jazz New Orleans, 1918–44*, Frémeaux.
2. Fletcher Henderson, *The Quintessence, 1924–36*, Frémeaux.
3. Charlie Johnson, *The Complete Sessions*, Jazz Archives.
4. The Red Heads, *The Complete*, Jazz Archives.
5. Johnny Dodds, *Story*, Jazz Archives.
6. Jimmie Noone *Apex Time*, Jazz Archives.
7. Jelly Roll Morton, *The Quintessence*, Frémeaux.
8. Duke Ellington, *Anniversary, Vol 11: Soloists*, Masters of Jazz.
9. Red Nichols, *His Best Recordings, 1927–31*, Best of Jazz.

bands. In New Orleans, however, the slide was used to spectacular effect and the 'tailgate style' earned trombonists the admiration of the crowds. While Kid Ory took full advantage of the technique, Honoré Dutrey, his main rival, preferred to merge into the ensemble.

Among the early trombonists, Charlie Green was the first to play solos – both with the Fletcher Henderson Orchestra and in a trio with Bessie Smith (replying to her vocals with great feeling). Trombonists use mutes too, and Bubber Miley was first joined in the use of the mute in Duke Ellington's band by the New Yorker Charles Irvis. In 1927, Irvis was replaced by Joe 'Tricky Sam' Nanton, a great virtuoso with the mute who remained with Ellington until his death in 1946. The first trombone soloists of any stature were two New Yorkers: Jimmy Harrison (black) and Miff Mole (white). Harrison's style demonstrated that Louis Armstrong's influence extended beyond the trumpet. Miff Mole's playing was quite different. He displayed a mastery of nuance and a fluency that were matched among black trombonists only by Benny Morton, although Mole's playing had more vigour. Morton, along with J C Higginbotham, provided a link between the trombone styles of the 1920s and 1930s. The white trombonist Jack Teagarden represented a kind of synthesis between the vigorous style of Jimmy Harrison and the elegance of Miff Mole. He is fundamentally uncategorizable, however, and he was so far ahead of the field in terms of fluidity of playing that he survived the whole of the 1930s without ever seeming old-fashioned – whether demonstrating the nobility of his sound (he was one of the pillars of the white jazz scene in New York) or his feeling for the blues (participating alongside Louis Armstrong in the New Orleans revival of the 1940s).

The clarinet

The 1920s were dominated by two figures – Johnny Dodds and Jimmie Noone. Sidney Bechet, a name all too often overlooked in this context, was constantly on the move and better known for his soprano saxophone playing. It was for his fervent, nuance-rich clarinet playing, however, that he had first become known. Johnny Dodds, a great blues performer who was much in demand for New Orleans collective-style work, had a harsher sound. At the opposite end of the scale was Jimmie Noone, widely regarded as an archetypal exponent of the Creole style of clarinet playing, whose earliest masters had been George Bacquet and the Tios (Luis, Lorenzo Sr and Lorenzo Jr). Although possessing the same rounded tone that finds its mellowest expression in the lower reaches of the instrument known as the 'chalumeau' register, he is something of an anomaly due to the fact that he spent almost his entire career in Chicago. Indeed, the music he played at the very chic Apex Club was far removed from the New Orleans model. With the saxophonist and clarinetist Doc Poston at his side, Noone led a band that dispensed with brass most of the time, thus anticipating the small groups of Benny Goodman and cool jazz.

For this reason Albert Nicholas or Omer Simeon are perhaps better examples of the Creole elegance that Barney Bigard later glorified in the music of Duke Ellington during the 1930s. The clarinet – either in a clarinet

LISTENING
GUIDE
Jimmy Dorsey: 'There'll
Come a Time' (with Red
Nichols, Brunswick, 29
May 1928)[1].
Stump Evans: 'Hyena
Stomp', 'Wild Man
Blues' (with Jelly Roll
Morton, Victor, 4 June
1927)[2].
Adrian Rollini: 'Ida',
'Feelin' No Pain' (with
Red Nichols, Brunswick,
15 August 1927)[1].
Benny Carter: 'Come On
Baby' (with Fletcher
Henderson, Columbia,
12 December 1928)[3].
Prince Robinson: 'Four
or Five Times' (with
McKinney's Cotton
Pickers, Victor, 11 July
1928)[4].
Bud Freeman: 'Rose of
Washington Square'
(with Red Nichols,
Brunswick, 12 June
1929)[1].
For Frankie Trumbauer
('Singing the Blues' with
Bix Beiderbecke), Stump
Evans ('Static Strut' with
Erskine Tate), Sidney
Bechet ('Cake Walking
Babies' with Clarence
Williams), Johnny
Hodges ('The Mooche'
with Duke Ellington),
Don Redman ('Stop
Kidding' with McKinney's
Cotton Pickers) and
Coleman Hawkins ('The
Stampede' with Fletcher
Henderson) see else-
where in this chapter.

CD GUIDE
1. Red Nichols, *His Best
Recordings, 1927–31*,
Best of Jazz.
2. Jelly Roll Morton, *The
Quintessence, 1923–40*,
Frémeaux.
3. Fletcher Henderson,
*The Quintessence,
1924–36*, Frémeaux.
4. McKinney's Cotton
Pickers, *1928–30*,
Classics.

trio (a combination dear to Don Redman) or as part of a wider reed section (where it was gradually knocked off its pedestal by the saxophone) – had a strong presence in the early big bands; not least in the Fletcher Henderson Orchestra, in which it was played with great virtuosity by Buster Bailey throughout the 1930s.

The instrument can also boast a number of noteworthy white performers, such as Leon Roppolo of the New Orleans Rhythm Kings, who recorded some fine solos in the Creole tradition in 1922. Names that stand out among the white Chicagoans are Frank Teschemacher (faithful to the Louisiana tradition), Benny Goodman (who found his own way forward in the 1930s) and the unclassifiable Pee Wee Russell (a complex figure who pleased the traditionalists during the New Orleans revival but immediately started playing Ornette Coleman when 'free jazz' arrived on the scene).

The saxophone

Closely related to single-reed woodwind instruments, the saxophone made its debut in New Orleans jazz bands after 1915. The wide range of instruments in the saxophone family (bass, tenor and soprano in Bb, alternating with the baritone and alto in Eb) had already won many admirers, but it took a while for musicians to work out how to use them. The first successful saxophonist was Rudy Wiedoeft, who played a variety of syncopated music on the C-melody sax (a C saxophone between tenor and alto). Wiedoeft's honeyed tone, virtuoso tonguing and jerky staccato were extremely influential. Frankie Trumbauer (C-melody sax) retained Wiedoeft's tenderness of timbre and phrasing, and Jimmy Dorsey added an energetic virtuosity. In the 1930s, these two white musicians inspired Lester Young's alternative to Coleman Hawkins's dominant style. Another white saxophonist, Adrian Rollini, liberated the bass sax from its role as a substitute for the double bass by playing melodies on it. Among the black players, 'Stump' Evans made a speciality of the 'slap' phrasing (a kind of virtuoso percussive staccato) widespread among saxophonists at the time. Sidney Bechet was a major influence, notably on Johnny Hodges, to whom he gave soprano saxophone lessons. In the 1930s, Hodges was Benny Carter's main rival for the title of leading saxophonist of the day. It was tenor saxophonist Coleman Hawkins, however, who turned his back on the instrument's tendency towards sentimentality, transforming its sound through growling effects and a powerful vibrato that endowed it with an inner passion. He influenced the majority of tenor and baritone saxophonists, leading them to abandon the archaic, jerky phrasing of the 1920s. Just two tenor sax players, Prince Robinson and Bud Freeman, escaped his influence.

The rhythm section

The banjo, double bass and bass drum provided the jazz band with its heartbeat, and the chords played on the piano, banjo and double bass also provided its harmonic framework. The sound engineers of the 1920s preferred wind basses (tuba or sax), but the arrival of electrical recording led to a rediscovery of the bowed or 'slapped' (in which the strings are made to snap back against the fingerboard) double bass of Wellman Braud

LISTENING
GUIDE
Baby Dodds: 'Oriental
Man' (Dixieland
Thumpers, Paramount,
December 1927)¹.
Zutty Singleton: 'No One
Else But You' (with Louis
Armstrong, Okeh, 5
December 1928)².
Tony Spargo: 'Dixie Jass
Band One Step' (ODJB,
Victor, 26 February
1917)¹.
Vic Berton: 'Delirium'
(with Red Nichols, Victor,
11 February 1927)¹.
Paul Barbarin: 'Sugar
Hill Function' (with
Henry Allen, Okeh, 18
February 1930)².
Kaiser Marshall:
'Sensation' (with
Fletcher Henderson,
Vocalion, 19 March
1927)¹.
Sonny Greer:
'Washington Wobble'
(with Duke Ellington,
Victor, 6 October 1927)¹.
Johnny Saint-Cyr: 'Willie
the Weeper' (with Louis
Armstrong, Okeh, 7 May
1927)³.
Lonnie Johnson: 'Hot
Fingers' (with Eddie
Lang, Okeh, 9 October
1929)⁴, 'Away Down in
the Alley Blues' (Okeh,
21 February 1928)⁴.
Joe Venuti and Eddie
Lang: 'The Wild Cat'
(Victor, 21 June 1928)⁵,
'Running Ragged
(Bamboozlin' the
Bassoon)' (Okeh, 18
October 1929)⁵.
Earl Hines (see
'Weatherbird' with Louis
Armstrong), Wellman
Braud (see Duke
Ellington, Pops Foster
with Louis Armstrong),
Quinn Wilson (see Jelly
Roll Morton), Harry Hull
(see Johnny Dunn), etc.

CD GUIDE
1. Anthology of Jazz
Drumming, Vol 1,
Masters of Jazz.
2. Anthology of Jazz
Drumming, Vol 2,
Masters of Jazz.
3. Louis Armstrong, The
Quintessence, 1925–40,
Frémeaux.
4. Great Blues Guitarists,
String Dazzlers,
Columbia.
5. Violin Jazz, Frémeaux.

and Pops Foster. The banjo, generally preferred to the guitar, was often left to mark the four beats of the bar while the double bass and bass drum emphasized the main beats in the manner of ragtime.

The result was a kind of alternating bass, which the stride pianists maintained until the arrival of the 'trumpet piano' style of Earl Hines, one of the fathers of modern jazz piano. In this style the hands were more independent of each other. The right was freer in terms of melodic possibilities, while the left acquired more rhythmic options as well as a bolder and more precise harmonic role.

Drums were used to articulate and underline the melody. Drawing on a wide range of sounds (produced by different stick strokes and the use of various accessories), drums could also complement or comment on the tune, introducing timing shifts and polyrhythmic effects inspired by ragtime. Unfortunately, at a time when the drum kit was being extended, notably by Duke Ellington's colourful drummer Sonny Greer, sound engineers all too often favoured small percussion instruments. The hi-hat, a double cymbal operated by the left foot, was introduced around 1926. Baby Dodds and Zutty Singleton were leading lights in a little-known world where white drummers (Tony Spargo, Vic Berton, Ray Bauduc) and black drummers (Paul Barbarin, Kaiser Marshall, George Stafford, Sonny Greer) vied for stardom.

Strings and other oddities

A number of unusual practices survived at the Creole dance halls in New Orleans and at the large venues in New York. The jazzmen of the 1920s were often multi-instrumentalists, frequently putting their main instrument aside and picking up some other, possibly unusual instrument (at least unusual in jazz). Examples include Don Redman (oboe with Fletcher Henderson), Sidney Bechet (sarrusophone with Clarence Williams), Frankie Trumbauer (bassoon with Joe Venuti), Fats Waller (organ with Fletcher Henderson) and Ira Moten (accordion with Benny Moten). Jazz also borrowed the improvised instruments of the 'spasm bands' or 'jug bands' that were all the rage in Memphis. Banjos and guitars with six or occasionally four strings (known at the time as tenor guitars) were confined to an accompanying role punctuated by occasional bursts of virtuoso ornamentation. Solos, on the rare occasions they came around, posed a problem for musicians such as Johnny Saint-Cyr, Bud Scott and Buddy Christian. The banjo was powerful but somewhat brutal, while the guitar permitted more nuanced playing but could not be heard. It was for this reason that solos were often reserved for the 'stop chorus' – that is, they were totally unaccompanied. Eddie Lang, widely regarded as the first great jazz guitarist, was able to make himself heard within the slightly more muted context of the white jazz band. Nevertheless, when he recorded duos with the black guitarist Lonnie Johnson, who came from a blues background, it was his extraordinary skill as an accompanist that prevailed, while his opposite number demonstrated his immense talent as a soloist capable of self-accompanied melodic improvisation.

Eddie Lang's greatest musical partner was his childhood friend Joe Venuti, the first solo violinist in the history of jazz. Despite the instrument's modest volume, many multi-instrumentalists carried a violin with them in their luggage (for example, Edgar Sampson, who played with Charlie Johnson, or Juice Wilson, one of the two violinists in Noble Sissle's orchestra in 1929). They all made use of both classical technique and the technique of country fiddle.

Hot jazz conquers the world

After the war, venues in Paris fought over the various black groups doing the rounds, some of which had made a name for themselves in the trenches. French ensembles – from accordion bands to music-hall orchestras – adopted *le jâse*. This meant the drum kit, for it was with that instrument that jazz was initially associated in France. Even in the United States the genre was not yet very well known and what was being discovered in France was jazz of a fairly primitive kind that succeeded nevertheless in stunning the audience with its exotic sound world and rhythmic movements.

Jean Wiener and Clément Doucet gave their first 'mixed' concert (in which they performed the new syncopated music and classical pieces on the same stage) on 6 December 1921. Led by Jean Cocteau, the intellectual elite became interested for a while in the new rhythms and the blue note without really knowing what to do with them. Those who worked in the music hall had more of an idea. Maurice Chevalier was one of the first to realize which way the wind was blowing.

Musicians in the capital's orchestra pits studied the new music carefully. The West Indians at the Bal Nègre on the Rue Blomet in the 15th arrondissement in Paris felt an affinity with it, as did the black Brazilian flautist and composer Pixinguinha when he passed through Paris in 1922. Inspired by the black revues and later, from 1926, by Paul Whiteman's orchestra, new bands (Ray Ventura and His Collegians, for example, or Gregor et Ses Grégoriens) triumphed at the music hall.

A smaller public, however, was discovering Louis Armstrong through his early recordings and starting to learn about a more authentic strain of jazz that it

LISTENING
GUIDE
Marcel's Jazz Band des
Folies-Bergère: 'For Me
and My Gal' (Pathé,
January–February
1919)'.
Ray Ventura and His
Collegians: 'I'm Afraid of
You' (Columbia, 1
December 1928)'.
Jean Cocteau with Dan
Parrish and his
Orchestre du Grand
Écart: 'La Toison d'Or'
(Columbia, 2 December
1929)².

CD GUIDE
1. *Jazz and Music Hall,*
Swing.
2. *Americans in Europe*
(1917–39), Swing.

regarded as a major art form. In a society intoxicated by the charleston on the one hand and mourning its war dead and dressing its wounds on the other, real jazz fans had to fight a battle on two fronts: against the infatuation of those who saw jazz as nothing more than an excuse to let off steam and against the contempt of those who regarded it as an incitement to debauchery.

The debate spread through Europe in the wake of the American tours. The battle raged as far as the Soviet Union, whose ideologues were puzzled by jazz. Was it bourgeois or proletarian, decadent or revolutionary? Maxim Gorky formulated the official anti-jazz line but the German composers Kurt Weill and Hans Eisler demonstrated that jazz was perfectly capable of serving the socialist cause. Fewer scruples were in evidence in the British colonies in Africa: the black inhabitants of the ghettos of South Africa reinterpreted ragtime according to its own traditions, and in Accra (in present-day Ghana), the High Society Club was entertained by a local band called the Jazz Kings.

Context

SOCIETY. The Stock Market Crash of 24 October 1929 had a serious knock-on effect. By 1932 there were eleven million unemployed in the United States alone. A crisis of confidence in free-market economics brought the Democrats to power, where they stayed for twenty years (1933–52). Hardest hit by unemployment was the black population (representing 38% of the unemployed with no means of support, rising to 80% in certain cities). For the first time ever, black voters turned their backs on the Republican party and voted Democrat. Franklin Roosevelt's New Deal policy and the appointment of black leaders to a number of public positions gave the black community a glimmer of hope, but the ensuing measures were of only limited benefit. The black churches helped make up for the deficiencies of the system through vital charitable and social work. They were also active in the political sphere, supporting the various boycott movements designed to pressurize companies into recruiting more black workers. Black activism was split between the middle-class desire for integration, the welfare aspirations of the proletariat and the radical positions of the black nationalists. The big black ghettos sank into poverty.

After Chicago, New York was the next city to put an end to the reign of the gangsters (already weakened by a spate of gangland killings) by means of a series of anti-corruption campaigns and the abolition of prohibition in December 1933. In Kansas City, the mobsters enjoyed the protection of the politician Tom Pendergast and held out until 1939.

THE MUSIC INDUSTRY. Not only did gramophone records suffer in the economic crisis, they also faced competition from talking pictures. The success of radio made matters worse. The technology for relaying concerts had made considerable progress since the first live broadcasts in 1923. Sixteen-inch discs, playing at 33⅓ rpm and holding 15 minutes of music per side, enabled prerecorded concerts to be broadcast. Jukeboxes, originally invented in 1899, became widespread in the early 1930s. Their success in the bars of the black ghettos would help promote the black music labels.

Small labels (including Gennett and Paramount) went bankrupt or were swallowed up by their larger competitors. The jazz record market came to be dominated by Victor-RCA, Columbia and the American arm of Decca. Serial takeovers and the

A soup kitchen during the Great Depression, 1931.

creation of overseas subsidiaries would later be the bane of collectors' and discographers' lives. Both in the United States and in Europe, jazz lovers became collectors, and the art of discography took off following the publication of Charles Delaunay's *Hot Discography* in 1936. Suddenly collectors wanted to know the recording dates of their discs and the names of all the musicians playing on them. Old records became valuable, and the reissuing of unsold stocks heralded the era of the rerelease. The magazine *Down Beat* was founded in 1934. Use of the microphone became widespread among announcers and singers. At a time when patent applications were flooding in for guitar resonators (the Dopera Brothers' Dobro and National models had been manufactured in the United States since 1926, and Mario Maccaferri's Selmer guitar went into production in France in 1932), a number of acoustic engineers (including Lloyd Loar and George Beauchamps) started to look closely at electric amplification. Launched in the early 1930s by Rickenbacker and Gibson, the electric guitar first seduced the world of Western swing and then the world of jazz. In 1935, Hammond launched an electric organ based on phonic wheel technology.

RELATED MUSICAL GENRES. Talent scouts continued to recruit musicians in the south. The legendary Robert Johnson recorded his thirty or so sides in a mobile recording studio in Texas in 1936–7. The ethnomusicologists John and Alan Lomax discovered blues artists such as Leadbelly (1933) and Muddy Waters (1941) during their recording expeditions for the Library of Congress.

The focus, however, started to shift to the cities that were the magnets for the rural exodus. Their studios and producers presided over the emergence of a new style of band-based blues. While Houston was visited by guitar-playing bluesmen from the countryside, the rough-and-ready pianists of the Santa Fe school (who would later influence Californian rhythm and blues) were making a name for themselves in the dives around the station from which the Santa Fe train departed.

After being drawn to Memphis, the Delta bluesmen continued north. In a St Louis caught between ragtime and boogie-woogie, the bar-room piano freed guitarists from the necessity of playing simple chords, encouraging them to develop a more melodic form of expression as a counterpoint to their singing. Due to the lack of a recording studio in the city, the pianists Walter Davis, Roosevelt Sykes and Peetie Wheatstraw and the guitarists Lonnie Johnson and Henry Townsend moved further north – to Chicago, the meeting place for southern bluesmen.

Chicago blues was born at the instigation of Lester Melrose, a producer with Columbia and then Bluebird (Victor-RCA's 'race series'). Working with artists from the south such as Big Bill Broonzy, Tampa Red and John Lee 'Sonny Boy' Williamson, Melrose created a style that combined elements of the orchestral sophistication of 'classic blues', the improvised instrumentation of Memphis, the vigorous piano style of Saint Louis and the pungency of the Delta blues.

A pioneer of Chicago blues, Thomas Andrew Dorsey turned to gospel at the beginning of the 1930s. His song compositions revived what was an ossified genre in the south. At a time when more and more solo singers were emerging (such as Willie Mae Ford Smith and Sister Rosetta Tharpe, whose reputation was compromised by her secular work), Mahalia Jackson became his preferred performer.

Country music was also caught up in the vogue for swing. Milton Brown and Bob Wills invented Western swing, fronting bands that included wind instruments, piano, drums and the first electric guitars.

The big bands

The era of swing and the heyday of the big band are generally considered to
have been the 1930s. While it is true that both spilled over into the bebop
period, finally coming to an end around 1945, the vogue for swing was at
its height during the pre-war period, when America was trying to forget its
economic woes and to lose itself in intoxicating rhythms. The decade can
be divided into two halves. The first half saw New York's black big bands
consolidate their section work and put the finishing touches to their lush
writing style. It was during the second half of the decade that the swing era
proper started, when the white swing bands were in the limelight and Count
Basie defined the classic big band and drew attention to the Kansas City
scene. A number of conventions were established during the 1930s that
were to govern jazz until the end of the century.

Harlem: clubs and dance halls

With Chicago in decline, New York became the new capital of jazz. Black
musicians were among the first to suffer during the Depression.
Nevertheless, there was work around for the most creative and for those
most capable of adapting to the needs of the large Harlem clubs. These
were controlled by gangsters, who remained the main employers of jazz
musicians until the mid-1930s.

When, in 1933, Connie's Inn decided to desert Harlem for a site near
Broadway on 48th Street, the Cotton Club's victory over its main

LISTENING
GUIDE
Cab Calloway: 'Minnie
the Moocher'
(Brunswick, 3 March
1931)¹.
Benny Carter: 'Devil's
Holiday' (Columbia, 16
October 1933)², 'Keep a
Song in Your Soul' (with
Fletcher Henderson,
Columbia, 2 December
1930)³.
Fletcher Henderson:
'Chinatown, My
Chinatown' (Columbia, 3
October 1930)³, 'New
King Porter Stomp'
(Columbia, 9 December
1932)³, 'Shanghai
Shuffle' (Decca, 11
September 1934)³.
Chick Webb: 'Stompin'
at the Savoy' (Columbia,
18 May 1934)⁴, 'Harlem
Congo' (Decca, 1
November 1937)⁴, 'Liza'
(Decca, 3 May 1938)⁴.

CD GUIDE
1. Cotton Club, Harlem
1924–Broadway 1936,
Frémeaux.
2. Benny Carter, His Best
Recordings, 1929–40,
Best of Jazz.
3. Fletcher Henderson,
The Quintessence,
1924–36, Frémeaux.
4. Chick Webb–Ella
Fitzgerald, The
Quintessence, 1929–39,
Frémeaux.

commercial rival seemed complete. But the end of prohibition and the increased feuding between gangsters meant that fewer whites were visiting this black district, and the Cotton Club went the same way as Connie's Inn in February 1936. Unwelcome at the new upmarket addresses, the black public instead frequented the Savoy Ballroom, which hosted legendary battles between bands on its two stages. From 1934, the other mecca for black music in Harlem – as popular for its weekly talent contests (where artists such as Ella Fitzgerald and Thelonious Monk were discovered) as for its concerts – was the Apollo Theater.

Power and fluidity

In order to meet the demands of these venues, bands boosted their numbers: three trumpets, two and then three trombones, four reeds. Reeds were still relatively mixed sections made up of multi-instrumentalists who switched between different types of saxophone and who were constantly reaching for the clarinet (and occasionally, as in Duke Ellington's band, the bass clarinet; or – as in the bands of Jimmie Lunceford, Chick Webb and Benny Carter – even the flute). The rhythm quartet became more fluid after replacing the banjo once and for all with the guitar and the tuba with the string bass. These larger bands offered power, high-quality instrumental playing, colourful orchestration, a mischievous combination of timbres and sophisticated writing from a new generation of arrangers. These arrangers went in for virtuoso modulation, 'modernistic' harmonic effects or bold and original ideas that showed they had learned much from their classical contemporaries. The great bands had also to master the rhythmic bounce, which was now expected to be more fluid and less jerky than before. Indeed, the phrasing of the ensemble playing as a whole was smoother and less halting than it had been previously, thus benefiting dancers of the lindy hop and other variants of the jitterbug.

The great Harlem bandleaders

During the first half of the decade, Fletcher Henderson's band adapted to these new demands by revamping its rhythm section (with John Kirby on double bass and Walter Johnson on drums) and hiring cutting-edge musicians such as the trumpeter Henry 'Red' Allen, the trombonist J C Higginbotham, the tenor saxophonist Coleman Hawkins and the arranger Benny Carter. The difference this made can be heard by comparing the head arrangement of 'King Porter Stomp' of 1928 with that of the 'New King Porter Stomp' of 1932.

While Fletcher Henderson reigned supreme at Connie's Inn (1930–1), three stars battled it out at the Cotton Club: Duke Ellington, who gradually refined his 'jungle' style over the years (see p.61), the singer and entertainer Cab Calloway, who fronted an exceptional band, and, from 1934, Jimmie Lunceford (see p.79). Newly arrived from the provinces, Lunceford became Ellington's main rival. He shared the Duke's sense of orchestral colour and surpassed him in the perfection of his ensemble playing. Lunceford's band was also one of the two most popular with dancers. The other was the drummer Chick Webb's band, which played at the Savoy Ballroom.

While there were many other Harlem-based big bands of note (including Al Cooper and His Savoy Sultans, the Mills Blue Rhythm Band led by the showman Lucky Millinder, the arranger Don Redman's band – resident at Connie's Inn between 1932 and 1935 – Claude Hopkins's band at the Roseland Ballroom on Broadway and the various bands led after 1932 by Benny Carter, who was omnipresent as an arranger in the 1930s), the arrival of newcomers Andy Kirk and above all Count Basie in New York in 1936 signalled the importance of the breeding ground that was Kansas City.

The 'territory bands'

New York may have become the capital of jazz, but it did not have a monopoly on it. Many of the city's musicians came from the provinces, and its big bands were constantly on the road. As they passed through different towns, they encountered other, sometimes exceptional orchestras, such as that of Earl Hines, who had remained behind in Chicago, or McKinney's Cotton Pickers, based in Detroit, which Benny Carter took over in 1931–2. There were many provincial bands (including Harlan Leonard, Boots & Buddies and Alphonso Trent) that travelled the country and spent a lot of time touring the central plains circuit. These became known as 'territory bands'. They exchanged musicians and influences and were often to be heard on the radio.

In December 1933, Coleman Hawkins was passing through Kansas City, which had a reputation for producing tenor saxophonists. Three of them (Herschel Evans, Ben Webster and Lester Young) set a trap for him at a club in the city. In the course of a jam session that lasted until the early morning, his crown slipped a little and so did the reputation of New York City.

Kansas City

Under the corrupt administration of Tom Pendergast, Kansas City's thriving drinking establishments and nightclubs were an important source of work for musicians from the south who were steeped in the blues. They also served as essential stopping-off points for big bands touring the Midwest. Devoid of the splendour of the New York establishments, these second-rate venues opened their doors to boogie-woogie pianists such as Pete Johnson and blues shouters such as Big Joe Turner and Jimmy Rushing (who were capable of making themselves heard above a big band), and hosted formal and informal encounters between artists. It was in jam sessions of this kind – in which the participants improvised on popular tunes and blues while avoiding the structural complications of Harlem-style jazz – that soloists capable of taking on the likes of Coleman Hawkins learned their trade. The brass acquired the habit of accompanying soloists with repeated phrases – either in unison or in harmony – which they inflected as required by the harmonic framework. These riffs might be invented on the spur of the moment by one of the musicians and taken up by his colleagues, or taken from well-known compositions, or chosen from a repertoire of orally transmitted standard themes. Thrilling soloists and audiences alike, these ritornelli were subsequently adopted as a compositional element by Kansas City composers and arrangers and have remained a constant feature of jazz right up to the present.

JIMMIE LUNCEFORD AND HIS ARRANGERS

While it was his iron discipline that enabled Jimmie Lunceford to take a group of Memphis high-school students all the way to the stage of the Cotton Club (where he succeeded Duke Ellington and Cab Calloway in 1934), it was his arrangers Willie Smith, Edwin Wilcox and Sy Oliver who guaranteed him a place in the history books. The clarinetist and first alto Willie Smith brought the phrasing and articulation of his reed section to a state of polished perfection and introduced a highly nuanced style of playing. This can be heard in his imaginative versions of Duke Ellington numbers, such as 'Sophisticated Lady' — notable for the precision and cohesion of its ensemble playing in percussive staccato passages (1:04–1:11) and elegant glissades and pirouettes (1:31–2:12) — and 'Mood Indigo', which features a barrel-organ-like counter-melody played on the saxophone and clarinet (0:00–0:43). The pianist Edwin Wilcox was able to take advantage of the same cohesion in stunning reed slaloms ('Sleepy Time Gal', 1:11–2:01), which are then extended to the entire band (2:08 onwards). He also specialized in those modern, attention-grabbing effects that developed only too naturally behind nightclub dance routines performed in various states of undress. Lovers of zany humour will respond to his 'I'm Nuts about Screwy Music' with its yapping trumpets in the opening section and extravagant wind and drum interjections in the chorus sung by Willie Smith (1:29–1:33; 1:36–1:38; 1:45–1:50; 1:52–1:57; 2:13–2:17; 2:20–2:21). 'Stratosphere' contains some inspired ideas, including dissonant chords (0:21 and especially 1:07), a trumpet ensemble that simulates a mysterious echo (0:41–0:53) and a finale that borders on the atonal.

But the arranger who contributed most to the Lunceford sound was the trumpeter Sy Oliver — in moving from one key to another during the course of wonderful interludes ('The Lonesome Road', 0:54–0:58), in bringing out the full charm of various popular tunes of the day (such as 'Ain't She Sweet'), in featuring Trummy Young's sardonic trombone ('T'ain't What You Do') and in leading the vocal trio in 'Cheatin' On Me' with Willie Smith and the trumpeter Eddie Tomkins. In the introduction to 'Dream of You' he lights up the stars in the sky one by one with a repeated twinkling figure on guitar and piano (0:00–0:18), setting the scene for a romantic trumpet serenade, to which acquiescent saxophones moan a response. It was thanks to Sy Oliver that the band acquired its relaxed, cruising tempo built around a bass that often picked out just the main beats of the bar ('Rain'). How could dancers of the day resist a rhythmic bounce that was so laid back?

Jimmie Lunceford and his band

Bennie Moten, the Blue Devils, Count Basie and classic jazz

Unlike many of the city's musicians, who were more or less new arrivals, the bandleader Bennie Moten was a native of Kansas City, where he reigned supreme. Active from the end of the 1910s, he succeeded in poaching many musicians away from his main local rivals, the bass player Walter Page's Blue Devils – including the bandleader himself. In 1932, he formed a legendary big band with some of the best jazzmen of the day: the trumpeter Oran 'Hot Lips' Page, the trombonist, arranger and guitarist Eddie Durham, the tenor saxophonist Ben Webster, the singer Jimmy Rushing and the pianist and arranger Count Basie. Shortly after Moten's death in 1935, Basie formed his own band from former members of Moten's band and the Blue Devils for a residency at the Reno Club. They were soon joined by Lester Young, who had heard a broadcast from the club on the local radio station W9XBY while visiting the city. It was also on the radio (this time during a broadcast from Chicago) that the producer John Hammond discovered the band and took it into the recording studio at the beginning of 1937. Alongside the three trumpets that had become the norm under Bennie Moten, the trombones were increased to three and the saxophone section (without clarinets) benefited from the mellow tones of two tenors (Herschel Evans and Lester Young) led by Earl Warren. The fourth saxophone was Jack Washington, who gradually switched from alto to baritone. Given the sectional nature of much of the writing, this enabled the saxophone section to assert itself more effectively vis-à-vis the brass (trumpets and trombones).

The reinvigoration of the rhythm section was even more radical. Each of the four beats of the bar was stressed equally and evenly by Freddie

Count Basie

LISTENING
GUIDE
Earl Hines: 'Rosetta',
'Cavernism' (Brunswick,
13 February 1933)[1].
Andy Kirk: 'Moten
Swing' (Decca, 4 March
1936)[2], 'Bearcat Shuffle'
(Decca, 10 April 1936)[2].
For Moten and Basie,
see p.82

CD GUIDE
1. Earl Hines, *Rosetta*,
Jazz Archives.
2. Mary Lou Williams,
Story 1930–41, Jazz
Archives.

Green's guitar, Walter Page's double bass and Jo Jones's bass drum, and underlined by a type of rhythmic figure played on the hi-hat (known in France as a chabada – see p.99). By virtue of its economy of means and effectiveness in terms of swing, energy and power, Count Basie's band can be regarded as having laid the foundations for so-called 'classic jazz'.

Count Basie conquers New York

As early as 1936, Count Basie's band headed east and soon became a hit in New York's large dance halls. Basie and a few members of his band were even invited to perform alongside Benny Goodman at the Carnegie Hall on 16 January 1938.

They were not the only territory band to conquer New York. Andy Kirk's long-established Kansas City band The Clouds of Joy seduced audiences at the Apollo Theater with the lightness and elegance of the arrangements by its pianist Mary Lou Williams. Jay McShann formed his more blues-based band in Kansas City in 1937. The laid-back simplicity of his scores left the band's soloists – one of whom, a certain Charlie Parker, was soon to be 'discovered' – plenty of freedom.

The white big bands

By the beginning of the 1930s, Paul Whiteman's 'symphonic jazz' project had reached a dead end and it was the Casa Loma Orchestra, taking its inspiration from the Fletcher Henderson Orchestra and McKinney's Cotton Pickers, that blazed a trail for white jazz. The Casa Loma Orchestra's main arranger was the guitarist and banjo player Gene Gifford. Aware of the rhythmic developments taking place in the black bands, he achieved a quality of musicianship that in turn influenced Jimmie Lunceford. The number of large-scale white bands increased dramatically throughout the 1930s. Their aesthetic differed from that of the black bands in that they exhibited a degree of suavity and sophistication more in keeping with the atmosphere of the big hotels and casinos where they regularly appeared than with the clubs and dance halls of the black ghettos. A good number of these white bands occupied the middle ground between jazz and light entertainment. Others, though, helped to advance the cause of jazz, while at the same time profiting from the enormous popularity of swing among white Americans. This was certainly true of Benny Goodman, whose nickname the 'King of Swing' may seem puzzling to some. For white America, however, Benny Goodman represented the high point of the swing era. A native of Chicago who settled in New York, Benny Goodman based the band he formed in 1934 on the Fletcher Henderson Orchestra. He soon became the star of *Let's Dance*, a radio programme broadcast throughout the whole of America. Assisted by the impresario John Hammond, he performed as far afield as the West Coast in 1935, delighting white jazz lovers with the elegance of his playing and his ability to electrify an audience.

Goodman's success had such a serious knock-on effect that the word

COUNT BASIE: FOUR MASTERPIECES

'TOBY' [1]

Bennie Moten's Kansas City Orchestra. Soloists: Eddie Durham (guitar), Oran 'Hot Lips' Page (trumpet), Ben Webster (tenor sax), Eddie Barefield (alto sax, clarinet), Count Basie (piano), Dan Minor (trombone). Recorded for Victor in Camden (New Jersey), 13 December 1932.

Background. After training in New York in the 1920s with the masters of stride piano, Count Basie joined Bennie Moten's band, which dominated the Kansas City scene at the time.

The number. The rhythm section features the alternating stride bass that Count Basie perfected in his solos. The bustling tempo is typical of bands at the beginning of the 1930s; they even competed with each other to see who could achieve the fastest speeds. 'Toby' is constructed on the 32-bar AABA framework (see p.87) that was common in the 1930s. Although composed by Bennie Moten, what stands out most is the work of the arranger Eddie Barefield, who organized it into a succession of dazzlingly effective riffs. Initially, these riffs are distributed between the brass and the reeds on a chorus-by-chorus basis, but the last few choruses introduce a dialogue between different sections.

1. Count Basie, *Complete Edition, Vol 2, 1930–2*, Masters of Jazz

'ONE O'CLOCK JUMP' [2]

Count Basie and His Orchestra. Soloists: Count Basie (piano), Herschel Evans (tenor sax), George Hunt (trombone), Lester Young (tenor sax), Buck Clayton (trumpet). Recorded for Decca in New York, 7 July 1937.

Background. After Bennie Moten's death, Count Basie formed a band from a number of Moten's musicians along with some of the best of those who had recently appeared on the local scene.

The number. The tempo is rather more relaxed and the rhythm, having broken free of the alternating stride bass, somewhat more economical. Jo Jones's bass drum, Walter Page's double bass and Freddie Green's guitar articulate each of the four beats of the bar with equal weight. The band is propelled forward on the gentle cushion of the *chabada* played on the hi-hat. During the first few bars, the pianist's left hand plays a boogie-woogie walking bass figure that was very common at the time. This composition, which became the band's signature tune in 1938, is really nothing more than a series of riffs designed to test the imagination of the soloists one after the other as they slot into the blues framework. Credited to Count Basie, 'One O'Clock Jump' is really the collective work of a number of arrangers (mainly Buster Smith and Eddie Durham), while the final riff was borrowed from one of Fats Waller's favourite phrases.

2. Count Basie, *The Quintessence, 1937–41*, Frémeaux

'SHINY STOCKINGS' [3]

The Count Basie Orchestra. Soloist: Thad Jones. Recorded for Verve in New York, 4 January 1956.

Background. At the end of 1951, after leading an octet for a while because of money problems, Count Basie reformed his big band with new musicians and recorded a number of masterpieces released on the album *April in Paris*.

The number. Although the younger musicians introduced a hint of bebop into the new band, the improvisers played only a secondary role in it, and the trumpet solo in this arrangement by Frank Foster is merely ornamental. Like the other arrangers who made a name for themselves with Basie after 1950

(Neal Hefti, Ernie Wilkins, Thad Jones, Frank Wess, Quincy Jones and, in the 1960s, Sammy Nestico), Foster made extensive use of ensemble phrasing, writing for all the wind instruments together rather than setting one section against another.

The twelve saxophonists, trumpeters and trombonists respond efficiently and as a single body to the arranger's demands for particular nuances — at times the mellow tones of the saxes are expected to dominate and at others the brass are required to use their combined forces to shake the building to its foundations. With an easy tempo, in which the steady rhythm section precludes any potential pitfalls, the band moves forward like a big cat, sometimes on soft paws, sometimes letting fly with powerful claws. Count Basie's orchestra has been called a swing machine. If so, it is a machine of flesh and muscle.

3. Count Basie, *April in Paris*, Verve

'THE KID FROM REDBANK'[4]

Count Basie Orchestra. Soloist: Count Basie. Recorded at a concert at the Paris Olympia on 9 or 12 December 1957.

Background. Neal Hefti's arrangements on the album *Atomic Basie* have become big band classics. Having been overexposed to these pieces — as background or title music or else simply played unimaginatively — without ever hearing them live, it is all too easy for us to look down on them (just as we might dismiss the *Mona Lisa* having only ever seen it in poor-quality reproductions). It is therefore well worth making the effort to listen to this live version.

The number. The sound was recorded close to the band — we can hear various band members grunting with pleasure — right next to Freddie Green's guitar. This allows us to hear how much the efficiency of the band depends on the quality of the beat set by this instrument. Eddie Jones's double bass and Sonny Payne's cymbal playing seem to sound from 'within' the guitar. The bass drum no longer systematically accentuates the beat but waits on the sidelines, ready to enhance the contours of the arrangement where necessary. As so often, Count Basie gets the rhythm going on the piano. For four whole choruses he prepares the ground, initially playing just a few notes on the keyboard and then phrasing more abundantly. Later on he even reverts to the prolixity of stride piano, a style he never fully abandoned. In the first few choruses, however, his main concern is to give the rhythm section enough space to find themselves, gather momentum and settle comfortably into their beat. Only then is the rest of the band — lined up like Formula 1 cars raring to start — given the green light.

4. Count Basie, *Autumn in Paris*, Magic

LISTENING
GUIDE
Gene Gifford:
'Chinatown' (Casa Loma
Orchestra, radio, mid-
1934)[1].
Bill Finegan: 'Lonesome
Road' (recorded by
Tommy Dorsey, Victor, 1
May 1939)[2].
Jerry Gray: 'Begin the
Beguine' (recorded by
Artie Shaw, Victor, 24
July 1938)[3].
Fletcher Henderson:
'Wrappin' It Up' (Decca,
12 September 1934)[4],
'King Porter Stomp'
(recorded by Benny
Goodman, Victor, 1 July
1935)[5].
Horace Henderson,
'Christopher Columbus'
(recorded by Fletcher
Henderson, Vocalion-
Okeh, 27 March 1936)[4].
Jimmy Mundy:
'Cavernism' (recorded
by Earl Hines,
Brunswick, 13 February
1933)[6], 'Sing, Sing,
Sing' (recorded by
Benny Goodman, Victor,
6 July 1937)[5].
Sy Oliver: 'Stomp It Off'
(recorded by Tommy
Dorsey, Victor, 20 July
1939)[1].
Edgar Sampson: 'Don't
Be That Way' (recorded
by Benny Goodman,
concert, 16 January
1938)[1].

CD GUIDE
1. Swing Era Big Band,
Frémeaux.
2. Tommy Dorsey,
Masterpieces, Jazz
Archives.
3. Artie Shaw, His Best
Recordings, Best of Jazz.
4. Fletcher Henderson,
The Quintessence,
Frémeaux.
5. Benny Goodman, His
Best Recordings, Best of
Jazz.
6. Earl Hines, Rosetta,
Jazz Archives.
7. Chick Webb–Ella
Fitzgerald, The
Quintessence, Frémeaux.

'swing', besides its other meanings, came to refer to the wave of white bands that washed over America between 1936 and the end of the war. Based on a long-standing partnership, the Dorsey brothers' big band (led jointly by the trombonist Tommy and the saxophonist Jimmy) performed regularly between Spring 1934 and September 1935, when the brothers fell out. They went on to lead their own bands, with Tommy's eclipsing Jimmy's in popularity. Tommy Dorsey's music is smoother than Benny Goodman's; indeed it is halfway between Goodman and Glenn Miller. Miller was famous for the suave combination of sax and clarinet that can be heard in 'Moonlight Serenade', but his popularity did not really take off until the end of the 1930s. It blossomed further when he joined up and became head of the Army Air Force Band. The clarinetist Artie Shaw embodied flawless writing and musical direction. Rather unusually, sometimes he led a proper big band and sometimes he led a mixed group with strings. His modern ideas anticipated certain aspects of cool jazz. The saxophonist Charlie Barnet, on the other hand, took his inspiration directly from black music sources, combining the influences of Duke Ellington and Count Basie (when he was leading the band) with those of Coleman Hawkins and Johnny Hodges (when playing the saxophone). The band fronted by Bob Crosby revived the New Orleans repertoire within the context of a big swing band, featuring the very Dixieland drumming style of Ray Bauduc.

Black arrangers

There were already a number of excellent arrangers in the white bands of the 1920s (Bill Challis, Fud Livingstone, Lennie Hayton) who had their worthy successors in the 1930s (Bill Finegan, Billy May, Jerry Gray, Joe Lipman), but by and large the white bands called on the services of a handful of black arrangers who were already being fought over by the black bands – notably Fletcher Henderson, Horace Henderson, Eddie Durham, Andy Gibson, Buster Harding, Jimmy Mundy, Sy Oliver, Edgar Sampson and Benny Carter. It was also fairly common practice for the white arrangers simply to plagiarize the work of their black counterparts. Glenn Miller's famous riff in 'In the Mood', for example, was borrowed from 'Hot and Anxious', a Horace Henderson arrangement from 1931.

The discography on this page is listed by arranger.

The combo

LISTENING
GUIDE
Fats Waller:
'Honeysuckle Rose'
(Victor-RCA, 7 November
1934)¹, 'The Joint Is
Jumping' (Victor-RCA, 7
October 1937)¹.
Teddy Wilson: 'I've
Found a New Baby'
(Brunswick, 1 June
1937)³, 'Fine and
Dandy' (Brunswick-
Decca, 31 March 1937)³.
Rex Stewart: 'Linger
Awhile' (Victor, 2
November 1940)².
The Chocolate Dandies:
'Six or Seven Times'
(Okeh, 18 September
1929)⁴, 'Krazy Kapers'
(Okeh, 10 October
1933)⁴, 'Smack'
(Commodore, 25 May
1940)⁴.
Lionel Hampton:
'Buzzin' Around with the
Bee' (Victor, 14 April
1937)⁵, 'When Lights
Are Low' (Victor, 11
September 1939)⁵.
Benny Goodman
Quartet: 'Avalon' (Victor,
30 July 1937)⁶.
Stuff Smith and His
Onyx Club Boys: 'Old
Joe's Hittin' the Jug'
(Vocalion, 1 July 1936)⁷.
John Kirby: 'Rehearsin'
for a Nervous
Breakdown', 'From A
Flat to C' (Decca, 28
October 1938)⁸, 'Minute
Waltz' (Vocalion, 19
May 1939).

The word 'combo' (from 'combination') refers to the small jazz groups of the 1930s that comprised a few brass players and a rhythm section. The combo, which thrived on the margins of the big bands, was often used in a kind of scam. Inspired by the after-hours jam sessions which jazzmen often engaged in, someone had the idea of getting together small, informal groups of musicians who could record the hits of the day as quickly as possible, without the help of an arranger but sometimes with a sung chorus. In this way the record industry responded to its crisis by reducing the cost of its recording sessions. This approach also satisfied the need that musicians had to express themselves more freely than they could in a big-band context. In a sense they were reviving the unrestrained New Orleans style, but using the language of the 1930s.

The first beneficiary of this new market was Fats Waller. In 1934, he formed the band Fats Waller And His Rhythm, which consisted of trumpet, clarinet or saxophone, guitar, bass and drums, centred around the leader's virtuoso piano and witty vocals. In 1935, the pianist Teddy Wilson formed the first of many small groups that often featured a female singer (Billie Holiday made a name for herself with his band). By bringing together soloists from various big bands, these informal recording sessions gave improvisers the opportunity to compare their talents.

One soloist after another

Benny Carter had started assembling small groups of musicians from different bands (under the name The Chocolate Dandies, previously used for contractual reasons by McKinney's Cotton Pickers) as early as 1929. Recordings by this variable line-up were made at various times throughout the 1930s and gave listeners the opportunity to discover soloists – such as Coleman Hawkins, Chu Berry and Benny Carter himself – when freed from the constraints of the big-band set-up. From 1937, the best instrumentalists of the decade also featured, one after another, in the one-off groups formed by Lionel Hampton. RCA-Victor gave Hampton the freedom to bring to the studio whomever he liked, whenever he liked. In addition to soloists, he also brought arrangers such as Edgar Sampson and the ubiquitous Benny Carter. Individual members of big bands also formed smaller

Benny Goodman

In the 1930s, jazz acquired a new repertoire from the world of musical theatre. This has provided jazzmen with a common currency right up to the present: when two musicians meet for the first time, they have a reservoir of standard themes to fall back on. Even if one of them does not know the melody, he will be familiar with the structure and the harmonic vocabulary.

CHORD PROGRESSIONS

Composers of musicals used the tonal system with ease. They added colour to the I–IV–V7 chord progression (see p.28) by replacing it with the progression I–VI–II–V7. This sequence entails a progressive increase in tension from the stability of the first degree (I) to the instability of the dominant seventh (V7). It occurs in the opening bars of numerous jazz themes, including George Gershwin's 'I Got Rhythm'.

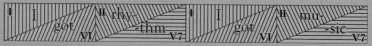

Chord progression in the first four bars of I Got Rhythm (George Gershwin)

In this example, the final tension of the progression leads back to the stability of the first chord (V7 → I). A similar progression is illustrated by this example from Charles Trenet's popular French song, *Douce France*.

Douce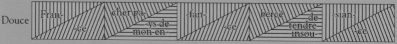

Chord progression in Douce France (Charles Trenet)

In many cases, however, the fifth chord will sever the link that attaches it to the original scale, providing an opportunity for a change of key. This involves moving to a scale (or ladder, to continue the acrobat analogy used on p.28) which is identical but situated at a different height. Later, one of the main preoccupations of improvisers – always impatient to break away and do their own thing – would be to experiment with the different ways of seizing this opportunity. The central phrase of 'I Got Rhythm' consists of a tumbling succession of V7 chords in adjacent keys. It is as if we were falling from the branch of a tree and trying to grab hold of a more solid-looking lower branch (I) that also breaks (it turns out be just a V7 chord in another key). We finally return to the original key after the scare and excitement of this eight-bar tumble, which has turned out to be nothing more than a diversion designed to dispel any monotony. Modern jazz musicians would later indulge in even more distant and exciting escapades.

Old man	trouble	I don't	mind him	you don't	find him	round my	door

The central phrase of 'I Got Rhythm'

THE IMPROVISER AND HARMONY

This chord progression (often abbreviated to II–V7) is the most common of a small number of formulae that make up the harmonic vocabulary of the standard repertoire. Combined with one another on what are themselves standard frameworks, they provide the jazzman with a springboard for improvisation.

The New Orleans 'collective' style involved each musician playing around the melody and contributing more or less spontaneous ornaments and variations of his own devising that were not always in keeping with the chords being played in the background. Louis Armstrong was probably the first to take advantage of the chords supplied by the piano, and Earl Hines was the first pianist to provide him with a logical harmonic structure that allowed for genuine interaction between soloist and piano.

After Armstrong, improvisers became real acrobats, ready to leap from one 'ladder' to another at their accompanists' invitation, moving around them on the rungs corresponding to the notes of the scale. As soloists' awareness of harmony developed, however, they sought to enrich the harmony (with passing chords, enriched chords and substitute chords) and then to liberate themselves from it altogether (the ambiguity of the blue note being a permanent invitation to transgress in this way). This would become one of the main features of bebop.

STRUCTURES OF THE JAZZ STANDARD

The soloist plays a theme and then improvises, while the double bass, piano and guitar repeat in a loop the sequence of chords that accompany the theme. The harmonic structure can be set down on paper in the form of a harmonic grid that an improviser can follow if he does not know the piece. The chords are written in the boxes representing the bars as follows (to be read left to right, top to bottom):

The grid of 'I Got Rhythm'. The names of the chords have been replaced by patterns and colours in order to provide a visual representation of the harmonic movement.

At the beginning of the 1920s, when improvisation took the form of simple variations and was often limited to short breaks, the ragtime framework – a succession of themes and harmonic patterns in different keys, sometimes separated by an interlude – was ideally suited to maintaining interest. As improvisers broke away from melody in the 1930s, they looked for more sophisticated harmonies but at the same time simpler, standardized structures that made it easier for them to get their bearings within a piece. From this point of view, songs from musicals represented the ideal repertoire. These songs were made up of a verse (similar to the recitative in opera in that they shared an uncertain tempo) and a chorus with a regular tempo (like an opera aria). This same structure can be found in George Gershwin's 'I Got Rhythm' from the musical *Girl Crazy*. After a brief orchestral introduction, the singer (Judy Garland in the film version) launches into the verse ('Days can be sunny...') at 0:13. The chorus (see above) begins at 0:55. It comprises an eight-bar A section (0:55–1:02), a repeat of the A section (1:03–1:10), an eight-bar B section, called the 'bridge' (1:11–1:19) and finishes with a reprise of the A section (1:19–1:29), with an additional two bars for the final reprise of the phrase 'Who can ask for anything more?' (not used by jazzmen when they play the piece). In the version selected in the Listening Guide, after a four-bar interlude (1:29–1:33) the piano repeats the whole of the chorus, playing variations. This is what jazzmen call 'taking a chorus'.

LISTENING GUIDE
Judy Garland :
'I Got Rhythm'
(Decca, 4 nov. 1943)[1].
Lester Young:
'Lester Leaps In'
(with Count Basie's Kansas City Seven, Vocalion, 5 September 1939)[2].

CD GUIDE
1. George Gershwin *To Broadway from Hollywood*, IMP / Chansons-Cinéma.
2. Lester Young, *The Quintessence*, 1936–1944, Frémeaux.

During the 1930s, the verses gradually disappeared (with a few exceptions, including the standard 'Tea for Two' and the ballad composed by Billy Strayhorn for Duke Ellington's band, 'Lush Life', whose verses continued to serve as an introduction). Improvisers focused on the chorus, which became the standard unit of measurement in jazz. With the exception of the twelve-bar blues structure, which continued to be used, the choruses in jazz were normally made up of 32 bars divided into four eight-bar sections following various patterns: ABA'C ('The Sheik of Araby'), ABAB' ('Whispering'), ABCD ('Strike Up the Band') and, most commonly, AABA ('I Got Rhythm', 'Body & Soul'). These structures provided the framework for a variety of harmonic progressions, including that of 'I Got Rhythm' (described above), one of the most common.

Lester Young improvises on 'I Got Rhythm'

When composing their own pieces, jazz musicians often borrowed from this repertoire of standard harmonic formulae, sometimes adopting entire structures from standard themes and superimposing their own melodic lines on them. Lester Young's 'Lester Leaps In', based on 'I Got Rhythm', is a case in point. The version of 5 September 1939 takes the following form:

Intro (0:00–0:06)

Statement of theme (0:06–0:37)

    AA (riff harmonized by the wind) B (piano) A (riff)

1st saxophone chorus

    A (0:37–0:44) A (0:45–0:53) B (0:53–1:00) A (1:01–1:08)

2nd saxophone chorus

    A (1:09–1:16) A (1:17–1:24) B (1:24–1:32) A (1:32–1:40)

Series of '4 x 4' between piano and sax (1 chorus, each instrument taking 4 bars)

    A (1:40–1:47) A (1:48–1:55) B (1:56–2:03) A (2:04–2:11)

The last two choruses finish on the same pattern with a series of 'traded fours', the sax and the piano alternating with the band's riffs in the A sections, and the piano reserving the B sections for itself.

The grid-based improvisation practised by Lester Young (standard harmonic progressions, 32-bar structure, traded fours) served as a framework for jazz improvisation until at least the end of the 1950s and is still used today by many jazz musicians in a more or less creative or revivalist spirit.

groups. Thus various bands drawn from the 'Duke's men' thrived under the leadership of Barney Bigard, Johnny Hodges, Rex Stewart and Cootie Williams from December 1936 onwards. Count Basie got together his Kansas City Six, drawn from his big band in 1938, Benny Goodman toured with his sextet in 1939 and Artie Shaw formed his Gramercy Five in 1940.

Chamber jazz, zany singing and virtuoso scores

In 1935, Benny Goodman broke a white American taboo when he performed on stage in a small multiracial band with the black pianist Teddy Wilson and the white drummer Gene Krupa. This trio was soon joined by Lionel Hampton on vibraphone. The energy and refinement of this combination produced a chamber jazz of sparkling lightness that stood in sharp contrast to the grandness of the big bands, the musical licence of jam sessions and the wacky sung or spoken interventions that graced the performances of some of the other small line-ups. The latter were very much in the mould of Fats Waller, but it is also possible to see in them the seeds of rhythm and blues. The Spirits of Rhythm and the Onyx Club Boys of the violinist Stuff Smith were two such bands that performed regularly at the clubs that opened on 52nd Street ('Swing Street') in the vicinity of Broadway in the mid-1930s. The smaller outfits flourished in this area, particularly at the Onyx Club and the Three Deuces. The most famous of them was John Kirby's sextet, nicknamed 'the biggest little swing band in the land'. Kirby – a former double bass player with Fletcher Henderson's band – had got together the drummer O'Neill Spencer, the pianist Billy Kyle, the clarinetist Buster Bailey, the alto saxophonist Russell Procope and, most importantly, the trumpeter Charlie Shavers, who provided the band with virtuoso and witty scores that often borrowed from classical composers. It is possible to hear in their work the first tentative expressions of bebop, particularly in the opening bars (0:13–0:18; 0:22–0:26) of 'From A Flat to C', a title that sounds like a manifesto for extravagant harmonic modulation.

Duke Ellington

The soloists and sidemen of swing

LISTENING
GUIDE
Henry 'Red' Allen:
'Queer Notions' (with
Fletcher Henderson,
Columbia, 22 September
1933)[1], 'Wrappin' It Up'
(with Fletcher
Henderson, Decca, 12
September 1934)[1].
Roy Eldridge: 'Wabash
Stomp' (Vocalion, 23
January 1937)[2], 'After
You've Gone' (Vocalion,
28 January 1937)[2].
Rex Stewart: 'Boy Meets
Horn' (with Duke
Ellington, Brunswick, 22
December 1938)[3], 'Solid
Old Man' (Swing, 5 April
1939)[3].
Cootie Williams: 'Echoes
of Harlem' (with Duke
Ellington, Columbia, 27
February 1936)[4].
Jonah Jones: 'Drum
Stomp' (with Lionel
Hampton, 16 August
1937, Victor)[5].
Hot Lips Page:
'Lafayette' (Decca, 11
November 1940)[6].
Buck Clayton: 'Swingin'
at the Daisy Chain' (with
Count Basie, Decca, 21
January 1937)[7].
Harry 'Sweets' Edison:
'Jive at Five' (with Count
Basie, Decca, 4 February
1939)[7].

A number of talented musicians made names for themselves in the wind sections of the big bands. They were improvisers who, used to the strict discipline of the large orchestras, nevertheless hankered after the freedom of expression possible in the smaller groups. Soloists had been confined to short breaks in the 1920s, but now the break became a platform for improvisation (listen to the two bars of the break at the beginning of Roy Eldridge's solo following the vocal introduction to his 'After You've Gone' of 1937, 1:22–1:24). Thereafter, it was not unusual for soloists to be given a free hand for the entire duration of a chorus or even longer.

The trumpet

Louis Armstrong was still the main point of reference, but a number of trumpeters were beginning to move away from his style. One of them was Henry 'Red' Allen, the son of Henry Allen Sr, leader of the New Orleans Brass Band. Having initially imitated the power and lyricism of Armstrong's playing, Allen gradually developed a more individual style based on an unprecedented assimilation of harmonic resources. When Coleman Hawkins composed his futuristic 'Queer Notions' for the Fletcher Henderson Orchestra, Allen was the only other member of the band able to find his way around the piece's convoluted harmonies (but they still had to return to the studio to put the finishing touches to a first recording). His great facility on the trumpet enabled him to use unusually wide intervals when playing a melody, to introduce unexpected rhythmic asymmetry into his playing, and above all to play with a fluidity that frequently verged on glissando. Armstrong's art was based firmly on the (often repeated) note, each note having its own value and place in a clearly articulated melody. Red Allen moved from this to a phrase-based style that remained at the forefront of developments and can still be found in the clusters of notes that are a feature of contemporary jazz. The trumpet playing of the day was also influenced by the fluidity of the reeds. Roy Eldridge – often suggested as the missing link between Louis Armstrong and Dizzy Gillespie – was impressed by the fieriness of the early playing of Rex Stewart and the virtuoso phrasing of the saxophonists

Roy Eldridge

(continued)
Charlie Shavers: 'Sweet Georgia Brown' (with John Kirby, Vocalion, 19 May 1939)[8].
Harold 'Shorty' Baker: 'Baby Dear' (with Mary Lou Williams, Decca, 18 November 1940)[9].
Bobby Hackett: 'A String of Pearls' (with Glenn Miller, Victor, 3 November 1941)[10].
Bunny Berigan: 'I Can't Get Started' (Victor, 7 August 1937)[11].
Harry James: 'Muskrat Ramble' (with Lionel Hampton, Victor, 21 July 1938)[5].

CD GUIDE
1. Fletcher Henderson, The Quintessence, 1924–36, Frémeaux.
2. Roy Eldridge, The Quintessence, 1936–45, Frémeaux.
3. Rex Stewart, His Best Recordings, Best of Jazz.
4. Duke Ellington, The Quintessence, 1926–41, Frémeaux.
5. Lionel Hampton, The Quintessence, 1930–44, Frémeaux.
6. Hot Lips Page, His Best Recordings, Best of Jazz.
7. Count Basie, The Quintessence, 1937–41, Frémeaux.
8. John Kirby, The Chronological, 1938–9, Classics.
9. Mary Lou Williams, Story, 1930–41, Jazz Archives.
10. Glenn Miller, Swing For Victory, Frémeaux.
11. Bunny Berigan, 1937–9, Jazz Archives.

Coleman Hawkins and Benny Carter. These he reproduced on his trumpet, adding his own characteristics of youthful impatience and enthusiasm. Eldridge had Louis Armstrong's ability to 'tell a story' – he could hold listeners spellbound even within the minimalist harmonic framework of 'Wabash Stomp' – but before he could make full use of it another trumpeter had caught his attention: Red Nichols, who was white. Rex Stewart's playing had become more nuanced since the 1930s, but he still favoured the cornet, which his contemporaries had by now abandoned. By pressing the valves of the instrument only halfway down, he obtained unusual distortions of timbre. In Duke Ellington's orchestra, the delicacy of Stewart's playing, frequently reminiscent of Bix Beiderbecke's, contrasted strongly with the radiance and violent expressiveness of Cootie Williams, who was very much in the mould of Bubber Miley, Louis Armstrong and King Oliver. The extended palette of big-band trumpet sections and the extremely varied way in which Armstrong's message had been interpreted thus allowed the arrangers of big-band music to 'blow hot and cold'. There was indeed little common ground between the hot-headed swing of Jonah Jones or 'Hot Lips' Page, the virtuoso elegance of Charlie Shavers and the tender, smouldering style of Buck Clayton or Harry 'Sweets' Edison, stoked up by Count Basie's orchestra.

Miles Davis and Clark Terry described themselves as having been raised in the St Louis school of trumpet playing exemplified by Harold 'Shorty' Baker during the second half of the 1930s. The full sound of the trumpeters of St Louis was probably inherited from the New Orleans trumpeters who passed through on the Mississippi riverboats, but the fluidity of their playing came from somewhere else. In addition to Shorty Baker, Miles Davis's teacher also introduced him to the playing of Bobby Hackett, a white trumpeter from Massachusetts and the most direct of Bix Beiderbecke's swing-playing heirs. On the white New York jazz scene, Bunny Berigan combined the influences of Armstrong and Beiderbecke, while Harry James regarded Louis Armstrong as his main model (although he betrayed his model with a fondness for commercial repertoire and flashy effects).

The trombone

In the 1930s, trombonists, like trumpeters, were preoccupied with speed. J C Higginbotham was a transitional figure who tackled the problem with a fiery power that linked him to the trombone style of the 1920s and to Louis Armstrong, who hired him a number of times. It is instructive to compare Higginbotham's solo on Fletcher Henderson's 'New King Porter Stomp' (1:47–2:24) with Sandy Williams's solo on the same track (1:09–1:28). The fluidity of Williams's solo gives it a more modern feel. Trummy Young can be thought of as the trombone equivalent of Roy Eldridge. Like Eldridge he prepared the way for bebop, playing with Higginbotham's vigour supplemented by a masterful technique that enabled him to perform musical acrobatics despite the limitations of the slide. Vic Dickenson was no less skilled, and if he spent the 1930s as a relatively anonymous section player, his disarmingly laid-back style and droll 'growl' – much in evidence on the recordings he made with his septet in 1953

LISTENING
GUIDE
J C Higginbotham: 'New
King Porter Stomp' (with
Fletcher Henderson, Okeh,
9 December 1932)[1].
Trummy Young: 'Margie'
(with Jimmie Lunceford,
Decca, 5 November
1937 and 6 January
1938)[2].
Vic Dickenson: 'Let Me
See' (with Count Basie,
Okeh, 19 March 1940)[3].
Bennie Morton:
'Swinging the Blues'
(with Count Basie,
Decca, 16 February
1938)[3].
Dicky Wells: 'Dicky's
Dream' (Kansas City
Seven, Vocalion, 5
November 1939)[4].

CD GUIDE
1. Fletcher Henderson,
The Quintessence,
1924–36, Frémeaux.
2. Jimmie Lunceford,
The Quintessence,
1934–41, Frémeaux.
3. Count Basie, *The*
Quintessence, 1937–41,
Frémeaux.
4. Lester Young, *The*
Quintessence, 1936–44,
Frémeaux.

and 1954 (see p.145) – brought him recognition as a soloist in the 1940s. Nevertheless, trombones are not really 'star' instruments and the general public has never really known much about them. For example, very few of the jazz fans wishing to assess Benny Morton – one of the first trombonists to master the instrument's higher register (compare his solo on 'Sugar Foot Stomp', 1:29–2:37, with that of Claude Jones, 0:44–0:56) – will have the rare recordings to hand that would allow them to do so. Even more than with the trumpet and reed sections, listeners have to be able to appreciate the background combinations that the different personalities within the trombone section have inspired arrangers to create. In the opening bars of 'Jumpin' at the Woodside', for example, there is an effective contrast between the smack of the trombones and the gentle breeze of the saxophones, and on 'Swinging the Blues' the few bars assigned to Benny Morton (0:34–0:36; 0:47–0:50) and his teammates (0:38–0:46) can, as it were, be enjoyed in passing. By immersing themselves in the overall acoustic mixture, listeners can attempt to identify its different components. Despite the trombone's lack of star status, between 1938 and 1946 Count Basie's band was able to provide a showcase for Dicky Wells, who had already made a name for himself playing with the main New York bands. Initially he stood out on account of his good musical taste. Rejecting the showy slide effects inherited from the 'tailgate' style, his extremely fluid slide and lip work enabled him to go beyond Jimmy Harrison's 'trombone-trumpet' style. His very free handling of time, weightless glissandi and soft, well-rounded tone blossomed above all in the small groups in which he played alongside Lester Young.

Of Duke Ellington's trombonists, Joe 'Tricky Sam' Nanton kept faith with 'jungle' colour while at the same time bringing his playing up to date, and Lawrence Brown adopted a romantic style that was much commented on by critics – some of them accusing him of playing with a sentimentality devoid of swing, others praising him for his nuanced mastery of the instrument. Juan Tizol, who played alongside him, introduced the valve trombone (which never really caught on). Confined to section roles, Tizol's main impact on the music of Duke Ellington came from the Cuban flavour of his writing ('Caravan', 'Conga Brava').

Among the white trombonists, Tommy Dorsey swelled the ranks of his trombone section

Jack Teagarden

LISTENING GUIDE
Barney Bigard: 'Clarinet Lament' (with Duke Ellington, Columbia, 27 February 1936)[1].
Johnny Hodges: 'Jeep's Blues' (on soprano sax, Vocalion, 28 March 1938)[2], 'I Let a Song Go Out of My Heart' (on alto sax, with Duke Ellington, Columbia, 3 March 1938)[2].
Benny Carter: 'Cocktails for Two' (Bluebird, 19 November 1940)[3].
Willie Smith: 'Uptown Blues' (with Jimmie Lunceford, Vocalion, 14 December 1939)[4].
Hilton Jefferson: 'Wrappin' It Up' (with Fletcher Henderson, Decca, 12 September 1934)[5].
Buster Smith: 'Squabblin'' (with Walter Page, Vocalion, 10 November 1929)[6].
Herschel Evans, Jack Washington and Lester Young (playing in this order): 'Doggin' Around' (with Count Basie, Decca, 6 June 1938)[7].
Ben Webster: 'Stardust' (with Duke Ellington, in concert, 7 November 1940)[1].
Chu Berry: 'Body and Soul' (Commodore, 10 November 1938)[8].
Harry Carney: 'Frustration' (with Duke Ellington, Radio, 7 August 1945)[1].
Earl Carruthers: 'Running a Temperature' (with Jimmie Lunceford, Decca, 26 December 1936)[4].
For Benny Goodman, Artie Shaw, Russell Procope and Buster Bailey (with John Kirby), see elsewhere in this chapter.

For CD GUIDE, see the following page.

to four in 1938. Dorsey displayed great technical mastery of the instrument, maintaining the elegance of his tone even during the most spirited swing numbers and often providing a contrast to energetic arrangements. His sophisticated legato is much in evidence in the ballads that earned him his reputation as the 'gentleman of the trombone'. Dorsey's technique and style had a considerable influence on the young Frank Sinatra, who sang with the band during the early stages of his career. Jack Teagarden was himself a wonderful singer. As a trombonist (see p.69), he was perfectly in tune with the swing era and formed his own big band in 1939.

The reeds

The swing era represented the clarinet's final glory years: in bebop and later developments it no longer played a leading role. The clarinet owed its success in the 1930s, for the most part, to the personality of Benny Goodman, who made it the star attraction of both his large and small bands. While it was also a leading instrument for the bandleader Artie Shaw, it eventually started to be regarded as an accessory that was occasionally used by saxophonists merely to provide colour. It was the only member of the reed family whose biggest stars were white. The few black jazzmen who continued to favour it (Barney Bigard in Duke Ellington's band and Buster Bailey in Fletcher Henderson's band and John Kirby's band) were musicians who had emerged in the 1920s and who were able to adapt their style of playing to the latest developments in jazz.

The soprano saxophone, championed by Sidney Bechet in the New Orleans style, remained relatively uncommon, although it did figure in the saxophone sections of a few big bands. Johnny Hodges, a disciple of Sidney Bechet, continued to use it as a solo instrument before abandoning it for good in the 1940s.

In the absence of the soprano sax, the alto sax was the highest of the saxophones in the section Hodges directed as first alto – a role in which Willie Smith, in Jimmie Lunceford's band, was unsurpassable. The leading improvisers, meanwhile, were Hodges and Benny Carter.

Johnny Hodges was in a class of his own. His historical importance is largely due to the colour he lent to Duke Ellington's band. While his vibrato, learned from Bechet, is at times reminiscent of the 1920s, the effectiveness of his phrasing in faster tempi locates him firmly in 1930s swing. The highly individual lyricism with which he performed ballads – evoking the mystery of the jungles dreamed up by Duke Ellington (either the imagined jungles of Africa or the urban savagery of New York) and occupying an ambiguous position between a naively sentimental romanticism and a clammy sensuality – is completely timeless.

Benny Carter also made a name for himself on the trumpet, clarinet and saxophone, and above all as a chief arranger. The words that describe his work in each of these roles are 'grace' and 'elegance'. His well-rounded, elastic sound gave swing a dynamism based on sinuous phrasing that was perfectly articulated in a stunning succession of glissandi, changes of direction, sudden accelerandos and virtuoso pirouettes. Carter happily shared all of these stylistic devices with the saxophone sections he led.

Space does not permit us to list the multitude of Hodges- and Carter-influenced alto saxophonists who worked in the big-band sections of the day. It is, however, worth mentioning two sax players who were omnipresent on the New York scene: Russell Procope, who stands out for his work with John Kirby's sextet (he also played with Duke Ellington between 1946 and 1974), and Hilton Jefferson, who was in great demand as a first alto. In Kansas, the main point of reference was Buster Smith, who also inspired Charlie Parker. However, the tenor saxophone was now the 'king of jazz', and Coleman Hawkins and Lester Young embodied the two main playing styles (see the following pages). While Coleman Hawkins could be said to have 'invented' the tenor saxophone in the 1920s, he encountered fierce competition from Kansas City in the 1930s. In Count Basie's big band, Herschel Evans – the precursor of the forceful Texan school of saxophone playing – represented the more rugged style presided over by Coleman Hawkins, in contrast to the smooth style of Basie's other star tenor, Lester Young. Count Basie maintained this contrast throughout the whole of his career, replacing Herschel Evans (who died in 1939) with another Texan, Buddy Tate.

Two major figures managed to emerge from the shade cast by Lester Young and Coleman Hawkins. Leon 'Chu' Berry combined Hawkins's voluble delivery with a playful, baroque lyricism very different to the fierce determination with which Hawkins went about dissecting harmony. Ben Webster made a name for himself in Bennie Moten's band in Kansas City with a relentless sound using generous vibrato which was reminiscent of Coleman Hawkins. His attachment to melody, however, meant he had more in common with Lester Young, while other aspects of his playing recalled Johnny Hodges. His lyricism, which could easily descend into sentimentality, made him a master of languorous ballads, which he interpreted with a gentle yet virile sensuality, exhaling the breath from the corner of his mouth in a way that transformed his blustery vibrato into an irresistibly tender caress.

While the bass saxophone had all but disappeared from its one-time double-bass role, the baritone sax gradually became a more or less regular feature of saxophone sections, providing them with a certain solidity. Occasionally, Jimmie Lunceford even doubled the size of Earl Carruthers' baritone sax parts ('Running a Temperature'). As is so often the case for the lower-register instruments, the baritones (despite their importance) spent most of their time occupied with sectional duties. While Jack Washington pioneered this role with Bennie Moten and later with Count Basie, Harry Carney managed to carve out a solo role for the instrument in Duke Ellington's band, using a majestic, masculine style of delivery that was to influence every one of his successors.

LESTER YOUNG AND COLEMAN HAWKINS

Two ways of wearing a hat, two different aesthetic approaches to the jazz saxophone, and, most importantly, two different approaches to improvisation. Jazz would fluctuate between these two approaches from then on.

Coleman Hawkins

It is said that he never removed his hat before playing and that when invited to perform in Paris he asked for the first row of seats to be occupied by the city's most beautiful women. In the hands of Coleman Hawkins (nicknamed 'The Hawk'), the saxophone was without doubt a male instrument. Hawkins's playing has been called rugged, and his sound is certainly relentless, gruff, constantly on the verge of breaking into angry growls and enlivened by a rapid, impatient vibrato. The Hawk turned this impatience into a style, but his phrasing is restless for a reason: it serves his desire to unpick the harmonic framework methodically, a passion that stems from his early studies of music theory and his taste for the classical music of the turn of the century. An associate of Fletcher Henderson during the early days, he learned much from Louis Armstrong during the trumpeter's brief spell with Henderson's band. Having acquired the title of leading saxophonist of the day as early as the 1920s, in 1933 Hawkins wrote 'Queer Notions', a work which anticipated the harmonic systems of later jazz. The following year, he left for Europe after his supremacy was brought into question during a Kansas City jam session with Lester Young. By the time he returned to the United States in 1939, his phrasing had become considerably more fluid. In 'Body and Soul', which experimented with various techniques that the beboppers later made their own, he recorded the first masterpiece of pre-bebop harmonic improvisation.

Lester Young

Lester Young's famous 'pork pie' hat was very different to Hawkins's choice of headgear. Inspired by a photograph of Victorian women, it was made specially for him. It was the prop of an amiable eccentric, designed to hide his profound discontent. When he played with Fletcher Henderson in 1934, Henderson's wife badgered him to listen to the recordings of Coleman Hawkins, who had just left the band. Young, however, was a very different sax player to Hawkins (whose hat matched his macho style). He had learned to play by listening to the white saxophonists Jimmy Dorsey and, in particular, the rather delicate Frankie Trumbauer, retaining their nonchalant elegance and a smooth, misty tone often free of vibrato. His phrasing, which featured unusual note placement, floated above the tempo – all melody but full of ambiguities (alternative fingering) and innuendo (ghost notes). Even when Count Basie was leading his band at breakneck speed, Young would offer a tender vision of things that contrasted strongly with the forcefulness of Herschel Evans's playing. He shared this vision and a susceptibility to the cruelty of the world with his great friend Billie Holiday. He called her his 'Lady Day' and she called him 'The President' (or 'Prez'). While the beboppers combined the influence of Lester Young (melodic and rhythmic ambiguity) with that of Coleman Hawkins (harmonic expertise and impatience), the exponents of cool jazz had only one president: Lester.

Two versions of 'The Man I Love'

'The Man I Love'. Coleman Hawkins (tenor sax), Eddie Heywood (piano), Oscar Pettiford (bass), Shelly Manne (drums). Signature, 23 December 1943.

What is immediately striking about Coleman Hawkins's interpretation of 'The Man I Love' is his lack of interest in the tune, which is not even stated at the beginning of the piece. As for Ira Gershwin's romantic lyrics, the double-quick tempo would seem to indicate that they are considered irrelevant. George Gershwin's tune is used merely as an excuse for a series of improvisations by the pianist, the double-bass player (the first great bebop bassist) and the saxophonist. The latter launches himself into this with all his might, breathily hurtling up and down the harmonies that underlie the theme, whose innermost recesses he explores with the feverish impatience of someone for whom time is in short supply. Had he planned a final statement of the tune, a short conclusion to placate his listeners? When the sound engineer signals from the control room that they are approaching the end of the record, instead of initiating some kind of landing manoeuvre he goes flat out in order to get to the end of his chorus and then simply stops in full flight.

LISTENING GUIDE

'The Stampede' (with Fletcher Henderson, Columbia, 14 May 1926).
'Queer Notions' (with Fletcher Henderson, Columbia, 22 September 1933).
'Honeysuckle Rose' (Swing, 18 April 1937).
'Body and Soul' (Victor-RCA, 11 October 1939).
'The Man I Love' (Signature, 23 December 1943).

CD GUIDE

Coleman Hawkins, *The Quintessence, 1926–44*, Frémeaux.

'The Man I Love'. Lester Young (tenor sax), Nat King Cole (piano), Buddy Rich (drums). Cléf-Verve, March–April 1946[1].

'When Lester plays, he almost seems to be singing', said Billie Holiday, 'one can almost hear the words…'. And Lester Young himself claimed that it was impossible to interpret a melody without knowing the words. Here, he clearly knows them and uses them as inspiration for telling his own story. He also sticks closely to George Gershwin's tune, respecting the original tempo and mood and taking time to caress the contours of the melody. There is no headlong rush into an exploration of the vertical structures of the harmony. The 'horizontal' variations inspired by the melody are sufficient to reveal the splendour of the harmonic foundation beneath the apparent ambiguities. Lester was a man who took his time. For a broken man, nothing is urgent. His tone, which seems to emerge from the mist, the nonchalance of his phrasing, which makes the merest of contact with the bar line before drifting off again, the discreet vibrato that escapes here and there like a barely concealed sob – all of this contributes to a sense of despair that resulted in Young being rejected by fundamentalists who saw 'true' jazz as something energetic and joyous. As with Billie Holiday, there is a dramatization of the thematic material, a sense of theatrical construction and spaciousness that was to become one of the obsessions of modern jazz.

LISTENING GUIDE

'Oh! Lady Be Good' (with Jones-Smith Incorporated, Vocalion, 9 November 1936)[2].
'He's Funny That Way' (with Billie Holiday, Vocalion, 13 September 1937)[3].
'Lester Leaps In' (with Count Basie, Vocalion, 5 September 1939)[2].
'Tickle Toe' (with Count Basie, Columbia, 19 March 1940)[4].

CD GUIDE

1. Lester Young, *The Complementary Works, Vol 8*, Masters of Jazz.
2. Lester Young, *The Quintessence, 1936–44*, Frémeaux.
3. Billie Holiday–Lester Young, *Lady & Pres, 1937–41*, Frémeaux.
4. Count Basie, *The Quintessence, 1937–41*, Frémeaux.

LISTENING GUIDE
Art Tatum: 'Tiger Rag', 'Tea For Two' (Brunswick, 21 March 1933)¹, 'Wee Baby Blues' (Decca, 21 January 1941)¹.
Teddy Wilson: 'I Wished on the Moon' (Brunswick, 2 July 1935)², 'Sweet Sue' (with Benny Goodman, Victor, 18 November 1936)³.
Teddy Bunn: 'I Got Rhythm' (Five Spirits of Rhythm, 24 October 1933)⁴.
Al Casey: 'Blue Turning Grey over You' (with Fats Waller, Victor, 11 June 1937)⁵.
Charlie Christian: 'Good Enough To Keep', 'Solo Flight' (with Benny Goodman, Columbia, 11 June 1940, 4 March 1941)⁶, 'Pagin' the Devil' (with the Kansas City Six, Columbia, 24 December 1939)⁶.
Gene Krupa: 'I Hope Gabriel Likes My Music' (Victor, 29 February 1936)⁷, 'Sing, Sing, Sing' (with Benny Goodman, Victor, 6 July 1937)⁸.

The rhythm section

The piano was the maverick of the rhythm section. Its role was to colour the work of the section freely but sparingly, adopting the alternating bass of stride piano or the rolling figures of boogie-woogie, regularly punctuating the beat with bass lines that often featured tenths (the top note a third in the octave above) or with freely voiced chords that were often peppered with melodic ornaments. Many pianists – notably Billy Kyle, Kenny Kersey and Mary Lou Williams – adopted the 'trumpet piano' style of Earl Hines, whom they nicknamed 'Fatha', and demanded a soloist's role on a par with that of the wind players. In addition to the two great leading pianists of this era, Count Basie and Duke Ellington, two other names dominated piano playing in the 1930s: Art Tatum and Teddy Wilson. While the stunning virtuosity of Art Tatum meant that he was highly respected by the great concert pianists of the day, he was also, like Coleman Hawkins, one of the precursors of bebop-style harmony. Teddy Wilson was the exact opposite. His more discreet style was based on economy and delicacy of touch and he favoured melody and rhythmic detail.

The replacement of the banjo by the more subtle guitar helped to introduce a greater suppleness into rhythm sections. Freddie Green was Count Basie's specialist in setting a steady pulse. Other, such as the black guitarist Al Casey and the white guitarists Dick McDonough and Karl Kress were able to play acoustic guitar solos in smaller line-ups, but most American guitarists (with the exception of the black guitarist Teddy Bunn) were primarily chord players during the 1930s. It was on the other side of the Atlantic that the first virtuoso player of melodic lines, Django Reinhardt, made a name for himself. In the United States it was only with the adoption of the electric guitar in the second half of the decade that home-grown single-note virtuosity developed in the figure of Charlie Christian, who got to occupy centre stage in 1939.

By the 1930s, the double bass was firmly established as the definitive bass instrument, although its place was occasionally taken by the tuba. The most common bass line was the 'walking bass' (one note per beat) but it was not unusual for bassists (notably Moses Allen in Jimmie Lunceford's band) to play on the strong beats alone in order to create a more relaxed feel. Supported by the guitar and bass drum, the double bass was still often 'slapped' (the strings made to snap back against the fingerboard) in order to make it more audible.

Slapped or not, the strings (which are raised some way above the

Art Tatum

(continued)
Dave Tough: 'The Blues in Your Flat', 'Sugar' (with Benny Goodman, Victor, 25 March 1938)[5].
Cozy Cole: 'Drum Stomp' (with Lionel Hampton, Victor, 16 August 1937)[9].
Sidney Catlett: 'Haven't Named It Yet' (with Lionel Hampton, Victor, 12 October 1939)[9], 'Summertime' (with Sidney Bechet, Blue Note, 8 June 1939)[10].
Wayman Carver: 'Sweet Sue, Just You' (with Chick Webb, Decca, 1 November 1937)[11].
Ray Nance: 'Moon Mist' (with Duke Ellington, Victor, 21 January 1942)[12].
Eddie South: 'Eddie's Blues' (Swing, 29 September 1937)[12].
Stuff Smith: 'Midway' (Asch, 8 September 1944)[12].
Red Norvo: 'Knocking on the Wood' (Brunswick, 8 April 1933)[13].
Lionel Hampton: 'Hot Mallets' (Victor, 11 September 1939)[9], 'Dinah' (Victor, 27 August 1936)[9].
For Moses Allen see Jimmie Lunceford; for Slam Stewart see Slim Gaillard; for Walter Johnson see Fletcher Henderson; for Freddie Green, Walter Page and Jo Jones see Count Basie.

CD GUIDE
1. Art Tatum, The Quintessence, 1933–45, Frémeaux.
2. Billie Holiday, The Quintessence, 1935–44, Frémeaux.
3. Benny Goodman, The Trio & Quartet, Jazz Archives.
4. Anthology of Scat Singing, Vol 3, Masters of Jazz.
5. Fats Waller, The Quintessence, 1929–43, Frémeaux.
(continued on the following page)

fingerboard) were plucked with the inner edge of the hand along the length of the index finger. In terms of melody, bass playing was not terribly sophisticated, and players such as Walter Page and John Kirby were valued above all for their steady pulse. However, Kirby – along with Israel Crosby, Billy Taylor, Milt Hinton and others – aspired to greater things. Slam Stewart even took to playing solos with the bow while humming the same tune an octave higher in order to make himself more audible.

The playing of the various drums and cymbals that make up the drum kit depends on a strict bass-drum beat. While the virtuosity of the two great drummer-bandleaders of the swing era (the black drummer Chick Webb and the white drummer Gene Krupa) was based on an extension of the New Orleans drum roll, their phrasing had become more fluid. This development is particularly evident in Dave Tough's use of brushes and in the drumming of those who choose to play a *chabada* rhythm on the hi-hat with their right hand. This old rhythmic figure, consisting of one long beat followed by two short beats, was transformed under the influence of irregular phrasing (*da-a-a ch-a ba da-a-a ch-a ba da…*) and accented on the weak beat (*cha*) by the closing of the hi-hat. Already used in the 1920s, this formula was systematized by Walter Johnson. It was subsequently adopted by many drummers, including Cozy Cole, who often retains just the *chaba* part played over and over again (a 'shuffle'). Whether he was playing with sticks on the hi-hat or with brushes on the snare drum, Jo Jones turned the *chabada* into a soft carpet that he unrolled beneath the stride of the band while developing the independence of his left hand. Sidney Catlett was largely responsible for the transition between this fluidity, ideal for the dancers of the day, and the daring innovations that would later make jazz fans want to sit down to listen to bebop.

Other instruments

While saxophone sections might still call upon the services of the less common woodwind instruments from time to time, this was only ever to provide occasional colour. The flute became a solo instrument in the hands of Wayman Carver, however, and Harry Carney was known to play choruses on the bass clarinet. The electric Hammond organ responded better to the needs of jazz in terms of rhythmic precision than the pipe organ, but no convincing players had yet come to the fore. The violin and the vibraphone, on the other hand, inspired a number of enthusiastic and talented performers.

It was in Europe that the violin experienced its greatest success (see pp103–4), but nevertheless a number of contrasting styles were in evidence among American players. The violin continued to serve as an additional instrument for the trumpeter Ray Nance and the saxophonist Darnell Howard, both exponents of a warm style with rustic overtones. Eddie South, who was black and therefore unwelcome in the classical milieus in which he hoped to make a career, retained a nostalgia for European music. He travelled to Paris to study with Firmin Touche at the Conservatoire and then to Budapest to take lessons from gypsy violinists. His slightly mannered lyricism was very different to the virile playing of Stuff Smith, who sought to reproduce the 'growl' effects of wind instruments and the percussiveness of the cymbals. This led him to electrify his violin in the 1940s.

(continued)
6. Charlie Christian, *The Quintessence*, Frémeaux.
7. *Anthology of Jazz Drumming, Vol 3, Masters of Jazz.*
8. Benny Goodman, *His Best Recordings, Best of Jazz.*
9. Lionel Hampton, *The Quintessence, 1930–44,* Frémeaux.
10. Sidney Bechet, *The Quintessence, 1932–43,* Frémeaux.
11. Chick Webb–Ella Fitzgerald, *The Quintessence*, Frémeaux.
12. *Violin Jazz,* Frémeaux.
13. Red Norvo, *The Chronological, 1933–6,* Classics.

LISTENING GUIDE
Adelaide Hall: 'The Blues I Love to Sing' (with Duke Ellington, Victor, 26 October 1927)[1].
Louis Armstrong and the Mills Brothers: 'Darling Nelly Grey' (Decca, 7 April 1937)[2].
The Mills Brothers: 'I've Found a New Baby' (Decca, 11 September 1934)[3].
Ethel Waters: 'Stormy Weather' (Brunswick, 3 May 1933)[4].
Maxine Sullivan: 'Who Is Sylvia?' (Columbia, 1 August 1940)[5].
Ella Fitzgerald: 'A-Tisket, A-Tasket' (Decca, 2 May 1938)[6].
Billie Holiday: 'Billie's Blues' (Vocalion, 10 July 1936)[7].
Big Joe Turner: 'It's All Right Baby' (Vanguard, 23 December 1938)[8].
Jimmy Rushing: 'Stealin' Blues' (Vanguard, 23 December 1938)[8].
Fats Waller: 'The Joint Is Jumping' (Victor, 7 October 1937)[9].
Cab Calloway: 'Jumpin' Jive' (Victor, 17 July 1939)[4].
Slim Gaillard: 'The Flat Foot Floogie' (Columbia, 19 January 1938)[10].
Leo Watson: 'Ja-da' (Decca, 22 August 1939)[3].

The vibraphone is a keyboard of metal bars that are struck with mallets. Underneath each bar is a resonator whose opening is fitted with a cap that continually opens and closes, producing a vibrato-like effect. The instrument is also equipped with a damper controlled by a pedal. In jazz, the vibraphone was preceded by the xylophone (which has wooden bars), a percussionists' accessory which the white musicians Adrian Rollini and Red Norvo turned into a melodic instrument. The drummer Lionel Hampton came across a vibraphone by chance in the corner of a studio in 1930. He brought his virtuosity as a drummer to this new instrument and was given a featuring role playing it in Benny Goodman's chamber jazz line-up as well as in his own white-hot groups. Red Norvo also took up the vibraphone but played it without vibrato and with the damper closed in order to stay closer to the dry tone of the xylophone.

Singers

Although female singers of classic blues anticipated the arrival of sung jazz, the first jazz vocalists as such were instrumentalists. These demonstrated the extent to which jazzmen transposed the inflections of the human voice to their instruments when they periodically put their instruments down and (more or less seamlessly) began to sing. This continuity between the two forms of expression was even stronger when the singer abandoned words in favour of an onomatopoeic vocabulary known as 'scat'. The invention of scat has been credited to Louis Armstrong (see p.52), although the technique is known to have been used before him and may have developed from African practices or even originated in the British Isles (Irish 'lilting'). In any case, scat is a reminder of the continual interaction in jazz between singing and the playing of instruments: while instrumentalists have sought to 'vocalize' their delivery, singers have always taken inspiration from the art of instrument playing. Duke Ellington was one of the first to give singers a purely instrumental role within his band ('The Blues I Love to Sing' with Adelaide Hall in 1927), and in the 1930s the Mills Brothers vocal quartet imitated jazz instruments. However, there was more to jazz singing than the instrumentalization of the voice. What distinguished jazz singing from the singing of light music was its swing and the ability to improvise the placing and pitch of a note based on what might well be a rudimentary score. Scat singer or straightforward performer of songs, the jazz singer was first and foremost a musician. In the 1930s, the majority of jazz singers were female. In the large clubs they graced the stage for the same aesthetic reasons that dancers did. They also accompanied bands on tour as a featured attraction. In this sexist context, female singers had to win the respect of the instrumentalists through their musicianship. Some bands dispensed with the services of singers altogether, and instead bandleaders would ask the players themselves to sing.

Ethel Waters, whose background was in vaudeville and who began to sing classic blues on a regular basis in the early 1920s, triumphed on the stage of the Cotton Club in 1933 with the song 'Stormy Weather' and went on to dominate the first generation of true jazz singers. Maxine Sullivan, a musician to her fingertips, was the antithesis of Waters, whose art was heavily influenced by the variety tradition. Waters was a major influence on the young Ella Fitzgerald. Having been spotted during a New York amateur night, Fitzgerald joined Chick Webb's band in 1935, taking the reins after his death in 1939. Although she was already famous, her art – which was to earn her a place in the pantheon of female jazz singers (see p.124) – was still in its early stages. On the other hand, when Billie Holiday made a name for herself with Teddy Wilson at the age of 20 in 1935, the consistent and highly individual features of her art, shaped by the tragic facts of her existence, were already in place. It was Billie Holiday's musical ability rather than her biography, however, that earned her the respect of her peers. In Kansas City, singing was the business of big-voiced men capable of competing with the loudness of the big bands and the noisy atmosphere of the clubs. One such singer was Big Joe Turner, who got himself noticed at the Sunset Bar, where he sang while mixing cocktails or drumming up business in the street. Less crude than it might at first seem, often tender or good-natured with a knowing, fluid swing feel, this tradition of the blues 'shouter' was represented in Count Basie's band between 1936 and 1950 by Jimmy Rushing.

While the female singers made their audiences dream, the men sang their hearts out or made people laugh. Black entertainers were no longer expected to make up as Negroes. They were black and that was enough. Fats Waller was said to be hurt that he was always seen as an entertainer rather than the great pianist he aspired to be. Yet there was no denying the brilliance of the off-the-cuff put-downs he directed at disruptive members of the audience.

Ethel Waters

A kind of revenge of the black American spirit is detectable behind the zany energy invested by Cab Calloway in his 'jive talk'. And there was an element of subversion in the way Slim Gaillard took the logic of light entertainment to absurd extremes by inventing an imaginary language called *vout*, or when the singer Leo Watson (with the Spirits of Rhythm) dislocated his phrasing, breaking up the words with bizarre sounds, interjections and linguistic fragments.

Enduring values

The economic crisis came as a cruel blow to the veterans of New Orleans jazz. Kid Ory took to breeding chickens, Baby Dodds became a taxi-driver, Meade 'Lux' Lewis did excavation work, Sidney Bechet became a tailor and King Oliver died in poverty in 1938. Some survived by adopting the language of swing. Louis Armstrong published his memoirs (*Swing That Music*) in 1936, made numerous screen appearances, led a number of big bands, took up a residency at the Cotton Club and toured as far afield as Europe, despite suffering from lip trouble that often led him to sing rather than play the trumpet. Others got back on their feet by updating the New Orleans message. Sidney Bechet – whose recording career, although it was to remain patchy until 1937, got underway in 1932 with his recordings with Tommy Ladnier and the New Orleans Feetwarmers – was one such. Jelly Roll Morton, on the other hand, did not emerge from oblivion until Alan Lomax's 1938 recordings for the Library of Congress. Lomax's research coincided with a change in America's attitude towards jazz. Regarded hitherto as a fashion statement, with the new eclipsing the old, jazz now came to be seen as an integral part of America's cultural heritage. Entertainment became an art form. Transcriptions of solos started to be

The New Masses Presents
AN EVENING OF AMERICAN NEGRO MUSIC

"From Spirituals to Swing"

(DEDICATED TO BESSIE SMITH)

FRIDAY EVENING, DECEMBER 23, 1938

Carnegie Hall
SEVENTH AVENUE AND 57TH STREET, NEW YORK CITY

LISTENING
GUIDE
Louis Armstrong: 'Swing
That Music' (Decca, 18
May 1936)¹.
Sidney Bechet: 'Shag'
(Victor, 15 September
1932)², 'Summertime'
(Blue Note, 8 June
1932)²·⁴.
Albert Ammons, Meade
'Lux' Lewis: 'Jumpin'
Blues' (Vanguard, 23
December 1938)³.

CD GUIDE
1. Louis Armstrong, *The
Quintessence, 1925–40*,
Frémeaux.
2. Sidney Bechet, *The
Quintessence, 1932–43*,
Frémeaux.
3. *From Spirituals to
Swing*, Vanguard.
4. Sidney Bechet, *Jazz
Classics, Vol 1*, Blue
Note.

published in music magazines such as *Down Beat* and *Metronome*. Inspired by the Hot Club of France and the publication of Charles Delaunay's *Hot Discography*, the United Hot Clubs of America, with collectors in mind, started to distribute stocks of old sides deleted by Okeh and Vocalion from their catalogues. The first specialist jazz outlet, the Commodore Music Shop in New York, also handled mail-order sales.

Following the success of Benny Goodman in opening up Carnegie Hall to his black colleagues in January 1938, the producer and talent scout John Hammond organized the first 'From Spirituals to Swing' concert there on 23 December of the same year. This concert was in effect a survey of the history of jazz. One of the things the New York audience discovered – or in this case rediscovered – was boogie-woogie, as played by Pete Johnson, Albert Ammons and Meade 'Lux' Lewis. Two weeks later, the German immigrant Alfred Lion brought Ammons and Lewis together in the recording studio. This session provided the Blue Note label with its first release, soon followed by others featuring Sidney Bechet.

The development of jazz outside America

Louis Armstrong toured Great Britain in 1932 and France in 1934. Duke Ellington toured Europe in 1933. Coleman Hawkins and Benny Carter lived in Europe between 1935 and 1939. These and others met with a warm welcome from an enthusiastic public familiar with specialist books such as *Das Jazzbuch* by Alfred Baresel (1926), *Jazz* by the Czech author Emil F Burian (1927) and *Aux Frontières du Jazz* by the Belgian Robert Goffin (Brussels, 1932). In France, the hub of the American tours, the public had access to serious critical works that included *Le Jazz* by André Schaeffner and André Cœuroy (1926), *Le Jazz Hot* by Hugues Panassié (1934) and Charles Delaunay's *Hot Discography* (1936). Following the example of *La Revue du Jazz*, (which was founded in 1929 and changed its name to *Jazz Tango* a year later), *Jazz Hot*, the organ of the Hot Club of France (founded in 1932), appeared in 1935. Under its sponsorship, the Quintet of the Hot Club of France was formed in 1934.

The Quintet of the Hot Club of France

Django Reinhardt was born in Belgium in 1910 to a family of itinerant gypsy musicians. He grew up in the Paris area and played the banjo in an accordion dance band, acquiring virtuosity in a style devised by gypsy guitarists and banjo players. He was on the point of being hired by Jack Hylton, a British bandleader and a disciple of Paul Whiteman, when he was badly injured in a caravan fire in 1928 and had to learn to play all over again with a partially paralysed left hand.

He discovered the recordings of Duke Ellington and Louis Armstrong, which moved him to tears. He began improvising offstage with the self-taught violinist Stephane Grappelli, whom he often met when playing at dances.

Django Reinhardt and Stephane Grappelli

They both loved jazz, but played instruments that struggled to be heard above the drums. They therefore formed a band without drums or trumpets, the rhythm section consisting of a double bass and two accompanying guitars. In addition to jazz standards, they also performed their own compositions. Their music has the flavour of the popular music with which they grew up: central European folk music, the French *chanson*, popular accordion music, dance-hall tunes and opera overtures. They created a distinctly European form of jazz that inspired musicians and coloured their playing. Their mastery of their respective instruments, unrivalled in the United States at the time, meant that Django Reinhardt and Stephane Grappelli were also able to extend their influence to the other side of the Atlantic. In response to invitations by the French record label Swing (founded by Charles Delauney in 1917), American musicians made a point of recording with them whenever they were passing through Paris.

Jazz under every regime

Django Reinhardt and Stephane Grappelli were not alone in playing jazz with a distinctly French character. Many others did so, including the pioneers of swing-singing Jean Sablon and Charles Trenet, music-hall ensembles such as that of Raymond Legrand, violinists (Michel Warlop, for example) and guitarists (such as the Argentinian Oscar Aleman, who was living in Paris at the time). Positioned – in keeping with the gypsy tradition – at the crossroads between different musical genres, gypsy guitarists such as the three Ferret brothers (Matelo, Baro and Sarane) initiated Louis Richardet, Charley Bazin, Gus Viseur, Tony Murena and other accordion players into the world of jazz harmony and the delights of improvisation. But France also boasted excellent orthodox jazzmen, including Alix Combelle and Philippe Brun (disciples of Coleman Hawkins and Bix Beiderbecke respectively).

Musicians throughout Europe answered the call to play jazz – Adi Rosner in Poland, Josep Puertas in Spain, Gustave Deloof (trumpet) in Belgium, the Scotsman George Chisholm (trombone) in Britain, the Danes Anker Skjoldborg (tenor sax) and Svend Asmussen (violin), the Swiss Eddie Brunner (clarinet) and Teddy Stauffer (bandleader) and the Italian Gorni Kramer (accordion). The influence of the Quintet of the Hot Club of France could be heard in the bands of the Norwegian guitarist Robert Norman and the Spanish violinist Mestre Demon. In Hungary, many violinists (among them Gabor Radics) turned their backs on the national style after Eddie South's visit to the country or after listening to the recordings of Joe Venuti.

In Germany, Joseph Goebbels prohibited the broadcasting of 'Judaeo-Negroid' music on the radio, but jazz continued to be played thanks to the keen interest of many of his countrymen, including a number of Nazi dignitaries. Nevertheless, in order to escape persecution, Weintraub's Syncopators – a band made up of Jewish musicians – went on permanent tour. This tour took them to the Far East, but they were not the first jazz musicians to visit that part of the world. The American pianist Teddy Weatherford had been playing in the international hotels of Singapore, Manila, Shanghai and Calcutta since 1926. In Tokyo, it was the Japanese themselves who took up jazz – in spite of increasing pressure from the authorities. The true capital of jazz in the Far East, however, was Shanghai, where the Russian bandleader Oleg Lundstrem made a career for himself after discovering the records of Ellington and Armstrong in Manchuria. In Russia, jazz musicians and fans were decimated by Stalin's purges in the years after 1936, but despite his steadfast pro-Americanism, the bandleader Alexander Tsfasman remained immune thanks to high-level protection within the state machinery. After all, did not the German ambassador report to the authorities in Berlin that he had seen General Voroshilov dancing the foxtrot with his wife in the presence of Stalin and the Politburo during a reception for foreign diplomats in the Kremlin?

LISTENING GUIDE

Quintet of the Hot Club of France: 'Djangology' (Ultraphone, September 1935)[1], 'Sweet Chorus' (Gramophone, 15 October 1936)[1]. 'Minor Swing' (Swing, 25 November 1937)[1], 'My Sweet' (Decca, 31 January 1938)[1], 'Stockholm' (Swing, 30 June 1939)[1].

Philippe Brun: 'Philippe's Stomp' (with Gus Viseur, Columbia, 29 December 1939)[2].
Michel Warlop: 'Taj Mahal'[3], 'Christmas Swing'[3, 4] (Swing, 21 December 1937).
Svend Asmussen: 'My Melancholy Baby' (Odeon, 22 October 1940)[4].

CD GUIDE

1. Django Reinhardt, *The Quintessence,* Frémeaux.
2. *Jazz Accordion (1928–47),* Swing.
3. Django Reinhardt, *The Complete Django Reinhardt, Vol 7,* Frémeaux.
4. *Violin Jazz, 1927–44,* Frémeaux.

Context

SOCIETY. Europe and the Far East were invaded by the Axis powers. The entry of the Soviet Union and the United States into the war determined its ultimate outcome and the world was divided up between the two superpowers at the Yalta Conference of 1945. The first test of strength during the Cold War was the Berlin Blockade of 1948.

One month after the Japanese attack on Pearl Harbor on 7 December 1941, President Roosevelt set the national production targets for the year ahead: 60,000 aircraft, 45,000 tanks and 20,000 anti-aircraft guns. The United States put its economy on a war footing, thus boosting emigration from the south to the industrial cities of the north as well as to California. The black population of Los Angeles grew from 98,000 in 1940 to 211,000 in 1950. These demographic shifts resulted in frequent outbreaks of tension between the white and black communities, culminating in the Detroit and Harlem

Race riot in Detroit in 1943

riots of 1943. Langston Hughes has his hero Jesse B Simple say: 'Bebop originated with the police when they lay into the heads of the blacks. Each time a cop hits a black person with his stick the damned baton says: "Bop bop! … Bebop! … Mop! … Bop".' A caricature of the black Harlemite, Jesse B Simple represents a new generation of less fatalistic African Americans, who adopted a more challenging attitude towards white America and thought carefully about their destiny and culture. Founded in 1935, the CIO – the first trade union to accept black workers – advocated equality of pay between black and white. In 1941, its leader Philip A Randolph threatened the federal government with protest marches on Washington unless it agreed to open up the armaments industry to black workers. While championing liberty and the struggle against fascism, the United States made its black soldiers fight in separate units. In 1945, the United Nations Charter proclaimed the equality of peoples and the UN headquarters were set up in New York. Among the first issues to be debated was decolonization.

An interracial organization founded in 1942, CORE (Congress on Racial Equality) organized the Freedom Ride in 1947. This was a bus journey undertaken by an interracial group across the southern states in defiance of the local segregationist laws. A new generation of white artists (notably the painter Jackson Pollock, the composer John Cage and the choreographer Merce Cunningham) made New York the world capital of modern art. The beboppers of 52nd Street made an important contribution to the cultural influence exerted by the city.

THE MUSIC INDUSTRY. New record labels came into existence. Founded by jazz lovers, these labels took a greater interest in the real world of jazz, from its historical figures to the avant-garde. Milt Gabler of Commodore, founded in 1938, was the first to list all the band members on the disc labels of the records he produced. It was Commodore that brought out 'Strange Fruit' – Billie Holiday's 1939 recording of a song condemning the lynchings taking place in the south – when it had been rejected by Columbia. After Commodore and Blue Note, the labels Capitol, Keynote, Aladdin, Apollo, Guild (immediately bought up by Musicraft) and Clef (Norman Granz's label) all saw the light of day in quick succession. Nevertheless, there was a delay before any 'official' bebop recordings could be made due to a recording strike organized by the AFM (American Federation of Musicians) between August 1942 and November 1944. The only sound documents available from this time are recordings of radio programmes and 'V-discs' (Victory discs) intended for the armed forces. In 1946, the labels Dial and Savoy became embroiled in a dispute over who had the sole rights to Charlie Parker's recordings – this became a burning issue when even the alternate takes of bebop's biggest star began to be released.

In 1940, 'Body and Soul' was recorded by Earl Hines on an electric piano called the Storytone.

RELATED MUSICAL GENRES. In Chicago, the South Side ghetto became overpopulated as a result of the flood of immigrants from the south, who then gradually invaded the West Side. A number of young musicians were discovered who were direct descendants of the blues Delta tradition (Arthur 'Big Boy' Crudup, Robert Petway, Tommy McLennan, Muddy Waters, Little Walter). These freed themselves from the sophistication of the Bluebird label while retaining its band-based structure and rhythm section. Many new record companies were set up to record the new heroes of the ghettos. The electric guitar became widespread in the south as well as in Chicago. One of its leading players was the Texan Lightnin' Hopkins. In Memphis, Howlin' Wolf used the microphone to create a blues style of rare violence. In Los Angeles, the high level of immigration from Texas led to the development of a new blues scene. Characterized by the virtuosity of the Texan guitarists and the electric guitar of Charlie Christian, it owed its laid-back quality to swing and to Nat King Cole's early successes as a singer. Two of the most important exponents of this scene were the singer-guitarist T-Bone Walker and the singer-pianist Charles Brown.

In the world of gospel, Thomas A Dorsey was followed by other important composer-lyricists such as William Herbert Brewster, who was brought to public attention by Mahalia Jackson, and Roberta Martin, who updated the harmonic language of gospel and founded the first mixed choir. After the success of the Golden Gate Quartet in Carnegie Hall in December 1938, vocal quartets enjoyed unprecedented popularity. Sister Rosetta Tharpe abandoned secular music in order to form a gospel duo with Marie Knight. The 'Western swing' orchestras were forced to disband because of conscription, and country music was invaded by elements of boogie-woogie and swing, above all through the honky-tonk style which was the white equivalent of the new electric blues. In reaction to the commercialization of the genre in Nashville, bluegrass put an emphasis on acoustic instruments in string bands while adopting a repertoire and virtuoso style that owed much to jazz.

LISTENING
GUIDE
*La Grande
Anthologie du
Gospel, 1927–63,
Body & Soul.
Chicago Blues, 1940–7,
Frémeaux.
Rock n' Roll, 1938–46,
Vol 2, Frémeaux.
Rock n' Roll, 1948, Vol
4, Frémeaux.*

The birth of bebop

Inadequately documented on disc, the birth of bebop has intrigued music historians right up to the present day. Bebop has been portrayed as a sudden break with the past, and some have even attempted to demonstrate that bebop was not a type of jazz at all. It is tempting to see bebop as a plot involving a handful of musicians – the result of a pact made between Charlie Parker and Dizzy Gillespie in a hotel room in Kansas City in Autumn 1939. On their first meeting the pair had exchanged a number of views that would form the basis of the way ahead. But ideas of the same kind were germinating all over the country at this time – from the Midwest to New York.

The end of jazz as mere entertainment

Up to this point, necessity had always been the mother of invention. Along with crime and boxing, jazz was one of the few areas in which black Americans stood a chance of succeeding. If they became jazzmen, they wanted to be the best. In this competitive climate, black musicians of the pre-war years had had no more than a dim awareness of their status as creative artists and of their important role in the history of music. On the eve of World War II, however, their younger colleagues were starting to apply their minds to their music and to wonder about its future.

From this time on, the history of jazz can be seen as a succession of advances, keenly followed by a cultured, music-loving public. The young

Lucky Thompson, Dizzy Gillespie, Charlie Parker and Billy Eckstine in 1944.

musicians found new rhythmic and harmonic possibilities in the work of those members of the older generation closest to them (Coleman Hawkins, Lester Young, Art Tatum). Naturally they were unable to experiment with these possibilities within the context of the large bands that employed them, and in any case being a 'background' player or a mere entertainer no longer corresponded to their aspirations. There were numerous cases of lack of discipline, dismissals for failure to turn up on time, eccentric behaviour and unwelcome musical spontaneity. The young musicians looked forward to one thing – meeting up after hours away from the routine and constraints of the big bands (sections, scores, light repertoire, silly showmanship) in order to indulge in a free exchange of ideas.

Meetings of the young guard

For the first time in the history of jazz, a new generation began to form an avant-garde. Its members flocked from all over the country (many, like Charlie Parker and Charlie Christian, from the Midwest) to New York, where they adopted two clubs as their new home. At Minton's Playhouse in Harlem in 1940, the house band, which included the pianist-composer Thelonious Monk, was placed in the hands of the drummer Kenny Clarke. Minton's management announced that it would feed the musicians from the nearby Apollo Theater on Mondays, when the Apollo was closed, and Minton's became famous for its jam sessions as a result. In order to scare off any undesirables, the incumbents adopted the custom of playing very fast and adding unexpected twists to their harmonic grids. A lot of the older musicians lost heart, but others, including Lester Young, Coleman Hawkins, Roy Eldridge and Hot Lips Page, picked up the gauntlet thrown down by the young generation.

Charlie Christian acquired a second amplifier, leaving it at the club so that it would be ready to use after his early-evening concerts with Benny Goodman's band. Two young virtuosi were universally admired: Dizzy Gillespie and Charlie Parker. Parker was a regular at another club where after-hours jam sessions were held: Clark Monroe's Uptown House on 52nd Street, which opened at four o'clock in the morning.

A whole generation got to know each other – and got themselves known – in these clubs. Between 1942 and 1944, Bud Powell played with Cootie Williams, recording Thelonious Monk's 'Round About Midnight'. In 1943, Monk was playing with Coleman Hawkins; Max Roach and J J Johnson were playing with Benny Carter; and Fats Navarro was playing with Andy Kirk. The beboppers were everywhere, but the most popular meeting place (especially for the trumpeters Freddie Webster and Dizzy Gillespie, the saxophonists Charlie Parker and Wardell Gray and the singer Sarah Vaughan) seems to have been Earl Hines's big band. In 1944, Billy Eckstine formed a band made up almost entirely of beboppers.

The crux of bebop was the diminished fifth – the destabilizing interval in the V7 chord (and the interval between the final two notes on Gillespie's 'Shaw 'Nuff'). During breaks at the Cotton Club, where they were playing in a revue

LISTENING GUIDE
Charlie Parker: 'Blues for Alice' (Verve, 8 August 1951)[1].
Dizzy Gillespie: 'Shaw 'Nuff' (Guild, 11 May 1945)[2].

CD GUIDE
1. Charlie Parker, *Swedish Schnapps*, Verve.
2. Dizzy Gillespie, *The Quintessence, 1940–7*, Frémeaux.

as part of Cab Calloway's orchestra, Dizzy Gillespie dragged Milt Hinton and his double bass onto the roof to induct him into its secrets. Miles Davis recalled that during the bebop era he and his colleagues had their fingers permanently frozen into position for diminished fifths. The sudden appearance of this particular interval on the jazz scene caused such a scandal that the calypso singer Young Tiger was still singing: 'This modern music's got me confused ... they take a major seventh and a flatted fifth' in his 'Calypso Be' in 1953. The various realities behind the 'diabolic interval' all have the same purpose: to extend the improviser's melodic possibilities and thus release him from the straitjacket of a fixed key.

As chords are an accumulation of thirds (C, E, G, B, etc), it is perfectly possible to continue adding thirds into the next octave (D, F, A). Very different from the notes that define the character of the chord in the lower octave, these added notes are relatively autonomous and can be inflected in ways that are alien to the original scale (eg D♭, D#, A♭).

These procedures were not unknown in the 1930s, but it was the beboppers who systematized them. The added notes provided new melodic ideas, notably the famous diminished fifth, as well as the idea of replacing certain chords with others. Strings of truncated II–V7 progressions (instead of the full I–VI–II–V7) in different keys proliferated and the V7 chord with its diminished fifth was replaced by chords borrowed from keys diametrically opposed to the main key. The basic blues grid took on a rather complex aspect. One of the grids used by the beboppers was given the name 'Swedish blues' as a way of emphasizing its strangeness.

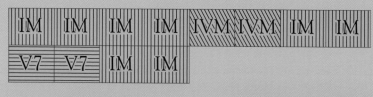

The original blues grid and the 'Swedish blues' grid ('Blues for Alice')

Dizzie Gillespie in 1948

Charlie Parker
and Dizzy Gillespie

The ideal quintet and its variants

LISTENING
GUIDE
Dizzy Gillespie: 'Salt
Peanuts', 'Hot House'
(Guild, 11 May 1945)[1],
'Anthropology' (RCA, 22
February 1946)[1], 'Oop
Bop Sh'Bam' (with
Sonny Stitt, Guild, 15
May 1945)[1].
Fats Navarro, Kenny
Dorham, Sonny Stitt:
'Fat Boy' (Be-bop Boys,
Savoy, 6 September
1946)[2].
Fats Navarro, Leo
Parker: 'Fat Girl' (Savoy,
January 1947)[2].
Howard McGhee:
'McGhee Special' (with
Andy Kirk, Decca, 14
July 1942)[3], 'Mad Hype'
(Modern Music,
September 1945)[3].
Freddie Webster:
'September in the Rain'
(with Frank Socolow,
Duke, 2 May 1945)[3].
Charlie Parker:
'Ornithology' (with
Lucky Thompson), 'Night
in Tunisia' (Dial, 28
March 1946)[4], 'Chasin'
the Bird' (Savoy, 8 May
1947)[4], 'Parker's Mood',
'Constellation' (Savoy,
18 September 1948).
See also pp113–14.
James Moody:
'Emanon', 'Ray's Idea'
(with Dizzy Gillespie,
Musicraft, 9 July and 10
November 1946)[1].
Wardell Gray & Dexter
Gordon: 'The Chase'
(Dial, 12 June 1947)[5].
See the following
page for CD
GUIDE.

A quick skim through jazz books might give the impression that a quintet once existed featuring Dizzy Gillespie on trumpet, Charlie Parker on alto sax, Bud Powell on piano, Oscar Pettiford on double bass and Kenny Clarke on drums. Apart from one important omission (Thelonious Monk was underrated at the time), this line-up includes all of bebop's founding fathers. However, this band never existed. Such strong personalities would never have been able to get on together in the long term. Bebop gave rise to a number of key talents and each one found among his followers the band members that suited him.

Dizzy Gillespie and the bebop trumpeters

The first 'official' bebop recordings were made in 1945 by Dizzy Gillespie at the head of various bands with differing musical outlooks. Two of them (a sextet in February and a quintet in May) brought together Gillespie and Charlie Parker, a combination which caused a sensation at the Three Deuces on 52nd Street (previously 'Swing Street' and now 'Bebop Street'). But Gillespie soon tired of his partner's uncontrollable behaviour and they went their separate ways, thereafter meeting only now and again.

Gillespie had a reputation as an eccentric who was always keen to provoke. There was also something of the showman about him, which suited his vocation as a bandleader. His superb ear for harmony inspired ingenious ideas that he delivered with an impatience and lightning speed inherited from Roy Eldridge. This speed let him down from time to time, making him the favourite target of bebop's opponents – until, that is, they discovered easier prey in the figure of his young and still inexperienced disciple Miles Davis. In the eyes of bebop's critics, Davis represented a new musical generation tainted by Gillespie's revolutionary ideas. Although lacking Gillespie's technique and range, Davis impressed Charlie Parker with his musicality and was engaged as Parker's opposite number in the saxophonist's own quintet. Fats Navarro, on the other hand, transformed Dizzy Gillespie's rapid runs into something more melodically and rhythmically precise. With Navarro and Kenny Dorham, modern jazz in the form of bebop acquired a more natural quality that anticipated hard bop.

CD GUIDE
1. Dizzy Gillespie, *The Quintessence, 1940–7,* Frémeaux.
2. Fats Navarro, *His Best Recordings,* Best of Jazz.
3. *Birth of Be Bop,* Frémeaux.
4. Charlie Parker, *The Quintessence, 1942–7,* Frémeaux.
5. Dexter Gordon, *Dexter Gordon, Cabu/Masters of Jazz.*

Howard McGhee, who had made a name for himself before discovering bebop, had a more dated approach to sound and rhythm, but was nevertheless a major influence on Fats Navarro. Freddie Webster was one of the first victims of the beboppers' fondness for hard drugs, dying in 1947 at the age of 31. He was mourned as one of the pioneers of bebop.

Charlie Parker and the bebop saxophonists

Charlie Parker embodied the spirit of jazz in the 1940s just as Louis Armstrong had done in the 1920s, and their respective masterpieces – 'Parker's Mood' and 'West End Blues' – can be seen as comparable achievements. Even the most obdurate opponents of bebop tend to go easy on Charlie Parker. Born in Kansas City, where he acquired the nickname 'Bird', he grew up in the blues tradition, rubbed shoulders with Lester Young and served his apprenticeship in the bands of Jay McShann and Buster Smith. Parker combined the fascination with harmony of Art Tatum and Coleman Hawkins (both of whom inspired in him a supreme mastery of extended chords) with the melodic and rhythmic ideas of Lester Young, whose laid-back approach he transformed into something faster-moving. He attained a phenomenal level of instrumental and harmonic virtuosity without ever abandoning the naturalness and spaciousness of Young's playing. Indeed, the silences that punctuated and structured his playing were almost as important as the notes themselves, with which he created a rhythmic architecture unfettered by the traditional eight-bar structural unit. His extremely reliable sense of tempo provided a firm foundation for even his most perilous acrobatics. His eight-bar break without rhythm section on 'Night in Tunisia' remains a classic of its type.

Charlie Parker's influence was overwhelming. Among his many disciples on the alto saxophone, two names that stand out are Leo Parker (no relation) and Cecil Payne, both of whom eventually made names for themselves on the baritone saxophone. Only Sonny Stitt assimilated Parker's alto style rapidly enough to be able to measure up to his model. On the tenor saxophone, Stitt was one of the many who continued to waver between the influences of Charlie Parker and Lester Young (and even the influence of Coleman Hawkins in the case of Lucky Thompson). This wavering by no means reduced the popularity of tenor sax cutting contests (also known as 'chases') that might, for example, set Dexter Gordon against Gene Ammons or Wardell Gray. The dual influence was also present in the playing of James Moody, who adapted Lester Young's style to the needs of Dizzy Gillespie's big band, in which he was one of the main soloists. Many white tenor saxophonists – Allen Eager, Brew Moore, the 'Four Brothers' in Woody Herman's band (see p.121) – anticipated the wave of white beboppers fascinated by Lester Young, whose work was later labelled 'cool jazz'.

Bud Powell and the bebop pianists

Thelonious Monk, the inventor of bebop piano, does not feature on the official photographs. He was probably not himself a bebopper (see p.118), but all beboppers, most of all Bud Powell, owe him something. Powell learned from Monk the ability to transform solid, granite-like rhythmic and harmonic material into displays of speed, volubility, precision and lightness.

CHARLIE PARKER: THE OTHER SIDE OF THE COIN

While wishing to avoid the voyeurism with which certain authors have scrutinized Charlie Parker's life, we cannot entirely overlook its inherent tragedy. It is impossible to disregard the numerous anecdotes testifying to his instability, his fondness for drugs, his sexual appetite, his teetering on the edge of life's abysses. These anecdotes say a lot about the extraordinary lucidity of this individual who survived on his wits – his saxophone often in the hands of the pawnbroker so that he could pay for a fix. In the middle of a chorus, when his audience thought he had retreated into another world entirely (a world from which he was sending extravagant, yet brilliantly articulated messages), he was capable of acknowledging those present through his playing – signalling the arrival of a pretty young woman by quoting 'A Pretty Girl is Like a Melody', for example, or greeting his female companion, who had turned up in a red dress, with a few bars of 'The Lady in Red'.

In the studio with Charlie Parker

The anecdotes that shed most light on Parker and bebop are those that relate to the recording studio (the best way to learn about musicians is to observe them at work). Parker's first session in his own name was held on 26 November 1945. It resembled numerous other sessions that have now become legendary: slapdash, unrehearsed, conducted in an atmosphere of urgency between a heroin high and the ensuing withdrawal symptoms; often inspired, occasionally third-rate. Miles Davis, ambitious and fearing the worst, could not stand Parker's suicidal attitude. Later, however, these sessions inspired him to impose a sense of urgency when recording with his own groups.

Parker had signed a contract for this first three-hour session. He was supposed to come up with four original numbers so that Herman Lubinsky, Savoy's boss, would not have to pay any royalties. He arrived

surrounded by a retinue of jazz enthusiasts, admirers and dealers, who continually came and went. Suffering from reed problems, Parker himself had to disappear several times to get the difficulty fixed. The pianist who was booked to play, Bud Powell, did not show up and someone left to find a replacement. While waiting, Dizzy Gillespie, who was among the crowd of supporters who had invaded the studio, sat down at the piano and produced an accompaniment that may not have been virtuosic, but was beautifully mischievous and revealed his harmonic skill.

Master takes and alternate takes

They started with a blues by Parker called 'Billie's Bounce', recording it in five takes. It was not unknown for Parker to record more than ten takes of the same piece, as he constantly sought to improve his playing. Miles Davis tired quickly of this practice, particularly as the take Parker chose as the master take was often not the one that showed Davis in his best light. In the case of 'Billie's Bounce', Davis was at his most inspired on the third take, but it was the fifth take that was released. Fortunately it was not long before the rejected (so-called 'alternate') takes started to be released too.

Is an interest in these alternate takes an unhealthy obsession or valid musicological curiosity? One admirer, Dean Benedetti, even took to following Charlie Parker around with one of the earliest available tape recorders. He collected the saxophonist's solos without recording anything else of the pieces to which they belonged. These recordings are now available as a set of seven compact discs. Since then the practice has become widespread. When reissuing old sessions today, record companies always try to include some unreleased take, even if incomplete or abortive, in order to tempt the jazz enthusiast.

Standards and plagiarism

As well as a themeless improvisation, two other original compositions by Charlie Parker were recorded that day based on the bebop model (unison theme statement by the two wind instruments; series of choruses taken by the different musicians; unison restatement of theme). By the end of the session, which overran the allotted three hours by some considerable time, Miles Davis had disappeared. He claimed to have fallen asleep exhausted in a corner of the studio but in all likelihood he was terrified by the introduction to the piece which had still to be recorded and which exceeded his still relatively modest technical skill. Fortunately, a pianist, Argonne Thornton, was eventually found and Dizzy Gillespie was able to play the trumpet part. After a stunning introduction by Parker and Gillespie, accompanied only by Max Roach on drums, the statement of theme was interrupted after a few bars. Having recognized the jazz standard 'Cherokee', the producer pointed out that the contract did not allow for the recording of standards. The musicians responded by repeating the introduction and then passing straight to the improvisations without stating the theme. The new piece was entitled 'Koko' without further ado.

This is typical of the way bebop made free with standards, using their harmonic grids as a framework for improvisation, either without quoting the theme or by replacing it with their own sharper-contoured compositions that were more in keeping with the new style. While the third number recorded at the session on 26 November 1945 bore the title 'Thriving on a Riff' (renamed 'Anthropology' at a later date), it was really nothing more than a carbon copy of 'I Got Rhythm', but with its melodic platitudes replaced by the virtuosic meanderings characteristic of bebop.

LISTENING GUIDE
Charlie Parker: 'Billie's Bounce', 'Now's the Time', 'Koko', 'Thriving on a Riff', 'Warming up on a Riff' (Savoy, 26 November 1945).

As both pianist and composer, Powell adapted this legacy to bebop's rapidity of thought, combining it with what he had learned from predecessors such as Art Tatum and Billy Kyle as well as from Charlie Parker.

Beaten up in 1945 during a police raid on a club and given poor treatment in a psychiatric hospital, Powell suffered from acute psychological problems throughout his career. A much sought-after accompanist, he only started recording under his own name in 1947, producing his most beautiful sides during the period which followed (see p.145). Throughout his career he remained faithful to one of the canonical line-ups of modern jazz: the piano–bass–drums trio.

Bud Powell was the intellectual leader of bebop piano during the 1950s. His influence extended to Europe – to the Catalan Tete Montoliu, the Frenchman René Urtreger – and even to Keith Jarrett. But he does not seem to have had an immediate influence on the earliest bebop pianists. His contemporaries, both black (John Lewis, Duke Jordan, Hank Jones) and white (Al Haig, Dodo Marmarosa, George Wallington), started off instead by combining the most recent developments with their own specific enthusiasms for the pianists of the 1930s.

Kenny Clarke and the bebop drummers

Until the end of the 1930s, jazz drummers marked the four beats of the bar on the bass drum, whose pedal they operated with their right foot. On the hi-hat (which they closed on the weak beats using their left foot), they played a *chabada* or swing rhythm with their right hand, which inevitably

Kenny Clarke

got in the way of what their left hand was doing. During the 1930s, a number of drummers started playing the swing pulse on a single cymbal (known as a 'ride' cymbal) positioned on the right. Kenny Clarke systematized this technique, creating plenty of room in front of him for his left hand, which now took on a far more active role. His left arm began to operate independently of his other limbs. Moreover, he became less strict in his marking of the four beats of the bar with his right foot (the trend among Clarke's successors was to suppress this altogether) in favour of free accentuation. Bandleaders accused Kenny Clarke of throwing 'bombs' onto the dance floor. However, the beboppers, who were not playing for dancers, appreciated his stimulating outbursts.

Kenny Clarke's earliest disciples were Art Blakey, Max Roach, Roy Haynes and Stan Levey (the first white drummer to adopt the bebop style). In the early days, these drummers came over as rather awkward on recordings that did them little justice. Their apprenticeship in bebop would continue until the end of the 1940s. Meanwhile, Dizzy Gillespie used transitional drummers such as Cozy Cole and Sidney Catlett on his first recordings.

Oscar Pettiford and the bebop bassists

As the bass drum was no longer marking the four beats of the bar, the 'walking bass' played by the double bass was suddenly able to make its melodic motifs heard. More precision, a less muted sound and greater melodic imagination were now required of double-bass players. No longer having to pull so hard on the string to be heard, they began to play with a greater fluency, while bebop's richer harmonies opened up new melodic perspectives.

Jimmy Blanton, Duke Ellington's bassist between 1939 and 1941, anticipated this technical revolution. He recorded a series of double-bass improvisations (sometimes using the bow) with Ellington which display a melodic ease worthy of a saxophonist. Blanton succumbed to tuberculosis in 1942 and so did not live to experience bebop, but he had a direct influence on Oscar Pettiford. Pettiford led the first bebop recording sessions with Dizzy Gillespie and was the first great double-bass player of the new style. He was a difficult man, remaining aloof from the hard core of bebop's initial phase, but he played a major role in the 1950s both as bandleader and sideman.

The bassist Tommy Potter was involved in many bebop recording sessions (notably as part of Charlie Parker's quintet), but he was not a great soloist and played a more discreet backing role, about which opinions are divided. While a number of musicians preferred the more open sound of Curley Russell, one bassist that everyone agreed about was Ray Brown. Having made a name for himself working with Dizzy Gillespie in 1946, Brown displayed a precision, power, fluency and reliability of tempo that remains a model even today.

The quintet gets bigger

While Charlie Parker remained more or less faithful to the quintet – the ideal laboratory for bebop's experiments – Dizzy Gillespie started performing with a sextet as early as 1945. In addition to the tenor saxophone, which often slipped in between the trumpet and the alto sax, various other instruments also took up the challenge of bebop. Trombonists, with their unwieldy slide, found the beboppers' speed rather intimidating. The first to put himself to the test was James Louis 'Jay Jay' (or 'J J') Johnson. With the exception of the white virtuoso Buddy DeFranco, the harmonic complexity of bebop seems to have frightened off clarinetists altogether, no doubt because of the instrument's complicated fingering. Post-Lionel Hampton, the vibraphone, on the other hand, had nothing to fear from bebop in terms of velocity. Milt Jackson's main contribution to the instrument was to modernize its sound by slowing down the vibrato and introducing a palette of unusual colours that he spent the 1950s perfecting. At the beginning of the 1940s, many guitarists turned to the electric guitar, continuing the work started by Charlie Christian but this time alongside the beboppers. While the evolution of the drums towards a more discreet marking of the beat made a rhythmic role for the guitar undesirable, melodic improvisation of the kind being undertaken by the wind instruments suited it well. Strangely, the pioneers of bebop guitar were white: Remo Palmieri, Bill DeArango, Arv Garrison, Chuck Wayne and others. Barney Kessel occupied a special place among them as he was a native of Oklahoma like Charlie Christian and shared Christian's authentic feel for the blues.

Bebop big bands and Latin rhythms

From the 1940s to the present day, the quintet (trumpet, saxophone, piano, double bass and drums) has, from the soloist's point of view, remained the ideal line-up – sometimes as a laboratory for experimentation and sometimes as a free, convivial space for interplay between soloists. In the second half of the 1940s, however, the beboppers sought to extend their work on harmony and rhythm to the area of form and to put their discoveries to the test on a larger scale – that of the big band.

LISTENING GUIDE
Dizzy Gillespie (and Gil Fuller): 'Ray's Idea', 'Things to Come' (Musicraft, 9 July 1946), 'Algo Bueno' (Victor, 22 December 1947); (with Chano Pozo) 'Manteca' (Victor, 30 December 1947). Dizzy Gillespie (and Tadd Dameron): 'Our Delight' (Musicraft, 10 June 1946). Dizzy Gillespie (and John Lewis): 'Two Bass Hit' (Victor, 22 August 1947). Dizzy Gillespie (and George Russell): 'Cubana Be Cubana Bop' (with Chano Pozo, Victor, 22 December 1947).

CD GUIDE
Dizzy Gillespie, The Quintessence, 1940–7, Frémeaux.

Dizzy Gillespie's big band

Billy Eckstine's big band, which in 1944 had included all the leading figures in bebop, was more like a loose collection of beboppers than a genuine bebop big band. In 1945, Dizzy Gillespie enlisted the services of the arranger Gil Fuller for an initial big-band experiment during the tour of the revue *Hepsations of 1945* – first with his sextet and then with the big band he formed in 1946.

In a manifesto entitled *What Is Bebop?*, distributed to audiences at the Royal Roost Club, Gil Fuller quoted Igor Stravinsky. There are indeed many similarities between the beboppers' preoccupations and those of the composer of *The Rite of Spring*: a rejection of romantic effusion, a desire to intensify contrasts and the use of harmonic tension and dissonance. All these elements are present in Gil Fuller's masterpiece 'Things to Come' and in the white arranger George Russell's finale for 'Cubana Bop'. The pianists Tadd Dameron and John Lewis also arranged for Dizzy Gillespie, working in a broadly similar style that can be seen as the culmination of aspirations

Dizzy Gillespie's big band, 1947

THE RECLUSIVE THELONIOUS MONK

He was a magician—monk with a taste for eccentric headgear. Those who said Thelonious Monk was slightly mad were not far wide of the mark. His demeanour could be alarming and his accompaniments were so strange that improvisers playing with him were often afraid of losing their bearings. As for his solos, they gave rise to a great deal of bewilderment, and many people still regard him as a wonderful composer but a mediocre pianist. He seems to have started out playing like Art Tatum before abandoning this technique and keeping only its essentials. Monk grew up in Harlem, the home of stride piano, and retained a certain taste for the alternating bass that was an important feature of that style. But speed was not his thing; his technique was governed by a different logic: the devising of unique, personal solutions to problems of execution. At the keyboard, beads of sweat forming on his forehead, Monk was like a scientist — testing explosive combinations, hesitating for a long time before adding a particular note to a particular chord and then pulling his hands back quickly to prevent them being burned by the resulting dissonance. Wrong notes also played a part in his system, representing so many problems to be solved. Silences too, because between each phrase, each chord, each note, he took time to listen to what he had just played and to ask himself what the next step should be. Thelonious Monk invented some of the harmonic material used by the beboppers, who constantly sought his advice while at the same time keeping him at arm's length. Way ahead of his time, he did not start recording until 1947 (for Blue Note). At the beginning of the 1950s, despite recording for Prestige, he sank into oblivion as a result of losing his 'cabaret card' (the permit that allowed him to work in the New York clubs) after being caught in possession of heroin. In the mid-1950s, when he was under contract to Riverside, his career finally took off again, and he employed some of the big tenor sax names of hard bop (John Coltrane, Sonny Rollins, Johnny Griffin). In 1959, he formed a regular quartet whose other permanent member was the tenor saxophonist Charlie Rouse. This group recorded for Columbia between 1962 and 1968, after which Monk's career went into gradual decline. In 1973, he withdrew into a total silence that lasted until his death on 17 February 1982. Since then, his work as a composer, finally included in the repertoire of jazz standards, has repeatedly caught the imagination of jazzmen from the most traditional to the most avant-garde.

LISTENING GUIDE

Thelonious Monk: *Genius of Modern Music, Vol 1* (Blue Note); *Solo 1954* (Vogue); *Brilliant Corners* (Riverside); *With John Coltrane* (Riverside); *Big Band and Quartet in Concert, Live in Tokyo* (Columbia); *The London Collection, Vol 1, Solo, The London Collection, Vol 2, Trio* (Black Lion). Charlie Parker and Dizzy Gillespie: *Bird and Diz* (Verve). Miles Davis: *Bags Groove, Miles Davis and the Modern Jazz Giants* (Prestige).

GENE NORMAN PRESENTS

DIZZY GILLESPIE and his orchestra

FEATURING CHANO POZO

evident in 'Queer Notions' (Fletcher Henderson) or 'Stratosphere' (Jimmie Lunceford).

The introduction of Afro-Cuban percussion instruments into Dizzy Gillespie's band in 1947 constituted the first real break with the jazz of the past. Irregular phrasing, which had characterized swing up to that point, was now under threat from the even beat produced by the percussionist.

Jazz and the Latin influence

The influence on jazz of the French and Spanish Caribbean could be heard in New Orleans at the beginning of the 20th century. It was evident in the left hand of Jelly Roll Morton and later spread to Chicago, where it made itself felt in the bass lines of the boogie-woogie pianist Jimmy Yancey. Conversely, Caribbean musicians looked longingly at New York and its big bands, adopting their instrumental sections during the 1920s. New York – or more specifically East Harlem, the neighbourhood known as 'El Barrio' or 'Spanish Harlem' – had become a major centre for Spanish Caribbean immigration, and in the 1930s many 'Latin' musicians such as the Puerto Rican trombonist Juan Tizol (with Duke Ellington) or the Cuban trumpeter Mario Bauza (with Chick Webb) occupied the desks of New York's big bands.

Jazz and Latin were very different, however. Jazz was based on a style of writing and a science of improvisation that were highly developed harmonically, and it was envied this by Latin musicians. On the level of rhythm, jazz improvisers stood out because of their characteristic irregular phrasing and the diversity of their note placement. This diversity was based, however, on a clear and relatively straightforward beat compared to the accompaniment provided by Caribbean rhythm sections. In jazz, soloists relied on the swing pulse known as the *chabada*, a short rhythmic figure that indicates the even and odd beats very clearly. Latin musicians, meanwhile, rely on the *clave* (a beat played by two sticks of wood struck against each other). Spread over a cycle four times as long as the *chabada*, the *clave* does not offer the same clarity of beat.

The *chabada/clave* divide

The *clave* is rendered even more difficult by the fact that it varies from piece to piece and is played over complementary and contradictory rhythmic motifs produced by other percussion instruments (congas and bongos), piano and double bass. Playing to a *chabada* rhythm (see p.99) is like walking on springy but firm ground; playing to the *clave* beat is like walking across a trampoline. Confronted with Caribbean rhythms, jazzmen soon lost their bearings. The first compositions to display a Latin character ('Caravan', for example, composed by Juan Tizol for Duke Ellington's orchestra) were merely exotic evocations that evaded these rhythmic problems.

Cubop

Section colleagues in Cab Calloway's band between 1939 and 1941, Dizzy Gillespie and Mario Bauza dreamed of uniting these two musical genres born of the Afro-American diaspora. Their dream took shape in 1940 when Machito formed a band called the Afro-Cubans under the musical direction of Bauza. While retaining a Latin rhythmic base, the band assimilated the jazz writing of the 1930s and subsequently the experiments of bebop and Gillespie's big band courtesy of the arrangements of René Hernandez. However, when Gillespie engaged Chano Pozo to play with his own big band, the other musicians found it difficult to adjust. While the bassist Al McKibbon immediately appreciated the relief provided by the Cuban ostinatos known as *tumbaos*, which took some of the pressure off his double-bass playing, Dizzy's band never entered fully into the rhythmic logic of the Caribbean. It was content simply to decorate the background without fundamentally modifying the way the wind instruments played. This meant the Latin percussionists themselves frequently had to give in to the demands of irregular phrasing.

The vogue for Latin music that filled New York's stages at the end of the 1940s had an influence on the jazz world that went far beyond Dizzy

Gillespie's big band. On the initiative of the producer Norman Granz, Charlie Parker embarked on a series of recordings with Machito's band for the Clef label in December 1948 and January 1949.

Many other soloists tried something similar, either for a single concert or in the course of more sustained collaborations. White musicians were by no means excluded from this. Stan Kenton recorded 'Machito' by the arranger Pete Rugolo as early as 1947, and, on a more modest level, Woody Herman recorded 'Bijou' ('Rhumba a la jazz') by the arranger Ralph Burns in 1945.

LISTENING
GUIDE
Machito: 'Nague' (Decca,
1941)¹, 'Cubop City'
(1948, Roost)², 'No
Noise Part 2', 'Mango
Mangue' (Clef, 20
December 1948)³,
'Tanga' (Clef, January
1949)⁴.
Stan Kenton: 'Opus in
Pastel' (Capitol, 4 May
1945), 'Artistry in
Percussion' (Capitol, 12
July 1946)⁵.
Woody Herman: 'Bijou'
(Columbia, 20 August
1945)⁶, 'Ebony
Concerto' (19 August
1946)⁶, 'Four Brothers'
(Columbia, 27 December
1947)⁶, 'Early Autumn'
(Capitol, 30 December
1948)⁶.
Boyd Raeburn: 'Boyd
Meets Stravinsky'
(Jewell/Savoy, 5
February 1946)⁷.
Buddy DeFranco: 'A Bird
in Igor's Yard' (Capitol,
23 April 1949).

CD GUIDE
1. *Machito & His Afro
Cubans, 1941,*
Palladium.
2. *Cuban Latino Jazz,*
Jazz Archives.
3. Charlie Parker, *South
of the Border,* Verve.
4. Machito, *The Original
Mambo Kings,* Verve.
5. *Artistry in Rhythm,*
Dutton Vocalion.
6. Woody Herman,
Woody Herman,
Cabu/Masters of Jazz.
7. *Swing Era Big Bands,
1934–47,* Frémeaux.

Breeding grounds for cool jazz

The initiatives of these two bandleaders said less about the advance of Latin music than about the change in mentality associated with the emergence of bebop. Even for the big bands formed during the swing era, light entertainment was no longer the name of the game. As early as 1941, Stan Kenton – heir to the Jimmie Lunceford tradition – displayed ambitions that would lead him four years later to hire the arranger Pete Rugolo, who was a pupil of Darius Milhaud and an admirer of Stravinsky. With Rugolo, Kenton recorded the 'Artistry in…' series ('Artistry in Rhythm', 'Artistry in Bass', 'Artistry in Bolero' etc). In 1947, with new personnel and a bigger band (including a five-strong trombone section that made systematic use of the bass trombone), he launched his Progressive Jazz Orchestra, which sought to combine the experimentation of 20th-century classical composers such as Stravinsky and Bartók with the timbres and rhythm of Afro-Cuban music and swing. Like many of Kenton's projects (*Innovations in Modern Music, New Concepts of Artistry in Rhythm*), his 'Wagner of jazz' concept was regarded with considerable disfavour but had the merit of opening up new avenues and bringing some of the future pillars of white 1950s jazz – so-called 'cool jazz' – to public attention.

Less ambitious than Kenton and more faithful to the swing tradition, Woody Herman's band, and his Second Herd line-up in particular, was another breeding ground for cool-jazz talent. Herman's saxophone section consisted of three tenors (Stan Getz, Zoot Sims and Herbie Stewart, the latter replaced by Al Cohn) and a baritone (Serge Chaloff). In the title of a well-known arrangement of 1947, Jimmy Giuffre nicknamed them the Four Brothers. The main bond between these four sax players was their love of Lester Young, but they also shared with the rest of the band, including the bandleader, an admiration for Charlie Parker. It was as one of the Four Brothers that Stan Getz had his first taste of success with a solo and a classic coda on 'Early Autumn', arranged by Ralph Burns.

The name of Igor Stravinsky deserves further mention here: in connection with Woody Herman, for whom he wrote the *Ebony Concerto*, premiered in Carnegie Hall in 1946; in connection with the bandleader Boyd Raeburn, of whom Barney Kessel said that he played popular music as if it had been arranged by Stravinsky; and in connection with George Russell, who composed 'A Bird in Igor's Yard' for the clarinetist Buddy DeFranco in 1949. Having liberated a great deal of energy that had been kept in check in the swing bands, bebop evidently also inspired ambitions of a more formalist nature.

Popular successes and enduring values

Bebop caused a split in the jazz audience. The concept of an 'avant-garde' was alien to most of the black community, who saw jazz as a way of life inseparable from dance. While the main thrust of jazz history now moved in a progressivist direction, a number of branches broke away and pursued a more popularist path.

The genesis of rock and roll and rhythm and blues

'To rock' is synonymous with 'to swing'. It also means 'to make love', and in the language of the bluesman a 'rocker' is a lover. In the 1920s, the word 'rocks' also started being used to describe the rolling bass line of boogie-woogie. Since the 1940s, while evoking the to and fro of both dancers and sexual partners, the term 'rock and roll' has been associated in dance halls throughout the world with the rhythm of boogie-woogie. In the 1940s, it had not yet come to refer specifically to a musical genre, but the black

singer Louis Jordan can be considered as the first popular figure in what would later become rock and roll. His saxophone playing and his band were merely a pretext for the performance of songs ('Caldonia', for example) that inspired the audience to dance, were bursting with humour and were delivered with an energy that anticipated Little Richard. Many black singers, such as Wynonie Harris and Roy Brown, followed a parallel route which led them from Slim Gaillard and Big Joe Turner to what had started being referred to as 'rhythm and blues' (see p.131). A number of female singers also played a part in these developments: for example, Helen Humes, who took the blues tradition to a new level with Count Basie, and Rosetta Tharpe, who sang with Lucky Millinder before dedicating herself to gospel.

Honking saxophones and block chords

The saxophone equivalent of the 'shouters' were the 'honkers'. Raising the volume of their instruments to its limits, these saxophonists delighted audiences with their acoustic contortions. Some of them, including the tenor saxophonist 'Big Jay' McNeely and the alto saxophonist Earl Bostic, retained the purely instrumental character of their performances. The Texan school, whose main exponent in the 1930s had been Herschel Evans (see p.94), was rediscovered around this time. This school of saxophone playing supplied Lionel Hampton with two particularly pungent tenor saxophonists: Illinois Jacquet and Arnett Cobb. Two of the main attractions of Hampton's big band, they helped it to move in a rhythm-and-blues direction that allowed Lionel Hampton to survive the decline of the big band. At the heart of the band was the pianist Milt Buckner. He helped to popularize the block-chord style, in which the hands – positioned side by side and moving in parallel – play large chords. Creating the impression that the melodic line is being harmonized by an entire orchestra, the block-chord technique has since been used by many pianists of differing styles, but in terms of economy and effectiveness Milt Buckner remains unsurpassed.

Scatters and crooners

At the same time on the west coast, Nat 'King' Cole was working his discreet, sensual, irresistible charm. A pianist who had only become a singer by accident, Cole suffered from a limited vocal range, but his tender yet virile timbre and the sly swing of his diction met with immediate success. Little by little, his singing took over from his piano playing, influencing the world of rhythm and blues from Charles Brown to Ray Charles. Before long, his only rival as a crooner was Frank Sinatra. This star of American popular music had come to public attention with Tommy Dorsey's band before branching out on his own in 1943. Sinatra's word placement, worthy of the greatest improvisers, met with approval from audiences and musicians alike. For the beboppers, songs were merely a pretext for improvisation. Nevertheless, they welcomed Sarah Vaughan (see p.125) as one of their own. Her early career had been sponsored by Billy Eckstine, himself a forceful if not universally admired crooner. In Kenny Hagood, Eckstine had a disciple who enjoyed a certain popularity among the beboppers. Most of all, however, the bebop age was the golden age of 'vocalese' (using the voice as an instrument) – one of whose originators was Eddie Jefferson (see p.161) – and scat. One of bebop's signature tunes, 'Oop-Pop-A-Da', made famous by Dizzy Gillespie, was composed by the extraordinary scat singer Babs Gonzales. In performing this sound-based song, or the song 'Ool Ya Koo', Gillespie was demonstrating that he had not forgotten the lesson of Cab Calloway (with his 'Hi-De-Hi-De-Ho' and 'Zah Zuh Zah'). These vocal performances can be seen as attempts to be provocative, but equally it could be said that Dizzy Gillespie was revealing a showmanship or sense of theatre on which his bebop colleagues had deliberately turned their backs. He often gave the last word to Joe Carroll, a member of his band who was a true scat virtuoso.

FOUR QUEENS OF JAZZ SINGING

In 1939, when Billie Holiday sang 'Strange Fruit', a song denouncing the lynchings carried out by the Ku Klux Klan, many of her former admirers felt betrayed. 'Strange Fruit' changed the status of the female jazz singer from mere attraction to artist in her own right.

Billie Holiday

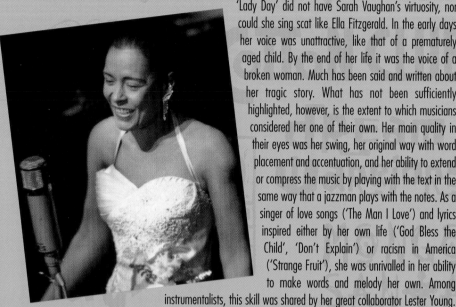

'Lady Day' did not have Sarah Vaughan's virtuosity, nor could she sing scat like Ella Fitzgerald. In the early days her voice was unattractive, like that of a prematurely aged child. By the end of her life it was the voice of a broken woman. Much has been said and written about her tragic story. What has not been sufficiently highlighted, however, is the extent to which musicians considered her one of their own. Her main quality in their eyes was her swing, her original way with word placement and accentuation, and her ability to extend or compress the music by playing with the text in the same way that a jazzman plays with the notes. As a singer of love songs ('The Man I Love') and lyrics inspired either by her own life ('God Bless the Child', 'Don't Explain') or racism in America ('Strange Fruit'), she was unrivalled in her ability to make words and melody her own. Among instrumentalists, this skill was shared by her great collaborator Lester Young.

LISTENING GUIDE
The Quintessence, 1935–44, Frémeaux. Lady and Pres, 1937–41, Frémeaux. Lady Sings the Blues (1956 concert), Verve.

Ella Fitzgerald

Ella Fitzgerald made a name for herself at the age of 16 with Chick Webb's big band, singing in a fresh, almost immature voice. Her first hit was the nursery rhyme 'A Tisket, A Tasket'. She was encouraged by Dizzy Gillespie, who introduced her to bebop. Her career really took off in 1945 with a scat version of 'Flying Home', and her scat singing continued to delight audiences throughout her career. She delivered it with a swing that put her on familiar terms with the greatest figures in jazz (from Count Basie to Louis Armstrong and the stars of Jazz At The Philharmonic). Her fresh voice gained depth over time, making her one of the great interpreters of the standard repertoire. With Louis Armstrong she made a recording of George Gershwin's *Porgy and Bess* that is considered by jazz lovers to have no equal.

LISTENING GUIDE
The Quintessence, 1936–48, Frémeaux. Pure Ella (1950 session), Decca/MCA. Ella in Berlin, Mack the Knife (1960 concert), Verve.

Sarah Vaughan

Beautiful and exceptionally gifted, Sarah was nicknamed 'The Divine'. While working as second pianist in Earl Hines's band, she was adopted by the elite of the young beboppers. She made a name for herself by singing 'Lover Man' with Dizzy Gillespie on one side and Charlie Parker on the other, clearly unintimidated by bebop's rhythmic and harmonic acrobatics. Her vocal range is characterized by an extraordinary ability to loop between low and high notes. A wonderful scat singer, she was able to bend lyrics to fit in with particularly daring musical ideas. In doing this, she gave precedence to sound over sense — something which met with disapproval from some quarters as well as accusations of frivolity. However, what her fans value most about her singing is her modern musicality, which is worthy of the greatest instrumentalists.

LISTENING GUIDE

The Quintessence, 1944–48, Frémeaux.
With Clifford Brown (1954 sessions), Emarcy.

Swingin' Easy (sessions from 1954 and 1957), Emarcy.

Dinah Washington

Nicknamed 'Queen of the Blues', Dinah Washington never forgot how much she owed to the 'Empress of the Blues', Bessie Smith. Discovered while singing with Fats Waller, Washington had her first taste of success with Lionel Hampton's band and devoted her first recordings under her own name to the blues, accompanied by young beboppers. The flexibility of her voice enabled her to work in every genre: jazz (with small groups or big bands), gospel, blues, rhythm and blues, and more commercial popular music with string arrangements. For this reason she was regarded by jazz audiences as a rather marginal figure but she was immediately adopted by the black public and had a major influence on soul singers such as Dionne Warwick and Diana Ross.

LISTENING GUIDE

The Queen Sings Jazz, 1943–8, Jazz Archives.
The Swingin' Miss 'D', (1956 sessions), Emarcy.

Dinah Washington Sings Bessie Smith (1957 sessions), Emarcy.

Zutty Singleton, Red Callender, Kid Ory, Charlie Beal, Bud Scott, Louis Armstrong and Barney Bigard in 1946

LISTENING GUIDE

Louis Armstrong: 'Do You Know What It Means to Miss New Orleans?' (Victor, 17 October 1946)[1].

Esquire All Stars: 'Mop Mop' (concert, 18 January 1944)[2].

Jazz At The Philharmonic: 'I Can't Get Started' (with Lester Young and Charlie Parker, concert, 28 January 1946)[3].

Coleman Hawkins: 'Drifting on a Reed' (Joe Davis, 19 October 1944)[4].

Budd Johnson: 'Little Benny' (1st tenor chorus, with Clyde Hart, Savoy, 19 December 1944)[4].

Don Byas: 'Be-bop' (with Dizzy Gillespie, Manor, 9 January 1945)[5].

Art Tatum: 'I Got Rhythm' (with Tiny Grimes, Brunswick, 5 January 1944)[6].

Erroll Garner: 'Loose Nut' (Dial, 10 June 1947)[7].

Gene Krupa: 'Lover' (Columbia, 26 September 1945)[8].

Artie Shaw: 'The Grabtown Grapple' (Victor, 9 January 1945)[9].

Glenn Miller: 'A String of Pearls' (Bluebird, 3 November 1941)[10].

Ancient and modern

Reaction against bebop boosted fans' interest in the history of jazz. Attempts were made to contrast bebop's values with the original values of 'real jazz' by forming veterans' bands within the context of a New Orleans revival (Bunk Johnson, Kid Ory, Sidney Bechet and others). After appearing in the film *New Orleans* at the head of the Dixieland Seven, Louis Armstrong broke up his big band and formed a new band, the All Stars, which adopted his Hot Seven format. However, a number of musicians of the swing generation, notably Coleman Hawkins, embarked on new careers accompanied by bebop rhythm sections.

Either way, jazz players both ancient and modern continued to rub shoulders with one another at parties or concerts organized by *Metronome* or *Esquire* magazines on the occasion of readers' or critics' polls. Devised by Norman Granz in 1944 and presented worldwide until 1967, the JATP (Jazz At The Philharmonic) evenings were designed to feature jam sessions between classic jazz and bebop musicians in a spirit of confrontation that was sometimes carried too far.

The unclassifiable

The combined and reciprocal influences of bebop and the beginnings of rhythm and blues easily crossed stylistic borders. This can be seen in the careers of the tenor saxophonists Gene Ammons (a bebopper seduced by the pugnacity of the 'honkers'), Budd Johnson and Don Byas (swing players who became heavily involved with bebop). Reconciling the irreconcilable, all three also combined the classic virility of Coleman Hawkins with the more feminine nonchalance of Lester Young.

A disciple of Teddy Wilson and apparently sharing none of the beboppers' preoccupations, Nat 'King' Cole had an influence on modern piano that extended into the 1950s. He also invented the piano–guitar–bass trio. Taken up by Art Tatum in 1943, this format became a runaway success and focused attention on a generation of black guitarists who had been won over by the electric guitar. These identified with Charlie Christian – less because of his pre-bebop heritage (to which they were not impervious) than because of his ability to update the language of the blues. Some of them (Al Casey and Tiny Grimes) advanced as far as the frontiers of rhythm and blues, while others adopted a typically Californian laid-back approach (Irving Ashby) or combined the fluidity of Charlie Christian's melodic lines with the harmonic needs of the band (Oscar Moore).

The leader of another piano–guitar–bass trio, the pianist Erroll Garner revealed himself to be a virtuoso at home in every style from boogie-woogie to bebop, although he had no desire to be affiliated with the latter. He created his own style based on the effect produced by the delay between his left hand, which marked each beat of the bar, and his right. As for the drummers of the swing era, they incorporated into their vocabulary a *chabada* played on the ride cymbal. Unclassifiable musicians such as these – black as well as white and receptive to bebop without being beboppers – could be found on every instrument: Joe Newman (trumpet), Red Callender (double bass), Bill Harris (trombone) and Buddy Rich (drums), to name but a few. The catch-all term that came to be used to describe the classic form of jazz developing in parallel with successive avant-garde movements was 'mainstream'.

The big bands of swing at the end of their reign

At a time when Duke Ellington had reached a turning point in his writing (see p.64), the big band line-up was also changing. It began to feature trumpet and trombone sections of up to four (or even five) players and standard saxophone sections of two altos, two tenors and a baritone. A sparser, more linear, more uniform style of orchestral writing aimed to create maximum impact, whether in Lionel Hampton's overheated black rock and roll on the one hand or the laid-back approach of the white bands under leaders like Glenn Miller on the other. Drummer-bandleaders such as Gene Krupa and Buddy Rich (both white), however, threw themselves into their performances. They led bands designed to highlight a virtuosity that was taking the art of the drum roll inherited from the military drum to new and sophisticated heights.

White bands not only employed black arrangers behind the scenes, they also began to welcome black musicians on stage. Benny Goodman and Artie Shaw even showed a mild interest in bebop by recruiting players from the younger generation. Although the big bands had been decimated by mobilization, the art of the big band underwent a precarious improvement in its fortunes while in the service of the military. This naturally came to an end with demobilization. Tastes had changed and television was starting to bring light entertainment directly into people's homes. The era of swing and the big band was drawing to a close.

Jazz during World War II

At the sound of Nazi jackboots, many foreigners deserted Europe. Oscar Aleman was among them and after returning to Buenos Aires his jazz took on a Latin flavour. War was declared while the Quintet of the Hot Club of France was in London. Stephane Grappelli decided to remain there, performing for the next four years with the up-and-coming pianist George Shearing. Django Reinhardt, meanwhile, chose to return to France, where French jazz, turned in on itself, prospered relatively well despite the curfew and the ban on dances.

French jazz under the occupation

It was French jazz, tolerated by the German authorities, that kept the occupying forces entertained (particularly the officers, many of whom were jazz enthusiasts). In Vichy France, jazz played up its national characteristics in order to circumvent the regime's mistrust of 'Judaeo-Negroid' music. English titles were translated into French and historians stressed the importance of the French influence in the New Orleans melting pot. 'National' jazz was very much to the fore, displaying a fondness for strings, as evidenced by Michel Warlop's string septet.

Nevertheless, the jazz of the French West Indies (Al Lirvat, Robert Mavounzy, Sylvio Siobud) flourished at the Parisian brasserie La Cigale, which also provided a refuge for the black American Harry Cooper and the Cameroonian Freddy Jumbo, both of whom had unwisely stayed behind in Europe. Django Reinhardt also bucked the trend, becoming more Americanized – albeit in a highly idiosyncratic way – by adopting the big-band format (along with drums) and replacing the violin in his quintet with a clarinet. This was an explicit reference to Benny Goodman, whose influence spread as far as the accordionists of the swing-style *musette* bands. But the world of jazz sought to distance itself from the fashion for swing launched in 1939 by Johnny Hess's song 'Je Suis Swing'. This song led to the 'zazou' movement, which took its name from Hess's onomatopoeic utterances (borrowed from Cab Calloway, the Cotton Club's star singer). Before long, in a reaction against the new national order, students started to advertise their enthusiasm for swing by donning eccentric outfits inspired by those worn by Calloway. This provoked an angry response from the Vichy press. Despite the difficulties, Johnny Hess's 'Ils Sont Zazous' was broadcast on Radio Paris in 1942, cleverly introduced as a parody.

Jazz at the front

Jazz played by 'Charlie and His Orchestra' was broadcast to other countries by German radio. The lyrics of jazz standards were altered in order to incorporate references to recent developments: 'Stormy Weather' was turned into a celebration of the invasion of Norway and 'Slumming' into a commemoration of the bombing of Mers-el-Kébir in Algeria. The *Reichsmusikführer* Baldur von Blodheim advised against the use of the saxophone and prohibited the playing of pizzicato on the double bass. Jazz

CD GUIDE
1. Oscar Aleman, *Buenos Aires–Paris, 1928–43*, Frémeaux.
2. Stephane Grappelli, *Grappelli Story*, Verve.
3. Tony Murena, *Valse et Swing*, Silex.
4. Django Reinhardt, *The Complete Django Reinhardt, Vol 12*, Frémeaux.
5. *Chansons Swing, 1931–66*, Swing.
6. *Antilles-Jazz, 1930–54*, Jazztime.
7. *Marabi Nights*, book with cassette, Ravan Press.

was nevertheless played throughout Europe – more or less clandestinely, but sometimes even by musicians wearing the *Wehrmacht* uniform or behind the barbed wire of the Teresienstadt ghetto, where the Ghetto Swingers were ordered by the Nazis to perform during a Red Cross visit. On the other side of the eastern front, jazz contributed to the war effort in the form of Soviet state jazz bands that adopted nationalist trappings such as Russian titles, folk tunes, balalaikas and accordions.

Founded by the first secretary of the regional Communist party, who was a jazz fan, the jazz orchestra of Byelorussia was placed under the musical direction of the exiled Polish trumpeter Adi Rosner. Rosner recruited Polish colleagues and the musical elite of the Baltic States, which had passed into Russian control, and made the band the best in the Soviet Union. He also gave a private performance for Stalin in an empty theatre. From 1942, American jazz scores were unofficially included in consignments of American aid, and the bands of the Red Army played Glenn Miller in the towns and cities they liberated. Jazz was present on every front, accompanying the American army in both Asia and Europe in the form of 'V-discs' (Victory discs), broadcasts by the Armed Forces Radio Service and concerts by military big bands (including Glenn Miller and the Army Air Force Band, and the Air Transport Command Band).

The battle over 'real jazz'

In France as all over Europe, interest in 'national' jazz waned after liberation. Concerts of the 'swing versus accordion band' type heralded the marginalization of the accordion in jazz, soon followed by that of the stringed instruments. Europeans now only had ears for the music of the liberators, for 'true' jazz. In France, Hugues Panassié took control of the regional Hot Clubs and declared war on bebop fans, whom he called the 'sour grapes'. The *Jazz Hot* magazine, which had remained in the hands of Charles Delaunay, fought back against the attacks of the 'mouldy figs'. In

1948, Panassié secured Louis Armstrong's All Stars and Claude Luter's revival band for the first Nice jazz festival. The same year, Delaunay invited Coleman Hawkins, Erroll Garner and Howard McGhee to the first festival in Paris. In February, Dizzy Gillespie's big band left Parisian audiences open-mouthed with amazement. In Ghana, on the other hand, once the port of Accra had been deserted by the troops, local bands abandoned swing in order to return to their favourite style of jazz, highlife. In South Africa, the Jazz Revellers and the Jazz Maniacs had been alternating the harmonies of American jazz standards with those of *marabi* (which combines the principles of European harmony with the underlying logic of the local polyphonic tradition) since the 1930s.

Context

SOCIETY. In 1949, Mao Zedong came to power in China. Communism now extended from Berlin to Beijing. In response, the Americans took charge of NATO in the west and the UN troops on the Korean front (which was yielding to Chinese pressure) in the east. A state of emergency was declared in the United States in 1950 and Senator Joseph McCarthy stepped up the hunt for communists he had started in 1947.

Bolstered by exceptional growth but paralysed by fear, America withdrew into the values that were to take the Republican Dwight D Eisenhower to power (1953–61). In the context of widespread suspicion, minorities and unconventional groups of any kind had to be discreet. Nevertheless, President Harry Truman advanced the cause of desegregation within the federal administration and the army. Black and white fought side by side in Korea.

In his novel *Invisible Man*, Ralph Ellison condemned the marginalization of the black American, a common theme in black literature (see also *The Man Who Lived Underground* by Richard Wright and *Nobody Knows My Name* by James Baldwin). This was echoed by the black Muslim leaders' habit of replacing their Anglo-Saxon surnames, which had been imposed on their ancestors by the slave owners, with an 'X'. Their leader, Elijah Muhammad, had some success in preaching the message that Christianity should be abandoned in favour of Islam. Criticizing the vanity of the integrationist policy of the black political class, he advocated a kind of reverse segregation – an autarchic withdrawal of the black community into the Nation of Islam and the creation of a black republic.

Jack Kerouac, Allen Ginsberg and William Burroughs became the heroes of the white students of the Beat Generation. They were fascinated by the margins of American society and the wandering tradition inherited from the pioneers of the West and the bluesmen. Bebop (particularly its sense of musical urgency and the nocturnal lifestyle associated with it) and hallucinogenic experiences were also sources of inspiration for these authors, who attempted to write in the way that jazz musicians improvised. Many poets even declaimed their work to the accompaniment of jazz.

THE MUSIC INDUSTRY. The replacement of shellac with Vinylite improved sound reproduction and made it possible to cut narrower grooves in records. The length of recordings was extended considerably by the introduction of playing speeds of 33rpm and an increase in diameter from 25cm to 30cm (the 12"LP). For his album *Masterpieces*, Duke Ellington came up with an arrangement of 'Mood Indigo' lasting 15 minutes. Miles Davis began extending his pieces by increasing the number of choruses. Recording onto magnetic tape replaced direct engraving. Tape recorders were economical and facilitated live recording. They also inspired a number of people to take up careers as sound engineers (notably Rudy Van Gelder, who made his first, historic recordings for Blue Note and Prestige in his parents' living room). Small labels keen to promote modern jazz sprang up all over the country: Prestige and Atlantic on the east coast, Pacific Jazz, Fantasy and Contemporary on the west coast. A number of musicians even

LISTENING GUIDE
The Beat Generation, Rhino.
La Grande Anthologie du Blues, 1925–62, Body & Soul.
Rock 'n' Roll, 1950, Vol 6, Frémeaux.
Perez Prado, Al Compas del Mambo, 1950–2, Tumbao.

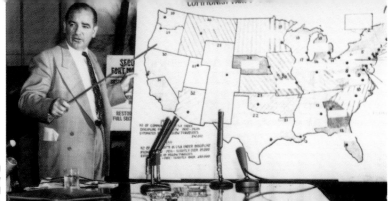

Joe McCarthy describing how the Communist party had penetrated the United States.

experimented with self-production (Dizzy Gillespie with the label Dee Gee, and Charles Mingus and Max Roach with Debut).

In 1951, Leo Fender invented the electric bass guitar (without a resonance chamber), intended to replace the double bass. Monk Montgomery started using it in Lionel Hampton's band in 1953.

RELATED MUSICAL GENRES. In Chicago, the pungency of the southern blues style was intensified by the introduction of electric guitars and basses, by powerful singing and by playing the harmonica close to the microphone, which created distortion. The unrivalled leader of the new Chicago blues and the star of the Chess label was Muddy Waters. His band brought the harmonica player Junior Wells, the guitarist Jimmy Rogers and the pianist Otis Spann to public attention. Other cities suffered from a lack of studio facilities. One such city was Detroit, where John Lee Hooker made his first recordings in the back of a shop before winning the support of the Chicago-based Vee-Jay label. Singers of Memphis blues, broadcast on local radio, were sought out by the Chess brothers from Chicago and the Bihari brothers from Los Angeles. The former signed Howlin' Wolf and the latter B B King. A guitarist inspired by the single-note style of Lonnie Johnson, T-Bone Walker and Charlie Christian, B B King was responsible for introducing the guitar solo into the blues. In New Orleans, the pianist Professor Longhair created an original style inspired by the rhythms of boogie-woogie, the Caribbean, Cajun music and the local parade tradition. The trumpeter Dave Bartholomew extended this style into a band format that was taken up by the singer and pianist Fats Domino.

In 1949, the music industry magazine *Billboard* replaced 'race records' with 'rhythm and blues' ('R & B') as a term to designate black music. Within this category, jazz rapidly ceded its pre-eminent position to popular secular forms inspired by the Negro spiritual, blues and boogie-woogie. Adapting to the market, Atlantic signed Ruth Brown (1950) and Ray Charles (1952). Many secular vocal quartets emerged at this time, including The Ravens, The Dominoes and The Platters. These groups popularized the *doo wop* style, which featured a soloist with onomatopoeic accompaniment.

In the world of gospel the vogue for male quartets soon came up against competition from female groups and choirs such as The Caravans. Soloists (including Sam Cooke and Bessie Griffin) started making a name for themselves within groups, the instrumental backing began to include electric instruments, and concerts featured the more spectacular aspects of black liturgy.

In New York, dancers deserted jazz in favour of the mambo. Popularized on the west coast by Perez Prado, this Cuban dance style proved a hit at the New York Palladium with Machito, Tito Puente and Tito Rodriguez.

White jazz in New York

On 3 January 1949, *Metronome* magazine got together in the studio a group of musicians who had been chosen in a readers' poll. While the predominant style of those chosen was bebop, black musicians (Dizzy Gillespie, Miles Davis, Fats Navarro, Jay Jay Johnson and Charlie Parker) were outnumbered by white musicians. The baritone saxophonist Ernie Caceres was a veteran of the swing era, the clarinetist Buddy DeFranco was a true bebopper, and the double-bass player Eddie Safranski and the drummer Shelly Manne had been working on giving their instruments more freedom in the Stan Kenton Orchestra ('Fugue for Rhythm Section'). The trombonist Kai Winding had transformed Kenton's big band sound with his smooth, vibrato-less style and was emerging as a direct rival to Jay Jay Johnson. The tenor saxophonist Charlie Ventura had set himself the task of popularizing bebop at the head of a small group called Bop for the People, which included Kai Winding and Shelly Manne. The alto saxophonist Lee Konitz and the guitarist Billy Bauer, meanwhile, were disciples of another poll winner, the pianist Lennie Tristano.

The Tristano school

Lennie Tristano brought a new sound to bebop. A great admirer of Charlie Parker, he believed that bebop represented not the culmination of something but a new point of departure. Starting from this conviction, he worked on an extension of Charlie Parker's harmonic and rhythmic legacy, thereby earning himself the reputation of being a cold theoretician. His entire system of teaching, however, was based on feeling. He banned his pupils from using scores and made them learn the solos of the great jazzmen without the help of their instruments by internalizing all the inflections and nuances of the music. This interiorization of tempo, articulation and harmonic substitutions was at the heart of his own extraordinarily forceful piano playing. To understand the depth of 'feeling' that sustained Tristano, who was capable of taking enormous risks,

Lennie Tristano

it is essential to listen to 'Requiem', his tribute to Charlie Parker. Ten years before the first recordings of 'free' jazz, his quintet recorded two collective improvisations without either theme or predetermined harmony ('Intuition' and 'Digression') that were rejected by his producer.

Tristano's 1949 quintet included his main disciples Billy Bauer (guitar), Lee Konitz (alto sax) and Warne Marsh (tenor sax). Unlike Charlie Parker, these two saxophonists rejected expressionistic technique. Their soft, evanescent sound, the absence of vibrato and their smooth phrasing recalled the nonchalance of Lester Young. Wayne Marsh favoured the upper register of his tenor sax, which made it sound like an alto. ('There's things going on up there man. Some of you guys are all belly,' Young is supposed to have replied to someone who expressed surprise at the alto-like sound he got out of his tenor sax.) Lennie Tristano's versions of the standards, weightlessly soaring above the original harmonies, suited the musicians' collective style and often inspired them to improvise some breathtaking counterpoint.

Miles Davis and the 'birth of the cool'

In 1946, a young white musician named Gil Evans settled in New York, attracted by the buzz of 52nd Street in the bebop era. A self-taught arranger, Evans had been working for some time for the Claude Thornhill orchestra, a rather curious big band that included two French horns, a tuba and a flute, and in which vibrato was not allowed. During his time with this outfit, Evans had been able to experiment with some unusual combinations of sounds and had decided to apply this orchestral treatment to the compositions of Charlie Parker. Lee Konitz had taken part in the experiment, as had a young white baritone saxophonist named Gerry Mulligan.

An arranger without a band, Mulligan was a regular visitor to Gil Evans's room, which was the meeting place of a number of beboppers, both white and black. These musicians reinvented the world of jazz while listening to the records of Charlie Parker, Lester Young, Alban Berg and Maurice Ravel. During 1948, Miles Davis, who had begun to tire of Charlie Parker's quintet, conceived with Evans and Mulligan the idea of a nonet comprising trumpet, trombone, French horn, tuba, alto sax, baritone sax, piano, double bass and drums. Favouring the mid-to-low range rather than the brilliance of the higher registers, the coloration produced by this band represented an extension of Davis's introverted instrumental style. Sonny Stitt was initially considered as the alto saxophonist, but Lee Konitz was eventually chosen in a deliberate attempt to distance the band from bebop. The band performed without any great success at the Royal Roost in New York, but succeeded in attracting the attention of an artistic director from Capitol, who got them into the studio on three occasions between January 1949 and March 1950. The resulting 78rpm sides were to have a considerable influence on the musicians of the West Coast. In 1954 these sides were brought together on a 25cm (10") LP under the title *Birth of the Cool*.

LISTENING GUIDE
Lennie Tristano Quintet: 'Subconscious-Lee' (Prestige, 11 January 1949)[1], 'Wow', 'Crosscurrents', 'Intuition' (Capitol, 4 March and 16 May 1949)[2].
Wayne Marsh and Lee Konitz: 'Marshmallow' (Prestige, 28 June 1949)[1].
Claude Thornhill/Gil Evans: 'Yardbird Suite', 'Anthropology' (Columbia, 4 September and 17 December 1947)[3].
Miles Davis: see the following pages.

CD GUIDE
1. Lee Konitz, *With Tristano, Marsh & Bauer*, Prestige.
2. Lennie Tristano, *Intuition*, Capitol.
3. Gil Evans, *1942–7*, Masters of Jazz.

'BOPLICITY' (Capitol, 22 April 1949)

From the initial statement of the theme, played at a medium tempo that provides a far from ideal basis for bebop-style acrobatics, the sound of the band seems firmly rooted in the lower registers and creates a mild sense of torpor, emphasized by Gerry Mulligan's completely laid-back solo. However, the main point of interest of the piece lies elsewhere. Swing and bebop have always been based on the same forms: either twelve-bar blues or 32-bar structures. Jazz improvisers are like judo experts. Their art is based on reflex, and in order to practise it they need to be able to find their way with ease around a familiar terrain. The beboppers, however, and a number of soloists before them, such as Lester Young, contrived to conceal these standard structures by shaping their phrases in a way that allowed them to straddle the customary subdivisions of four or eight bars in unusual ways.

Gil Evans's arrangement goes even further. The theme is classically constructed on a 32-bar AABA framework. The rules are first infringed when the theme is allowed to spill over into the first bar (0:57–0:58) of the following chorus. In this first variations chorus, the bridge (B, 1:26–1:43) exceeds the usual length of eight bars, lasting instead for ten, of which the band gets six (1:26–1:36) and the trumpet gets four (1:36–1:43). The trumpet then continues to play through the final A section of the chorus (lasting for the normal eight bars, 1:43–1:57) but now as part of the band rather than solo. This unison section then spills over into the first bar of the next chorus before the trumpet drops out completely (2:00). It then plays an unaccompanied solo during the second A section (starting 2:12). The trumpet thus underlines the fact that the final A section of the first variations chorus is carried over into the first A section of the final chorus, thereby helping to mask the break between the two.

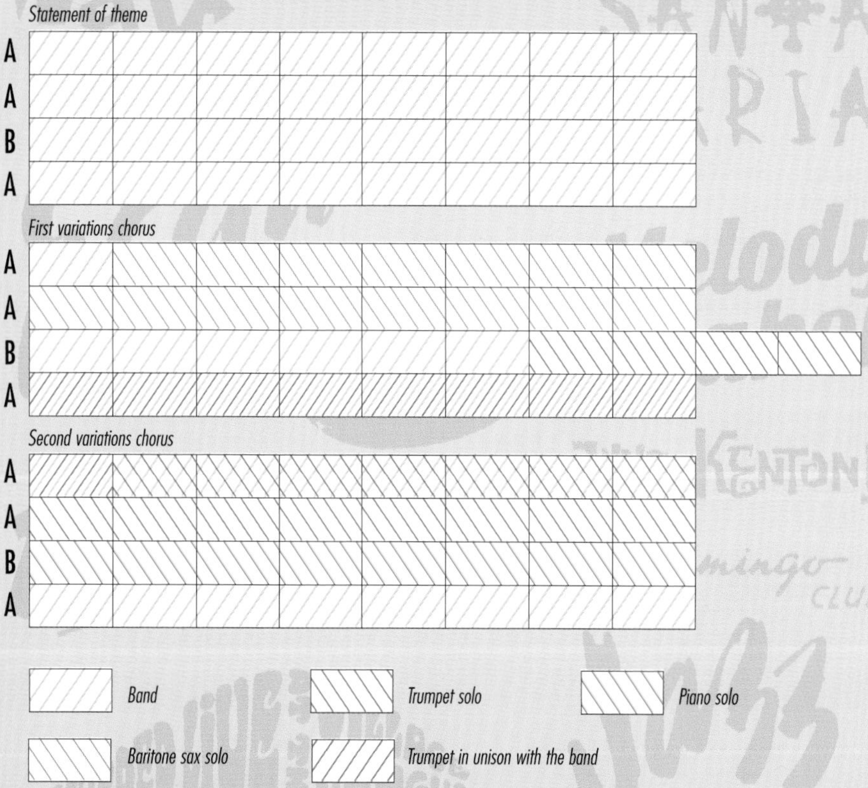

Statement of theme

A
A
B
A

First variations chorus

A
A
B
A

Second variations chorus

A
A
B
A

	Band		Trumpet solo		Piano solo
	Baritone sax solo		Trumpet in unison with the band		

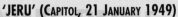

'JERU' (Capitol, 21 January 1949)

This arrangement by Gerry Mulligan displays the same ambition to liberate the music from traditional structural divisions. The composition is constructed on an AABA framework but the bridge (B, 0:21–0:35) is twelve bars long and the arrangement again spills over into the first bar of the following chorus (0:47) with the trumpet creating a feeling of continuity that helps to obscure the change of chorus. It is interesting to note that during the trumpet chorus the band reverts to the usual structure in order to help the improviser.

Gerry Mulligan also takes a radical initiative of a different kind by questioning the supremacy of 4/4 time in jazz. Back in 1942, Fats Waller had already broken a taboo with his self-composed 'Jitterbug Waltz'. Here, Gerry Mulligan threatens the rhythmic unity of the piece: the bridge of the opening statement contains five three-beat bars within a 4/4 phrase (0:26–0:30).

0:21			0:26					0:31			
4	4	4	3	3	3	3	3	4	4	4	4

Further on, the A sections of the third chorus begin with four three-beat bars followed by a bar of two beats, then followed by four bars of 4/4. These daring innovations were so far ahead of the jazz practices of the day that they were to remain uncommon for a long time to come. In fact, it was not until the 1960s that soloists dared to improvise on such uncertain territory.

1:31				1:35				
3	3	3	3	2	4	4	4	4

1:41				1:45				
3	3	3	3	2	4	4	4	4

'MOON DREAMS' (Capitol, 13 March 1950)

This arrangement by Gil Evans is a classic 32-bar ballad with an ABAC structure. The fully composed theme statement displays Evans's taste for unusual combinations of instruments and his ability to vary the ways in which the instruments enter and exit. The theme is followed by a lengthy coda that begins with four bars played by the baritone sax (the number's only solo). This coda, which takes up almost half the piece, is a slow tumble by all the musicians, a free-for-all in which one instrument seems to be trying to grab hold of the next. Its feeling of torpor and dejection represents the very opposite of the dynamism to which jazz had hitherto accustomed its audiences. It is easy to see how jazz lovers might have found it difficult to recognize their favourite type of music in these sides released by Capitol. Because of its radical questioning of traditional values, *Birth of the Cool* should perhaps be seen as the birth of modern jazz itself. Some, of course, saw it as its death warrant.

LISTENING
GUIDE
Miles Davis, 'The
Complete Birth of the
Cool', Capitol.

White west coast jazz

The word 'cool', in addition to all its other meanings and associations, brings to mind refreshing cocktails and a breeze blowing across a Pacific beach. Were New York's young white beboppers, imbued with Lester Young's laid-back style, attracted to California by its mild weather, its easy lifestyle and its location far away from the stresses of New York and the rigours of the east coast climate? Always on the lookout for good instrumentalists and composers, the film industry contributed to the establishment of a mixed community of white musicians in the Hollywood area. This community enjoyed its golden age during the first half of the 1950s, but it continued to thrive until the end of the decade.

Fertile terrain

The Californian jazz scene benefited from the wartime growth in the west coast's black population. Howard McGhee visited Los Angeles in 1944–6, and Charlie Parker and Miles Davis came in 1946. Many young musicians received the bebop message loud and clear. In particular, bebop inspired a group of black saxophonists who had already come under the influence of Lester Young (Dexter Gordon, Wardell Gray, Lucky Thompson and others). But Parker's Californian admirers also included a number of white

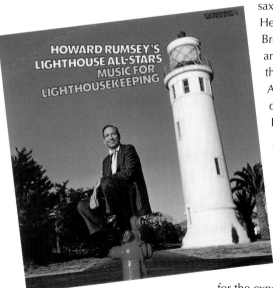

saxophonists, among whom Woody Herman had discovered his Four Brothers (see p.121). Stan Kenton and his men were also based on this side of the United States.

A former colleague of Kenton's, the double-bass player Howard Rumsey, launched Sunday evening jam sessions at the Lighthouse Café at Hermosa Beach in Los Angeles. This became a meeting place for Stan Kenton's musicians, particularly after the disbanding of Innovations in Modern Music (see p.121) in 1952. Before long, the Lighthouse became the venue for the experimentation of a hard core of musicians from both Kenton's and Herman's bands: Shorty Rogers (trumpet), Jimmy Giuffre (clarinet, tenor sax and baritone sax), Shelly Manne (drums) and the free spirit Art Pepper (alto sax). They recorded their manifesto, *Modern Sounds*, on 8 October 1951 under the name of Shorty Rogers & His Giants. The octet they formed for the occasion (which included a French horn and a tuba) was inspired by Miles Davis's nonet. However, it played a more dynamic form of swing, inherited from Count Basie, and showed a sense of balance that served as a model on the west coast.

Variables and constants

The west coast was a mosaic of often very different styles based around a number of constants. These constants were inherited from Lester Young and were common to the so-called 'cool' jazz of both seaboards: lighter vibrato, a soft tone and laid-back phrasing. The taste for counterpoint displayed by the white east coast jazzmen was reflected on the west coast in a tendency to give improvisations an orchestral setting, using a style of writing inherited from the big bands of Woody Herman and Stan Kenton. And while California may have started off as a venue for various one-off reunions, during the course of the 1950s the arrangers who were the real architects of the West Coast sound (notably Dave Pell, Lennie Niehaus, Manny Albam, Bill Holman, Pete Rugolo and Bill Byers) started to make their mark there. Many of them came from classical backgrounds and exploited this in their use of classical forms such as the fugue and counterpoint. Some turned to serialism or atonality for inspiration, but most seemed closer to the neoclassical composers (such as Darius Milhaud) and Bach, who was an omnipresent point of reference in the jazz of this period. Highly inventive in the area of orchestration, these arrangers introduced new colours into the jazz band, adding the entire woodwind family (clarinet, flute, oboe and cor anglais) to the French horn and tuba already used by Claude Thornhill. They also experimented with every possible combination of the existing big-band sections, exaggerating the size of one, eliminating another entirely and often reducing them to one instrument per family. Thanks to their skill in orchestration, these arrangers were able to make a medium-sized group sound like the most powerful of big bands, although more often than not they chose to create something akin to the intimacy of chamber music – possibly in reaction to Stan Kenton's love of large formations, but also in memory of the small groups formed by the vibraphone player Red Norvo on the west coast in the 1940s.

Although they adopted the rhythmic efficiency of the swing bands, they were accused of toning it down through introspection and mannerism. It is almost impossible to describe this mannerism in terms of a single, uniform trend. The accusation of affectation could hardly be levelled at Marty Paich's muscular arrangements or the increasingly hard bop practised by the Shelly Manne quintet from the second half of the 1950s onwards or the light, humorous style of Barney Kessel's small formations. And accusations of aesthetic timidity (compared to the risks taken by bebop) could be countered by the example of The Three. Six years before the explosion of free jazz, with no support from either piano or double bass, the trio The Three (Shelly Manne, Jimmy Giuffre and Shorty Rogers) juggled with free improvisation ('Abstract No. 1') and the twelve-tone scale ('Three on a Row') while using the drums as a melodic instrument ('Pas de Trois').

The Gerry Mulligan and Dave Brubeck quartets

Gerry Mulligan arrived on the west coast in 1952. Engaged to play at the Haig Club in Los Angeles, he experimented with a number of different line-ups before settling on a quartet with no piano. This option proved important for the future of jazz (see p.143). It offered a totally open space in which the interaction between Mulligan and the trumpeter Chet Baker (a romantic disciple of Miles Davis's introverted style of playing) could unfold. In a muted, chamber-music-like atmosphere, Mulligan's themes provided the basis for elegant counterpoint along compositional lines followed by both front-line players during their improvisations. Attracted to the west coast by an engagement with Stan Kenton's orchestra, Lee Konitz regularly added a third voice to the group. Mulligan provided Kenton with a number of scores.

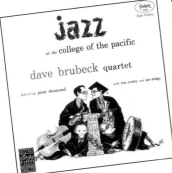

While studying music, the pianist Dave Brubeck was heavily influenced by encounters with Arnold Schoenberg and in particular Darius Milhaud. Indeed, it was with pupils of Milhaud that he formed his first group – an octet that allowed him to experiment with counterpoint, the fugue, polytonality and different time signatures. These remained constant preoccupations in the quartet he formed at the beginning of the 1950s on the west coast. While Brubeck was a favourite target of the detractors of West Coast jazz, who criticized the stiffness of his phrasing and his lack of swing, Paul Desmond's alto sax was virtually irresistible. Desmond was able to transform Brubeck's ideas into pure emotion with an impalpable, misty tone and a melodic logic of almost literary sophistication. Despite the criticism, by performing on university campuses the quartet succeeded in acquiring a loyal following that soon enabled them to start recording for Columbia.

The soloists and sidemen of cool jazz

Prominent among the exponents of cool jazz are a number of legendary musicians – those tragic, misunderstood artists whose work is appreciated only by dedicated jazz fans, and those ill-fated figures in the Chet Baker and James Dean mould who were icons for a generation of American rebels. An examination of cool jazz instrument by instrument, however, reveals a diversity of musical personalities, thus putting into perspective the stereotypes that have become associated with the genre. Cool jazz is often identified, for example, with an absence of vibrato inherited from Lester Young. Yet vibrato continued to be used, regularly and systematically, by a

Chet Baker

number of musicians (including the trumpeter Conte Candoli), and selectively, varying in both frequency and width, by others (such as Stan Getz), as a way of colouring the end of a long note.

Brass

The trumpeters of cool jazz were not necessarily that cool. Not all of them came into the category of meditative melodists (Chet Baker, Tony Fruscella, Don Joseph) in the Miles Davis tradition. At different times during his long career, even Baker abandoned his fondness for romantic outpourings and adopted a more boppy aggressiveness.

In Stan Kenton's orchestra, numerous west coast trumpeters even acquired a powerful, precise and brilliant playing style. Among them were the Candoli brothers (Pete and Conte), Maynard Ferguson and Buddy Childers (a specialist in 'first trumpet' roles).

Kai Winding, Bill Harris and Jack Teagarden were the main influences on the virtuoso trombonists of the west coast – a group which included Frank Rosolino, Carl Fontana and Milt Bernhart. Bob Brookmeyer (who joined Gerry Mulligan's quartet in 1954) and Bob Enevoldsen helped bring the hitherto underused valve trombone to a wider audience. Other rarities were dusted off, including the tuba (Gene Englund) and French horn (John Graas), inspired by Miles Davis's nonet, and even the bass trumpet (Cy Touff).

Reeds

A coterie of white tenor saxophonists, all disciples of Lester Young, formed around Woody Herman's Four Brothers (see p.121). In addition to those already mentioned, the main figures were Richie Kamuca, Bob Cooper, Bill Perkins and Bill Holman. This family of sax players also extended to the east coast, where the 'cool connection' had many offshoots and where it indulged in multiple betrayals of the fundamental style. Two of the family's founding members, Al Cohn and Zoot Sims, adopted a harder tone during the course of their many and varied collaborations. And Stan Getz, for all his swooning sonority and highly romantic sense of melody, used energetic phrasing that opened the door to collaborations with authentic beboppers. Having liberated the baritone sax from its rather passive big-band role and the rugged classic style invented for it by Harry Carney, Gerry Mulligan found he had rivals in Serge Chaloff (the baritone player of the Four Brothers) and Jimmy Giuffre (also tenor sax and clarinet). Alto saxophonists were clearly heavily influenced by Charlie Parker, but they did not escape the influence of Lester Young either, and in the case of Art Pepper the influence of Benny Carter was added to the brew. Bud Shank, Buddy Collette (one of the first black musicians allowed into the film studios) and Bob Cooper answered Hollywood's call by doubling up or tripling up on other instruments: flute in the case of Shank, flute and clarinet in the case of Collette, bassoon and cor anglais in the case of Cooper. Sam Most and Herbie Mann even made the flute their main instrument.

The rhythm section

The demand on the west coast for the black rhythm section of Carl Perkins (piano), Curtis Counce (bass) and Lawrence Marable (drums) demonstrates the permeability of the frontier between black and white jazz. Hampton Hawes, the pianist of the Lighthouse All Stars and originally a disciple of Bud Powell, can no more be considered an exponent of cool jazz than he can a member of the white jazz scene. Jazz piano on the west coast was very varied (Russ Freeman, André Previn, Pete Jolly and others), but a general history of jazz such as this is not the right place to explore its many different aspects.

PACIFIC JAZZ 1224

CHET BAKER & CREW

The first half of the 1950s was a period when the double bass, under the influence of Ray Brown, truly came of age in every area of jazz. In the absence of a pianist in Gerry Mulligan's quartet, its bassist had a heavy responsibility. Plucking the strings not with the index finger alone but with the index and middle fingers alternately, Red Mitchell brought to the double bass a melodic dimension that would become a feature of the more virtuoso white school of double-bass playing.

LISTENING
GUIDE
Chet Baker–Russ
Freeman, Quartet,
Pacific.
Tony Fruscella, Tony
Fruscella, Atlantic.
Stan Kenton (with Conte
Candoli in 'Portrait of a
Count', with Maynard
Ferguson in 'Invention
for Guitar and Trumpet',
and with Frank Rosolino
in 'Frankly Speaking'),
New Concepts of Artistry
in Rhythm, Capitol.
Art Pepper, Discoveries,
Savoy.
Bob Cooper, Shifting
Winds, Capitol.
Bill Perkins (with Bud
Shank, Carl Fontana and
Red Mitchell), On Stage,
Pacific.
Stan Getz (with Jimmy
Raney and Tiny Kahn),
Live at the Storyville,
Roost.
Al Cohn (with Bill
Perkins and Richie
Kamuca), The Brothers,
RCA.
Al Cohn and Zoot Sims,
Al and Zoot, Coral.
Shelly Manne (with Bob
Enevoldsen, Bob Cooper,
Jimmy Giuffre and
Curtis Counce), West
Coast Sound, Pacific.
Jimmy Raney (with Red
Mitchell), Visits Paris, Vol
1, Vogue.
Red Norvo (with Tal
Farlow), The Savoy
Sessions, Savoy.
Anita O'Day, Anita,
Verve.
June Christy, This Is June
Christy, Capitol.
Blossom Dearie, Once
Upon a Summertime,
Verve.
Helen Merrill, Helen
Merrill (featuring
Clifford Brown), Emarcy.
The Four Freshmen, And
Five Trombones, Capitol.
Mel Tormé, Live at the
Crescendo, Bethlehem.
Chet Baker, Sings,
Pacific.
For Chico Hamilton and
Hampton Hawes, see the
recordings of Gerry
Mulligan and Shorty
Rogers respectively.

Leroy Vinnegar, on the other hand, with his insistence on the instrument's rhythmic function and depth of sound, represented the black tradition on the west coast. He provided a solid rhythmic foundation in partnership with the drummer Shelly Manne, who exploited the various timbres of his drums to melodic effect. When not working with timbre in this way, the 'cool' drummers smoothed the ground under the musicians' feet (as opposed to bebop drummers who strewed it with pitfalls) by means of the discreet efficiency and flexibility of the brushes. On the west coast, the black drummer Chico Hamilton was able to play both ways. On the east coast, Tiny Kahn developed his own subtle method of breaking up the regular chabada rhythm.

The guitar no longer had an exclusively rhythmic function, starting instead to be used with greater facility in a solo role. The main agents of this change were white guitarists. Billy Bauer was a faithful interpreter of Lennie Tristano's logical approach. Johnny Smith was an expert at playing tunes in chords. Jimmy Raney, thanks to his perfect knowledge of the fingerboard and fluid plectrum technique, succeeded in bringing the dramatic qualities of Stan Getz's phrasing to the guitar. Tal Farlow was brought into Red Norvo's trio (with Charles Mingus and then Red Mitchell) because of his ability to play very fast. He acquired an extraordinary fluidity, which he facilitated by reducing the tension of his strings.

White voices

The vogue for cool jazz was a godsend for female white singers. Anita O'Day (who achieved success with Gene Krupa in 1941 and later with Stan Kenton in 1944) and Peggy Lee (who came to the fore with Benny Goodman between 1941 and 1943) were already known, but their models were the black singers. The white vocalists of the 1950s, however, were inspired by the white instrumentalists of the day. Succeeding O'Day in Kenton's band (before eventually handing over to Chris Connor), June Christy was the partner of the saxophonist Bob Cooper and was surrounded by the best musicians on the west coast. On the east coast, following the What's New album she made with the trumpeter Clifford Brown in 1954, Helen Merrill made a more lasting impression on jazz lovers with her breathy voice and long, drawn-out word placement that floated above the bar line. Blossom Dearie, by contrast, swung with a liveliness all her own, singing in a mischievous, high-pitched voice.

The white swing bands had worked with a number of vocal groups: The Boswell Sisters sang with Tommy Dorsey's band, The Rhythm Boys (including Bing Crosby) with Paul Whiteman, and The Snowflakes with Claude Thornhill. Two male vocal groups in particular kept this tradition alive in the 1950s: the Four Freshmen and the Hi-Los, each of which treated their combined voices like an instrumental section. The composer, arranger and remarkable scat singer Mel Tormé made a name for himself at the head of the vocal group the Mel-Tones. While the particular quality of his voice earned him the nickname 'Velvet Fog', his verve and humour placed him at the opposite extreme to Chet Baker, whose scat singing was a highly introverted extension of his trumpet playing.

A word that crops up repeatedly when jazzmen talk about their art is 'space', a confusing term covering a number of concepts that were already of relevance in the earliest days of jazz. It was only in the 1950s, however, that jazz musicians became fully aware of how important the notion of space was.

Time and space

As well as having to choose their notes, turn them into melodies and give them some kind of tangible shape, improvisers also need to regulate the flow of their melodic ideas in order to allow them to breathe. They need to incorporate breaks, pauses and breathing spaces into their playing. Improvisers seek to create space between both notes and phrases. The improvisations of Louis Armstrong or Count Basie are full of space. The lesson that Lester Young and Miles Davis taught the musicians of cool jazz was partly about this ability to 'take one's time' in order to control the passing of time. While Charlie Parker thought more quickly, producing a more rapid flow of ideas, he also knew how to take his time within this fast delivery and how to use silence in his construction of the music. This silence was also an integral part of Thelonious Monk's vocabulary.

The desire to take one's time and the preoccupation with silence also relate to a need to hold back time. Due to the lack of a written part, time eludes the improviser, who has to transform it into space in a process that is like fitting out a room. Space no longer has any temporal meaning. It is no longer a question of thinking of the music in terms of the way it unfolds in a linear sense; it needs to be thought of in terms of verticality or thickness.

Sound and space

The need for space can therefore affect the sound a musician makes (not just timbre itself but timbre combined with all the other elements of a musician's delivery). Slowing down the vibrato, using it only selectively and adopting a cooler, cleaner-lined, leaner sound in the middle registers rather than the higher registers can create a feeling of well-being, ease of breathing and spaciousness. If the middle register, on the other hand, is too rich, it can create an oppressive, stifling atmosphere.

Around this time, new technology allowed sound engineers to incorporate space into their recordings by placing instruments in larger or smaller spaces and using artificial reverberation, by altering the type or positioning of microphones, by adjusting the relative volume of the instruments, and later by careful positioning of individual instruments within the stereophonic image.

The band and space

Musicians also need to feel at ease and be free in their movements. Space has to be organized so that the players do not get in each other's way. From the first half of the 1950s onwards, the pianist Ahmad Jamal was a master of space in the way he organized his trio (with the double-bass player Israel Crosby and the guitarist Ray Crawford, and later the drummer Vernell Fournier). On both the temporal and the spatial level, Jamal's music continually offers the listener a feeling of spaciousness as a result of his careful organization of everything from the sound of the band to its intricately worked-out performances.

It has often been claimed that Jamal plays his audience more than he plays the piano. It could also be said that he plays his trio, such is the care he takes to ensure that each of his musicians has the space he needs. Miles Davis started listening to Ahmad Jamal in 1954 and saw his work as a permanent encouragement to develop further the sense of space he had already acquired from Charlie Parker.

Harmony and space

That same year, Miles Davis had the idea of increasing the number of piano entries and exits as a way of creating space and enhancing the soloist's freedom of movement. The soloist was no longer supported by a sequence of very precise harmonic instructions from the piano. This left just the bass line, which was far more suggestive as a result of being played just one note at a time (four per bar). Pianists

LISTENING
GUIDE
Ahmad Jamal, *The Three
Strings, The Ahmad
Jamal Trio, Columbia, At
the Pershing, But Not
for Me,* Argo.

were also moving independently in the direction of more open and suggestive harmonic utterances. They experimented with the 'voicing' of chords. This involves disregarding the usual hierarchical order when arranging the notes of the chord, placing a seventh note, for example, at the bottom. A C-major chord built not on the root (C), but on the third note (E) or the seventh note (Bb) releases the soloist from the strong pull of the root and gives him far wider melodic choices; all the more so if the pianist decides to leave out the root note altogether, to merely suggest the chord without playing all its notes, or to colour it using added notes from the octave above (9th, 11th, 13th, for example). This makes the harmony less thick, less restrictive and more suggestive, providing both listener and soloist with a feeling of space.

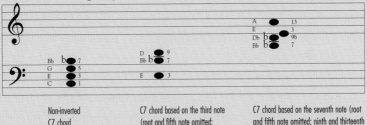

Non-inverted
C7 chord

C7 chord based on the third note (root and fifth note omitted; ninth note added).

C7 chord based on the seventh note (root and fifth note omitted; ninth and thirteenth notes added).

Underestimated by jazz historians because they were not the leaders of any major movements and because they did not fit easily under any heading, Erroll Garner and Ahmad Jamal were the precursors of this art of 'voicing', which was later taken further by Red Garland and Bill Evans. It was to have a decisive influence on the development of the soloist in the 1960s.

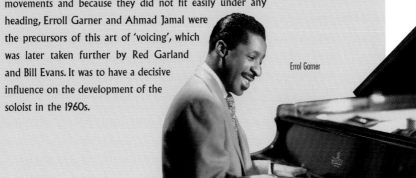

Errol Garner

Bebop's star wanes

Bebop was in crisis. Bud Powell was on the road to insanity. A whole generation of jazz musicians had followed Charlie Parker into drug addiction. For some this was fatal (Fats Navarro in 1950, Parker himself five years later), while others survived as criminals or dropouts. Between 1951 and 1954, Miles Davis was reduced to playing on borrowed trumpets. Dexter Gordon languished in jail from 1953 to 1955. Monk and Parker were banned from entering New York's clubs. Those on 52nd Street had closed as a result of police harassment. The success of Californian jazz kindled a lasting resentment of white musicians. Now marginalized, a number of beboppers converted to Islam, either because they agreed with the Black Muslims' ideas or in order to protect themselves from their self-destructive tendencies. Art Blakey took the name Abdullah Ibn Buhaina and Kenny Clarke became Liaquat Ali Salaam. Less self-destructive, Dizzy Gillespie nevertheless saw his career stagnate as his label Dee Gee suffered commercial setbacks.

Bebop infected by the preoccupations of cool

The Royal Roost on Broadway, however, had been presenting a bebop programme since 1948. Also on Broadway, the Birdland Club gave Charlie Parker a rapturous welcome when he played at its opening night in 1949. On the radio, the disc jockey Symphony Sid had proclaimed himself the ambassador of bebop, broadcasting live concerts on a regular basis. Labels such as Blue Note and Prestige championed bebop. Norman Granz had just taken Charlie Parker under his wing and recorded him with his regular bands as well as with other leading beboppers (the album *Bird & Diz*, for example, on which Thelonious Monk also plays). Granz provided him with sumptuous backing in the form of string sections, full-scale variety orchestras and choirs. Parker even recorded Latin American favourites such as 'La Cucaracha', which he completely transformed. In December 1950, he took part in the recording by Machito's orchestra of an ambitious work called *The Afro-Cuban Suite* by Chico O'Farrill, the first Cuban arranger to have fully assimilated orchestral bebop.

Whether as the result of a desire to take stock or a need to catch its breath, bebop's star began to wane. Now less unbridled and more formal, it adapted itself to the meticulous scores of the pianist Tadd Dameron, the trombonist J J Johnson, the alto saxophonist Gigi Gryce (who studied with Arthur Honegger and Nadia Boulanger in 1952) and the trumpeter Quincy Jones (who also studied with Boulanger, in 1957). In 1948, the pianist John Lewis took advantage of a trip to Paris to study with Germaine Tailleferre (a member, alongside Darius Milhaud, of the group of composers known as The Six). Assuming leadership of the Modern Jazz Quartet in 1952, Lewis began to explore baroque forms, suffusing them with the spirit of swing and the blues.

Bebop gains classic status

The beboppers reached maturity most obviously in the rhythm section. The

LISTENING
GUIDE
Bud Powell (with Sonny
Rollins, Roy Haynes and
Max Roach), *The
Amazing Bud Powell,*
Blue Note.
Charlie Parker (with
Chico O'Farrill), *South of
the Border,* Verve.
Charlie Parker, *Bird &
Diz, With Strings,* Verve.
Charlie Parker–Dizzy
Gillespie–Bud
Powell–Charles
Mingus–Max Roach, *The
Greatest Concert Ever,*
Prestige.
Tadd Dameron (with
Clifford Brown), *Clifford
Brown Memorial,*
Prestige.
J J Johnson (with John
Lewis, Percy Heath and
Kenny Clarke), *The
Eminent Jay Jay
Johnson, Vol 1,* Blue
Note.
Clifford Brown (with Gigi
Gryce and Quincy
Jones), *The 1953 Paris
Sessions,* Vogue.
The Modern Jazz
Quartet (with Percy
Heath and Kenny
Clarke), *Django,*
Prestige.
Vic Dickenson (with
Ruby Braff and Sir
Charles Thompson), *Vic
Dickenson Septet,*
Vanguard.

first disciples of Kenny Clarke (Art Blakey, Max Roach, Roy Haynes and Stan Levey) had now fully achieved their polyrhythmic ambitions.

Young bassists such as Percy Heath were continuing the work begun by Ray Brown and Oscar Pettiford, while Bud Powell became the key model for the younger generation of pianists. Sonny Rollins liberated the bebop tenor sax from Lester Young's influence, following directly in Charlie Parker's footsteps while adopting the gruff tone of Coleman Hawkins. Rollins and the trumpeter Clifford Brown helped the up-and-coming hard-bop generation to get noticed. Bebop became a classic alongside other classic jazz forms. No one was scared of it any more.

Its most brilliant exponents were now regulars of Jazz At The Philharmonic (see p.126). Even the JATP rhythm sections now included well-known figures from the bebop scene such as Hank Jones and Ray Brown. Oscar Peterson, a direct disciple of Nat King Cole and more or less JATP's permanent pianist from 1953, embodied the new mainstream, which combined the values of swing with those of bebop.

Mainstream and revival

After breaking up his big band in 1950, Count Basie himself called mainly on the services of beboppers when forming his octet, which had stylistic affinities with cool jazz. In 1951, he recruited his new big band from the young generation. Around the same time, Duke Ellington hired Louie Bellson to carry on the swing tradition of the big-band drummers while simultaneously modernizing it. Ellington had already eliminated the guitar, a typical component of swing rhythm sections, in 1949. Between 1951 and 1955, his faithful alto saxophonist Johnny Hodges went it alone at the head of a small band that included a saxophonist who was to become a leading figure in jazz in the 1960s – John Coltrane. In 1953, the label Vanguard started to offer 1930s veterans a second bite of the cherry. Record buyers were thus given a chance to rediscover the trombonist Vic Dickenson playing alongside Sir Charles Thompson (a pianist in the Basie mould but with a certain sympathy for bebop) and Ruby Braff (a white trumpeter of the bebop generation who favoured pre-bop trumpet styles, synthesizing them into something new). The Riverside label, which would later champion the bebop revival, started off by recording the unacknowledged veterans of New Orleans, such as George Lewis, and reissuing old Paramount and Gennett recordings.

Bebop goes international

Europe was submerged by a wave of revivalism. In Britain, the revivalist movement was led by two trumpeters, Ken Colyer and Humphrey Lyttleton. After his triumph at the Paris Jazz Festival, Sidney Bechet settled in France and played with the bands of Claude Luter and André Réwéliotty. Also playing at the festival, however, were Charlie Parker and Miles Davis.

LISTENING
GUIDE
Henri Renaud: 'Godchild'
(with Bobby Jaspar and
Jimmy Gourley, Saturne,
June 1951)[1].
Django Reinhardt:
'Nuages', 'September
Song' (with Maurice
Vander and Pierre
Michelot, Blue Star, 10
March 1953)[2],
'Impromptu' (with
Bernard Hulin, Hubert
Fol, Raymond Fol and
Pierre Michelot, Decca,
11 May 1951), 'Flèche
d'Or' (with Roger Guérin
and Raymond Fol,
Decca, 30 January
1953).
Lars Gullin: 'Galium
Verum' (with Åke
Persson and Bengt
Hallberg, Metronome, 3
June 1954).
The African Swingsters:
'Swazi Stomp' (African
Jive–His Master's Voice,
1952).
Bebo Valdés: 'Descarga
Caliente' (Mercury,
October 1952)[3].
Laurindo Almeida:
'Carinoso' (Pacific, 15
April 1954)[4].

CD GUIDE
1. Henri Renaud, *The
Complete Legendary
Saturne Picture Discs*,
Paris Jazz Corner.
2. Django Reinhardt,
Pêche à la Mouche,
Verve.
3. Bebo Valdés,
Descarga Caliente,
Caney.
4. Laurindo Almeida,
*Quartet Featuring Bud
Shank*, Pacific.

Western Europe under the influence of bebop

Bebop was played all over Europe. In Liège in Belgium, Jacques Pelzer (alto sax), Bobby Jaspar (tenor sax) and Sadi Lallemand (vibraphone) performed as the Bob Shots. The saxophonist Hans Koller moved from Austria to West Germany, where he formed the New Jazz Stars with the trombonist Albert Mangelsdorff and the pianist Jutta Hipp in 1953. From 1947, Parisian bebop was performed by The Bebop Minstrels, the Michel de Villiers quintet, the West Indian Robert Mavounzy and others. Django Reinhardt electrified his guitar and performed with the cream of French bebop, including Bernard Hulin, Roger Guérin (trumpet), Hubert Fol (alto sax), Raymond Fol, Maurice Vander (piano) and Pierre Michelot (double bass). A musician of international standing, Michelot became the preferred rhythm section partner of Kenny Clarke, who was based in Paris between 1948 and 1951, settling there permanently in 1956. French critics were divided on the subject of cool jazz, but its influence could be heard in Django Reinhardt's circle. A well-known disciple of Coleman Hawkins, the tenor saxophonist Jean-Claude Fohrenbach relinquished his audience to Guy Lafitte at the beginning of the 1950s, when he made a series of aesthetic choices similar to those made by Stan Getz and Warne Marsh. Based in Paris in 1951, the guitarist Jimmy Gourley introduced the city to a cool style of guitar playing that met with the approval of Bobby Jaspar and the pianist Henri Renaud. Jaspar was the first of many Belgian musicians who moved to the French capital.

In Sweden, Stan Getz discovered a whole generation of like-minded 'cool' musicians, including Åke Persson (trombone), Arne Domnérus (alto sax, musical direction), Bengt Hallberg (piano) and, most importantly, the baritone saxophonist Lars Gullin.

Eastern Europe under the inquisition

After the 1948 Prague Coup, Stalinism lay like a stifling blanket over eastern Europe. Wishing to close off its borders to all Western influences, entrench his power in the new republics and bring to order a population intoxicated by victory, Stalin initiated new purges which had a debilitating effect on jazz. As early as the end of 1946, his censors had started to hunt down the blue note, the double-bass pizzicato and the trumpet mute. The majority of jazzmen were sent to the gulag. In 1949, Moscow's saxophonists were summoned to the National Agency for Light Music, where their instruments were confiscated. Prokofiev's *Lieutenant Kijé*, which includes a saxophone part, was withdrawn from the official repertoire. Komsomol, the communist youth organisation, formed special brigades to carry out checks on music venues, and the Union of Soviet Composers sent 'inquisitors' to the USSR's eastern European satellite states. Despite these measures, jazz records still managed to find their way into the Soviet bloc, thanks mainly to Red Army officers posted in Berlin.

The only place in Russia where live jazz could be heard was the gulag. Upon arriving at Kolyma camp in 1946, Eddie (Adi) Rosner was given a cornet and started a new career under the protection of Alexander Derevenko, the despotic director of the gulag system. Jazz did manage to take root, however, in the peripheral regions that escaped the jamming of Western radio stations, such as the Baltic states. In Estonia in 1948, the Swing Club of Tallinn organized what would eventually become the Tallinn Jazz Festival. The young generation identified with bebop, which became a symbol of freedom and counter-culture.

Further east, Shanghai's jazz clubs were shut down when Mao Zedong came to power. Tokyo became Asia's new jazz capital, after recordings arrived in the kitbags of American GIs. The Japanese publication *Swing Journal* first appeared in 1947. The pianist Toshiko Akiyoshi formed his quartet in 1951 and the saxophonist Sadao Watanabe debuted with it two years later.

Jazz in the southern hemisphere

In South Africa, a trend developed around 1950 for street music played on the penny whistle (*kwela* music). Combining elements of jazz and *marabi*, *kwela* gradually developed into a form known as *mbaqanga* that became the dominant strand of South African jazz in the 1950s.

Descargas (jam sessions based on Cuban rhythms) had existed in Cuba since the 1940s, but it was not until 1952, under the musical direction of the pianist Bebo Valdés, that they were recorded. Brazilian *choro* music (a contemporary form of band-based music related to ragtime) developed among young musicians such as the saxophonist Paulo Moura, who performed in the jazz clubs of Buenos Aires, and Laurindo Almeida, who

played with Stan Kenton's big band. In Argentina, where jazz was first taken up by tango musicians, the Bop Club Argentino and the Hot Club of Buenos Aires became rivals in the battle for 'real jazz'. They were nevertheless championing the same idea: that jazz was a serious form of music that deserved to be heard. Around the same time, Astor Piazzolla was starting to dream of tango being given the same consideration.

Context

SOCIETY. After Stalin's death in 1953, the winds of change began to blow through eastern Europe. The eastern and western blocs settled into peaceful coexistence guaranteed by mutual fear. Decolonization provided the framework for a struggle for influence played out in a multitude of local conflicts in which the major powers avoided direct confrontation with each other. The foundations for the eventual outcome of the Cold War were laid in the cultural sphere. In 1955, the radio station Voice of America launched a jazz programme presented by Willis Conover.

In the United States, Joe McCarthy was repudiated by the Senate in 1954. Minorities began to raise their heads, and a judgement by the Supreme Court that same year put an end to segregation in public education. Although not

Martin Luther King

enforced in the southern states, this ruling represented the culmination of the legal battle waged by the NAACP (National Association for the Advancement of Colored People). It also highlighted the limitations of the NAACP's methods when faced with the blocking measures taken by American society. Black Americans now took their struggle to the street. In 1955, the Baptist minister Martin Luther King organized a boycott of public transport in Montgomery, the capital of Alabama, in protest against segregation. Influenced by Gandhi and the doctrine of non-violence, he became president of the SCLC (Southern Christian Leadership Conference), founded in 1957. The fight for civil rights was pursued with non-violent actions but provoked a violent reaction from the southern states. At the start of the 1957 academic year, the governor of Arkansas, Orval Faubus, prohibited African-American schoolchildren from attending Little Rock High School. The National Guard had to intervene in order to uphold the law.

THE MUSIC INDUSTRY. The post-war baby boom created a lucrative teenage market of which rhythm and blues and rock and roll were the main beneficiaries. The commercial potential of modern jazz, however, also proved attractive. It aroused the interest of the Riverside label and led to the revival of Atlantic's jazz division and the creation by Mercury of the Emarcy catalogue. It even caught the attention of Norman Granz and his new label Verve, which remained focused, however, on the two safe bets of bebop and swing. Blue Note's cardboard record sleeves became legendary – sacred icons to the hard-bop fan. Even the major companies were on the lookout for talent: Shorty Rogers was hired by Victor/RCA as a producer and Miles Davis, Dave Brubeck and Duke Ellington were signed by Columbia.

LISTENING
GUIDE
Sam Cooke, *With the Soul Stirrers*, featuring his first solo recordings, Specialty.
Ray Charles, *The Atlantic Years*, Rhino.
Little Richard, *The Essential*, Ace.
Willie Dixon, *The Chess Box*, Chess.
Chicago Boss Guitar, Paula/Flyright.

Since the early 1950s, magnetic tape had allowed music to be erased, corrected, cut, pasted and transferred from one tape to another. It was now possible to superimpose two parts recorded at different times. In 1954, Chet Baker played the trumpet accompaniment to his own singing on the album *Chet Baker Sings*. In a later release, his voice was replaced by Jimmy Giuffre on clarinet. 'Brilliant Corners' (1956), a piece that presented Thelonious Monk's fellow musicians with considerable technical difficulties, is assembled out of portions of tape from different takes that have been edited together. At Columbia, the producer George Avakian undertook an enormous feat of post-production on Miles Davis's 1957 album *Miles Ahead* (arranged by Gil Evans), linking the different pieces together with brief interludes in order to create a continuous suite. The scissors were also taken to pieces that were considered too long. Practised with varying degrees of precision and often perceived as an act of censorship, this cutting created great tension between musicians and producers. In 1959, Charles Mingus was asked to drop his intense sung diatribe that accompanied his satirical piece dedicated to Orval Faubus, 'Fables of Faubus'.

In 1954, Benjamin Miessner developed an electric piano that was marketed by Wurlitzer. Sun Ra used it as early as 1956, and it was soon embraced by rhythm and blues.

RELATED MUSICAL GENRES. Sam Cooke, star of the gospel quartet the Soul Stirrers, caused a scandal by recording secular music under a pseudonym. The dividing line between the two was so fine, however, that before long the new secular music adopted the name 'soul music'. Combining the ingredients of gospel and rhythm and blues and transposing religious exhilaration and the sacred hymn into the sphere of love and sex, this music celebrated the soul of the African-American community as it joyfully prepared itself to battle for its civil rights. The gradual shift towards soul music was embodied by Ray Charles on the Atlantic label and James Brown on King.

The dividing line between rhythm and blues and soul music is very indistinct – mainly because the term 'rhythm and blues' does not actually refer to any precise musical style. Fats Domino, Bo Diddley, Little Richard and Chuck Berry were the last black exponents of rock and roll – a term which was subsequently appropriated by rockabilly. This was a predominantly white fusion of country music, blues harmonies and the rhythm of boogie-woogie, brought to public attention by Elvis Presley in 1954.

The *éminence grise* of Chicago blues was Willie Dixon, a double bassist, singer, composer and producer for Chess. During the second half of the 1950s, however, it was B B King's guitar style, which had made its mark on the whole country, that inspired the city's young bluesmen (including Otis Rush, Magic Sam and Buddy Guy) to create the West Side Sound, named after Chicago's poorest ghetto. Sombre, poignant and tinged with gospel and soul, this new style was promoted by the Cobra label. In Louisiana, the accordionists Boozoo Chavis and Clifton Chénier popularized the 'zydeco' style, a hybrid of blues and Cajun music. The producer Jay Miller, meanwhile, was inspired by the obsessive blues style of Slim Harpo and the effects that could be obtained with amplification (echoes, vibrato and distortion) to create 'swamp blues', a musical evocation of the bayou country of southern Louisiana.

The hard bop sound

In 1954, black jazz took on a new lease of life. In reaction to cool jazz, hard bop reconnected with the relentless tone of bebop but broke (or pretended to break) with bebop's harmonic and rhythmic sophistication. Instead it went further back, to blues and Negro spirituals, for its inspiration – to the great satisfaction of the public, who to this day have continued to regard it as the most important expression of classicism in jazz.

Two previews

At the lowest point of his battle with drug addiction, Miles Davis was cut to the quick to find that he had been knocked off his perch by a greenhorn from the west coast: Chet Baker. Once he was clean again, Davis made it known in no uncertain terms that he was back. In March 1954, he recorded 'Blue Haze', a stripped-down, timeless blues that unfolds in a stifling, oppressive atmosphere created by a simultaneously minimalist and ponderous rhythm section (Horace Silver on piano, Percy Heath on bass and Art Blakey on drums). In April, he returned to the studio at the head of a sextet to record 'Walkin''. More uptempo, yet solid as a rock, the blues here has a hymn-like quality. Davis was not the only one to wake up with a start. On 21 February, Blue Note had recorded a concert at Birdland featuring the trumpeter Clifford Brown, the alto saxophonist Lou Donaldson, the pianist Horace Silver, the double-bass player Curly Russell and the drummer Art Blakey. Listening today to this recording – regarded as marking the birth of hard bop – one can hear the fast runs and urgency of bebop, but it is also possible to detect something new.

The hymns of 'churchy' jazz and the trances of funky jazz

Hard bop can be recognized from its compositional style. Its numbers are like anthems to the new-found confidence of the black community, to that community's pride in being black. While it is impossible to sing bebop's

Miles Davis and
Bud Powell

LISTENING
GUIDE
Art Blakey, *A Night at
Birdland* (Split Kick),
Blue Note.
Miles Davis, *Blue Haze*,
Prestige.
Miles Davis, *Walkin'*,
Prestige.
Horace Silver, *And the
Jazz Messengers* ('The
Preacher', 'Doodlin''),
Blue Note.
Art Blakey's Jazz
Messengers, *1958, Paris
Olympia* ('Moanin'',
'Whisper Not'), Fontana.

themes, those of hard bop can be hummed to blues harmonies ('Doodlin''
by Horace Silver) or gospel harmonies ('The Preacher', also by Silver).
On Bobby Timmons's 'Moanin'', the responses exchanged between the brass
and the rhythm section are reminiscent of black church services. This jazz
style, with its frequently explicit titles ('The Preacher', 'The Sermon'), has
been described as 'churchy'. Everything in Benny Golson's 'Blues March',
from its side-drum introduction to the triumphant melody with its strong
beat, evokes the parades of New Orleans. It seems designed to accompany
the inexorable march – head held high and chest puffed out – towards
recognition by the black American people. Even in Golson's 'Whisper Not',
whose harmonies are more in the bebop mould and whose general tone is
more restrained, the same confident dynamism, relaxed expectation and
sense of elation can be heard.

Hard bop has also been described as 'funky' (a US slang term meaning
'with a strong smell', referring specifically to the odours of the body). Funky
jazz had B.O. This label underlined the authenticity of the new music,
which was stripped of harmonic lingerie and unadorned by cosmetic
rhythmic effects. It swayed gently amid the rhythm-and-blues odours that it
exuded, enticing listeners to join in. Smelling sometimes of sweat and
sometimes of incense, hard bop was closely related to the burgeoning genre
of soul music. It could be seen as the instrumental reply to Ray Charles's
'Hallelujah I Love Her So'.

A collective sound

After the meticulous writing of cool jazz, improvisation now came back to
the fore – sandwiched between the two theme statements, as in early
bebop. The simplicity was only apparent, however. The vigour of the playing
was reinforced by a compact collective sound obtained by means of
economical, highly effective arrangements. These were based on: partial or
full harmonization of the theme, with two or three voices playing close
together in order to create a sense of harmonic density ('Doodlin''); precise
note placement by the rhythm section in response to motifs suggested by
the band (the piano on Horace Silver's 'The Preacher') or an inversion of
these roles, with the wind instruments responding to statements made by
the rhythm section ('Moanin'' by the Jazz Messengers); dance-like piano and
double-bass motifs inspired by gospel ('Doodlin'') or Latin music (Clifford
Brown's 'Delilah'); and the alternation of swing-type sections phrased in
irregular quavers and sections phrased in regular ('binary') quavers over a
Latin rhythm ('Split Kick', recorded at Birdland by Art Blakey's group).
This technique of alternation had already been used in bebop ('Night in
Tunisia' by Gillespie, Parker or Powell), where it was confined to the theme
statement. From the end of the 1950s onwards, soloists more and more
frequently took the risk of moving from one rhythmic mode to the other
during the course of their improvisation ('So Tired' by Art Blakey displays
irregular phrasing at 0:34–0:44 and 1:19–1:29, for example). The greater
length of LP records meant that improvisations tended to get longer. These
improvisations would be structured in such a way that players would
rendezvous at precise points indicated by specific rhythmic figures (at

1:20–1:23 and 1:38–1:41, for example, in the case of Horace Silver's 'Baghdad Blues'; at 1:00–1:22 in Clifford Brown's 'The Blues Walk'). They also made use of various signals, such as the piano entries and exits in 'Oleo' by Miles Davis.

The leaders of hard bop

The unifying group behind hard bop was Art Blakey's. It first went into the recording studio under the name of Horace Silver and the Jazz Messengers. In 1955, Art Blakey took over and Horace Silver formed his own group. Silver's new group was lighter, more jaunty, more cheerful and characterized by sly, mischievous writing and piano parts. Blakey's group seemed more solemn and dense on account of the wall of sound created by the vibration of the rivets of the cymbal known as the 'sizzle', the peremptory accentuation of the backbeat on the hi-hat and the continual cross-rhythms that rained down onto the other elements of the drum kit. All this was performed with an independent, laid-back air that made it seem extraordinarily simple. Although the Jazz Messengers were regarded as a training ground for musicians by several generations of jazzmen (see p.155), the group formed by Clifford Brown and Max Roach did not last long enough to assume such a role, as Brown was killed in a car accident in 1956. In addition to his tone, which was the exact opposite of Miles Davis's (in other words, full-bodied, grainy and coloured by a generous vibrato), Brown also possessed a facility with harmony that made him a natural successor to Fats Navarro. Shortly before his death in 1950, Navarro declared that only when his colleagues familiarized themselves with harmonic progressions would a truly modern jazz be achieved. Whereas these progressions were the cause of effort, abstraction and even excess and confusion among Parker and Gillespie's early successors, Brown tackled them with an ease, a lyricism and a sense of structure that marked him out as the embodiment of bebop in its fully

Max Roach

formed, classic incarnation – someone capable of taking modern jazz forward to the next stage in its development.

Even more importantly, the clarity of his trumpet diction seemed as natural as that of the spoken word, regardless of the complexity of the phrases he constructed or the speed with which he delivered them. Drummer Max Roach shared this ease and sense of architecture, which he learned while playing alongside Miles Davis in Charlie Parker's band from 1947 to 1948. By extending the sound palette of the tom-toms, he gave the drums a musicality that had previously been the preserve of the melodic instruments.

The Hammond organ – made for hard bop

Thanks to its volume, the bass provided by its pedal board, its wide range of timbres and the spectacular effects produced by its Leslie speaker cabinet (housing its set of rotating loudspeakers), the Hammond electric organ could sound like a full orchestra. The organ player Wild Bill Davis had been performing without a bass player since 1948, accompanied only by guitar and drums. It was with his trio that he created the resounding arrangement of 'April in Paris' that was adopted unchanged by Count Basie and his band. However, this one-man-band role was starting to feel dated and the instrument lacked the necessary attack to do anything other than produce massed instrument effects through the use of block chords. Hammond's launch of a new model, the B3, equipped with a 'percussion' effect that reinforced the attack of each note, allowed Jimmy Smith to rethink the sound and phrasing of the Hammond organ and to use his right hand in a similar way to a wind instrument. With the guitarists Quentin Warren or Kenny Burrell and the drummer Donald Bailey, Jimmy Smith adapted the Hammond organ so well to the hard-bop style that it became reminiscent of the organ as used in black churches and soul music.

Miles Davis and Charles Mingus: on the fringes of hard bop

Despite being the initiator of hard bop, Miles Davis was never fully a part of it. When he conjured up the black church, it was as a visionary poet ('All Blues') who looked beyond its clichés. He also liked to take a new look at songs from the shows, which hard bop had turned its back on ('If I Were a Bell', 'Bye Bye Blackbird' and others). When he formed his quintet in 1955, Davis asked the pianist Red Garland and the double-bass player Paul Chambers to recreate the harmonic and orchestral space that he so admired in Ahmad Jamal's work. The drummer Philly Joe Jones set this space ablaze, working in intimate collusion with Davis's trumpet. The tenor saxophonist John Coltrane brought him the contrast and sense of surprise he had been looking for since leaving Charlie Parker. In order to counterbalance Coltrane's destabilizing modernity, Davis anchored his music in the black tradition by adding the Parker-influenced alto saxophonist Cannonball Adderley. Inexpensively, using minimalist means and making full use of the available human resources to bring about a miracle based on the barest of instructions, Miles Davis took a highly personal approach to the density of sound that characterized jazz at the end of the 1950s.

Charles Mingus had studied the cello in his youth and retained a passion for the music of Béla Bartók. A friend advised him to abandon the cello and take up the double bass instead, claiming that the cello was not a black instrument. Mingus remained deeply hurt and outraged by this idea. Despite becoming one of the great double-bass players of bebop, he did not neglect his writing. Imbued with the colourful world of the blues and the Sanctified Church, he was torn between the injustice done to black Americans and his taste for the classical music of his youth, to whose more 'learned' forms he continued to aspire. He was influenced by Lennie Tristano's ideas and even sympathized with the 'third stream' (see p.163). Mingus expected his musicians to memorize complex episodic compositions without the help of a score and provided frequent opportunities for collective improvisation in his works. He had Ellington's skill as a colourist and was capable of bringing about explosions of sound that anticipated the anger of the black community in the 1960s. Part of hard bop's return to the sources of black music, his 'churchy' avant-garde appealed to audiences from both ends of the spectrum.

The soloists and sidemen of hard bop

Characterized first and foremost by a new collective sound and a new repertoire, the leading bands on the hard-bop scene offered new opportunities to a multitude of instrumentalists, who formed and reformed short-lived groups in response to the requirements of live engagements or studio sessions.

Trumpeters

Lee Morgan

Although Clifford Brown was the dominant influence on trumpet in the hard bop era, several other players also made their mark betewen 1954 and 1959: Blue Mitchell, Donald Byrd and Bill Hardman. The most brilliant of them, however, was also the youngest: Lee Morgan. Morgan made a name for himself well in advance of his peers Freddie Hubbard and Booker Little (born, like him, in 1938), who only came to the fore at the beginning of the next decade. Kenny Dorham, the most senior of the hard-bop trumpeters, was perhaps also the most captivating. Succeeding Clifford Brown in Max Roach's band, Dorham, who had originally come to attention as Miles Davis's successor with Charlie Parker, revealed himself to be a musical personality very different from either of these two diametrically opposed figures of the post-Gillespie era.

The flugelhorn and the cornet

Miles Davis's more insidious influence can be heard in the playing of Art Farmer, who gradually abandoned the trumpet in favour of the flugelhorn, a form of valved bugle from which he obtained a more mellow, almost cool sound.

The vintage years

Art Blakey's bands were a permanent training ground for young musicians. Special projects were undertaken (including big-band work and encounters with other percussionists) and there were several periods of uncertainty, but a number of line-ups stand out in particular:

1955: Kenny Dorham (trumpet), Hank Mobley (tenor sax), Horace Silver (piano), Doug Watkins (double bass). *The Jazz Messengers at the Café Bohemia*, Blue Note.
1958: Lee Morgan (trumpet), Benny Golson (tenor sax, musical direction), Bobby Timmons (piano), Jymie Merritt (double bass). *1958, Paris Olympia*, Fontana.
1959–61: Lee Morgan (trumpet), Wayne Shorter (tenor sax, musical direction), Bobby Timmons followed by Walter Davis (piano), Jymie Merritt (double bass). *A Night in Tunisia*, Blue Note.
1961–4: Freddie Hubbard (trumpet), Curtis Fuller (trombone), Wayne Shorter (tenor sax, musical direction), Cedar Walton (piano), Jymie Merritt followed by Reggie Workman (double bass). *Free For All*, Blue Note.
1966: Chuck Mangione (trumpet), Frank Mitchell (tenor sax), Keith Jarrett (piano), Reggie Workman (double bass). *Buttercorn Lady*, Limelight.
1977–9: Valery Ponomarev (trumpet), Bobby Watson (alto sax, musical direction), David Schnitter (tenor sax), Walter Davis and subsequently James Williams (piano), Dennis Irwin (double bass). *Gypsy Folk Tales*, Roulette.
1980–1: Wynton Marsalis (trumpet), Bobby Watson (alto sax), Bill Pierce (tenor sax), James Williams (piano), Charles Fambrough (double bass). *Album of the Year*, Timeless.

Throughout the 1980s and up to his death on 16 October 1990, Art Blakey was the teacher of a whole generation of young neo-boppers: the trumpeters Terence Blanchard, Philip Harper, Wallace Roney and Bryan Lynch, the saxophonists Branford Marsalis, Donald Harrison, Kenny Garrett, Javon Jackson and Jean Toussaint, the pianists Donald Brown, Mulgrew Miller, Benny Green and Geoff Keezer, and the double-bass players Charles Fambrough and Lonnie Plaxico.

It became relatively common around this time for trumpeters in big bands to be asked to play the flugelhorn as well as the trumpet. Miles Davis plays it throughout *Miles Ahead,* his first record arranged by Gil Evans. Clark Terry became a great virtuoso on the instrument from around 1957. Thad Jones was an enthusiastic player of both the flugelhorn and the cornet, which was on its way out but which Nat Adderley (Cannonball's brother) made his speciality.

Trombonists

Apart from J J Johnson and his successors Curtis Fuller and Slide Hampton, very few trombonists were able to compete with the speed of their colleagues on the trumpet. The warm tones of Charles Mingus's trombonist Jimmy Knepper are widely admired, while Willie Dennis's economical use of the slide combined with high speed (achieved by means of a virtuosic lip technique) has been largely neglected.

Tenor saxophonists

This period was dominated by two colossuses among tenor saxophonists. The older of the two, John Coltrane, was as yet unknown – to others and to himself – when he was hired by Miles Davis. Working with Davis and Thelonious Monk, he revealed himself to be a great mystic in love with the absolute. Coltrane played his instrument with an ascetic discipline, developing a technical mastery and power that would enable him to penetrate the secrets of the acoustic universe and releasing breathtaking 'sheets of sound' in order to approach harmony from every possible angle. The younger of the two, Sonny Rollins, began to earn a reputation for himself at the beginning of the 1950s as the heir to Charlie Parker and Coleman Hawkins. At the same time, he observed the rise of John Coltrane with a mixture of anxiety, impetuosity, fragility and power that led to many stylistic U-turns. In addition to the calypso, a form to which he applied his considerable rhythmic skill from 1955 onwards ('St Thomas'), and the waltz, for which he started a trend in 1956 (with 'Valse Hot'), he also experimented in 1957 with a pianoless trio. Here, his tormented harmonic inspiration frayed into long, breathless phrases or tied itself up in rhythmic-

Sonny Rollins

melodic knots punctuating his musical discourse. Free jazz was starting to emerge.

Johnny Griffin is worthy of mention alongside these two titans. Too mischievous, daring and unruly to play tragic roles, however, the 'Little Giant' preferred to enjoy himself with Monk. Other tenor saxophonists were also knocking on fame's door: the sensual Benny Golson, the limpid Harold Land, the nonchalant Hank Mobley and the mysterious John Gilmore – not forgetting Charlie Rouse, who placed his considerable musical skills entirely at the disposal of Thelonious Monk at the end of the 1950s.

Alto saxophonists

Perhaps because it was somewhat outdated and too closely connected with the bebop of Charlie Parker (which Cannonball Adderley and Lou Donaldson nevertheless managed to reinject into hard bop), the alto saxophone played more of a background role. Two musicians stood out: Gigi Gryce for his delicate phrasing reminiscent of cool jazz and Jackie McLean, a Charlie Parker follower, who played slightly off key. McLean liked to produce a full sound and was later receptive to the ideas of free jazz. Also among the elite of the Parker-inspired alto saxophonists was the white player Phil Woods.

Baritone saxophonists and miscellaneous wind

It was a white musician, Pepper Adams, who provided the most convincing alternative to the cool aesthetic of Gerry Mulligan and Serge Chaloff. The saxophone sections of the big bands were being expanded at this time and were encouraging their members to double on the flute, the clarinet or even the double reeds (oboe, bassoon etc). The flute even produced some soloists (such as the alto and tenor saxophonist Frank Wess with Count Basie, or the tenor saxophonist James Moody), some of whom gave it a saxophone-like expressivity by singing into it (the baritone saxophonist Sahib Shihab, for example). Later, the repertoire of flute techniques was extended even further due to the influence of contemporary music and non-European musics (breathing effects, percussive attack, rolling of the tongue and multiphonics).

Guitarists

Kenny Burrell, playing alongside Jimmy Smith, took the guitar as far as it would go as part of an organ trio, but the great revelation at the end of the 1950s was Wes Montgomery, who reinvigorated the instrument with incredibly dynamic phrasing obtained without a plectrum (instead he plucked the strings with a downward motion of the thumb). His mastery of octaves and chords, his feeling for the blues and song and his sense of architecture ensured that his improvisations were never less than thrilling. Montgomery made a name for himself on the west coast, playing alongside his brothers Buddy (on vibraphone) and Monk (on electric bass) in the Mastersounds, beefing up the delicate guitar–piano–vibraphone–bass–drums combination created by George Shearing in 1949. In 1959, Montgomery embarked on a career under his own name which was to exert a great influence over guitar playing at the end of the century.

Hard bop was a reaction both to cool jazz and to the excessive floridness and extreme harmonic mobility of bebop. Clifford Brown was a master at projecting this abundance and instability, as is evident in the cascades of more or less disguised I–VI–II–V7 chord progressions in 'Joy Spring' or the tumbling V7 chords of 'Jordu'. To take up again the metaphor of an acrobat picking his way around a series of ladders (see pp28–9), Brown would leap constantly from one ladder to another with astounding ease. In fact it had become almost too easy. John Coltrane sought to raise the stakes.

John Coltrane at the outer limits of functional harmony

In 1957, John Coltrane was working at the Five Spot Café in New York with Thelonious Monk, the great alchemist of bebop harmony. Monk used to leave the piano frequently and Coltrane would experiment with just the bass and drums. He used this as an opportunity to work out his own way forward, saturating the harmony with veritable 'sheets of sound' in the form of systematic exercises in corrupting the chord progression described above. His album *Giant Steps*, and above all the piece 'Countdown', can be seen as a summation of this work. The number 'Giant Steps' was conceived as a kind of bet. Coltrane seems to have been saying to himself: 'Let's take three keys as far away from each other as possible and see by what logic of functional harmony we can move from one to another as quickly as possible.' Exploring at great speed the chords proposed by the piano, he managed to create long phrases whose lyricism makes it easy to forget the systematic, almost gymnastic nature of the task he set himself.

However, in view of the repetitions that recur in the various takes of 'Giant Steps', the question arises of whether the very tight grid of this piece might not actually constitute a prison for the soloist. John Coltrane must have felt he had pushed functional harmony to its utmost limits. As a result he had to change systems. This is a similar realization to that which had already led hard-bop composers to return to blues and gospel harmonies and which had prompted Miles Davis's interest in modes.

Miles Davis and modal jazz

Miles Davis felt that bebop's excessively detailed harmonies hindered his melodic imagination. He got into the habit around 1956, notably in 'Oleo', of asking his pianist to stop playing from time to time. Playing without the piano liberates the music, he claimed, likening it to walking down a street on a bright, sunny day with nothing and nobody in one's way. He introduced interludes suspending harmonic movement into his solo grids, as can be seen in his compositions 'Milestones' and 'So What'. Although based on a classic AABA structure, parts A and B are in separate keys stripped of all harmonic progression. The musicians pass from one to the other without any predetermined transitions: it is up to the soloist to make his own way there. In each section the soloist finds himself within a particular mode. This modal system is practised above all in traditional Indian music – a scale, or mode, is selected and the musicians focus on its melodic colour for the whole of the piece in order to extract its essential qualities.

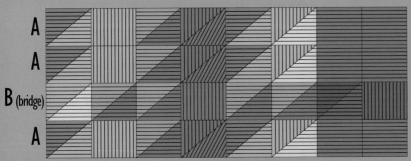

A
A
B (bridge)
A

Comparison between a bebop grid ('Jordu', above) and a modal grid ('So What', below). What is immediately striking is 'Jordu''s multicoloured grid and the relatively smooth colour progressions. In 'So What' the harmony is static and the tonal functions have disappeared. The hatching that represents the tonal functions in the 'Jordu' grid now indicates the type of scale (two 'Dorian' modes in this example), while the colour indicates the notes on which these scales start (D and Eb). The soloist passes from one scale to the other without any formal transition.

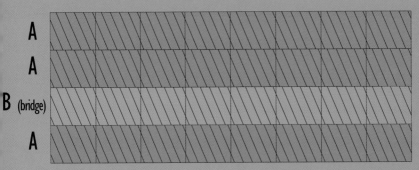

A
A
B (bridge)
A

This provided an opportunity for musicians to discover modes other than our own major scale. John Coltrane had started to examine this same territory with his teacher Dennis Sandole. The saxophonist Yusuf Lateef explored it on a range of flutes as well as on the *arghul*, the Egyptian double clarinet. There was a lot of talk at the time about George Russell's work on modal music, and Bill Evans conducted the experiment of improvising alone for nearly seven minutes on a single mode with a static left-hand accompaniment ('Peace Piece'). While recording the album *Kind of Blue*, Miles Davis suggested to Bill Evans that they repeat the experiment as a quintet, taking as their starting point five different modes that each soloist would explore for as long as he wished, the only written instruction being that they had to string them together in a prescribed order. The resulting 'Flamenco Sketches' heralded the arrival of modal jazz.

LISTENING GUIDE

Clifford Brown, *Clifford Brown and Max Roach*, ('Joy Spring', 'Jordu'), Mercy.

John Coltrane, *Giant Steps*, ('Giant Steps', 'Countdown'), Atlantic.

Bill Evans, *Everybody Digs Bill Evans*, ('Peace Piece'), Riverside.

Miles Davis, *Kind of Blue* ('So What', 'Flamenco Sketches'), Columbia.

0:19   0:36   0:53   1:10   1:44

Diagram of Miles Davis's solo in 'Flamenco Sketches', showing the order of the different modes (Ionian starting on C, Mixolydian starting on Ab, Ionian starting on Bb, Phrygian starting on D, and Dorian starting on G). The other solos are constructed on the same principle but with different durations for each mode.

LISTENING
GUIDE
Sonny Clark (with Art Farmer, Jackie McLean, Paul Chambers and Philly Joe Jones), *Cool Struttin'*, Blue Note.
Phineas Newborn, *Phineas' Rainbow*, RCA.
Sonny Rollins (with Wynton Kelly, Doug Watkins and Philly Joe Jones), *Newk's Time*, Blue Note.
John Coltrane (with Tommy Flanagan, Paul Chambers and Art Taylor), *Giant Steps*, Atlantic.
Randy Weston, *Little Niles*, United Artists.
Sonny Rollins (with Wilbur Ware and Elvin Jones), *A Night at the Village Vanguard*, Blue Note.

Pianists

The funky aesthetic of black pianists such as Horace Silver, Bobby Timmons and Sonny Clark focused on the effects of blue notes as well as on melodic and rhythmic figures borrowed from gospel and Afro-Cuban music. Their accompaniment was based on alternate melodic outbursts, harmonic interjections and long silences. In accompaniments as well as solos, the use of block chords developed towards maximum density or, conversely, towards a luminosity created by airy voicing (Red Garland, Kenny Drew, Wynton Kelly and one of the few white hard-bop pianists, Bill Evans). The general characteristics of hard-bop piano should not, however, be allowed to overshadow individual qualities such as the delicate refinement of the playing of Tommy Flanagan (Ella Fitzgerald's favourite accompanist) or the omnipresent influence of Bud Powell and even Art Tatum in the playing of Phineas Newborn. Barry Harris constituted a kind of one-man archive of jazz piano. In addition to Thelonious Monk, who worked with the greatest instrumentalists of the day (Rollins, Coltrane, Griffin, Blakey and Roach), there were three pianists, active on the margins of hard bop, who became cult figures for future avant-gardists. Mal Waldron, the most soul-orientated of the three, was capable of remaining discreetly in the background when accompanying Billie Holiday or indulging in whirling dervish-like gyrations while creating trancelike music for Charles Mingus (alternating in this role with Horace Parlan). Randy Weston, who was interested in African culture, took Monk's work in new and unexpected directions in collaboration with the trombonist and arranger Melba Liston. Herbie Nichols achieved recognition by calling into question the AABA form.

Double bassists

Paul Chambers led double-bass players such as Doug Watkins towards a greater clarity of note (thanks to a more controlled plucking over the fingerboard), greater freedom of initiative and greater virtuosity (evident above all in his bowed solos). But at a time when the white double bassist Scott LaFaro, on the west coast, was experimenting with a totally melodic use of the instrument, there was a noticeable desire among Chambers's black colleagues not to go too far in terms of speed and exploration of the higher registers. They preferred to remain anchored in the lower registers with a short, firm sound that matched the weight of the instrument and underlined its role of providing a solid foundation for the other musicians.

Drummers

Roy Haynes and Philly Joe Jones vied with Art Blakey and Max Roach for the privilege of freeing the drums from their hitherto somewhat limited role. This liberating process involved various factors: the increasing integration of sounds taken from Afro-Cuban percussion in particular; a variation of the traditional *chabada* swing rhythm (inversion, suspension, change of timbre); a move towards a more independent use of the hi-hat; and greater autonomy for the four limbs, while seeking to maintain a continuity of phrasing using all the different elements of the drum kit. In this regard, the appearance of Elvin Jones alongside Sonny Rollins in 1957 looked ahead to the 1960s. Dannie Richmond, drumming for Charles Mingus, became interested in the superimposition of ternary and binary metres, which had caught his attention while he was on a trip to Mexico.

Less innovative drummers found their own paths through these new developments, offering a funkier efficiency (Louis Hayes), a more discreet elegance (Art Taylor), or a more dramatic framework (Jimmy Cobb and Connie Kay, who championed this particular style with the Modern Jazz Quartet).

Scat, variety and vocalese

The wave of white female singers that emerged with cool jazz did not completely overwhelm their black counterparts, but unless they chose rhythm and blues (like Esther Phillips or Lavern Baker) black female singers found that recognition was slow in coming. Betty Carter, who had learned to sing scat with Lionel Hampton's band, was discovered around 1955. Destined for a career as a great improviser, she benefited on her early records from arrangements by Gigi Gryce, Melba Liston and Benny Golson. On these recordings she alternated between words and scat, displaying an irresistible combination of freshness and musicality. Carmen McRae was another excellent scat singer who achieved fame in the mid-1950s. Having learned her trade among the beboppers (she was married to Kenny Clarke for a while), McRae combined a technique apparently inspired by Sarah Vaughan with a special, intangible quality (a rather acid timbre and a skill at dramatizing her lyrics) reminiscent of Billie Holiday. During this same period, Abbey Lincoln abandoned her role as a glamorous singer backed by Hollywood strings and revealed a new voice with a bitter edge – a foretaste of the anger to come.

Frank Sinatra, accompanied by the sumptuous orchestras of Nelson Riddle and Billy May, was a huge success for Capitol. Nat King Cole recorded his first genuine jazz session (*After Midnight*) only to devote himself thereafter to his career as a crooner. The singer-entertainer Sammy Davis Jr proved a hit on Broadway with a style somewhere between jazz and variety. Joe Williams, half crooner and half blues shouter, was the star singer with the Count Basie Orchestra.

The real innovation of the day was vocalese (singing lyrics to an existing instrumental tune or recorded solo). This new singing style had been created by Eddie Jefferson at the end of the 1940s when he put words to Coleman Hawkins's famous solo on 'Body & Soul'. King Pleasure followed close behind. In 1957, the black singer Jon Hendricks joined up with two white singers, Annie Ross and Dave Lambert, to record a collection of Count Basie numbers in vocalese. In 1959, the French singer Mimi Perrin took the experiment further, writing lyrics to accompany the arrangements and solos of Quincy Jones's big band. These lyrics were designed to reflect the precise timbres, inflections and articulation of the instruments. By recording six male singers and six female

LISTENING GUIDE
Betty Carter, *Out There With Betty Carter*, Progressive Jazz.
Abbey Lincoln, *That's Him*, Riverside.
Carmen McRae, *By Special Request*, Decca.
Sammy Davis Jr and Carmen McRae, *Boy Meets Girl*, Decca.
Frank Sinatra, *Come Dance With Me!*, Capitol.
Nat King Cole, *Welcome to the Club*, Capitol.
Joe Williams, *Count Basie Swings & Joe Williams Sings*, Clef.
Eddie Jefferson, *The Jazz Singer*, Festival–Inner City (also known under the title *Hipper Than Thou*, Bear/Zu-Zazz).
Lambert, Hendricks & Ross, *Sing a Song of Basie*, ABC/Paramount.
Double Six, *The Double Six*, BMG.

161

singers twice over (hence their name, the Double Six), Perrin took the art of vocalese to its peak.

On the margins of hard bop

All generations benefited from the jazz revival. Louis Armstrong reinterpreted the music of W C Handy at the head of his All Stars. Up to his death in 1956, Art Tatum recorded prolifically for Norman Granz, either by himself or in the company of prestigious guests such as Ben Webster or Buddy DeFranco. Oscar Peterson and Erroll Garner had become classics. The big bands of Ellington and Basie enjoyed a new lease of life thanks to the arrival of new recruits who had grown up under bebop (see p.64 and p.82). The vibraphone player Cal Tjader spiced up West Coast jazz with Cuban percussion. After moving to the east coast, the flautist Herbie Mann composed the suite *With Flute To Boot* for Machito's band, with guests Johnny Griffin and Curtis Fuller.

The beboppers and the young generation

Because the division between bebop and hard bop was fairly fluid, the beboppers were able to benefit doubly from the new interest in jazz. Bud Powell recorded for Blue Note with Paul Chambers and Art Taylor. Even Coleman Hawkins worked with the avant-garde, elbowing his way in between John Coltrane and Thelonious Monk. And Monk finally found,

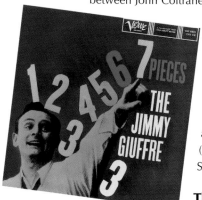

among the young generation, the interpreters his music deserved (see p.118). In 1956, Dizzy Gillespie started recruiting new members from among the hard boppers and jammed in the studio with Roy Eldridge, Sonny Rollins and Stan Getz. This gave Getz the opportunity to show that he was just as capable of assuming a harder edge as the other West Coasters who had moved east (notably Gerry Mulligan with Thelonious Monk and Serge Chaloff with Sonny Clark).

The role of cool jazz in film and experimental music

Meanwhile, Lennie Tristano, the godfather of the white New York school, continued with his experiments. In 1955, he made 'Turkish Mambo' by overdubbing a number of piano parts with different, uncommon metres. On 'Line Up', he tampered with the tape speeds in order to obtain the exact articulation he was after, which he could not achieve in real time.

Cool jazz thrived on the west coast. Dave Brubeck had a hit with 'Take Five', a five-in-a-bar number penned by Paul Desmond. Large and medium-sized bands based in and around Hollywood prospered thanks to the 1953 film *The Wild One* (with music by Shorty Rogers), which created a trend for jazz in the cinema. Rogers himself, monopolized by the studios, was no longer available (see p.136), but Jimmy Giuffre continued to attempt the impossible in the company of the guitarist Jim Hall, forming bands without drums or bass that were inspired by the idea of chamber music. The black west coast drummer Chico Hamilton was doing something similar by introducing a cello into his band (in which Eric Dolphy played alto sax, flute and bass clarinet). Dolphy would later become one of the leaders of the black avant-garde, which was already represented by Ornette Coleman on the west coast label Contemporary with the seminal albums *Something Else!!!* and *Tomorrow Is the Question*. On the east coast, the pianist Cecil Taylor began his recording career in 1955, releasing the albums *In Transition* and *Looking Ahead*.

The 'third stream'

LISTENING
GUIDE
Louis Armstrong, *Plays W C Handy*, Columbia.
Art Tatum, *The Art Tatum–Ben Webster Quartet*, Pablo.
Oscar Peterson, *At the Stratford Festival*, Verve.
Erroll Garner, *Concert by the Sea*, Verve.
Machito, *With Flute To Boot*, Palladium.
Dizzy Gillespie, *For Musicians Only*, Verve.
Serge Chaloff, *Blue Serge*, Capitol.
Lennie Tristano, *Tristano*, Atlantic.
Dave Brubeck, *Take Five*, Columbia.
Jimmy Giuffre, *Western Suite*, Atlantic.
Chico Hamilton, *The Hamilton Man*, Pacific.
Ornette Coleman, *Tomorrow Is the Question*, Contemporary.
Cecil Taylor, *Looking Ahead*, Contemporary.
Modern Jazz Quartet, *Pyramid*, Atlantic.
Outstanding Jazz Compositions of the 20th Century, Columbia.
George Russell Smalltet, *Jazz Workshop*, RCA/Victor.
Gil Evans, *Miles Ahead*, Columbia.

One of Ornette Coleman's first champions was the pianist John Lewis. Reinterpreting the forms of classical music at the head of the Modern Jazz Quartet, Lewis was one of the founders of the 'third stream'. This answered the desire of many jazzmen to combine the expressive vigour and spontaneity of jazz with the harmonic and formal structures of classical music. The other founder of the third stream was the composer and cornet player Gunther Schuller. The trend assumed concrete form between 1955 and 1957 in a series of recordings for Columbia which were brought together on the album *Outstanding Jazz Compositions of the 20th Century* after having been partially released under the title *Music for Brass*. They included ambitious works by J J Johnson, John Lewis, Teo Macero, Charles Mingus, Duke Ellington, Gunther Schuller and George Russell.

Two maverick composers: George Russell and Gil Evans

The most convincing work in this series was probably George Russell's. Well known for his contribution to the repertoire of Dizzy Gillespie as well as for his theoretical work on modes, George Russell never really claimed to be a member of the third stream, but his work from the 1950s (*Jazz Workshop* and *New York, NY*) demonstrates a capacity to renew the relationship between composition and improvisation which he has maintained throughout his career.

The impact made by *Music for Brass* provided an opportunity for Miles Davis to renew his acquaintance with Gil Evans, who had fallen into relative obscurity since their 1949 collaboration. In 1957, the two men made *Miles Ahead*. This was followed a year later by *Porgy & Bess*, in which Gil Evans completely redefined the big-band concept by adding flute and bass clarinet to the sax section and two French horns and a tuba to the brass. A mood magician and an alchemist with combinations of timbre, Evans was also in tune with Davis's preoccupation with mode. He managed to steer clear of the more ponderous aspects of the third stream to compose works of astounding depth.

Bebop from Europe to South Africa

In 1956, while passing through Thailand, Benny Goodman took part in a jam session with the King of Thailand, Bhumibol Adulyadej, a keen amateur saxophonist. While their recordings have been kept secret and no doubt deserve to remain so, they do at least show that jazzmen on tour, whether beboppers or exponents of the mainstream, could now expect to find local jazz partners anywhere in the world.

European students of the American school

When in Europe, Miles Davis used the trio of the French pianist René Urtreger. Chet Baker recorded arrangements by the Frenchman Pierre Michelot and the Belgians Francy Boland and Bobby Jaspar when he was in Paris. Following the example of Sidney Bechet and Kenny Clarke, Americans enjoyed extended stays in Europe. Bud Powell took up residence in Paris, the hub of the European jazz scene. Oscar Pettiford settled in Copenhagen, an essential stopping-off point on the way to Norway and Sweden, and Stan Getz settled in Stockholm. In 1958, the International Youth Band at the Newport Festival included the Yugoslav Dusko Goykovich and the Frenchman Roger Guérin on trumpet, the German Albert Mangelsdorff on trombone, the Swede Bernt Rosengren and the Pole Jan Wroblewski on sax, the Swiss George Grüntz on piano and the Hungarian Gabor Szabo on guitar.

Many Europeans crossed the Atlantic in the opposite direction. The Belgian harmonica player Toots Thielmans played guitar in George Shearing's quintet from 1953. Henri Renaud, the favourite pianist of Americans passing through Paris, recorded in New York. The Austrian pianist Friedrich Gulda performed at Birdland. Bobby Jaspar played in the bands of J J Johnson and Miles Davis. Gabor Szabo and the Japanese pianist Toshiko Akiyoshi studied at the Berklee School of Music in Boston. The Austrian pianist Joe Zawinul had barely arrived at Berklee before he was hired by the trumpeter Maynard Ferguson.

Towards an original form of expression

Some preferred to stay in Europe, where the large permanent orchestras such as those attached to Germany's regional radio stations or the RAI in Italy represented a regular source of work. The French pianist Claude Bolling formed his first big band. The British trumpeter Humphrey Lyttelton progressed from a Hot-Five style to more of a swing band, in which the saxophonist and clarinetist Tony Coe was given his first break. The Charlie Parker-influenced saxophonist John Dankworth brought his wife, the singer Cleo Laine, to public attention and employed the Canadian trumpeter Kenny Wheeler from 1959. The saxophonist Ronnie Scott opened his own club in London in 1959, after a number of years co-leading the Jazz Couriers, pioneers of British bebop, with Tubby Hayes (tenor sax, vibraphone and flute). In Italy, the bebop scene was dominated by the trumpeter Oscar Valdambrini and the tenor saxophonist Gianni Basso. Panned by the critics, Stan Kenton nevertheless had many European disciples, including the German Kurt Hedelhagen and the Frenchman Christian Chevallier. The

message of cool jazz reached the Baltic Republics (nicknamed the Russian West Coast) and was also heeded by Keitaro Miho's Japanese nonet.

In Brazil, the muted tones and harmonic sophistication of West Coast jazz inspired João Gilberto and Antonio Carlos Jobim to create a new samba-derived song form called the bossa nova. In Argentina, Gato Barbieri played the music of Basie and Gillespie in Lalo Schifrin's big band. However, a number of musicians started to break with the American model. In 1959, Joe Harriott, a Jamaican Parker-influenced saxophonist living in London, started to free his writing from the rhythmic regularity and cyclical harmonic structure of jazz. The quintet he led was proof of the vitality of the London-based West Indian scene. In Paris, the pianist Martial Solal showed himself to be just as bold while remaining faithful to the rhythmic and harmonic language of bebop, which he deconstructed and reconstructed with a stunning combination of humour and virtuosity. The drummer of the quintet that recorded *Suite en ré bémol* (*Suite in D Minor*) in 1959 was Daniel Humair, who had recently arrived from Switzerland. In 1954, André Hodeir, a theoretician of musical language in general and swing in particular, started composing ambitious works in which he transposed into the written score the energy and momentum of improvisation. For this he used a technique he called 'simulated improvisation'. In 1957, at the San Remo jazz festival, the pianist Giorgio Gaslini performed 'Tempo e relazione', which he had composed using the twelve-tone scale.

The East breathes, Africa speaks and America answers

In Poland, where the Soviet stranglehold had started to loosen, the Polish Jazz Federation and the Sopot jazz festival were founded in 1956. Warsaw's first Jazz Jamboree was held in 1958. It revealed a very lively bebop scene centred around the pianists Krzysztof Komeda and Andrzej Trzaskowski. De-Stalinization freed Russian jazz from ideological harassment, enabling it finally to concentrate on problems of a musical kind. Whether revivalist, cool jazz or hard bop, the bands that emerged placed great emphasis on improvisation and began to build up good rhythm sections. Vyosmorka ('The Eight') followed in the footsteps of the Jazz Messengers and the trumpeter German Lukianov's quintet took its inspiration from Miles Davis's quintet. In South Africa, the trumpeter Hugh Masekela formed a bebop band named the Jazz Epistles with the pianist Dollar Brand in 1959. While touring in Ghana, Louis Armstrong met the leading exponent of the highlife style, the saxophonist E T Mensah. The drummer Kofi Ghanaba recorded *Africa Speaks, America Answers* in 1956. After settling in New York in 1958, he made a significant impression on the city's black musical community. Yusef Lateef introduced the Yoruba drummer Babatunde Olatunji to John Coltrane.

FREE JAZZ: THE TASTE OF FREEDOM
(1960–1968)

Context

SOCIETY. Decolonization led to the emergence of the Third World, which was racked by coups d'état, plagued by anti-imperialist guerrillas and wooed by the superpowers. The United States sponsored the fight against Castroist rebels in South America and became embroiled in the Vietnam War in 1964.

While young Americans were preoccupied by conscription and Vietnam,  elsewhere in the developed world a whole generation – split between pacifism and violent action – rose up against imperialism, the consumer society and middle-class morality. An interest in the Chinese Cultural Revolution, solidarity with liberation movements and the quest for artistic, political, sexual and spiritual freedom made for a volatile mixture that exploded in 1968. In America, black organizations came together within the Civil Rights Movement

Demonstration by the Black Panthers

to remind John Kennedy of his electoral pledges. As the non-violent actions of the movement were met with acts of criminal brutality (lynchings, attacks and assassinations) in the south, young black Americans adopted a more radical stance and riots occurred with increasing frequency. They culminated in explosions of anger against the assassination of Martin Luther King in 1968. Three years earlier, 'Black Power' had been proclaimed by new black leaders, most prominently those of the Black Panthers, an organization advocating armed self-defence, rejection of conscription and solidarity with revolutionary groups in the Third World. Black intellectuals adopted the slogan 'black is beautiful' to celebrate the values of their community, which they contrasted with the ethical and aesthetic values of white society.

THE MUSIC INDUSTRY. Adopting a cautious attitude towards the new directions in which jazz was moving, the record companies began to show a preference for rock, which was booming. Columbia tried to act as if nothing had changed, while Verve, which had been taken over by MGM, adopted a bold eclecticism that embraced both classic jazz and the more moderate avant-garde. The success of John Coltrane had encouraged the Impulse label to open up its lists to free jazz. Blue Note wavered between hard bop and libertarian tendencies. Strongly supportive of the black cause, Atlantic issued seminal free-jazz recordings, while devoting itself primarily to soul. Prestige took a punt on soul jazz. Riverside went bust.

The chain of responsibilities involved in the production of a record became more complex. Four-track or even eight-track stereo recording allowed sound engineers to indulge in all kinds of manipulation.

Special care was paid to packaging (for example, the Impulse label's gatefold sleeves or Miles Davis's covers featuring photographs of his wives). Credited on the back of the sleeve, artistic directors began to wield greater power. Discrepancies developed between the need for profitability and the preoccupations of the artist, with artists turning increasingly to new independent labels (ESP, Candid) or even self-managed labels (JCOA Records).

The electric guitar market was booming. Many different models of electric piano were launched. In 1965, Harold Rhodes and Leo Fender brought out a portable electric keyboard marketed as the Fender Rhodes piano.

RELATED MUSICAL GENRES. Atlantic turned to southern studios such as Stax (Memphis) or Fame (Muscle Shoals) for complete teams of technicians, instrumentalists, arrangers and even composers, who guided and defined the music of great rhythm-and-blues singers like Otis Redding, Wilson Pickett and Aretha Franklin. The New Orleans style, as sung by Lee Dorsey, was shaped by the black producer and composer Allen Toussaint. In contrast to these robust productions with their southern roots, the black Detroit record company Tamla Motown employed sophisticated production techniques and a team of composers and lyricists (Smokey Robinson and the Brian Holland–Lamont Dozier–Eddie Holland trio, for example) to mould the sound of both singers and groups (Marvin Gaye, Stevie Wonder, the Temptations and the Four Tops, to name but a few), thereby giving the genre a new lease of life while watering it down to some degree. James Brown's forceful style managed to escape the clutches of the producer, and in 1968 he was able to record his famous song 'Say It Loud, I'm Black and Proud'. Faced with the defection of its best musicians to soul, gospel also updated its sound, thanks largely to James Cleveland, who formed mass choirs made up of singers from various black churches.

After the success of the West Side Sound at the beginning of the 1960s, and despite the interest of the Stax label in bluesmen such as Albert King, who appealed to soul-music audiences, the blues went into decline. However, two militant white anti-racists, the musicologist Alan Lomax and the singer Pete Seeger, had been making the young white generation aware of America's multiracial roots. From 1959 onwards, white folk singers shared the stage of the Newport Folk Festival (organized by George Wein on the fringes of the jazz festival) with black bluesmen. The subsequent blues revival led to the rediscovery of old Delta singers such as Skip James and Bukka White as well as the waning stars of the Chicago scene, who converted back to the acoustic guitar.

In Great Britain, the tours undertaken by various bluesmen fuelled the music of the new British groups. The guitarist Jimi Hendrix – a link between British rock (the Beatles and the Rolling Stones) and American rock (the Doors and Jefferson Airplane) and between the black musical legacy and the new psychedelic trend – was a prime example of the interaction involved in the simultaneous development of rock music and the new forms of black popular music. Self-taught skills and collective songwriting enhanced the status of 'the group' and contributed in the short term to the development of unpredictable work free from any hint of academicism.

LISTENING GUIDE
The Blues at Newport, 1964, Vanguard.
James Brown, The James Brown Show Live at the Apollo, King.
Jimi Hendrix, Electric Ladyland, Reprise.
Otis Redding, The Dock of the Bay (The Definitive Collection), Atlantic.
The Temptations, Anthology, Tamla Motown.

Free jazz: wiping the slate clean

Dewey Redman and Ornette Coleman

The most spectacular event of the 1960s was the emergence of the black avant-garde. Called initially the 'new thing' and then 'free jazz', it reflected the political radicalization of black Americans. This new avant-garde received the unconditional support of a generation of fundamentally Marxist critics who were opposed to the old musical order. While the 1960s cannot be reduced to a simple opposition between free jazz and reactionary tendencies (certainly not without looking at the alternatives that emerged on the fringes of free jazz: see p.175), it is nevertheless true that freedom – freedom of conscience, freedom of the body, freedom in terms of production methods – was the guiding principle on all creative fronts in the 1960s. The first person to associate the word 'free' with the word 'jazz' was the alto saxophonist Ornette Coleman, in the title of his December 1960 album *Free Jazz*.

The ramblings of Ornette Coleman and Don Cherry

The title of one of his pieces, 'Ramblin'', says much about the technique into which Ornette Coleman initiated his first regular collaborators from 1958 onwards. These were the trumpeter Don Cherry, the bassist Charlie Haden (one of the rare white musicians among the early activists of free jazz), and the drummer Ed Blackwell. 'Ramblin'' is a blues number and provides an example of Coleman's frequent use of standard structures (blues, AABA) in his early work. But these structures are not strictly measured and, particularly in 'Ramblin'', are therefore relatively elastic. The solos themselves do not respect the structure, which plays the role of a springboard without offering a rigid framework or precise harmonic support. Ornette Coleman's improvisation technique could be described as 'digressive'. His melodic line generally conforms to a series of 'tonal centres', key notes around which the soloist gravitates, moving from one to the next by means of a simple association of ideas. A succession of melodic motifs forms around each of these tonal centres. Based on the variation principle, one motif engenders another.

The system relied on the melodic sense of the double-bass player and soloist and their ability to listen to each other. They had to adapt their playing to one another constantly. This need to listen, which also operated on a rhythmic level between the soloist and the drummer, was frequently extended to the entire group (notably in 'Free Jazz', a 37-minute collective improvisation by two juxtaposed quartets) and refers back to the New Orleans collective style.

Don Cherry drew on what he had learned from working with Ornette Coleman in 'Togetherness', a suite developed by Cherry while he was living in Europe in 1965, in collaboration with the Argentinian saxophonist Gato Barbieri, the German vibraphone player Karl Berger, the French double-bass player Jean-François Jenny-Clark and the Italian drummer Aldo Romano. Recorded in New York later in the year under the title 'Complete Communion', the improvisation in this piece is polythematic. It was based on a principle already explored by Charles Mingus that lay at the heart of much of the jazz starting to be played around this time. In 'Complete Communion', the improvisers take the basic material for their solos not from a particular key or mode but from the succession of themes. This constituted a new framework, destined to replace the old harmonic grids.

LISTENING GUIDE
Ornette Coleman, The Shape of Jazz to Come, 'Lonely Woman', Atlantic.
Ornette Coleman (with Don Cherry, Charlie Haden and Ed Blackwell), Change of the Century ('Ramblin''), Atlantic.
Ornette Coleman (with Charlie Haden and Scott LaFaro, Free Jazz, Atlantic.
Ornette Coleman (with David Izenzon and Charles Moffett), An Evening with Ornette Coleman, Black Lion.

Rejecting the Western notion of 'completeness'

The shifting and superimposition of the melodic material – and even the rhythmic material (listen to the contradiction in the rate of delivery between the opening theme statement and the drumming on 'Lonely Woman') – produce a feeling of instability, indeterminacy and modal ambiguity. This is fundamental to the poignant charm of Ornette Coleman's music, which is permanently and irresolutely suspended between elation and despair. It may seem astonishing that a musician as moving as this tightrope-walker-cum-poet of the written and improvised melodic line, whose compositions now belong to the standard jazz repertoire, could have provoked so much antipathy among his contemporaries. This rejection was due mainly to the fact that Coleman's indeterminacy offended the notion of 'completeness' of a work of art inherent in Western aesthetic criteria.

Ornette Coleman's sound is not 'pretty'. While this was not in itself new in jazz, Coleman went further, rejecting the solidity of timbre and articulation that had prevailed from Louis Armstrong to Charlie Parker. Jazz's swing was being undermined not only by calling into question the idea of metric unity and continuity but also by a rhythmic precipitation and violent melodic and rhythmic discrepancies that produced a feeling of inarticulacy. The intonation itself was imprecise – 'out of tune' to the ears of Coleman's detractors, but 'human', 'subjective' and 'untempered' to those who saw in his music the raw art of the bluesman. The shout, the moan and the growl were re-entering black American music at a time when African Americans were making their anger and dissatisfaction heard. From 1962, together with the drummer Charles Moffett and the white double-bass player David Izenzon – an interpreter of Western contemporary music (which made greater use of the bow) – Coleman radicalized his approach even further. He also took up the trumpet and violin at this time, maintaining that his lack of expertise on them helped to preserve spontaneity.

Cecil Taylor and free-jazz piano

From the mid-50s, Cecil Taylor's work, like that of Ornette Coleman, began to display some of the main features of free jazz. Taylor was an exception in a number of ways, however. He was a pianist, whereas Coleman had excluded the piano as a symbol of Western bourgeois aesthetics and regarded its harmonic function as being over-protective of the soloist. Taylor's early influences included Dave Brubeck and Lennie Tristano, two of the 'whitest' of jazz pianists. Indeed his early solos share a certain stiffness with Brubeck, although they also at times recall Thelonious Monk, in particular in the dissonances and clusters of notes (escaping the classic rules of harmony) that Monk liked to create with the flat of his hand or with his forearm. Hearing these clusters in the work of the various 20th-century Western classical composers whose music informed his writing, Taylor adopted them. He gradually moved away from jazz standards and traditional harmony, retaining only the raw material of extended or compressed chords (freed from conventional harmonic syntax), natural or altered scales, and his own individual melodic clichés. These he hammered out on the keyboard with virtuosic gestures that recalled the 'dripping' technique of the painter Jackson Pollock and the vigorous brushstrokes of Willem de Kooning.

LISTENING GUIDE
Cecil Taylor, *Love for Sale*, United Artists. Cecil Taylor (with Bill Dixon, Jimmy Lyons, Alan Silva, Henry Grimes and Andrew Cyrille), *Conquistador, Unit Structures*, Blue Note.

In Ornette Coleman's work, swing, although under threat, is nevertheless present – in the phrasing as well as in the drumming of his swing-orientated drummers Billy Higgins, Ed Blackwell and Charles Moffett. In Cecil Taylor's music, swing has been replaced by a flood of energy, a momentum that permits the gestural treatment of dense sounds and textures. Whether with a band or (as has increasingly been the case since the 1970s) on unaccompanied piano, his performances, like action painting, represent a physical struggle with matter. His music needs to be experienced live on stage for its full force to be appreciated.

Free jazz's new recruits

A whole wave of musicians surged through the breach opened up by Ornette Coleman and Cecil Taylor. John Coltrane (see pp176–7) was also instrumental in this development – his 'sheets of sound' encouraging all kinds of risks to be taken. Often taking short cuts that allowed them to avoid a bebop apprenticeship and occasionally overusing a vocabulary of multi-purpose scales, many musicians moved straight into free jazz from rhythm and blues or Dixieland. Frequently displaying a very close relationship with their instrument, they placed great emphasis on spontaneity of gesture and authenticity of expression, thus turning to their advantage any imperfections such as squeaking reeds, spontaneous harmonics, tuning differences or noises beyond their control.

Although concerned with the political radicalization of the black movement, many free-jazz musicians displayed not so much their political commitment as a form of mysticism that synthesized elements of Islam,

Buddhism and African animism. The quest for their African roots fused with a feeling of solidarity with and curiosity for the Third World. On stage, this manifested itself in the adoption of traditional costumes and an array of ethnic instruments that were deployed as part of an often amateurish multi-instrumentalism.

Free jazz gets organized

Various stylistic persuasions gradually emerged, initially along purely regional lines. Ornette Coleman left behind a significant but largely underrated following on the west coast, including the trumpeter Bobby Bradford and the clarinetist John Carter, who were co-leaders of the New Art Jazz Ensemble, and the alto saxophonist Sonny Simmons, who often played with the flautist Prince Lasha. Chicago's free-jazz musicians joined forces to fight the indifference of the record labels and to organize the dissemination and teaching of what they called 'the Great Black Music'. This they did within the context of the AACM (Association for the Advancement of Creative Musicians), founded by the pianist Muhal Richard Abrams. This cooperative and the Black Artists Group of Saint Louis, based on the same model, were to play an important role in the 1970s. In New York, Bill Dixon's Jazz Composers' Guild temporarily brought together Sun Ra, Archie Shepp, John Tchicai, Cecil Taylor and three white musicians: Paul Bley, Carla Bley and Michael Mantler. Carla Bley and Michael Mantler formed the Jazz Composers' Orchestra, which in turn set up a non-profit-making foundation (the JCOA) to promote the creation, recording and publication of concertante works for jazz orchestras and soloists.

Free jazz initially favoured small groups – jazz laboratories along the lines of the bebop quintet. While some exponents of free jazz aspired to liberate themselves from thematic material of any kind, others strove to re-establish the relationship between writing and improvisation within a compositional framework. This took the form of orchestral suites with marker themes that served to launch the improvisers or call them back in, pivot themes to articulate the different movements, and thematic grids that unfolded in the background. The exponents of free jazz also had ambitions to produce bigger and denser massed sounds. Wanting to liberate individual energies in order to create a more intense collective sound, they sought to shape the new material by introducing a structure for collective improvisation. However, big bands were rare during the early years of free jazz, and sadly there are no recordings of the Experimental Band that Muhal Richard Abrams directed as early as 1961. By contrast, plentiful recordings allow us to track the career of the mysterious Sonny Blount, alias Sun Ra, who adopted the persona of an extraterrestrial seer.

Having begun his career back in 1930s Chicago, Sun Ra formed his first

LISTENING GUIDE
John Carter–Bobby Bradford (New Art Jazz Ensemble), *Seeking*, Hat Hut.
Michael Mantler (with Gato Barbieri, Pharoah Sanders, Larry Coryell, Don Cherry, Cecil Taylor, Roswell Rudd and Steve Swallow), *The Jazz Composers' Orchestra*, Watt.

Sun Ra in 1970

band, the Arkestra, around 1955. Up to his death in 1993, he was the guru of a community whose most faithful members were the alto saxophonist Marshall Allen and the tenor saxophonist John Gilmore, both converts to the multi-instrumentalism that was standard practice in the band. Starting off in the style of Tadd Dameron's bebop arrangements and passing through rhythm-and-blues and doo-wop phases, Sun Ra started to move closer to New York's free-jazz scene around 1961, presenting imaginary intergalactic extravaganzas in a series of sumptuous visual and acoustic rituals.

Brass

Brass instruments were the poor relations of the first generation of free jazz. This may have been because of the level of technical expertise required and the length of the apprenticeship needing to be served before an expressive response could be obtained from the chosen instrument. Alongside Bobby Bradford and Don Cherry, Bill Dixon was one of the most convincing of free-jazz trumpeters. Activist, unifying force, composer and teacher, Dixon possessed a talent for organization – a quality evident in both his composition and his trumpet playing. At the Cellar Café in 1964, he organized a series of concerts (the 'October Revolution in Jazz') that served as a showcase for the New York avant-garde. While the trombonist Grachan Moncur III defected from hard bop, Roswell Rudd came straight from traditional jazz. His playing harked back to the hearty slide effects of the 'tailgate style' and the expressive sounds of the Ellingtonian jungle.

The free-jazz tenor saxophonists

Free-jazz saxophonists, on the other hand, were legion and showed a marked preference for the tenor sax. A number of them, such as Sam Rivers and John Gilmore, had taken a detour via bebop, but among the great charismatic free-jazz tenor saxophonists – Albert Ayler, Pharoah Sanders and Archie Shepp – more of a honking rhythm-and-blues background can be detected. Albert Ayler was the first to interpret themes from popular forms such as military marches, calypsos, gospel songs, nursery rhymes and funeral dirges. He played these with all the fervour of a preacher, forcing the melodic paraphrase and the timbre and intonation of his instrument into a scream in his frantic quest to express the inexpressible. He alternated

Albert Ayler (with Gary Peacock and Sunny Murray), *Spiritual Unity*, ESP.
Albert Ayler (with Alan Silva and Milford Graves), *Love Cry*, Impulse.
Pharoah Sanders (with Sonny Sharrock and Henry Grimes), *Tauhid*, Impulse.
Archie Shepp, *Archie Shepp–Bill Dixon Quartet*, Savoy.
Archie Shepp (with Grachan Moncur III, Roswell Rudd, Howard Johnson and Beaver Harris), *Mama Too Tight*, Impulse.
Archie Shepp, *The Way Ahead*, Impulse.

melodic variations played at maximum volume with monochrome sounds with distorted textures that he kneaded like dough.

A similar alternation between fervent melodies and acoustic chaos, though with a firmer sax sound, can be heard in the music of Pharoah Sanders. The concept behind his group was clearly inspired by John Coltrane (Sanders became Coltrane's regular collaborator in 1965). Based on fluid drones or ostinatos played by the band, his use of modes is nevertheless more naïve than Coltrane's and draws in a highly imaginative way on African, Eastern and Far-Eastern musical and spiritual traditions. Tormented atmospheres resolve into soothing incantations, and rubato movements with no strict pulse form a prelude to highly articulated trancelike rhythmic passages. Archie Shepp represented the very opposite of this mysticism. Along with Bill Dixon, whom he partnered at the beginning of the 1960s, Shepp was one of the most political and intellectual of the free-jazz musicians. All the same, his music is comprehensible, immediately captivating and rooted in tradition. Influenced by the Marxist critique of history, he put the roots of black American music into a new perspective with his evocations of Africa, the blues and New Orleans marches and his reinterpretations of the repertoire (notably the music of Duke Ellington). On the tenor sax, his generous sonority makes direct reference to Ben Webster, his eruptive phrasing often recalls Sonny Rollins, his melodic line combines the digressive melodic style of Ornette Coleman with John Coltrane's saturation effects, and his interweaving of composed and improvised sections is reminiscent of Charles Mingus's colourful style.

The other saxes

The free-jazz alto saxophone occupies a less prominent place in the history of jazz. Players included: Jimmy Lyons, who remained faithful to the orchestral textures of Cecil Taylor; John Tchicai, whose pirouetting phrases could be heard in the New York Contemporary Five, to which Archie Shepp and Don Cherry belonged; Marion Brown, whose troubled fragility contrasted with the clamorousness of free jazz; and Giuseppi Logan with his frenetic expressionism. Following in the footsteps of John Coltrane, many saxophonists also turned to the soprano sax, which had been neglected since Sidney Bechet's day. It was Steve Lacy, however, who inspired Coltrane to take up the instrument and make it a part of modern jazz. Originally a Dixieland player, Lacy took a long detour via Thelonious Monk, playing with the pianist and studying his music. From Monk he developed a minimalist, rigorous style that found its place both in the heat of free jazz and in combination with Gil Evans's smoother playing.

Archie Shepp

Archie Shepp at the Panafrican Festival
in Algiers in 1969

The versatile Howard Johnson – able to play in
conventional big bands, rock groups, blues
bands and variety orchestras – was one of the
few baritone saxophonists (and tuba players)
during the early years of free jazz who kept his
career going over the following decades. Pat
Patrick, a multi-instrumentalist who played
baritone sax in the totally unstructured sax
section of Sun Ra's Arkestra, sought to force the
instrument out of its usual register by exploiting
its ability to produce shrill sounds.

The rhythm section

The piano was generally unpopular as an
element in free jazz. The few free-jazz pianists
other than Cecil Taylor included Richard
Abrams, Dave Burrell, Don Pullen and Horace Tapscott. They worked in
areas close to those explored by Cecil Taylor, while exploiting many
elements of the traditional jazz-piano vocabulary. It was mainly during the
following decade that they became known.

The guitar was just as unpopular as the piano, perhaps because it was so
closely associated with the overwhelming success of rock music. Sonny
Sharrock nevertheless occupied an important place in Pharoah Sanders's
band, exploiting the instrument's potential for distortion with an almost
instinctive style that involved rubbing the strings in a violent and chaotic
manner.

Freed from their harmonic function, the double-bass players of the black
avant-garde were encouraged to play in a way that involved a greater
degree of interaction with the soloist. In many free-jazz groups, however,
they were still expected to provide a regular pulse in the form of an old-
fashioned ostinato or walking bass based on relatively large intervals; and
where they were not expected to provide a pulse, bassists produced a kind
of continuous drone. The bow might also be used to texture the resulting
background with shrieking harmonics. Black bassists such as Henry Grimes,
Lewis Worrell and Ronnie Boykins continued to favour the instrument's
lower register, providing bands with energy, mass, depth and a solid
foundation. This contrasted with the lighter playing style of the white
bassists of the LaFaro school (see p.182), who were more willing to perform
acrobatics on the higher notes. Charlie Haden was an exception,
performing a very different function in the double quartet that recorded the
album *Free Jazz* from that discharged by his opposite number Scott LaFaro.
In Cecil Taylor's band, Alan Silva provided a voluble bass (with a
predilection for excitedly bowed high notes) that contrasted strongly with
the bass previously supplied by the traditionalist Henry Grimes. Also worthy
of note are the many black bassists recruited from the margins of free jazz,

LISTENING
GUIDE
The New York Art
Quartet (with Roswell
Rudd, John Tchicai,
Lewis Worrell and
Milford Graves), *The
New York Art Quartet*,
ESP.
Marion Brown (with
Dave Burrell), *Three for
Shepp*, Impulse.
Giuseppi Logan (with
Don Pullen and Milford
Graves), *The Giuseppi
Logan Quartet*, ESP.
Steve Lacy and Roswell
Rudd (with Henry
Grimes and Dennis
Charles), *School Days*,
Hat Hut.

such as Reggie Workman, Cecil McBee and Richard Davis.

There were two schools of free-jazz drumming. The first, which included drummers such as Dennis Charles, remained attached to traditional methods of marking the beat. This they treated in a more or less allusive, continuous manner while varying their (often Africa-influenced) timbres through the use of tom-toms, snare drum without snare, felt sticks or their bare hands. Charles Moffett and Ed Blackwell, Ornette Coleman's drummers, were veritable dancers. Blackwell successfully combined the phrasing of New Orleans-style drumming with configuration inherited from Max Roach. Other drummers, however, saw tempo as a form of alienation and considered themselves as soloists in their own right, free to intervene as they saw fit without having to provide any kind of beat or accompaniment. Shifting his centre of gravity from the snare drum to the cymbals, Sunny Murray created a haze of sound made up of murmurings, rustlings and crashes. Milford Graves played in an airier manner based on a wider and more detailed range of drums and accessories. Andrew Cyrille maintained an ambiguous relationship with tempo and the vocabulary of bebop, which he learned from Philly Joe Jones. Jones and a number of his colleagues were happy to accept invitations from the free-jazz scene, either as occasional defectors like Joe Chambers or as genuinely versatile musicians like Beaver Harris.

Controlled freedom

The term 'free jazz' was so attractive that musicians hesitated for a long time over what to call the music being made on the fringes of the free-jazz movement, pretending to see it as nothing but an extension of bebop. It is sometimes referred to as 'modal jazz' contemporaneous with free jazz, although this is an ambiguous term. The musicians in Miles Davis's second quintet (1964–8) described themselves as practising 'controlled freedom', condescendingly insinuating that free jazz was uncontrolled. But a number of free jazz musicians did openly express their aversion to instrumental discipline. Sonny Sharrock even declared that the greatest artists were those with no technique. Despite this, there was no unbridgeable gulf between the two aesthetic approaches.

Charles Mingus and Eric Dolphy: the temptation of free jazz

The hard boppers were unsettled by the arrival of free jazz. Many were jealous of the success achieved by the exponents of free jazz using the minimum of technique – a success which called into question their own hard-won musicianship. But while some denounced free jazz as a fraud, others could relate to it. From 'Pithecanthropus Erectus' to the tormented

THE ASCENSION OF JOHN COLTRANE

Despite his hypertechnical schooling in bebop and hard bop, John Coltrane was revered by the free-jazz musicians because he transcended traditional harmony: the 'sheets of sound' he derived from it blurred the legibility of conventional chord progressions. He himself forged strong links with the free-jazz movement. In June 1965, he even invited some of its leading lights into the studio to see what he could learn from them. The resulting long, turbulent collective improvisation was released under the title *Ascension*. When he died in 1967, the music at his funeral was provided by the Ornette Coleman and Albert Ayler quartets.

The turning point of modal jazz

The year after making *Giant Steps* (see p.158) – an album that was a summation of his work up to then – was a period of withdrawal and preparation for Coltrane. During it he experimented intensively before setting off in a new direction. He formed a pianoless quartet (with Don Cherry), spent time looking for the right rhythmic support, sought new ways of harmonizing the blues and experimented with harmonics and multiphonics. In Autumn 1960, he recorded the new Broadway hit 'My Favourite Things' on the soprano saxophone, as if no longer satisfied with the high, shrill notes obtainable on the tenor. He dismantled the number's AAA'B structure, replacing its cyclical form with a continuous form whose B section (12:33–12:48), instead of being trivialized by its inclusion in each chorus, is postponed until the end of the piece, when it has the full force of a dramatic denouement. The A melody serves as an interspersed leitmotif based on a persistent two-chord structure, sometimes minor (2:35–3:08, 7:26–9:41) and sometimes major (3:25–5:56, 9:59–12:15), around which the soloists express themselves for as long as they wish, improvising in one mode and then the other. The hypnotic character of the harmonic ostinato tirelessly repeated by the rhythm section had a certain resonance with a public that was starting to appreciate the attractions of Indian music. Jazz was finally moving away from the logic of harmonic mobility that had culminated in bebop. Coltrane immerses the listener in a unique atmosphere for nearly 14 minutes.

Playing 'out' and polymodalism

Having found the ideal rhythm section (McCoy Tyner on piano, Jimmy Garrison on double bass and Elvin Jones on drums), Coltrane began over the course of several months to depart from the strict diatonicism (exclusive use of the notes belonging to a particular mode) of traditional modal music. Just as he had superimposed chords within the context of functional harmony, he was now tempted to superimpose different types of modes (polymodalism) and even to depart completely from the chosen mode – but not without also exploiting the results of his harmonic experimentation on *Giant Steps*. This resulted in a feeling of extraordinary tension, intensified by the combination of the melodic line with his sax sound, which he constantly reinvented (using growls, shrieks and multiphonics), and an extremely dense rhythmic division of the phrase. The members of the rhythm section multiplied their entries in a polyrhythmic sharing of the space and a permanent sense of harmonic irresolution.

The final quest

And yet Coltrane still felt that McCoy Tyner's chords were too legible, too directive. As early as 1963, in 'Impressions', while respecting the strict AABA structure borrowed from Miles Davis's 'So What', Coltrane made the piano and then Jimmy Garrison on double bass stop playing (6:33 and 7:29 respectively), so that he alone confronted the wave of energy created by Elvin Jones on drums. In June 1965, he recorded 'Vigil', a duet for saxophone and drums. This was followed a few days later by *Ascension*, made with the leading exponents of free jazz. That autumn he brought Pharoah Sanders into the band and added a second percussionist, Rashied Ali. Elvin Jones could not stand the totally free playing of his new colleague and left the band.

Finally, Coltrane's second wife, Alice, replaced McCoy Tyner on piano. The rhythm section was no longer about articulation, but about setting the space around the soloist vibrating in sympathy with the chosen modal landscape. The regular pulse gave way to a rubato pulse (already experimented with by his first quartet) that proceeded in huge waves with an irregular, slow backwash. For some, this was the end of the road. The history of jazz stopped here, with the disappearance of swing. Nevertheless, some irreducible momentum remained, some plastic rhythmic quality that was already present in the introduction to Louis Armstrong's 'West End Blues', and this continued to differentiate jazz from any other music.

LISTENING
GUIDE
John Coltrane, *Coltrane Jazz*, Atlantic.
John Coltrane, *My Favourite Things*, Atlantic.
John Coltrane, *Afro Blue Impressions* ('Impressions'), Pablo.
John Coltrane, *Love Supreme*, Impulse.
John Coltrane, *Ascension*, Impulse.
John Coltrane, *Expression* ('Offering'), Impulse.

John Coltrane began listening to the records of Ravi Shankar in the early 1960s and became interested in Indian, Algerian, Chinese and Japanese modes, all of which helped to enrich his vocabulary. He was particularly interested in the pentatonic modes, whose roots went back to the ancient musics of Europe and Africa. Since the 1950s, Africa had been the inspiration for many of Coltrane's pieces, and his association with Babatunde Olatunji in the 1960s inspired a number of orchestral, structural and polyrhythmic ideas that he shared with his rhythm section. His fundamental preoccupation, however, lay elsewhere and his music gradually acquired the air of a sacred offering, an interior journey towards fundamental truths that would allow him to enter into sympathetic vibration with the cosmos. This is the feeling conveyed by 'Offering', recorded in 1967 a few months before his death.

Charles Mingus

suite 'Meditations on Integration', Charles Mingus had anticipated free jazz with his questioning of formal structures, his acoustic excesses, his use of collective improvisation and his generally subversive approach.

His time with Charlie Parker and his experience as a frustrated classical cellist had left him with a highly developed critical faculty. Mingus sympathized to some extent with the aims of free jazz, but he criticized the tendency to make no distinction between truly creative artists and imposters.

Mingus's new collaborator Eric Dolphy (alto saxophone, flute and bass clarinet) was involved with the avant-garde movement. Hailing from the west coast, he played in Ornette Coleman's double quartet (*Free Jazz*) before joining John Coltrane's quartet for several months and helping to take it in the direction of free jazz. Dolphy's tuning was not always exemplary. As with Ornette Coleman and Charles Mingus, his poetic personality meant that he had little time for matters such as technical perfection. He liked to step beyond the confines of melodic and rhythmic contours – just as painters had been doing throughout the century. As both soloist and leader, he found his most committed disciples among the exponents of free jazz. While his playing style was directly influenced by Charlie Parker and grid-based improvisation, and while he respected the relevant procedures, he also twisted them around, indulging in alterations of timbre, rushed or abruptly terminated lines and vertiginous leaps from the lower to the upper registers. A leap just as big took him to the threshold of free jazz on his album *Out To Lunch*, recorded in 1964 a few months before his death.

LISTENING GUIDE
Charles Mingus (with Eric Dolphy and Jaki Byard), *The Great Concert, Paris, April 1964*, America.
Eric Dolphy (with Booker Little and Jaki Byard), *Far Cry*, Riverside.
Eric Dolphy (with Freddie Hubbard, Bobby Hutcherson, Richard Davis and Tony Williams), *Out To Lunch!*, Blue Note.

On the margins of free jazz

Within Dolphy and Mingus's circle were many musicians who had learned their trade under bebop and who walked the line between free jazz and the rest of modern jazz. One of them was Booker Little (d.1961), a direct descendant of Kenny Dorham and Clifford Brown. His playing had a sombre, mysterious, languid quality which contrasted strongly with Clifford Brown's optimism and poetic loquaciousness. A regular collaborator of Eric Dolphy, Little liked to claim that there was no such thing as a wrong note. He invented new forms in order to break away from the repetitive chorus structure and experimented with less common metres (5, 7 and 9 beats in a bar) that gradually acquired currency during the 1960s. He passed freely from one time signature to another ('Moods in Free Time') and interrupted regular tempi with drawn-out flights of fancy of great poignancy ('Quiet Please'). Jaki Byard, a regular collaborator of Mingus and Dolphy, covered the whole gamut of jazz piano from Earl Hines to the avant-garde in an astonishing stylistic kaleidoscope. Playing in the band of the hard bopper

LISTENING
GUIDE
Booker Little (with Eric
Dolphy), *Out Front*,
Candid.
Booker Ervin (with Jaki
Byard, Richard Davis
and Alan Dawson), *The
Freedom Book*, Prestige.
Roland Kirk, *The
Inflated Tear*, Atlantic.
Jackie McLean, *New &
Old Gospel*, Blue Note.
Bobby Hutcherson (with
Freddie Hubbard, Sam
Rivers, Andrew Hill,
Richard Davis and Joe
Chambers), *Dialogue*,
Blue Note.
Sam Rivers, *Fuchsia
Swing Song*, Blue Note.
Andrew Hill (with Kenny
Dorham and Eric
Dolphy), *Point of
Departure*, Blue Note.

Booker Ervin – a candid, driving tenor saxophonist of the Texan school – he led a remarkably subversive rhythm section.

Byard, the bassist Richard Davis and the drummer Alan Dawson never missed an opportunity to pull the rug from under the leader's feet or trip the saxophonist up in order to challenge his technical assurance and stimulate his poetic imagination.

Playing in a style that encompassed free jazz, hard bop and rhythm and blues, Roland Kirk used Jaki Byard as his pianist on several occasions. Kirk took multi-instrumentalism to extreme lengths. In addition to the flute, he played two or three saxophones simultaneously and often resorted to rare or improvised instruments, adding a wide range of accessories of his own. Drawn to free jazz, Jackie McLean even invited Ornette Coleman to play trumpet on his album *New and Old Gospel* in 1967. He was not, however, the first artist from the Blue Note stable to turn his attention to free jazz. Freddie Hubbard had already played in Coleman's double quartet and Bobby Hutcherson played vibraphone with Archie Shepp for a while in addition to making his own highly ambiguous recordings for Blue Note. The label welcomed the leaders of free jazz (Cecil Taylor, Ornette Coleman and Don Cherry) as well as 'in-between' players (such as the pianist Andrew Hill and the saxophonist Sam Rivers) into its studios.

Emancipation through assimilation

Many of those who aspired to be progressive nevertheless refused to completely dismiss their harmonic inheritance. They preferred assimilation to flat rejection, absorbing the musical languages to which their curiosity led them. This curiosity was far from alien to the free-jazz musicians, but in their case it was accompanied by a tendency to reject the old. It also often operated on a spontaneous basis, as theory was suspect in their eyes. George Russell, on the other hand, arrived at this deconditioning of the reflexes inherited from tonal harmony through his theoretical work on modes. In his case it took the form not of a rejection but of a broadening of perspective. Bill Evans undertook his own reappraisal of functional harmony and its relationship with individual initiative within the band (see p.185). The outcome of this was patient discipline rather than loud spontaneity. John Coltrane's approach may have led in the end to free jazz (see pp176–7) but it too got there through a mastery of the instrument and modal vocabulary that had little to do with free jazz's reappraisal of the beat and emphasis on gestural spontaneity. McCoy Tyner, the pianist in Coltrane's first quartet, helped him to free himself not by replacing a harmonic style with a percussive one (Cecil Taylor's approach), but by replacing the old harmonic progressions with new chord sequences drawn from a modal vocabulary. Alternating an emphasis on the first beat of the bar with polyrhythmic ambiguity, his accompaniments relied on Jimmy Garrison's solid pulse on the double bass. The drummer Elvin Jones, the

LISTENING
GUIDE
George Russell (with
Don Ellis and Eric
Dolphy), *Ezz-Thetic*,
Riverside.

third member of the rhythm section, divided the irregular note values of the *chabada* rhythm into equal triplets and redistributed them among all the different elements of the drum kit. He thereby produced a tumultuous acoustic and rhythmic swell which, while not exactly stating the beat, nevertheless hinted at its presence.

LISTENING GUIDE

Miles Davis (with George Coleman and the Miles Davis Quintet), *The Complete Concert 1964: My Funny Valentine + Four and More* ('Stella by Starlight'), Columbia.

Miles Davis (with Wayne Shorter and the Miles Davis Quintet), *ESP* ('Eighty-One'), Columbia.

Miles Davis (with Wayne Shorter and the Miles Davis Quintet) *Cookin' at the Plugged Nickel*, Columbia.

The new Miles Davis quintet

A former student of Alan Dawson, Tony Williams transposed this effervescence into predominantly 'binary' phrasing based on the even quavers of Latin music and rock (compare this with the irregular phrasing on 'Eighty-One', in which a transition from one to the other is made within each solo). Attracted for a while by free jazz, Williams juggled with different forms of phrasing, superimposing them and breaking them down. He would divide the beat up into smaller and smaller values before simplifying it again, creating deceptive note values based on a playful, virtuosic arithmetic which the other members of Davis's quintet either joined in with or gleefully resisted.

On the face of it, Ron Carter embodied the black double-bass tradition, decrying the frivolity of the white school of bass playing led by Scott LaFaro. But although he produced a round, full, dark and deep sound and was the mainstay around which the others rallied in moments of confusion, his playing was generally far removed from the strict articulation of the beat typical of the walking-bass style. His lines and note placement could even become extraordinarily complex at times. Under his fingers, 'Stella by Starlight', a song familiar to every jazz fan, plunges the listener into an almost unbearable state of uncertainty.

Herbie Hancock, the remaining member of Davis's rhythm section, was heir to three traditions: Horace Silver's funky piano, the kind of harmonic and rhythmic support provided by McCoy Tyner, and the impressionistic style of Bill Evans. Influenced by Evans and encouraged by his former leader, the trumpeter Donald Byrd, Hancock became interested in early 20th-century French music, from Claude Debussy to Lili Boulanger. To its harmonic evasiveness (displacement, superimposition, suggestion, silence), he added a rhythmic quality, in collaboration with Carter and Williams, that delighted Miles Davis.

Herbie Hancock

After working for a while with the tenor saxophonist George Coleman, a great second-generation hard bopper who feigned a lofty indifference to the whims of Davis's rhythm section, Williams, Carter and Hancock found their ideal opposite number in the figure of Wayne Shorter. Having been the musical director of Art Blakey's Jazz Messengers for five years, Shorter was experiencing a second flush of youth, reinventing not only his playing but also his writing. This provided the quintet with some of its most beautiful numbers, unsettling compositions that at the same time sound like classics.

Miles Davis intensified this element of mystery and emphasized the strangeness of the moods created by the band by issuing enigmatic instructions. He also knew how to give his collaborators a free hand,

Initially, modal jazz involved suspending all harmonic movement, instead providing the improviser with a reference point in the form of an ostinato, a persistent sounding of the tonic. Later, harmonic progressions (sometimes of a radical nature) were reintroduced above a bass pedal-note, a kind of drone in the lower register, played more or less continuously without modulation. The rhythm section would avoid any sequence of notes or chords capable of evoking functional harmony, in particular the II–V progression and even the V7 chord (see p.86). If this chord was needed, its third was replaced by a fourth, which effectively removed any major or minor character. McCoy Tyner was the expert in chords built on successive fourths. Even in their melodic playing, both improvisers and composers tended to favour the fourth (the opening notes of 'ESP' and 'Maiden Voyage', for example), thereby breaking with the traditions of tonal music, which is built around the third.

Wayne Shorter

While free jazz adopted a kind of harmonic atheism, modal jazz cast an agnostic eye over the dogma of tonal harmony. The music acquired a heightened sense of mystery and the soloist benefited from greater freedom.

The musicians were even able to regain a total harmonic freedom of movement by using the new modal colours in accordance with a new form of harmonic syntax that was often allusive, elliptical and highly abstract. Soloists tackled this new mobility by relying on their knowledge of the different modes, particularly the pentatonic scales. This knowledge allowed them to deal with harmonic turbulence without changing scale or, conversely, to move from one scale to another and play in several at the same time with astounding ease.

Rhythm was affected by similar changes. In addition to the emergence (under the influence of rock music and Caribbean and Brazilian musics) of metres other than 4/4, composers and members of rhythm sections were tempted to abandon the division of the beat into uneven quavers in favour of a division into two, or sometimes three, even quavers. The new generation took a greater interest in the specifics of Latin rhythms than the early beboppers had done. On *Inventions and Dimensions*, Herbie Hancock and Paul Chambers respond (with no prior compositional framework) to the polyrhythmic playing of Willie Bobo and 'Chihuahua' Martinez, two percussionists active on the New York Latin scene. For their part, the jazz drummers, while not yet possessing an organic understanding of the rhythms of the African diaspora, derived from them a new imaginative vocabulary – as illustrated by Joe Chambers on Wayne Shorter's 'El Gaucho' and by Elvin Jones on John Coltrane's 'Africa'.

LISTENING GUIDE

Miles Davis, *ESP*, Columbia.
Herbie Hancock, *Maiden Voyage, Inventions and Dimensions*, Blue Note.
Wayne Shorter, *Adam's Apple*, Blue Note.
John Coltrane, *Africa/Brass*, Impulse.

appealing to their sense of 'controlled freedom' or 'extrasensory perception' (whence the album title *ESP*). The instruction for this was 'time no changes' (in other words a fixed tempo with no predetermined harmonic progression). On stage, Davis's musicians could digress so far that they completely lost their bearings and even the tempo, the restatement of the theme being the final signal for any possible regrouping. They had come round to Ornette Coleman's style of digressive improvisation, which Miles Davis had criticized at the beginning of the 1960s as a dead end. A decade later, he confessed to feeling very close to Don Cherry.

Black and white

Only rarely venturing near such extreme approaches as this, Blue Note's back catalogue nevertheless reflects the development of the black scene on the margins of free jazz under the intersecting influences of John Coltrane's quartet and Miles Davis's quintet during the 1960s. The members of these two groups were constantly renewing partnerships with former collaborators, with the result that their names appear on the backs of numerous record sleeves. The names of other important musicians also feature. These include the trumpeters Woody Shaw and Freddie Hubbard, the saxophonists Joe Henderson and James Spaulding, the pianist Cedar Walton, the organist Larry Young, the double-bass players Reggie Workman and Richard Davis, and the drummers Joe Chambers and Pete LaRoca. While black jazzmen seemed to have regained their position as the true leaders of modern jazz, a number of white musicians were also to be found among the 1960s avant-garde. Their preoccupations were often similar to those of their black counterparts but they brought a different sensibility to their work, as illustrated by the revolution brought about by Scott LaFaro in double-bass playing. By the end of the 1950s, LaFaro had acquired a fluency on the instrument that allowed him to abandon the walking bass and to phrase instead as though he were playing a wind instrument. Although gaining in speed, he lost the power and depth that characterized the playing of his black colleagues (something his successors compensated for with amplification). Killed in a road accident in 1961, LaFaro spawned a long line of virtuoso white double bassists, including Gary Peacock. The drummer Paul Motian, who played alongside LaFaro in the Bill Evans trio, also stopped accentuating the beat, transforming the drum kit instead into a chamber-music instrument – something which did not prevent him from sympathizing, like Peacock, with Albert Ayler and Don Cherry.

LISTENING GUIDE
Wayne Shorter (with Reginald Workman and Joe Chambers), *Adam's Apple*, Blue Note.
Joe Henderson (with McCoy Tyner and Elvin Jones), *Inner Urge*, Blue Note.
McCoy Tyner (with Joe Henderson, Ron Carter and Elvin Jones), *The Real McCoy*, Blue Note.
Larry Young (with Woody Shaw, Joe Henderson and Elvin Jones), *Unity*, Blue Note.

Chamber jazz and early jazz-rock

This 'chamber jazz' approach was the preserve of a considerable number of white musicians who were the successors to the West Coast tradition. They included Jim Hall, who in the 1960s was to Wes Montgomery's guitar what Bill Evans was to McCoy Tyner's piano. Jimmy Giuffre, one of Hall's former collaborators, invented a kind of free chamber jazz based on half-tones. This he did together with the pianist Paul Bley (a one-time disciple of Oscar Peterson before converting to the ideas of Ornette Coleman) and the double-bass player Steve Swallow (positioned stylistically halfway between LaFaro and Haden).

Alternating with Gary Peacock in Paul Bley's trios (alongside Paul Motian and later Barry Altschul on drums), Steve Swallow joined the vibraphone player Gary Burton, the guitarist Larry Coryell and the drummer Bob Moses to play music that was very free but at the same time impregnated with rock music, country music and the folk songs that young singer-songwriters had been inspired to write upon coming into contact with these two genres. From 1965, as improvisation started to occupy an important place in rock music and Frank Zappa's musical plunderings began to include jazz, attempts increased to bring jazz and rock together. These attempts were centred in San Francisco and New York, around the black pianist and saxophonist John Handy, the flautist Jeremy Steig and the vibraphone player Mike Mainieri. While Gary Burton was revolutionizing the vibraphone with his four-stick technique and extremely muted, vibrato-less sound, Mainieri was continuing Milt Jackson's legacy, but on an amplified instrument. The use of amplification was already gaining enthusiastic support from all types of instrumentalists (such as the black saxophonist Eddie Harris, the trumpeter Don Ellis and a growing number of double-bass players) and the electric piano was also starting to become widespread (for example, Joe Zawinul with Cannonball Adderley).

Influenced by Stan Getz and John Coltrane, the tenor saxophonist Charles Lloyd exuded a kind of musical ecstasy that was closer to Californian 'flower power' than 'black power'. Recalling the groups of John Coltrane and Miles Davis, his quartet was a big hit with the hippie generation, thanks mainly to support from the pianist Keith Jarrett, whose playing was marked by folk, rock and soul influences, but thanks also to the contribution of the black drummer Jack DeJohnette, who pushed the binary energy of rock and the ternary polyrhythms of jazz to the limits of the rational.

The other star of jazz piano in the second half of the 1960s was Chick Corea. Of Italian ancestry, influenced by his contact with Latin jazz and combining the legacies of McCoy Tyner, Bill Evans and Bud Powell, Corea contributed to the piano–bass–drums catalogue with his album *Now He Sings, Now He Sobs*, recorded with the black drummer Roy Haynes and the double-bass player Miroslav Vitous, who was of Czech origin.

Large and medium-sized groups

LISTENING
GUIDE
Gary Burton–Carla Bley,
A Genuine Tong Funeral,
RCA.
Gil Evans, The
Individualism of Gil
Evans, Verve.
Don Ellis, Electric Bath,
Columbia.

With George Russell and Charles Mingus, the problems of jazz composition were refocused on smaller big bands with severely reduced sections. Continuing work done with a nine-piece band in the 1940s and a ten-piece band in the 1950s, Gil Evans used larger groups that went beyond big band conventions in that they were open to all members of the wind family (including clarinets, flutes and double reeds). He obtained fascinating textures based on extended tempi. These perfectly captured the vulgar accents of Kurt Weill's 'Bilbao Song' and 'Barbara Song'.

Despite denying that Weill was an inspiration, the self-taught composer Carla Bley produced music that was often reminiscent of his works. It was based on dramatic and mischievous writing incorporating elements of the waltz and the tango, the nightclub and the bandstand, Satie's 'pear-shaped pieces' and tacky operetta. Bley's music was much performed at the time (especially by her first husband Paul Bley and Art Farmer's quartet), and her success allowed her to realize her own orchestral projects either with the Jazz Composers' Orchestra or based around Gary Burton's quartet.

Having experimented in various ways (including twelve-tone improvisation, variations of tempo and metrical superimposition) with small groups in the company of Jaki Byard and Paul Bley at the end of the 1960s, the trumpeter Don Ellis led a big band that included electric keyboards, an Indian sitar and Latin percussion, using metres from India and the Middle East.

On the margins of the avant-garde

LISTENING
GUIDE
John Coltrane and
Johnny Hartman,
Impulse.
Sonny Rollins (with Don
Cherry), Our Man in
Jazz, Victor/RCA
Sonny Rollins (with
Herbie Hancock), Now's
the Time, Victor/RCA.
Oscar Peterson, Mellow
Mood, MPS.
Dexter Gordon (with
Herbie Hancock), Takin'
Off, Blue Note.

In July 1960, Charles Mingus and Max Roach organized a parallel event at the Newport Jazz Festival in protest against the conformism of the official programme. The alternative bill featured Booker Little, Eric Dolphy and Jimmy Knepper side by side with Coleman Hawkins, Roy Eldridge and Jo Jones. During the decade, the veteran jazzman Pee Wee Russell would perform pieces by Ornette Coleman, and Duke Ellington would record with Charles Mingus and Max Roach and separately with John Coltrane. Coltrane would even accompany the crooner Johnny Hartman. Searching furiously for an identity, Sonny Rollins recorded with Don Cherry one moment and Coleman Hawkins the next, alternating standards – reharmonized by Herbie Hancock or Jim Hall – with calypsos performed with choir and percussion. Oscar Peterson showed himself to be receptive to the music of Bill Evans. Having survived the horrors of prison, Dexter Gordon recorded with different rhythm sections made up of Blue Note artists ranging from Bud Powell to Herbie Hancock.

Soul jazz and commercial temptations

There was no clear dividing line between the founders of hard bop and their successors. Indeed, the innovations in playing and writing made by the new soloists (Woody Shaw, McCoy Tyner and Wayne Shorter, to name just three) could be enjoyed by the veterans of hard bop (including Art Blakey and

BILL EVANS: THE OTHER REVOLUTION

At the beginning of 1965, the double-bass player Gary Peacock and the drummer Paul Motian left Bill Evans in order to return to the avant-garde. Asked by Jean-Louis Ginibre about the meaning of the word 'free', Bill Evans replied: 'For me, "freedom" is to make room where there isn't any to start with. You take a music part. It seems there's no freedom in there, but if you take the time, and if you understand what's in the part, you'll find as much freedom as you want. You can also throw the part away, sit down on the piano, play with your elbows and say: "This is freedom". Not for me. The most valuable freedom is the one which has strength, because it is won against something solid, something rigid.'

The phrase 'quiet revolution' has often been used in connection with Bill Evans. During the 1960s, however, he was considered as more of a lounge pianist. The clamours of free jazz drowned out the discreet confidences of this white pianist, who, after having started out as a firm-handed successor to Bud Powell and Lennie Tristano, introduced a new quality of touch into jazz. In the 1970s, it became clear that he had influenced a sizeable majority of the pianists who followed him. His heirs included not only pianists but also guitarists, double-bass players, drummers and even saxophonists and trumpeters. This was because Bill Evans had been the first to allow the other members of his trio to speak with an equal voice and because the principle on which his trio functioned was interaction between the musicians. With Evans, instead of simply providing the harmonic and rhythmic décor, the bassist Scott LaFaro and the drummer Paul Motian made their instruments sing. Formed at the end of 1959 (and hit hard by LaFaro's death in 1961), Bill Evans's trio opened up territory for the circulation of ideas — ideas that modern jazz seized upon.

Bill Evans's quiet revolution was also directed at harmonic content — through his mastery of voicing, through the melodic quality of his progressions and through the way in which he multiplied the possibilities of functional harmony exponentially by drawing on the modal vocabulary. He brought to his improvisation and real-time experimentation the modal expertise of the masters of classical piano from the beginning of the 20th century: Scriabin, Fauré, Debussy, Satie and Ravel.

LISTENING
GUIDE
Bill Evans (with Scott LaFaro and Paul Motian), *Waltz for Debby*, Riverside.
Bill Evans (with Scott LaFaro and Paul Motian), *Sunday Evening at the Village Vanguard*, Village.
Bill Evans (with Gary Peacock and Paul Motian), *Trio 64*, Verve.

LISTENING
GUIDE
Horace Silver, *Song For My Father*, Blue Note.
Lee Morgan, *The Sidewinder*, Blue Note.
Cannonball Adderley (with Joe Zawinul), *Mercy, Mercy, Mercy*, Capitol.
Stan Getz, *Focus*, Verve.
George Benson, *It's Uptown*, Columbia.
Wes Montgomery (with Oliver Nelson), *Goin' out of My Head*, Verve.
Oliver Nelson, *The Blues and the Abstract Truth*, Impulse.
Quincy Jones, *Quintessence*, Impulse.
Thad Jones and Mel Lewis, *Live at the Village Vanguard*, Solid State.
Mongo Santamaria, *Mongo*, Fantasy.
Cal Tjader (with Eddie Palmieri), *El Sonido Nuevo*, Verve.
Stan Getz, *Getz/Gilberto*, Verve,
Gerry Mulligan, *Concert Jazz Band*, Verve.
Paul Desmond, *Take Ten*, Victor/RCA.
Lee Konitz, *Motion*, Verve.
Max Roach, *We Insist!*, Candid.
Nina Simone, *Live at the Village Gate*, Colpix.
Jeanne Lee, *The Newest Sound Around*, RCA.
Mark Murphy, *Rah*, Riverside.

Horace Silver) as well as by their earliest disciples (Donald Byrd, Lee Morgan and others). At the same time, the Adderley brothers' quintet, the Jazz Crusaders and a whole host of organists (including Jack McDuff and John Patton) and guitarists (including Grant Green and George Benson) were cultivating the special empathy that existed between hard bop and soul music, not infrequently allowing themselves to be seduced by the latter's musical simplicity and commercial potential.

Wes Montgomery and Jim Hall were the godfathers of the next generation of guitarists, those of the 1970s. Montgomery had no qualms about assuming the role of musician-as-product that the producer Creed Taylor foresaw for him. On Verve, and then on his own label CTI, Taylor promoted highly commercial ventures backed up with monumental arrangements (scoring a few happy successes along the way – Eddie Sauter's string arrangements on Stan Getz's *Focus*, for example). The arranger Oliver Nelson was sidetracked from pursuing a career as a musical innovator in the same way. Quincy Jones, the other orchestra leader and promising arranger from the beginning of the decade, was sucked into both the music industry (as vice-president of Mercury) and the film industry. The responsibility of rejuvenating the big-band tradition while preserving its orchestral principles fell to the black trumpeter Thad Jones and the white drummer Mel Lewis.

Latin jazz, bossa nova and the rebirth of cool

Contaminated by soul music, Latin jazz found itself some new leaders (the percussionists Ray Barretto, Willie Bobo and Mongo Santamaria, and the pianist and arranger Eddie Palmieri), but remained torn between its various stylistic elements. It was also frequently compromised by commercialization. In 1962, an encounter between Stan Getz and the Brazilian singer João Gilberto led to an instant infatuation with the rhythms and repertoire of the bossa nova on the part of jazz musicians from Coleman Hawkins to Archie Shepp. The alto saxophonist Paul Desmond seized upon the discreet elegance of the bossa nova as an opportunity to further underline the desperate sense of detachment in his character. Lee Konitz, by contrast, flirted with the avant-garde, recording in a trio with Elvin Jones and in a duo with Jim Hall and later Joe Henderson. While West Coast jazz was being swallowed up by Hollywood, Gerry Mulligan rediscovered his talent as an arranger when he led the Concert Jazz Band, which he formed in 1960. Chet Baker quit the scene in 1966 after having his jaw shattered by drug dealers, and Art Pepper went off to jail.

New voices

Although largely neglected by free jazz, black female singers were certainly not untouched by the radicalization that was under way. Abbey Lincoln eschewed any attempt at charm and lyricism in her rendition of *We Insist: Freedom Now Suite* composed by Max Roach. Nina Simone, mixing jazz, variety, blues and folk song, adopted a caustic, corrosive tone that spoke of the hurt and bitterness of her community. Far removed from the usual mannerisms of sung jazz, Jeanne Lee emphasized the tender, fragile aspects of the black American singing tradition, drawing on blues, cradle songs, rural laments and urban ballads.

After re-examining, in the company of the pianist Ran Blake, the conventions governing the interplay between singer and accompanist, Lee worked in Europe with the clarinetist and vibraphone player Gunter Hampel, exploiting the different expressive possibilities of the voice in her improvisations while rejecting the instrumental imitations of scat. Among white singers, Sheila Jordan's introverted singing style was not without a certain aesthetic radicalism, and Mark Murphy reinvented the art of the crooner, adding his highly developed musicality and sense of drama.

From American hegemony to global hybridization

Although it became an international language in many parts of the world, jazz failed to fully establish itself in countries with their own strong popular traditions. In Jamaica, jazzmen went into the studio to make records featuring ska (a mixture of rhythm and blues and local rhythms). In Cuba, which was now in the grip of communism, cymbals were regarded as symbols of jazz and therefore imperialist. Towards the end of the 1960s, the saxophonist Paquito D'Rivera, the pianist Chucho Valdés and the drummer Enrique Pla trod a delicate path between officially sanctioned traditional Cuban music and state-controlled jazz. In Africa, the music that was sold as jazz (for example, the Bembaya Jazz National in Guinea) was more a mixture of African and Caribbean music and rhythm and blues.

From South Africa to Western Europe

The pioneers of South African 'township bop' fled apartheid and left the country. The trumpeter Hugh Masekela moved to the United States. Dollar Brand, who had caught the attention of Duke Ellington in Zurich, took the same route. The group of the white pianist Chris McGregor, the Blue Notes, was banned in South Africa because of its multiracial composition and moved to London, where it embraced the influence of free jazz. This enabled the saxophonist Dudu Pukwana and the trumpeter Mongezi Feza to mix with a lively, decompartmentalized scene that was particularly receptive to rock music through the medium of blues bands such as that of Alexis Korner. The British jazz elite of the 1970s was centred around Korner's band and large groups with varying stylistic outlooks (from the big band of John Dankworth to the more progressive groups of Mike Westbrook and Graham Collier). While the alto saxophonist Peter King – the magazine *Melody Maker*'s 'new star' of 1960 – remained faithful to Charlie Parker's example, the guitarist John McLaughlin moved back and forth between bop, rock and free experimentation. London's free-jazz scene really began to develop in 1966 with the creation of the drummer John Stevens's Spontaneous Music Ensemble. This group had a variable line-up that included at one time or another the trumpeter Kenny Wheeler, the saxophonist Evan Parker, the guitarist Derek Bailey and the double-bass player Dave Holland.

On the other side of the Channel, a number of jazzmen who were no longer all the rage were recruited by the yé-yé singers (the French 'girl groups' of the 1960s). It was under the baton of the arranger Jef Gilson, however, that the new leaders of jazz emerged – from the clarinetist Michel

Jean-Luc Ponty

Portal, who was also a classical soloist with an international reputation, to the drummer Bernard Lubat.

Under Gilson, Jean-Luc Ponty came to the attention of the public with an amplified vibrato-free violin style that was closer to John Coltrane than Stephane Grappelli. This brought him into contact with some of Europe's most talented jazz musicians, including the German pianist Wolfgang Dauner, the Danish double-bass player NHOP (Niels-Henning Ørsted Pedersen), the Martinican organist Eddy Louiss and the Swiss drummer Daniel Humair. In 1966, André Hodeir composed *Anna Livia Plurabelle*, a 'jazz cantata' based on the principle of simulated improvisation. Far removed from this highly directive approach, and yet more closely written than the work of Ornette Coleman, *Free Jazz* was recorded by the pianist François Tusques with the trumpeter Bernard Vitet, the clarinetist Michel Portal, the saxophonist François Jeanneau, the double-bass player Beb Guérin and the drummer Charles Saudrais. With equally contrasting styles, Martial Solal and later the Kühn brothers (pianist Joachim and clarinetist Rolf, originally from East Germany) were invited to play at the Newport Jazz Festival. The Kühn brothers' drummer was Aldo Romano, who played alongside the double-bass player Jean-François Jenny-Clark in Paris and Rome with Don Cherry and Gato Barbieri. Cherry and Barbieri both contributed to the pianist and composer Giorgio Gaslini's album *Nuovi Sentimenti*, on which the trumpeter Enrico Rava also plays.

The North-East Passage

Sponsored by Kenny Clarke, the Belgian arranger Francy Boland convincingly combined the legacies of Basie, Ellington and Kenton, recruiting the best jazzmen on the European scene (including a number of expatriate Americans) for his big band. His compatriot, the guitarist René Thomas, was among the best of the contemporaries of Jim Hall and Wes Montgomery. But throughout Europe the up-and-coming generations were becoming increasingly radical as they listened to the American avant-garde. In the Netherlands, the saxophonist Willem Breuker, the pianist Misha Mengelberg and the drummer Han Bennink formed a society called the Instant Composers Pool (ICP) in 1967. In Germany, Alexander von Schlippenbach's Globe Unity Orchestra caused a stir at the 1966 Berlin Jazz Festival. In Scandinavia, a whole generation of musicians (including the Norwegian saxophonist Jan Garbarek, the Danish trumpeter Palle Mikkelborg and the Swedish trombonist Eje Thelin) made the most of George Russell's visits to that part of the world. Central Europe provided a number of tremendous double bassists, including Miroslav Vitous and George Mraz from Czechoslovakia and Aladar Pege from Hungary. Even the previous generation had its followers of the new avant-garde: for example, the French saxophonist Jean-Louis Chautemps, the German trombonist Albert Mangelsdorff and the Polish pianist Krzysztof Komeda. The Polish scene in particular was extremely dynamic and quick to interpret and assimilate the new signals coming from the United States.

The trumpeter Tomasz Stanko made a name for himself with the pianist Adam Makowicz's Jazz Darings, possibly Europe's first free-jazz group. The saxophonist Zbigniew Namyslowski toured the United States with the pianist Andrzej Trzaskowski's Wreckers.

The Russian scene benefited from the détente between East and West, but was nevertheless subject to lurches to the left caused by the vicissitudes of the Cold War, protests from the elite and accusations of revisionism from China. Borders opened up hesitantly, although the tour undertaken by Charles Lloyd's quartet kept the KGB on their toes. The Jazz Researchers' Group circulated photocopies of specialist works that it got its members to translate. Indeed, the knowledgeability of the jazz fans acted as an effective stimulant on the musicians – whether they were exponents of an orthodox jazz of increasing quality (such as the Muscovite pianist Vadim Sakun, who worked with the trumpeter Valery Ponomarev), flirted with the avant-garde (the saxophonists Roman Kunsman from Leningrad and Vadim Vyadro from Estonia) or explored their own roots (the Azerbaijani pianist Rafik Babaev).

LISTENING GUIDE
Krzysztof Komeda (with Tomasz Stanko and Zbigniew Namyslowski), Astigmatic, Muza.
Vadim Sakun's Sextet, Muza.
Ahmed Abdul-Malik, East Meets West, RCA.
Ravi Shankar, Improvisations, World Pacific.
The Joe Harriot–John Mayer Double Quintet, Indo-Jazz Fusions, Lansdowne.
Pedro Iturralde–Paco de Lucia, Flamenco Jazz, MPS.

First steps towards world music

Outside the United States, jazzmen started to turn their attention to their own roots (notably with *Swinging Macedonia*, recorded by the trumpeter Dusko Goykovich in 1966). They were encouraged in this by the process of reappraisal undertaken by free jazz, by the quest for African origins and by the interest of modal jazz in non-European traditions and even American country music (which inspired Charlie Haden, Jimmy Giuffre and Gary Burton). The first experiments with fusion took place in the United States, conducted by Yusuf Lateef, who borrowed prolifically from the music of the Middle East, and by Ahmed Abdul-Malik, a double-bass player of Sudanese origin who also took up the oud (Arab lute). The sitarist Ravi Shankar, whose visits to America met with greater and greater success, jammed with Bud Shank and got on well with John Coltrane. Encounters of this sort proliferated in the United States (Buddy Rich and the tabla player Alla Rakha) and Britain (the saxophonist Joe Harriott and the sitarist Diwan Motihar). In 1965, Joachim Ernst Berendt, artistic director of the Berlin Jazz Days, organized encounters between jazz musicians and traditional musicians from various parts of the world. These led to the *Jazz Meets India* and *Japan Meets Jazz* recordings. Another recording was *Flamenco Jazz*, which combined a German quartet with the Spanish saxophonist Pedro Iturralde and the flamenco guitarist Paco de Lucia. In the same vein, the Catalan pianist Tete Montoliu performed at the Village Gate with Richard Davis and Elvin Jones. In Japan, the arranger Toshiko Akiyoshi worked in the West Coast tradition, but a highly original free-jazz scene grew up in Tokyo around the pianist Masabumi Kikuchi, the drummer Masahiko Togashi and the guitarist Masayuki Takayanagi.

Context

SOCIETY. Following the gradual withdrawal of the United States from South-East Asia, the Soviet Union started to take advantage of the aspirations and instability of the Third World in order to extend its influence, thereby bringing to an end the period of détente between East and West. The dividing line between the different spheres of influence ran through the Israel–Palestine region and the neighbouring oil-producing countries. Threatened by rising petrol prices and under pressure from terrorism, Western society fell back into recession, unemployment and insecurity. The splintering of the anti-establishment movement into small groups from 1968 onwards fed the terrorist networks. The Soviet intervention in Czechoslovakia in August 1968 and the genocide in Cambodia in 1975 dealt severe blows to the prestige of communist ideology. The revolutionary ideal gradually gave way to the concept of counter-culture and to a multiplicity of alternative projects in the ecological, humanitarian and spiritual domains. From rite-of-passage pilgrimages to Katmandu to regular tourism, the young people of the West beat a path to every corner of the earth in order to 'find themselves'.

In the United States, the FBI conducted an out-and-out war on anti-establishment elements. Outwitted by the opponents of the Vietnam War, it succeeded in eliminating black radicalism by using every possible means (infiltration, false evidence and assassination). The black community went through a period of profound disenchantment. Despite the positive effects of 'affirmative action', which encouraged greater levels of recruitment from the ethnic minorities, there were still many barriers to integration, particularly in the sphere of education. The black majority was plunged into unrelieved poverty, while the political class lost interest in social problems.

The medallists Tommie Smith (gold) and John Carlos (bronze) avert their gaze from the Stars and Stripes and raise their fists in a Black Power salute during the playing of the US national anthem at the 1968 Olympics in Mexico.

THE MUSIC INDUSTRY. The commercial decline of jazz in the face of competition from rock music was aggravated by soaring costs that pushed up break-even points. The arrival of multitrack recording (using 8, 16, 24 and 32 tracks) meant that studios were required to spend larger and larger sums on equipment. As a major consumer of vinyl, the industry was also hit by rising petrol prices. While Columbia and Polydor fought over the jazz-rock market, the other branches of jazz took refuge with smaller, occasionally independent labels such as Horizon, Artist House, Flying Dutchman, Muse, Concord, Nessa and Arista. Polydor was content to exploit the back catalogue of its new acquisition Verve, while Norman Granz continued to produce the big stars of classic jazz on his new label Pablo.

American musicians discovered a rapidly developing scene in Europe, with interest in their music coming from many independent labels: MPS, ECM and Enja in Germany; Steeplechase and Storyville in Denmark; Timeless in the Netherlands; Black Saint in Italy; Byg, Futura, Owl and Musica in France; and Hat Hut in Switzerland. Some of these labels, including FMP (Free Music Production) in Germany, ICP (Instant Composers Pool) and BVHaast in the Netherlands and Incus in Britain, were even run by the artists themselves.

The electric piano market took off in a big way. There were crazes for the Rhodes piano and the Mini Moog, the first ever portable synthesizer. Synthesizer technology continued to develop throughout the decade.

RELATED MUSICAL GENRES. While gospel remained the preserve of black artists, the blues only survived thanks to the interest of white music fans such as Bruce Iglauer of the Alligator label and the founders of *Soul Bag* magazine in France.

Like swing in the 1930s, 'groove' became the watchword of the latest incarnation of rhythm and blues, which was called 'funk'. Funk was a stripped-down style, based on a forcefully syncopated polyrhythmic structure suggestive of Black America's disenchantment. Having come of age in the Stax studios and in the music of its great master, James Brown, funk was adapted by the Meters to the rhythms of New Orleans and used by George Clinton as the basis for his extravagant groups such as Parliament and Funkadelic. Midway between funk and psychedelic rock, Sly Stone proved a hit with the mainly white audience at Woodstock in 1969, assuming a harder edge in 1971 with *There's a Riot Goin' On*. While generally more soothing than funk, soul music also reflected the racial tension of the day. There was a common desire among artists to escape the control of their record companies: Marvin Gaye produced his album *What's Going On* himself, Stevie Wonder recorded in the privacy of his own studio (*Songs in the Key of Life*) and Curtis Mayfield founded his own label in order to record 'The Other Side of Town'. A large proportion of black music nevertheless gave in to the most commercial aspects of soul, eventually descending into the commonplaces of disco.

'Rapper's Delight' was recorded in 1978 by the Sugar Hill Gang, but rap had many antecedents within the black American tradition – notably the Last Poets of Harlem, who recorded 'When the Revolution Comes' in 1970. In Jamaica, where Bob Marley was winning over Western audiences to the music of the Third World urban scene, DJs started to comment on the records they played, acquiring the name 'toasters'. These records would often be dubs – remixes of original recordings, frequently with the words removed, thus leaving only the rhythms and added effects. This marked the birth of a new culture of sound manipulation, which was to dominate the final years of the 20th century.

A multitude of genres – traditional or progressive to varying degrees and occasionally receptive to jazz – emerged in the field of rock music. The despair of the British working classes in the wake of the first oil crisis led to the excesses of the punk movement, which had a lasting impact on a number of artistic fields. From New York to Puerto Rico, salsa blended the exuberance of Caribbean rhythms with tight brass and electric-bass playing that displayed both jazz-rock and soul influences.

LISTENING GUIDE
James Brown, *Love Power Peace*, Polydor.
Parliament, *Mothership Connection*, Casablanca.
Curtis Mayfield, *Curtis*, Curtom.
Last Poets, *Last Poets*, Douglas.
Fania All Stars, *Jerry Masucci Presents Salsa Greats*, Fania.

Jazz-rock

The slogan adopted by the French protesters of May 1968 – 'Power to the Imagination' – could have been invented for the jazz musicians of the 1970s. They were freeing themselves from the final remaining codes and conventions of jazz as well as from its geographical origins. Throughout the world, observers witnessed an explosion of styles and fusions with other genres. The genre that exerted the strongest pull on jazz musicians was rock, the most popular music in the world.

Miles Davis goes electric

LISTENING GUIDE
Miles Davis, *Filles de Kilimanjaro, Bitches Brew, Jack Johnson, On the Corner, Agharta,* Columbia.

Pressed by Columbia to justify his financial demands, Miles Davis decided to use his December 1967 recording sessions (in which he took up the electric piano) for a change of direction. He was intrigued and at the same time irritated by the success of rock. His favourite rock musician was Jimi Hendrix, the demiurge of the electric guitar and a black hero in a field dominated by white musicians. He also loved the funk of James Brown and Sly and the Family Stone. In the summer of 1968, in order to complete his album *Filles de Kilimanjaro,* he reinvigorated his quintet – paradoxically through the addition of two white musicians, Chick Corea (piano and electric keyboards) and Dave Holland (double bass and electric bass). Shortly afterwards, Tony Williams was replaced on drums by Jack DeJohnette.

While this new rhythm section was able to indulge in its penchant for free-jazz-style excesses on stage, in the studio it was neutralized as part of expanded formations such as those used on the album *Bitches Brew.* Depending on his needs, Davis was able to call upon the rhythm-and-blues-tinged playing of the British guitarist John McLaughlin and double or even triple the size of the rhythm section. His thematic material consisted of a number of short phrases shared out at the last minute between the horn players and the rhythm section. The harmonic material was reduced to one or several modal colours which were splashed over the backdrop, as it were, by the electric keyboards, hinted at by the ostinatos played on the bass and hammered out in binary phrasing by the drummers and other percussionists. The horn players improvised freely during long takes that were then reworked during post-production (using cuts, edits, additional instruments and special effects) by the producer Teo Macero, who was effectively the co-composer of the album *Jack Johnson*. In 1971, Davis started to electrify his trumpet so that he could pull his phrasing around using wah-wah effects. He introduced Michael Henderson, who had a soul background, on electric bass, used tablas and a sitar for a while (notably on the album *On the Corner*) and brought in various keyboard players (including Keith Jarrett) before replacing the keyboards with two or even three guitarists and adding a permanent percussionist to the rhythm section (on the album *Agharta*). His musical world was becoming ever more dense, sweaty and violent. Like Ellington, Davis produced music that evoked the jungles of Africa and the jungle of the black neighbourhoods, but the voluptuous exoticism of the earlier bandleader was replaced by an emphasis on the resentments of black America and the hidden menace of a mysterious, rebellious Africa.

Jazz-rock and the legacy of Miles Davis

By the time Miles Davis was forced to stop playing for health reasons in 1975, many musicians had passed through his various bands and been strongly influenced by the experience. Around 1969, following the example of Tony Williams, they had begun to get together in essentially electric line-ups under the leadership of the double bassist Miroslav Vitous, the saxophonist Wayne Shorter or the pianist Joe Zawinul. In 1971, these three formed Weather Report (see p.195) and John McLaughlin formed the Mahavishnu Orchestra. The latter explored the richness of Indian metres combined with an ecstatic virtuosity, a forceful beat and a saturated sound evoking the ruggedness of hard rock. Following a brief detour into a more free-jazz style with Anthony Braxton (see p.208), Chick Corea formed the group Return to Forever. Saxophone and flute (played by Joe Farrell) were soon replaced by electric guitar (Bill Connors and then Al Di Meola), giving rise to an electric music of supercharged virtuosity in terms of both writing and execution. The group's work featured strong references to Afro-Latin and Spanish music. It also borrowed from classical composers and displayed an interest in elaborate forms of 'progressive' rock (Emerson, Lake & Palmer, Yes, King Crimson). Aimed at the white audiences of the large festivals established in the wake of Woodstock (1969), jazz-rock was a music of dreams and oblivion whose performers were often closely associated with a guru or sect. Influenced by Buddhism, Herbie Hancock was no less interested in the race issue. He adopted the Swahili pseudonym 'Mwandishi' in order to connect with a black audience. From 1969, he started using more and more funk musicians and funk sounds and exploiting the playful polyrhythmic aspects of rhythm and blues. These ideas culminated in the formation of a new group, the Headhunters. Accentuating the dance aspects of his music, Hancock even forged links with commercial disco in the second half of the 1970s.

LISTENING GUIDE
The Tony Williams Lifetime, *Emergency!*, Polydor.
Miroslav Vitous, *Mountain in the Clouds*, Atlantic.
John McLaughlin and the Mahavishnu Orchestra, *Birds of Fire*, Columbia.
Chick Corea, *Where Have I Known You Before*, Polydor.
Herbie Hancock, *Sextant, Headhunters*, Columbia.

Jazz-rock rhythm sections

Although the genre had been invented by a trumpeter, the jazz-rock of
Miles Davis's direct descendants did not give prominence to wind
instruments. The very high sound volume most of the bands went in for did
not suit such instruments, but it helps to explain the widespread adoption of
the soprano sax, whose high-pitched sound was better able to make itself
heard above the high decibel count (for example, Wayne Shorter in Weather
Report and David Liebman with Miles Davis). However, jazz-rock presented
some of the instruments that had remained in the background throughout
the history of jazz with an opportunity to get their own back. Drummers
had always delighted audiences with their solos. Surrounded by a forest of
drums and cymbals, over which their sticks flitted with phenomenal speed
and power, jazz-rock drummers (most of whom were black) became stars in
their own right. It was from them that the groups drew their energy: Al
Foster in Miles Davis's band, Billy Cobham in the Mahavishnu Orchestra,
Lenny White in Return to Forever, and Harvey Mason in the Headhunters.
Most also followed the example of Tony Williams and Lifetime and led their
own groups.

Billy Cobham

Influenced by their funk colleagues (James Jamerson, Larry Graham),
electric bassists such as Alphonso
Johnson (Weather Report) adopted
a completely new approach to the
instrument, abandoning the
walking bass and contributing
with virtuosic mobility to the
polyrhythmic fabric of the band.
Stanley Clarke (who also played
the double bass) carved out a
place for himself as a soloist
alongside Chick Corea. And the
emergence of Jaco Pastorius
revolutionized the world of the
bassist (see p.196).

Electric keyboard players made an important contribution to the emergence
of jazz-rock through their prolific use of the Rhodes piano with its
distinctive sound (the keyboard used on Miles Davis's *Bitches Brew*). This
instrument, already susceptible to natural distortion, was subjected on
Weather Report's *I Sing the Body Electric* and elsewhere to a host of special
electronic effects. Other keyboards were also used, such as the Clavinet
(which provides the shrill accompaniment to the solos on 'Sly' from the
album *Headhunters*), or even bottom-of-the-range organs of the Farfisa type,
such as those Davis got his pianists to play on several occasions (Herbie
Hancock's solo on 'Right Off' from the album *Jack Johnson*). In Tony
Williams's group Lifetime, Larry Young on the Hammond organ provided a
passionate alternative to Jimmy Smith's classical approach. But the really
new thing was the synthesizer, which was capable of generating an infinite
number of original or imitative sounds. The first portable model, the Mini
Moog developed by Robert Moog, was popularized by the Czech émigré
Jan Hammer in the Mahavishnu Orchestra. Initially monophonic (allowing
only one note to be played at a time), the synthesizer became polyphonic in

WEATHER REPORT: A BRIEF SURVEY

The Austrian émigré Joe Zawinul made a significant contribution to Miles Davis's 1969 sessions, both on keyboards and as a composer. Having played the electric piano in Cannonball Adderley's band since 1967, he now became interested in the possibilities of electronics. In January 1971, he convinced Columbia to sign up the group he had just founded with the black saxophonist Wayne Shorter, the Czech double bassist Miroslav Vitous, the black drummer Alphonse Mouzon and the Brazilian percussionist Airto Moreira. Weather Report was born. Except for the permanent members Joe Zawinul and Wayne Shorter, the group underwent numerous personnel changes and carried on until 1985.

The first steps

Named after the band and developed around embryonic thematic material often without a fixed metre, their first record was based on an extensive collective freedom – in which the solo's importance was only relative – alongside funk polyrhythms and mellow moods.

Recorded in the studio and in concert during the winter of 1971–2, the group's second album, *I Sing the Body Electric*, introduced the first personnel changes with the arrival of the drummer Eric Gravatt and the Brazilian percussionist Dom Um Romão. The music on this record confirmed a number of tendencies present on the first album, particularly the highly evocative character of the melodic and rhythmic elements and of the special sounds used, which are often descriptive (desolate laments, sirens and a martial-sounding trumpet and side drum on 'Unknown Soldier'). It also revealed a new structural imperative formulated by Joe Zawinul that would be pursued in the following albums.

Maturity

Over the following years a succession of drummers played with the group. Occasionally two drummers were used together in order to satisfy Zawinul's contradictory rhythmic requirements. Zawinul wanted to obtain the punch of rhythm and blues without sacrificing the sophistication of jazz, which meant incorporating both binary and ternary phrasing. Miroslav Vitous, a bassist in the Scott LaFaro mould, did not fit in and was replaced in 1974 by Alphonso Johnson, a virtuoso black bassist with a background in both jazz and rhythm and blues. The fourth album, *Mysterious Traveller*, was the group's first great classic. It displays a balance between Joe Zawinul's structural requirements and the suppleness of the ensemble playing, confirming the lesser importance of solo expression. The

Weather Report performing at Chateauvallon in 1973. Left to right: Joe Zawinul, Wayne Shorter, Greg Errico and Miroslav Vitous

breadth of the group's musical references means it is impossible to attach a label to it, but it confirms its strong attachment to the black tradition through its references to jazz and rhythm and blues as well as through the very deliberate inclusion of Afro-Brazilian and Afro-Cuban percussion.

Using recording techniques to highly creative effect, Joe Zawinul exploits the full range of sounds made possible by the synthesizer, injecting his melodic genius into the music in the form of interjected phrases and ostinatos that provide a framework for impressive musical frescoes. Set well back from the others but totally at one with the music, Wayne Shorter adds the bittersweet lyricism and extreme concision of his sax playing. As a composer of enigmatic melodies, he contributed open, interactive works which were put together with the precision of a watchmaker yet which preserved the freshness of the group. With *Mysterious Traveller* – a hit that even the biggest rock group would have been proud of – Weather Report achieved the ideal balance between creativity and commercial appeal.

World music but still jazz

With the exception of its last album, *This Is This* (1986), which can be seen as the fulfilment of contractual commitments by a band that had run out of steam, Weather Report managed to maintain this equilibrium. Served up by a succession of percussionists (including Alyrio Lima, Alejandro Acuna, Don Alias, Bobby Thomas and Mino Cinelu), the black rhythms of the African diaspora constituted a springboard for Joe Zawinul's ambition to embrace the whole range of world musics. Thus the album *Black Market* includes evocations of various places (the harbour atmosphere in the introduction to 'Gibraltar'; the explosions of war forming the conclusion to the African panorama of 'Black Market'). But the relationship with jazz was also maintained – through oblique tributes ('Cannonball') or explicit evocations scattered throughout the later albums ('Birdland', 'Rockin' in Rhythm'), with a bank of synthesizers playing the part of a big band.

LISTENING
GUIDE
Weather Report (1971), *I Sing the Body Electric* (1972), *Mysterious Traveller* (1974), *Black Market* (1976), *Heavy Weather* (1977), *Night Passage* (1980), *Sportin' Life* (1985), Columbia.

Two rhythm teams brought the instability of the band's line-up to an end: Jaco Pastorius and Peter Erskine between 1978 and 1981; and Victor Bailey and Omar Hakim between 1982 and 1985. The first, the group's only white rhythm section, was to become legendary. In addition to his qualities as a composer and performer, Jaco Pastorius revolutionized the electric bass. He obtained an acrobatic lyricism from his fretless instrument and propelled the band with an efficiency all the more astounding as his bass lines were built around elaborate pirouettes and restatements of the thematic material. In the drummer Peter Erskine he found his ideal partner. Erskine was able to encourage his spirited playing while also providing a solid foundation for his more daring gestures. A former big-band drummer, Erskine reintroduced a jazz tempo to the group and was the perfect partner for the bassist in their exploration of the ambiguities of ternary and binary phrasing.

Herbie Hancock

the mid-1970s, turning Joe Zawinul in Weather Report into a virtual one-man band.

A host of innovations allowed the interconnection of several keyboards, the operation of the synthesizer by an instrument other than the keyboard (for example, guitar or saxophone) and the pre-setting of sequences using a 'sequencer'.

Europe: violins and progressive rock

Having been mainly marginal figures in the history of jazz, guitarists were now its new heroes (see p.199), but there was also new-found enthusiasm for an instrument that had been all but forgotten since bebop: the violin. As demonstrated by Jerry Goodman in the Mahavishnu Orchestra, amplification now allowed the violin to match the volume of the most powerful drumming. In 1969, during a visit to the United States, Jean-Luc Ponty collaborated with Frank Zappa and founded a group called the Jean-Luc Ponty Experience, whose music made explicit reference to the funkiest aspects of Herbie Hancock. In 1972, after another spell in Europe, Ponty settled in America, where he played with the new Mahavishnu Orchestra in 1974 and embarked upon a career as the leader of exclusively jazz-rock-oriented bands in 1975.

The 'electric' violin was taken up with great enthusiasm, often within a jazz-rock context and particularly in Poland, where Michal Urbaniak and Zbigniew Seifert switched from the sax to the fiddle. Towards the end of the decade, the French double-bass player Didier Levallet formed a string ensemble, the Swing Strings System, in which the violinist Didier Lockwood played briefly at a time when his career had a strong jazz-rock orientation. Elsewhere in Europe, the jazz-rock influence often had less to do with the mass electrification of bands than with the rhythmic vocabulary they adopted – binary rhythms and the virtuosic application of uneven metres. This resulted in many original approaches and varying stylistic mixes, ranging from the groups led by the Belgian guitarist Philip Catherine and the Dutch pianist Jasper Van't Hof to the German guitarist Volker Kriegel's group Spectrum and the French saxophonist Yoshk'o Seffer, who explored his Hungarian roots with the band Zao.

LISTENING
GUIDE
Jean-Luc Ponty,
Experience, Pacific.
Didier Levallet (with
Didier Lockwood), Swing
Strings System, Original
Sessions, Evidence.
Zbigniew Seifert,
Passion, Capitol.
Philip Catherine,
September Man,
Atlantic.
Yoshk'o Seffer,
Retrospective,
Frémeaux.

197

A number of French groups of the free-jazz persuasion, such as the Dharma Quintet or the Cohelmec Ensemble, were allergic to the formalism of jazz-rock but not indifferent to the acoustic jungles dreamed up by Miles Davis. The progressive rock of the group Magma took its inspiration from John Coltrane, sharing musicians such as Didier Lockwood and Yoshk'o Seffer with the French jazz scene. These exchanges had some influence on groups with more of a free-jazz tendency, such as Perception. In Britain, where jazz and rock already enjoyed a close relationship, a scene as odd as it was varied emerged when jazz came into contact with the progressive rock of the so-called 'Canterbury' school, which was developing around the group Soft Machine. Soft Machine had a permanent saxophone soloist, Elton Dean, and even a wind section, while the trumpeter Ian Carr and his group Nucleus demonstrated that having a jazz background did not preclude a band from embracing the rhythmic characteristics of rock.

LISTENING GUIDE
Soft Machine, *Third*, Columbia.
Nucleus, *Elastic Rock*/*We'll Talk About It Later*, BGO.

The other American jazz-rock

In the 1960s, in their quest for alternative locations in which to work and exhibit, New York artists had started to take over industrial buildings and entire apartment blocks in Manhattan, converting their lofts into living and working spaces. At the end of the 1960s, these lofts (as well as recording studios during quieter periods) hosted jam sessions led by young musicians who had come to try their luck in the city. Mostly white, they generally possessed good technical skills acquired at the best schools, such as the famous Berklee School of Music in Boston. They were wide-ranging in their experiments, some drawing on free improvisation, others combining rock or rhythm-and-blues rhythms with large brass ensembles in the manner of rock groups such as Chicago Transit Authority and Blood Sweat & Tears, whose combinations of this kind were very popular with the public. It was in this way that the informal, legendary big band White Elephant came together around the vibraphone player Mike Manieri. Its members included the drummer Steve Gadd, the pianist Warren Bernhardt, the trumpeters Lew Soloff, Jon Faddis and Randy Brecker, and the tenor saxophonist Michael Brecker.

Another name should be added to the names of these musicians, who were highly sought after as session players due to their versatility in the fields of rock and funk – that of the alto saxophonist David Sanborn, a figure familiar to blues and soul bands. Sanborn and Michael Brecker introduced a new approach to sax playing at a time when the saxophone world was traumatized by the loss of John Coltrane. Michael Brecker declared that he had started out playing 'rock-and-roll tenor' and that his earliest influences had been singers and guitarists. Indeed his sax sound, biased towards the higher register, possessed a vibrato that was reminiscent of soul voices and was perfect for penetrating the wall of sound created by the new bands. The astounding precision of his note placement and articulation even in extremely fast phrases recalled the skill of the rhythm-and-blues bands rather than the utterances of free jazz.

THE NEW GUITARISTS

Underemployed in jazz, in rock the guitar became a loudhailer, a standard, a weapon. A prop for symbolic (mainly sexual and warlike) gesticulation, the guitar exploited electric energy (power of sound, special effects) and corrupted the instruments that surrounded it (the double bass, when it was electrified, became in effect a bass guitar, and keyboards started to be worn slung over the shoulder). The new generation of white jazz guitarists had grown up surrounded by the cult of rock music and its guitar heroes.

The first jazz guitarists to own up to an interest in rock guitar were the American Larry Coryell and the Briton John McLaughlin. Reworking the rhetoric of country music and blues, Coryell developed a style of phrasing made possible by the secondary effects of amplification, which gave his guitar sound a more sustained quality. This new approach allowed McLaughlin to integrate into his playing the 'sheets of sound' devised by John Coltrane. Guitar phrasing acquired a torrential fluidity that only Tal Farlow had previously managed to come anywhere near.

While John McLaughlin was moving in the direction of a mastery of staccato phrasing (each note individually attacked), other guitarists adopted the rock guitarists' method of stringing their instruments with flexible strings close to the fingerboard. They adopted a legato (smooth and flowing) style. The movements of the left hand on the neck of the guitar were enough to set the strings in motion and the plectrum was used by the right hand simply to accentuate the phrase. The champion of this style was the British guitarist Allan Holdsworth, who achieved an unrivalled fluidity. Initially under the influence of John McLaughlin, John Abercrombie adopted this new type of phrasing in reaction to the overblown excesses of jazz-rock. His aim was to develop a freer form of music and reintroduce the notion of space that was dear to Bill Evans. Along with the two main exponents of jazz guitar in the 1960s — Jim Hall and Wes Montgomery — Bill Evans became one of the essential points of reference for a generation that had grown up listening to rock and adoring Jimi Hendrix but that had learned its trade from the masters of controlled freedom. Before devoting himself to teaching, Mick Goodrick made a name for himself during a brief spell in Gary Burton's quartet and was the spiritual leader of the majority of guitarists who emerged in the 1970s. His successor in Burton's group was Pat Metheny, who divided his career between the free meanderings of Ornette Coleman and a group that was heavily influenced by rock and American folk music. John Scofield, whose style was a mixture of controlled freedom and deep blues roots, emerged at the end of the decade in David Liebman's group.

LISTENING GUIDE

Larry Coryell, *Lady Coryell*, Vanguard.
John McLaughlin, *Extrapolation*, Polydor.
Tony Williams, *Million Dollar Legs*, Columbia.
John Abercrombie, *Gateway*, ECM.
Gary Burton (with Mick Goodrick and Pat Metheny), *Dreams So Real*, ECM.
Pat Metheny, *Bright Size Life*, ECM.
David Liebman (with John Scofield), *If They Only Knew*, Timeless.

Pat Metheny

199

Whether in the group Dreams, which recreated the convivial atmosphere of the New York loft scene, or in studio session work, Michael and Randy Brecker worked together a lot of the time. They formed the jazz-rock group the Brecker Brothers, in which they altered the sound of their instruments using the wah-wah pedal.

Towards a European chamber jazz

LISTENING GUIDE
Chick Corea, *My Spanish Heart*, Polydor.
Shakti, *A Handful of Beauty*, Columbia.

Towards the middle of the 1970s, a rift opened up between the music press and a young public dazzled by jazz-rock. Whether their heroes had been Louis Armstrong or the Rolling Stones, Albert Ayler or the Doors, the rock and jazz cognoscenti alike found the newcomers rather insipid compared to the legendary figures who inhabited their own personal halls of fame. They were nostalgic for the whiff of the subversive, the scandalous and the forbidden that had accompanied the century's music up to the 1960s – from the foxtrot to free jazz and from rockabilly to acid rock. They could not understand a generation whom they saw as passive consumers of strong emotions, special effects and hollow virtuosity. The jazz-rock musicians themselves felt trapped by their success, the overemphasis on technique and the demand for an ever higher decibel count. They criticized the term 'jazz-rock' as too simplistic and proposed 'fusion' instead. This was rapidly adopted as a new label. At the same time, they started to give acoustic instruments a bigger role in their bands (Chick Corea's *My Spanish Heart*) and returned to more intimate forms (the piano solos of Chick Corea and Herbie Hancock), more natural forms or even totally acoustic forms (John McLaughlin's group Shakti, the Larry Coryell–Philip Catherine duo), alternating styles and often leading parallel careers.

Keith Jarrett

The new apostles of controlled freedom

When exactly the new trend for acoustic instruments began is not clear. As early as 1970, John McLaughlin recorded *My Goal's Beyond*, which alternates guitar solos with pieces performed by a small acoustic band inspired by Indian music. The vibraphone player Gary Burton, a forerunner of the blending of jazz and rock, performed solo from 1971 and recorded in a duo with Chick Corea in 1972 (*Crystal Silence*). Acoustic interludes, providing moments of relief, had been common from the earliest days of jazz-rock. In parallel with a phase of anarchic experimentation in the lofts of New York, notably in the company of Dave Holland and Barry Altschul, Corea began recording his own

LISTENING
GUIDE
Chick Corea and Gary
Burton, *Crystal Silence*,
ECM.
Cecil Taylor, *Air Above
Mountains*, Enja.
Mal Waldron, *The
Opening*, Futura.
Chick Corea, *Piano
Improvisations, Vol 1*,
ECM.
Paul Bley, *Open To Love*,
ECM.
Keith Jarrett, *Facing
You*, ECM.
David Liebman (with
Lookout Farm), *Sweet
Hands*, Horizon.
David Liebman and
Richard Beirach,
Forgotten Fantasies,
Horizon.
Gary Burton (with Steve
Swallow and Roy
Haynes), *Times Square*,
ECM.

Piano Improvisations in March 1971, starting a trend for the piano solo – a form whose previous practitioners covered a very wide aesthetic spectrum (Cecil Taylor, Mal Waldron, Dollar Brand, Joachim Kühn). Impressionistic or romantic, classical piano seems to have exerted a significant influence on jazz piano around this time. This was evident in the highly economical, almost Monk-like playing of Paul Bley (following his period of experimentation with his Synthesizer Show), in the very engaging, very Latin playing of Chick Corea, and in the whimsical, ecstatic playing of Keith Jarrett with its echoes of folk, soul and funk as well as ragtime, bebop and free jazz. In January 1975, at the Cologne Opera, Jarrett recorded the continuous suite *Köln Concert*. His early admirers accused him of overdoing the effusive, ecstatic mode, but the general public was very enthusiastic about this classical music that 'let its hair down'.

Keith Jarrett was typical of a generation of white musicians torn between different influences in an all-inclusive, varied culture whose musical references included Schumann and Debussy, Aretha Franklin and Joni Mitchell, Bill Evans and Ornette Coleman, the electric and acoustic recordings of Miles Davis, latter-day folk music and non-European musical traditions. Jarrett ('Long As You Know You're Living Yours') and Steve Swallow ('Falling Grace') enriched the jazz repertoire with compositions that had more in common with the new composers of pop songs – James Taylor or Carole King – than with the composers of musical theatre. While Jarrett, in spite of his time with Miles Davis, was resistant to electric instruments, others used them without being dogmatic about it. Thus Steve Swallow switched to the electric bass, but transformed it into an ambiguous instrument with the register of the cello and played with a plectrum like the guitar, and Gary Burton was happy to recruit rock-influenced guitarists.

A pioneer of the loft scene, David Liebman was the first occupant of a building on 19th Street where he was joined by Chick Corea, Dave Holland and later Michael Brecker. The president of a musicians' cooperative (Free Life Communication), Liebman set up numerous jam sessions inspired by John Coltrane's free-jazz period. Together with the pianist Richard Beirach he founded the group Lookout Farm, located stylistically somewhere between Coltrane, Bill Evans and the acoustic and electric groups of Miles Davis. These were the main influences on this first 'loft generation', which had grown up listening to rock and learning from jazz. On the fringes of jazz-rock (to which it contributed), this generation took the controlled freedom of the previous decade to a new level, bringing to it a fresh sensibility that opened up new horizons.

The European temptation

Although Roy Haynes could be found playing with Burton and Corea and although Jack DeJohnette was also closely involved, these circles were nonetheless dominated by white musicians. The influence of country music was often more important than that of blues. References to classical piano and a propensity to understate swing and groove, to make rhythm sections lighter (pursuing the direction taken by the Bill Evans trio) or to

ECM

In the 1970s, a new type of record sleeve started to appear in the jazz section of music shops. And, on playing the record inside, listeners were struck by the recording quality, the precision with which the most lightly played harmonic was captured, the detail with which each contour was crafted (particularly the sculpted sound of the cymbals) and the careful placing of each instrument within the stereophonic image. The space between the instruments as well as the space between notes was able to breathe thanks to a judicious use of artificial reverberation. Whereas the legendary Blue Note recordings seemed to recreate the muted, confined, smoky atmosphere of the jazz club, ECM's recordings reproduced the sound of the modern (classical) concert hall or even a natural, open-air acoustic.

The main ambition of the founder of ECM (Edition of Contemporary Music), Manfred Eicher, was to record jazz to the same high standards that were expected for classical music. Even the name of the label, founded in 1969, was significant. Contemporary Music: Eicher was distancing himself from jazz. Edition: there was something literary about his work as a producer, a relationship with the written word and paper. The sleeve designs revealed an art lover with a knowledge of photography and cinematography. Flicking through the ECM catalogue today, one is struck by the comparative diversity of the cover art. At the time, the eye was caught by a few sleeves in particular: coloured balloons floating on an expanse of water, misty sunsets, icy landscapes wreathed in freezing fog... Far removed from clammy, polluted New York, Eicher and the music he recorded transported the listener to the virgin spaces of northern Europe.

It was there, mainly in Scandinavia, where he found a good number of the artists in his catalogue: the trumpeter Palle Mikkelborg, the saxophonist Jan Garbarek, the pianist Bobo Stenson, the guitarist Terje Rypdal, the double-bass player Palle Danielsson and the drummer Jon Christensen. When he looked elsewhere, it was for the piano of Keith Jarrett or Paul Bley, the vibraphone of Gary Burton or the acoustic guitars of Ralph Towner. Eicher was accused of favouring soothing, emotionless music, but this view failed to take into account that the music was also among the most innovative of the decade.

It was ECM that gave a platform to the new guitarists John Abercrombie and Pat

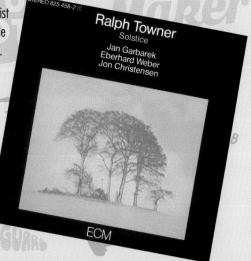

Metheny and presented the drummer Jack DeJohnette in the best possible light. Its list also featured plenty of free-jazz-style music – Garbarek's first recordings, the Art Ensemble of Chicago, Derek Bailey's extreme experimentation, the group Circle (to which Anthony Braxton and Chick Corea belonged), and Keith Jarrett's American quartet. There were times when Eicher tried rather heavy-handedly to make the music sound the way he thought it should, but overall, by exploiting the full resources of high fidelity, he revealed himself to have a genuinely musical ear, surveyed the contemporary scene with great insight and showed a new respect for jazz. No doubt referring to the science of ecology that had recently come to public attention, he invented an 'ecology of jazz' offering the new avant-gardes an environment more favourable to their growth. Those who liked jazz for the whiff of booze and debauchery that went with it, or for the scandals surrounding the legends, listened to ECM's releases differently. But Eicher opened up opportunities for a host of European producers. Of course, it was not long before imitators appeared on the market, but labels such as Enja, Owl, Black Saint and Hat Hut had learned from ECM that it was perfectly possible for a record company to operate independently while looking after the wellbeing of both its artists and its public.

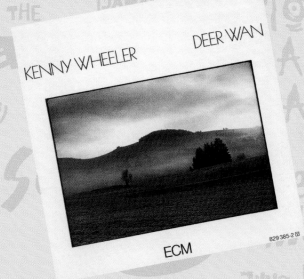

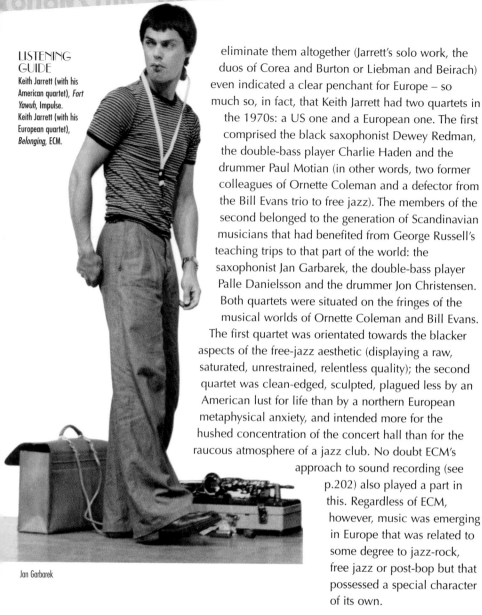

Jan Garbarek

eliminate them altogether (Jarrett's solo work, the duos of Corea and Burton or Liebman and Beirach) even indicated a clear penchant for Europe – so much so, in fact, that Keith Jarrett had two quartets in the 1970s: a US one and a European one. The first comprised the black saxophonist Dewey Redman, the double-bass player Charlie Haden and the drummer Paul Motian (in other words, two former colleagues of Ornette Coleman and a defector from the Bill Evans trio to free jazz). The members of the second belonged to the generation of Scandinavian musicians that had benefited from George Russell's teaching trips to that part of the world: the saxophonist Jan Garbarek, the double-bass player Palle Danielsson and the drummer Jon Christensen. Both quartets were situated on the fringes of the musical worlds of Ornette Coleman and Bill Evans. The first quartet was orientated towards the blacker aspects of the free-jazz aesthetic (displaying a raw, saturated, unrestrained, relentless quality); the second quartet was clean-edged, sculpted, plagued less by an American lust for life than by a northern European metaphysical anxiety, and intended more for the hushed concentration of the concert hall than for the raucous atmosphere of a jazz club. No doubt ECM's approach to sound recording (see p.202) also played a part in this. Regardless of ECM, however, music was emerging in Europe that was related to some degree to jazz-rock, free jazz or post-bop but that possessed a special character of its own.

The European creators

Who were the exponents – whether young newcomers or veterans – of this new European jazz that was too varied to be given a label but sufficiently interesting to intrigue American musicians? Some obvious names come to mind. On trumpet: Palle Mikkelborg (Denmark), Tomasz Stanko (Poland), Enrico Rava (Italy), Kenny Wheeler (Canada/UK); on saxophone: Juahni Aaltonen (Finland), Jan Garbarek (Norway), John Surman (UK), Zbigniew Namyslowski (Poland), Heinz Sauer (Germany), François Jeanneau (France); on guitar: Philip Catherine (Belgium), Terje Rypdal (Norway), Allan Holdsworth (UK), Christian Escoudé (France); on violin: Zbigniew Seifert (Poland), Didier Lockwood (France); on keyboards: Joachim Kühn (Germany/France), Bobo Stenson (Sweden), John Taylor (UK), Eddy Louiss (Martinique/France), Michel Graillier (France), Adam Makowicz (Poland), Franco D'Andrea (Italy); on double bass: Henri Texier, Jean-François Jenny-

Clark, Beb Guérin (France), Arild Andersen (Norway), Palle Danielsson (Sweden), Eberhard Weber (Germany), Freddie Deronde (Belgium), Giovanni Tommaso (Italy); and on drums: John Marshall (UK), Daniel Humair (Switzerland/France), Aldo Romano (Italy/France), Edward Vesala (Finland), Jon Christensen (Norway), Czeslaw Bartkowski (Poland). Because of the wide range of their aesthetic approaches, it is impossible to describe these musicians en bloc. Many of them, including Joachim Kühn, also moved from one style to another, from jazz-rock to Europe's very active free-jazz scene (see p.211) and back again. Their common fund of influences included Miles Davis, John Coltrane, Bill Evans, Ornette Coleman and Cecil Taylor, but beyond this they all defined themselves in terms of their personal preoccupations, the prevailing socio-economic conditions and the local cultural environment (jazz antecedents, proximity to distinctive free-jazz or rock scenes, preponderance of popular or classical traditions, and so on).

One of the main differences between 'old' Europe and 'new' America was the substantial cultural heritage of the former compared to the relative cultural poverty of the latter. A number of musicians continued to plough the bop furrow while exhibiting an apparent indifference towards all that was happening around them, but the most inventive, such as Martial Solal, were constantly being ambushed by their history. A forerunner of the European scene, Solal took an almost Cartesian approach to his dissection of the certainties of bop (while Joachim Kühn reworked Schumann's legacy through the prism of McCoy Tyner and Cecil Taylor). To do this, Solal deliberately used musicians who were at the forefront of the contemporary scene, such as Jean-François Jenny-Clark, Henri Texier and Daniel Humair. As early as 1969, he took the bold step of stripping the trio of its drums and replacing them with a second bass – a line-up far removed from the orchestral canvas of bebop. With his new trio Solal turned his attention to the 'thematic suite' dear to Don Cherry and which he had himself helped to pioneer in 1959. After playing in a variety of contexts, the virtuosic Danish double-bass player Niels-Henning Ørsted Pedersen, on the other hand, was apparently tempted by an American-style career, having been wooed by American musicians as they passed through Copenhagen. Musicians on the American scene acknowledged the originality of European jazz, which was open to fusions of all kinds. At the same time they often deplored its lack of swing and the weakness of its rhythmic base. Some, however, were already jettisoning their prejudices and beginning to see qualities where before they had only seen defects.

The legacy of free jazz

In Paris, where the embers of May 1968 continued to glow for some considerable time, free jazz was seen as a political symbol and was often contrasted by the militant activists with rock: a music of commitment versus

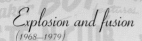

one of mass consumption.

The musical extremism of Albert Ayler and his disciples invited many comparisons with the political extremism of the Black Panthers. The discovery of Ayler's body in New York's East River in November 1970 and the suspicions that hung over the police were much commented on in the French music press. Just like the black movement, free jazz was showing signs of flagging. This could be seen in the recent work of Pharoah Sanders and Albert Ayler, which revealed a need to return to relative rhythmic and melodic clarity, to adopt more acceptable structures (borrowing from rock and the more soothing aspects of non-European ritual music) and to eliminate the more obdurate aspects of their music in favour of something increasingly devotional.

LISTENING
GUIDE
Pharoah Sanders, *Jewels of Thought*, Impulse.
Albert Ayler, *New Grass*, Impulse.
The Byg/Actuel Catalogue of 1969–71, Charly.

Rendezvous in Paris

Fleeing the indifference and even animosity they encountered in America, many musicians who refused to compromise arrived in Paris in 1969. Mixing with the French avant-garde and welcomed as messiahs by a boisterous public who saw themselves reflected in their riotous music, these ambassadors of free jazz recorded intensively throughout the summer of 1969 for the new label Byg, a partner of the underground newspaper *Actuel*. Depending on the listener's point of view, the many tracks recorded by these artists and by various others on the same label can be considered as examples of a free jazz that was either running out of breath or brimming with energy. While they contain moments of extreme sonic turmoil and apocalyptic instrumental excesses, it is also possible to hear in them a desire to explore and shape the material. Interest in form had never been totally absent from free jazz, particularly within the AACM (see p.171). A significant number of the musicians who had arrived in Paris were members of this Chicago cooperative. Their music exhibited a need on their part to construct, organize, compose, reintroduce nuance, silence and song, abandon the notion of wiping the slate clean, reconnect with their musical heritage and convention, and reduce the sometimes unbearable density and intensity achieved by free jazz from 1965 onwards. After the indifference shown towards it in America, the welcome it received in Europe helped free jazz to enter a new and positive phase.

The Art Ensemble of Chicago and the Great Black Music

This is what happened with the Art Ensemble of Chicago, founded in 1967 and made up of AACM members: the trumpeter Lester Bowie, the saxophonists Joseph Jarman and Roscoe Mitchell, the double-bass player Malachi Favors and, from 1970, the drummer Don Moye. In fact, each of these musicians was a multi-instrumentalist and the group's concerts resembled a large-scale display at some museum of ethnomusicology, adding a visual element to performances that were akin to *happenings*. The musicians played in costume and exotic make-up, influenced in all likelihood by Jarman, who had experience of multidisciplinary practices combining poetry, theatre and music. Free jazz thus took a decisive turn towards the creation of an acoustic theatrical experience with a major visual impact.

Under the banner 'Great Black Music' (it rejected the term 'jazz' as too pejorative and wanted moreover to take account of the black American musical heritage in its entirety), the Art Ensemble gave many black musicians the opportunity to play a reinvigorated form of free jazz that took much of its inspiration from Eric Dolphy and Charles Mingus. Its chief exponents included Leo Smith (a trumpeter and composer who used a highly conceptual musical system based on aspects of non-European music and with a syntax that made much use of silence), Leroy Jenkins (a rural fiddle sound adapted for contemporary music-making), Anthony Braxton (see p.208) and the trio Air, composed of the saxophonist and flautist Henry Threadgill, the double-bass player Fred Hopkins and the drummer Steve McCall (sophisticated polyphony with subtle combinations of timbre, and drumming from a colourist who caressed his instruments). 'Great Black Music' seemed to be developing into a kind of sophisticated chamber music.

The 'second loft generation'

Back home after its extended stay in Paris, the black American avant-garde continued to pay regular visits to Europe, where it had a relatively large audience. Members of the AACM returned to Chicago before large numbers of them moved to New York. Marginalized by the indifference of promoters, New York's black musicians fitted out their own lofts, such as Ornette Coleman's Artists House or the saxophonist Sam Rivers's Studio RivBea. Rivers was one of the Blue Note artists who in the mid-1960s had sought an alternative way forward somewhere between free jazz and modal jazz. In the 1970s, he became the mentor to a new wave of musicians. Heirs to the free-jazz tradition, they were nevertheless critical of the genre's excesses. This new wave of musicians is often referred to as the 'loft generation'. In order to distinguish it from the New York loft scene of the end of the 1960s (see p.198 and p.201), we shall refer to it here as the 'second loft generation'.

David Murray, a disciple of Duke Ellington's saxophonist Paul Gonsalves, became a prominent figure on the RivBea scene. Having learned his trade on the west coast with the Californian veterans of free jazz (Bobby Bradford, John Carter and Charles Tyler), Murray employed many of the stylistic traits of free jazz but aspired to assimilation rather than wiping the slate clean. He belonged to the first generation of jazzmen to learn to play by systematically studying the greats, from Ben Webster to Albert Ayler. He intensified Ayler's power and lyricism in the context of a less feverish and more structured line, approaching the fundamentally inimitable with very different technical resources and an encyclopedic knowledge of the history

LISTENING
GUIDE
Art Ensemble of Chicago,
Message to Our Folks,
Byg.
Leo Smith, *Creative Music*, Kabell.
Anthony Braxton (with Leo Smith and Leroy Jenkins), *Silence*, Black Lion.
Air, *Air Lore*, Novus.

ANTHONY BRAXTON, THE SEARCHER

Taking on the most ambitious challenges of free jazz, Anthony Braxton reformulated the perennial problems with which jazz had been preoccupied throughout its history: the relationship between improvisation and composition, between spontaneity and premeditation and between the African roots of black Americans and the European heritage. He had a significant and lasting influence on both sides of the Atlantic on the various forms of music that developed out of free jazz.

The soloist

It was as a soloist that Braxton first attracted attention. One of his early records, made in autumn 1968, was a collection of alto sax solos entitled *For Alto*. The idea of improvising on a melodic instrument without any harmonic or rhythmic support whatsoever resurfaced throughout his 1970s recording work. It revealed a desire not so much to free the present moment from predetermined external guidelines as to renew the framework for improvisation. Admittedly, many of the stylistic elements of free jazz were present (the effects of extreme timbres on the melodic line, explosions of sound, multiphonics, hurried phrasing), specific points of reference being the work of Ornette Coleman (melodic rambling), Eric Dolphy (undulating phrasing favouring large intervals) and Cecil Taylor (the effects of melodic saturation). These elements that connected Braxton to the free-jazz movement contrasted, however, with a definite penchant for 'cool' sax players such as Lee Konitz, Warne Marsh and Paul Desmond (because of their delicacy of sound, clarity of melodic line and expressive restraint). This contrast was reinforced by the staccato detailing of his melodic lines (each note detached and individually voiced), which was occasionally subjected to confused articulation and which alternated with legato phrases that seemed sometimes to float and sometimes to bite. With their rhythmic phrasing, which often eludes rational analysis, his improvisations unfold in a manner that hints at the existence of pre-established, notated guidelines or points to a reasoned spontaneity having less to do with totally unhindered improvisation than with an instantaneous act of composition.

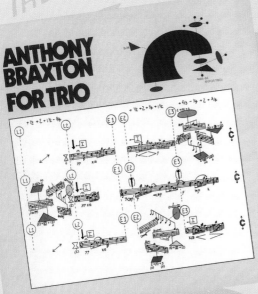

The composer

The solo pieces that Braxton wrote throughout the 1970s were conceived mostly for the saxophone (mainly alto and sopranino) but also for the flute, the clarinet and oddities such as the contrabass clarinet. They fall into the same category as his duos and trios in that they are reminiscent of 20th-century chamber music, which serves as a constant reference point for the compositions and improvisations included on the album *The Complete Braxton* (1971) as well as for the repertoire of the quartet Circle. Circle included Chick Corea at a time when he was experimenting with impressionism and free jazz, immediately before indulging in the more immediate pleasures of jazz-rock.

LISTENING
GUIDE
Circle, *Circle*, ECM.
Anthony Braxton (with
various groups including
quartet, tuba quintet
and duos with Chick
Corea), *The Complete
Braxton*, Arista.
Anthony Braxton (with
various groups including
quartet, saxophone
quartet and clarinet-
synthesizer duo), *New
York, Fall 1974*, Arista.
Anthony Braxton,
*Creative Orchestra
1976*, Arista.
Anthony Braxton,
*Dortmund (Quartet)
1976*, Hat Hut.
Anthony Braxton, *Alto
Saxophone
Improvisations, 1979*,
Arista.

When Corea moved on, Braxton formed a more or less regular quartet with the trumpeter Kenny Wheeler and the Circle rhythm section (Dave Holland on double bass and Barry Altschul on drums). This quartet produced the albums *New York, Fall 1974* and *Five Pieces, 1975*, which include some of the key pieces of 1970s free jazz. Later, the trumpet was replaced by a trombone (George Lewis or Ray Anderson) and then by a piano (Anthony Davis or Marilyn Crispell). Bebop influences (the occasional use of standards and the frequent adoption of a swing feel by the rhythm section) were combined with attempts to achieve a balance between free improvisation and formal constraints that would provide the improviser with a constantly renewed expressive context. These constraints might relate to the general structure of the piece, to the inclusion of the improvisation in the compositional material or to giving the improviser notated guidelines that would replace the conventional harmonic and rhythmic accompaniments. Some scores were incomplete, perhaps with one of the parameters (rhythm, melody, order of notes within a thematic unit, tempo) left open for the performer to choose. Certain acoustic moods were indicated merely by metaphors, or a series of extremely uncommon metres might be used. While these compositions – with titles incorporating enigmatic diagrams and sketches – referred back to Eric Dolphy and Charles Mingus, they also made reference to the 20th-century composers that Anthony Braxton liked to talk about in interviews, in particular John Cage, Iannis Xenakis and Karlheinz Stockhausen. The pieces were based on an analysis of the processes of musical creation, whose basic parameters Braxton had dissected and catalogued using his own system of classification before endlessly reassembling them within a range of extremely varied forms, including tuba quintet, saxophone quartet, duo for clarinet and synthesizer, big band (the Creative Orchestra), string quartet and quadruple symphony orchestra.

A member of the AACM, Braxton had been part of a major delegation of black American avant-garde musicians that had visited France in 1969. Throughout 1970, he remained a regular visitor to Europe, where his approach served as a model for the pioneers of improvised music. Performances by his quartet, his big band the Creative Orchestra and numerous other combinations with which he was involved were acclaimed by a sizeable and enthusiastic public. Over the last few decades of the century, however, his work met with relative indifference and he devoted himself to teaching.

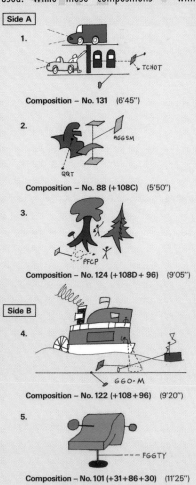

Side A

1. TCHOT

Composition – No. 131   (6'45")

2. AGGSM
QQT

Composition – No. 88 (+108C)   (5'50")

3. PFCP

Composition – No. 124 (+108D + 96)   (9'05")

Side B

4. GGO-M

Composition – No. 122 (+108 + 96)   (9'20")

5. FGGTY

Composition – No. 101 (+31 + 86 + 30)   (11'25")

All compositions by Anthony Braxton, Synthesis Music – BMI

Hamiet Bluiett, David Murray, Julius Hemphill and Oliver Lake

of jazz.

Fifteen years older than Murray yet achieving fame at the same time as him, Hamiet Bluiett also took a member of Duke Ellington's band as his model, in this case the baritone saxophonist Harry Carney. Having learned his trade in a wide variety of bands, from the Thad Jones–Mel Lewis Big Band to Charles Mingus's group, Bluiett was capable of playing with great fluidity in the baritone saxophone's highest register. He was a member of BAG, the Black Artists Group of Saint Louis, modelled on the AACM. With David Murray and two other members of the BAG, the alto saxophonists Julius Hemphill and Oliver Lake, he founded the World Saxophone Quartet. The band's structure was inspired by the classical quartet tradition and drew on the New Orleans collective style, the tradition of big-band sax sections and the fruits of free-jazz experimentation on the saxophone. The quartet's original repertoire was generated by the band members themselves – particularly Julius Hemphill, a highly regarded composer rediscovered after his death by the younger generations of the 1990s. A prominent member of other groups that Hemphill directed was the cellist Abdul Wadud, one of the revelations of the New York loft scene.

LISTENING GUIDE

Sam Rivers, *Contrasts*, ECM.
David Murray, *Sweet and Lovely*, Black Saint.
David Murray, *Flowers for Albert*, India Navigation.
Hamiet Bluiett, *Endangered Species*, India Navigation.
The World Saxophone Quartet, *Steppin' with the World Saxophone Quartet*, Black Saint.
Julius Hemphill (with Abdul Wadud), *Coon Bid'ness*, Arista.

Harmolodic funk and formal abstraction

Ornette Coleman was at this time recharging his batteries: engaging with funk at the head of Prime Time, which comprised two electric guitarists, an electric bass and one or two drummers. This line-up, which was to evolve over the following decade into a band with two electric rhythm sections, revived some of the principles of the free-jazz double quartet and allowed Coleman to draw a range of conclusions based on his theory of polyphonic improvisation known as 'harmolodics'.

His playing had hardly changed, but the term 'harmolodics' soon became all the rage – not as a way of designating Coleman's musical system but as a label for the appearance of electrofunk in the work of his new disciples, such as the guitarist James Blood Ulmer.

Anthony Braxton, by contrast, brought into the limelight young musicians who were less exclusively preoccupied with the roots of Afro-American music. The pianist Anthony Davis, for example, who preferred a style of counterpoint free from all harmonic functions, shared with the flautist James Newton a real interest in the music of Olivier Messiaen. The great trombonist George Lewis, who had come up through the free-jazz movement, became interested in the use of computers in music through his work with Richard Teitelbaum, a white musician who was one of Anthony Braxton's regular collaborators. Teitelbaum had been involved with a group of improvisers called Musica Elettronica Viva and approached the synthesizer less as an electric piano than as a machine to generate and freely organize extraordinary sounds.

Anthony Braxton helped to bring many white musicians to the fore, including the trombonist Ray Anderson, the double bassist Mark Helias and the drummer Gerry Hemingway. By the end of the decade the music performed by these three took the form of a very free interpretation of Mingus's colourful style and funk. They drew attention to a white American scene that, while assimilating certain aspects of free jazz, brought to it a less 'African' sensibility, adopting a more intellectual approach close to that of contemporary classical music. The work of the saxophone quartet Rova (Jon Raskin, Larry Ochs, Andrew Voigt and Bruce Ackley), for example, was based less on the impetus of improvised music and the African-American collective memory than on an exploration of form and structure that took them along similar paths to many European improvisers.

LISTENING GUIDE
Ornette Coleman, *Body Meta*, Artists House.
James 'Blood' Ulmer, *Are You Glad to be in America*, Rough Trade.
Anthony Davis and James Newton, *Hidden Voices*, India Navigation.
George Lewis, *Homage to Charles Parker*, Black Saint.
Ray Anderson, Mark Helias and Gerry Hemingway, *Oahspe*, Auricle.
Rova, *This, This, This, This*, Moers Music.

Libertarian Europe

Many pioneers of the free-jazz movement remained behind in Europe, thereby ensuring a certain continuity between the avant-gardes of the two continents. John Tchicai, a Dane with a Congolese father, had by now returned to Denmark. Don Cherry wandered the world, using Sweden as his home base. Steve Lacy assembled the hard core of his sextet, whose music combined the influence of Monk and the wider world of the arts and literature. The double bassist Barre Phillips and the drummer Stu Martin formed The Trio, representing a link between the latest developments on the Coltrane-inspired scene and the new European jazz, with the Briton John Surman on soprano and baritone saxes and bass clarinet. This link was evident in the trio's encounter with two defectors from classical contemporary music, the clarinetist-saxophonist Michel Portal and the percussionist Jean-Pierre Drouet.

LISTENING GUIDE
John Tchicai, *Real Tchicai*, Steeplechase.
Steve Lacy, *The Way*, Hat Hut.
The Trio, *The Trio*, Dawn-Sequel.
Michel Portal, *Alors!*, Futura.

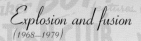

Free jazz and stylistic fragmentation

Free jazz was paradoxical. At the same time as it rallied musicians to its cause, it encouraged emancipation and stylistic fragmentation. In 1972, John Surman started to distance himself from the Coltrane model, turning instead to a more pastoral style inspired by British folk music. In France, the Free Jazz Workshop changed its name to the Workshop de Lyon in order to position itself more firmly in the here and now. Interested in the political dimension of free jazz, Michel Portal pondered the question of how legitimate it was for a European to play this music and attempted to anchor his work in his own personal history. Some years later, the Russian avant-garde also asserted its independence from the American model and even from Western European forms. From Paris to Leningrad, people started to avoid using the word 'jazz'. It was a word that referred to a music whose values had been undermined not only by free jazz but also by the exponents of controlled freedom. As soon as rhythm sections started merely hinting at harmony and the beat, they became optional, and bands with new and original line-ups began to appear in large numbers – solos, duos, trios without bass or drums, saxophone quartets, double-bass quartets, and so on. These bands, knocking on the door of contemporary classical music, were far removed from the rhythmic efficiency of hot jazz and swing. Europe's 'new improvised music' led to many exchanges between Britain, Italy and Germany. Whether spontaneous or composed, this music involved practices specific to each different community of musicians (made up of a number of more or less stable groups) and was so disparate that it is still difficult to describe today. However, the role of memory in improvisation provides a starting point that allows a few initial characteristics to be identified.

Improvisation and memory

In Britain, at the opposite end of the spectrum to imaginary folk music (see p.223), the guitarist Derek Bailey and the saxophonist Evan Parker excluded all use of memory from their improvisations, banishing from their work not only jazz conventions but also habit, thematic material, repetition, cyclical structures and metre. This constant quest for the unprecedented led them to discover unexplored aspects of their instruments (the sounds obtained by rattling the saxophone keys and tapping on the body of the guitar, for example). Evan Parker's extraordinary technique was the culmination of the liberties taken by black American musicians with instrumental timbre since the beginning of the century. This former disciple of John Coltrane seemed to decompose Coltrane's sound in the same way that one might obtain abstract pictorial material from an examination of the figurative masterpieces of the past with one's eye close to the canvas. The acoustic material obtained by Evan Parker reflected the direction taken by painting in the 20th century, in which there is a tendency for the subject to disappear behind the texture of the picture.

Many guitarists (including the German Hans Reichel, the Briton Fred Frith and the Americans Eugene Chadbourne and Henry Kaiser) were attracted by this approach. They availed themselves of the whole gamut of extraneous noises that could be produced on the guitar, reinvented rare techniques and

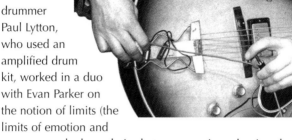

Derek Bailey

devised 'prepared' instruments. The British drummer Paul Lytton, who used an amplified drum kit, worked in a duo with Evan Parker on the notion of limits (the limits of emotion and annoyance, the boundaries between music and noise, the maximum resistance of skins and reeds).

Many musicians were tempted on a more or less long-term basis by the concept of total improvisation. Founded by Derek Bailey in 1976, the group Company featured improvisers from all over Europe as well as Americans such as Anthony Braxton, Leo Smith and even Lee Konitz. But work on texture was also carried out by musicians inclined towards composition, such as the English double bassist Barry Guy or, from the end of the 1970s, the Dutch double bassist Maarten Van Regteren Altena as the leader of small chamber groups.

In the German-speaking countries, musicians placed an emphasis on energy, urgency and physical exertion. Less methodical than the Britons, and more anarchic, the Germans Peter Brötzmann (saxophone) and Peter Kowald (double bass) and the Dutchman Han Bennink (drums) pushed the innovations of Cecil Taylor and Albert Ayler to their logical extremes. But behind the frenetic acoustic gesticulation and frequent resurfacing of aspects of the European musical heritage (the Belgian Fred Van Hove, the Dutchman Willem Breuker), a hint of jazz was still discernible in the work of these former admirers of Coltrane, Dolphy and Mingus. Bennink, a multi-instrumental bruitist, also identified with Baby Dodds, while his countryman Misha Mengelberg made repeated references to the music of Thelonious Monk. The work of the Swiss pianist Irene Schweizer, which combined her experience of hard bop with the influence of Cecil Taylor, revealed an interest in jazz's rhythmic values. Double bassists attracted by the possibilities of the bow (such as Barre Phillips and the Swiss Léon Francioli) and drummers interested in contemporary percussion (such as the Swiss Pierre Favre and the Italian Andrea Centazzo) continued to be influenced by the legacy of jazz.

Political circumstances and musical theatre

The political circumstances of the day were often reflected in the titles of pieces (for example, 'La fabbrica occupata' by Giorgio Gaslini and 'Libérez Michel Le Bris' by François Tusques) and the aim of much musical or theatrical activity was to ridicule social structures or reactionary artistic practices. The music of the Dutch saxophonist Willem Breuker recalled Soviet agitprop of the 1920s. Writing in the tradition of Kurt Weill for politically committed cinema or Brechtian theatre, as the leader of the

The Willem Breuker
Kollektief

Willem Breuker Kollektief he produced a form of musical theatre that borrowed from popular music and street theatre.

From the Brechtian cabaret of the British bandleader Mike Westbrook to the extreme happenings of the drummer Paul Lovens, this notion of musical theatre covered a wide range of different approaches. Many duos and trios stressed the dramatic qualities of collective improvisation, conceived as a dialogue or a theatrical event. The French scene that formed around the Cohelmec and Dharma ensembles drew on the dramatic aspects of Miles Davis's music but also reflected the experience of communal life. The exchanging of glances and visible signs of complicity sometimes assumed greater importance than the music. In the work of Bernard Lubat or the Workshop de Lyon, the theatricalization of musical exchanges could take on a playful, humorous dimension (gestures simulating anger, for example, or chases). The essentially visual nature of this explains why many recordings of this kind of music have aged badly.

The spirit of May 1968

LISTENING
GUIDE
Willem Breuker, *Music
For His Films*, BVHaast.
Willem Breuker, *Summer
Music*, Marge.
Workshop de Lyon, *La
Chasse de Shirah
Sharibad*, Move.

Even when used to ridicule the old order, the act of borrowing from popular music had an ambiguous function and, as with Albert Ayler, a certain seriousness of intent. In France perhaps more than elsewhere, this music perpetuated the spirit of May 1968: tributes to the working classes, nostalgia for a world of innocence, the quest for personal roots. Michel Portal's interjected themes sounded like impudent slogans or graffiti. His bandoneon, like the accordion of the drummer Bernard Lubat, was a call to musicians to reassert themselves in the sphere of dance and public festivities. Working on behalf of community associations in the area of music education and related activities, the new improvisers reinvented innocence, creating a repertoire of rickety nursery rhymes, improvising in a hopscotch-like fashion and gleefully cheating while theatricalizing their infringement of the rules. From public festivities it was a small step to psychodrama, group psychoanalysis and aesthetic debate. In their discussions, workshops, group activities and general hullabaloo, the new independent festivals revealed an intense nostalgia for the days when the Sorbonne was occupied.

Away from its more packaged and commercial manifestations, rock music

FREEING THE VOICE

Many singers embarked on the path taken by Jeanne Lee, freeing themselves from the three constraints of traditional song: words, music and a short, circular format. In 1971, the black singer Betty Carter set up her own record label, Bet-Car, in order to take personal charge of her career as an improviser and scat singer. In Austria at the end of the 1970s, Lauren Newton added her purely instrumental voice to the trumpet section of the Vienna Art Orchestra. While vocalese was being given a new lease of life by the group Manhattan Transfer, there was a tendency among vocalist improvisers to abandon the imitation of musical instruments. Performing with Pharoah Sanders, the African-American singer Leon Thomas took his inspiration from pygmy yodelling. The black singer Linda Sharrock began her career exploring the aesthetic qualities of the howl alongside her husband, the free-jazz guitarist Sonny Sharrock. The Polish singer Urszula Dudziak explored forms of articulation other than scat and used electronics to extend her vocal palette. Electronic techniques were frequently resorted to by jazz-rock keyboard players as a way of adding their distorted voices to the range of sounds that could be produced by their synthesizers (for example, Joe Zawinul at the end of 'Badia' on the album *Tale Spinnin'*).

The French singer Tamia worked less on phrasing than on the sound of the voice itself, focusing on contemporary developments as well as on non-European vocal techniques. Other vocalists, such as Maggie Nicols and Phil Minton in Britain, Annick Nozati in France and Lauren Newton in Austria, occupied a position halfway between theatre and music, using the intonations of speech and the semantics of articulate or inarticulate sounds, including shouts, whispers, interjections and mouth noises. Their work was closer to Luciano Berio and Georges Asperghis than Ella Fitzgerald. It was not too far removed, either, from some of the material collected by Alan Lomax, and it shared some of its techniques with Al Jarreau, who employed them in a more swinging, mass-market context.

More traditionally, the British singer Norma Winstone sang with the unadorned voice of a folk singer in her work with the trio Azimuth (alongside the trumpeter Kenny Lomax and the pianist John Taylor). The American singer Joni Mitchell, who came from a folk background, collaborated with Wayne Shorter and Jaco Pastorius. In the field of pure jazz, Dee Dee Bridgewater made a name for herself singing with the Thad Jones–Mel Lewis Big Band and went on to have a successful career as a scat singer and improviser.

Annick Nozati

THE NEW BIG BANDS

The large jazz orchestras such as the Thad Jones–Mel Lewis Big Band and the Buddy Rich and Woody Herman bands had become enormous, powerful machines that had incorporated a number of Gil Evans's innovations (expanding the saxophone section with other wind instruments, possible inclusion of French horn and tuba) and adopted the rhythms and instruments of rock music and Latin music (electric guitar, piano and bass, various percussion instruments). Gil Evans had also gone down the rock route, even dedicating an entire album to the compositions of Jimi Hendrix. In time his wind sections came to seem modest compared with his band's overdeveloped rhythm section (guitar, electric bass, electric piano and harp, and later synthesizers, drums and assorted percussion occasionally reinforced by a tuba). Initially rather unwieldy, this informal structure gradually became lighter and more supple over the years as Evans gave his group more and more freedom to improvise, based on a framework consisting of various signs and reference points. In this respect, Gil Evans had much in common with the large free-jazz bands, taking his inspiration from them and influencing them in equal measure.

The orchestra breaks ranks

The new big bands had emerged from behind the neat wooden stands – painted in the band's colours – of the swing era. As if to underline a band's democratic principles, the instrumentalists generally played standing up, either in a single curved line or grouped into sub-ensembles that once again called into question the traditional orchestral functions of the big band. The band members were even, from time to time, dotted among the audience, or they strolled together through the auditorium – ideas inspired by earlier experiments in contemporary music or by street parades. The big band sometimes provided a setting for collective improvisation, as was the case with the Celestrial Communication Orchestra, formed in France by Alan Silva, all of whose members seemed to be encouraged to give vent to their individual energy. This resulted in an intense ferment of sound based on the addition of individual voices or on approximate regroupings around a series of simple indications. Leaders would bring out certain details as they saw fit, as if operating a mixing desk. Other bands performed music that was far more closely composed and orchestrated within the context of highly conceptual formal experimentation. Composers often avoided traditional forms of notation, instead setting their work down in diagram form or directing it in a very gestural or physical manner.

These approaches and a number of customs inherited from big bands were combined in the black American bands (such as those of Anthony Braxton or Roscoe Mitchell) and the European bands (the short-lived Conflagration, centred around the John Surman Trio, Keith Tippett's gigantic Centipede, Jef Gilson's Europamerica with its overdeveloped sax section, and the Globe Unity Orchestra, which played both the freest kind of collective improvisation and music composed by its members).

However, it was probably the English double bassist Barry Guy's London Jazz Composers' Orchestra that took this interweaving of the roles of composer and improviser the furthest and on the most sustained basis, working on problems which Duke Ellington had also had to confront. Like Ellington, Guy composed for specific improvisers in a manner designed to stimulate and regenerate their potential. Also like Ellington, he took care that they would work together well in his large ensemble. More important than pitch in Guy's writing was the sculpting of the orchestral mass: its density, intensity, instrumental colour and flow – preoccupations similar to those of the symphonic composers of the 20th century. The effect on audiences of the sumptuous textures

The Globe Unity Orchestra, 1976

of his compositions and the incredible energy given off by his musicians recalled the effect produced fifty years earlier by *The Rite of Spring*. Added to these qualities was an element of chance, but supported by momentum and the collective science of improvisation — something all too often lacking in the work of contemporary classical composers who make use of random elements.

Festive brass and neoclassicism

The brass sounds of the big band were ideal for the free-jazz version of South-African jazz created by Chris McGregor and his Brotherhood of Breath, for the festive frolics of the big band La Marmite Infernale and for the oompah of Willem Breuker's music theatre. In the United States in 1969, Charlie Haden had recorded Carla Bley's arrangements of revolutionary songs of the Spanish Civil War. The following year, Bley assembled a huge line-up for her opera *Escalator Over the Hill*, but in general she preferred lighter, medium-sized groups that were better suited to the mischievous humour of her music. Her influence on large and medium-sized groups often combined with the influence of Gil Evans, George Russell and Charles Mingus — and also Frank Zappa, who was winning increasing admiration from jazz musicians for his virtuoso orchestration and the satirical quality of his music.

Even in Britain, whose large groups inspired many composers, the economic situation made big bands the exception. Often brought together on a one-off basis, they rarely had adequate rehearsal time, although this could obviously be of benefit to experiments based on spontaneity. In the second half of the 1970s, an increased number of projects was an indication that the economic situation had improved for jazz. This was true not only for the United States but also for Europe, which welcomed the big bands of Anthony Braxton, Roscoe Mitchell and Sam Rivers, and where new groups were emerging every year. A major turning point was the creation of the Vienna Art Orchestra by the composer Mathias Rüegg in Austria in 1977. Permanent and generously subsidized, the VAO stood in the same relation to the large free-jazz bands as the exponents of controlled freedom to free jazz. In France, the formation of François Jeanneau's Pandemonium in 1979 and the creation of Martial Solal's Dodecaband and Patrice Caratini's Onzetet in 1981 confirmed this new trend for large groups, although there were various aesthetic outlooks ('binary', modal and open to varying degrees). Their 1970s antecedents were the bands of the American George Russell, the Briton Mike Westbrook, the Dane Palle Mikkelborg, the Swiss George Grüntz and the Rhodesian expatriate Michael Gibbs, amongst others.

Carla Bley

interacted intensively with the new improvised music in the counter-cultural sphere. At the 1969 Amougies Festival in Belgium, Frank Zappa jammed at different times with Pink Floyd and members of the black American avant-garde based in Paris. Britain was particularly open to exchanges of this kind, which were organized by practitioners such as the singer Robert Wyatt, the groups that had sprung up around the Canterbury school, the guitarist Fred Frith (leader of the group Henry Cow) and the saxophonists Lol Coxhill and Trevor Watts. During the second half of the 1970s, a number of musicians (such as the British pianist Steve Beresford) turned their attention to the punk scene and its new-wave offshoots. They shared a desire with the free-jazz and rock scenes to respond to the deteriorating social climate and the prevailing tendency towards aesthetic normalization – whether with great intensity or total detachment, through provocation or derision. In France, the radical nature of certain improvisation-based groups at the end of the 1970s (for example, that of the trumpeter Jac Berrocal or the trumpeter Bernard Vitet's Drame Musical Instantané) was not unconnected to the tougher stance adopted by the autonomous leftist splinter groups. In the United States around the same time, the singer and saxophonist James Chance (aka James White) was playing music full of disenchantment, a combination of crazy funk and extravagant free jazz.

Respectability and counter-culture in the Soviet Union

LISTENING
GUIDE
Michel Portal, *Splendid Yzlment*, Columbia.
Michel Portal (with Bernard Lubat), *Chateauvallon 76*, L'Escargot.
Lol Coxhill, *The Joy of Paranoia*, Ogun.
Steve Beresford, *My Favourite Animals*, Nato.
Jac Berrocal, *Catalogue – Penetration*, Hat Hut.
James Chance *Buy the Contorsions*, Ze Records.
Ganelin Trio, *Catalogue: Live in East Germany*, Leo.

In the Soviet Union, as a consequence of the tougher line taken after the Prague Spring, the authorities displayed the same aversion to rock that they had previously shown to jazz. They banned electric groups that did not include at least three wind instruments – thereby promoting the development of Soviet jazz-rock. Jazz itself, having now become respectable, was included in the catalogue of the state record company Melodiya and was taught in music schools. Specialist jazz academies were established in the mid-1970s. Having grown out of the counter-culture, jazz saw its audiences getting older and older. The economic situation remained difficult for jazz, and many musicians emigrated to the United States. Among them was the trumpeter Valery Ponomarev, who joined Art Blakey's Jazz Messengers in 1977. The authorities attempted to delete their names from the Soviet jazz repertoire and writings on Soviet jazz history. Of those who remained behind, many were tempted by the commercial success of jazz-rock. The reaction of the Ganelin Trio (the pianist Viacheslav Ganelin, the saxophonist Vladimir Chekasin and the drummer Vladimir Tarasov) was more radical, demonstrating the need of the artistic avant-garde to break free from the oppressive constraints imposed on Soviet society by its ageing leaders.

The unclassifiable

A number of musicians on the European free-jazz scene from the end of the 1960s onwards were also active at the same time in jazz-rock and on the controlled-freedom scene. There were various reasons for this: they may have been only occasional guests on the free-jazz scene, they may simply have been interested observers or they may have felt somewhat limited in

LISTENING
GUIDE
*Humair Jeanneau
Texier,* Owl.
Enrico Rava (with Jean-
François Jenny-Clark
and Aldo Romano),
Enrico Rava Quartet,
ECM.
Kenny Wheeler (with
Evan Parker and Jean-
François Jenny-Clark),
Around Six, ECM.
Albert Mangelsdorff, *A
Jazz Tune I Hope,* MPS.
Jan Garbarek (with Arild
Andersen and Edward
Vesala), *Triptykon,* ECM.
John Surman, Mike
Osborne and Alan
Skidmore, *SOS,* Ogun.
Tomasz Stanko,
Baladyna, ECM.

range after putting so much energy into free jazz. The last reason is what led three Frenchmen – the saxophonist François Jeanneau, the double bassist Henri Texier and the drummer Daniel Humair – to form a trio that was very active at the end of the 1970s. Similarly, the trumpeter Enrico Rava participated in a very free-jazz Italian scene while also playing music of a less anarchic kind. The trombonist Albert Mangelsdorff and the trumpeter Kenny Wheeler, two veterans born in 1928 and 1930 respectively, were extremely active in elite free-jazz circles, conducting their own experiments in this field while also performing less radical music with American rhythm sections or in the company of artists in the ECM mould. Having served his apprenticeship in free jazz, the Norwegian saxophonist Jan Garbarek still continued to display the powerful influence of Ornette Coleman in his work with Keith Jarrett. The French double bassist Jean-François Jenny-Clark, the Italian drummer Aldo Romano, the German pianist Joachim Kühn, the British saxophonist John Surman, the Polish trumpeter Tomasz Stanko, the Finnish drummer Edward Vesala and the Norwegian double bassist Arild Andersen have all had careers that are difficult to label and that have varied greatly from one another.

Jazz and world music

Until well into the 1960s, the interaction between jazz and traditional forms of music had been modest, simplistic and a source of misunderstandings. For example, the jam sessions involving a contingent of black American free-jazz musicians and various traditional musicians at the Panafrican Festival in Algiers in 1969 revealed a mutual lack of understanding between the two camps. As ethnomusicological collections became more widespread, foreign travel became more popular and distant places became more easily accessible, music from all over the globe helped to enrich the musical vocabulary of the new improvisers, many of whom were the forerunners of the 'world music' of the 1980s.

Travellers and exiles

The first black American musicians to help change the nature of this interaction were travellers like Don Cherry (see p.220) or Randy Weston, who visited Africa a number of times from 1961 onwards before eventually settling in Tangiers for several years and founding the African Rhythm Club there. Things were very different for the Argentinian saxophonist Gato Barbieri and the South African pianist Dollar Brand. After adopting a bebop style in the late 1950s, Brand started to distance himself from any elements specific to South African jazz. But then, having fled South Africa and apartheid in the early 1960s, he felt a need to emphasize his roots. Little by little, the influence of Thelonious Monk in his piano playing was supplemented by a certain African character, and from 1965 onwards the references to Africa became explicit in albums such as *Anatomy of a South African Village*, *African Piano* and *African Sketchbook*. After converting to Islam and adopting the name Abdullah Ibrahim, Brand returned to South Africa in 1973. From this point on he had a dual career – making recordings in Europe (as a solo

DON CHERRY, WANDERING MUSICIAN

Don Cherry and Nana Vasconcelos at the Chateauvallon Festival in 1972

A former colleague of Ornette Coleman, Don Cherry started to collect musical instruments – Balinese gamelans, flutes of all descriptions, an Indian harmonium, gongs and small ritual instruments from the Far East – in 1968, thereby continuing the multi-instrumentalist tradition of free jazz. But beyond this self-consciously exotic collection, Don Cherry had a truly nomadic soul. Perhaps he owed this to his ancestry: with a black American father and an a Native American mother, he was almost predestined to cross boundaries. In 1968, his multi-instrumentalism took a remarkable turn in his response to a commission he received from the festival Berlin Jazztage. Played by a band of eight musicians, most of them European, and constructed on the architectural principle of his 'Complete Communion' (see p.169), the long suite *Eternal Rhythm* was based on the use of gamelan-like metallophones and the rhythmic and melodic vocabulary associated with them. This displayed a desire to go far beyond musical commonplaces, to break new ground at a time when musical tourism was largely focused on India. The following year, playing trumpet, flutes and piano in a duo with the drummer Ed Blackwell, Cherry made a double album (*Mu*) that drew on the discoveries he had made on a trip to Africa with Randy Weston. Having made Sweden his home, he travelled extensively, making many contacts in different cultures around the world. These contacts resulted in collaborations with the Indian percussionists Latif Khan and Trilok Gurtu, the Turkish drummer Okay Temiz, the South African double bassist Johnny Dyani, the Jamaican poet Linton Kwesi Johnson, the singer Lou Reed and the composer Krysztof Penderecki. In his group Codona, he played alongside the Brazilian percussionist Nana Vasconcelos and the sitar and tabla player Collin Walcott. This trio aptly illustrated Cherry's aspiration to live in a world without frontiers, whether political or aesthetic.

LISTENING
GUIDE
Don Cherry, *Eternal Rhythm*, MPS.
Don Cherry, *Mu*, Byg/Actuel.
Don Cherry, Collin Walcott and Nana Vasconcelos, *Codona*, ECM.
Don Cherry–Latif Khan, Europa.

the third world - Gato Barbieri

artist or in a duo or trio) and recording more dancelike music in South Africa with young local musicians (*African Marketplace*). Having worked with Don Cherry and been a disciple of Ornette Coleman before moving closer to John Coltrane and Pharoah Sanders, Gato Barbieri followed a similar path. A series of duos recorded in 1968 with Dollar Brand marked a major turning point of his career. The following year he recorded *The Third World*, the first album in an oeuvre that was now focused exclusively on the music of Latin America.

LISTENING GUIDE

Randy Weston, *African Nite*, Owl.

Abdullah Ibrahim (Dollar Brand), *African Piano*, Japo.

Gato Barbieri and Dollar Brand, *Confluence*, Black Lion.

Gato Barbieri, *The Third World*, Flying Dutchman.

Okay Temiz, *Oriental Wind*, Sonet.

John Surman, *Upon Reflection*, ECM.

Vagif Mustafa Zadeh, *Vagif Mustafa Zadeh*, Melodiya.

Jim Pepper, *Pepper's Pow Wow*, Embryo.

Tete Montoliu, *Catalonian Folk Songs*, Timeless.

Ralph Towner, *Solstice*, ECM.

Gary Burton, *Tennessee Firebirds*, RCA.

Egberto Gismonti, *Circense*, EMI.

Hermeto Pascoal, *Zabumbê-bum-a*, Warner.

David Grisman, *Quintet 80*, Warner.

Jerry Gonzalez, *Ya Yo Me Cure*, American Clave.

The search for roots

While London's South Africans (including the saxophonist Dudu Pukwana, the trumpeter Mongezi Feza and the double bassist Johnny Dyani) fraternized with the British capital's free-jazz scene as members of Chris McGregor's Brotherhood of Breath, many other musicians were incorporating elements of their own musical heritage into their playing. Among them were the Turkish drummer Okay Temiz (with the group Oriental Wind), the British saxophonist John Surman, the Azerbaijani pianist Vagif Mustafa Zadeh, the Native American saxophonist Jim Pepper, the Catalan pianist Tete Montoliu, the Scottish drummer Ken Hyder, the Polish violinists Michal Urbaniak and Zbigniew Seifert and the young North Americans influenced by country music and folk guitar (Pat Metheny, Ralph Towner and, from the 1960s onwards, Charlie Haden and Gary Burton). By contrast, performers of traditional musical forms facing the threat of dilution or even extinction saw jazz as a good model to follow. Getting away from the packaged formats of mass-market traditional folk music, musicians such as the Brazilian multi-instrumentalists Egberto Gismonti and Hermeto Pascoal, the flamenco guitarist Paco de Lucia, the southern Indian violinist Lakshminarayana Shankar and the bluegrass revivalists Tony Trischka (five-string banjo) and David Grisman (mandolin) carved out niches for themselves on the contemporary jazz scene.

The interplay between jazz and Latin enjoyed a new lease of life as a reaction to the overly flashy vogue for salsa. The pianist Chucho Valdés formed Irakere, a Latin-jazz band with drums, in Cuba in 1973. This group began touring outside the island in 1976, bringing the trumpeter Arturo Sandoval and the saxophonist Paquito D'Rivera into the public eye. At the end of the 1970s, a number of young musicians belonging to New York's Bronx-based Latin community also turned away from salsa in a double-pronged movement towards jazz, whose drum kit they adopted, and the ancient sacred music of the Caribbean. Of Puerto Rican ancestry, the Gonzalez brothers (trumpeter-percussionist Jerry and double bassist Andy) were at the forefront of this development.

Ways of borrowing and coming together

The new generation of jazzmen took advantage once more of jazz's ability to assimilate. After modal systems and traditional metres, they turned their attention to instrumental variety (Michel Portal tried out the Romanian taragot and the Basque tenora), new techniques of sound production (the trombonist Albert Mangelsdorff's multiphonics and John Surman's circular breathing, based on the bagpipe principle, which enabled him to breathe without interrupting the flow of music) and new, exotic ways of playing European instruments (double bass played with strings off the bridge, producing a sound close to that of the African thumb piano; clarinet without mouthpiece played like an oblique flute or didgeridoo; percussive playing on the clarinet to produce drumlike noises).

In this way, working practices and musical rituals within the band were given new life. With its fits of laughter and moments of great seriousness, the music of the Workshop de Lyon and the Marvelous Band hinted at the impact the world-music label Ocora would have. The label covered music that was functional, ritual, playful, sacred and initiatory. The borrowing of procedures and musical vocabularies sometimes gave way to veritable pastiches (including imitations of pygmy chants in the opening to 'Watermelon Man' by Herbie Hancock's Headhunters) or the adoption of traditional themes (the Native American theme of Jim Pepper's 'Wichi Tai To', which became something of a jazz standard in the 1970s).

At other times simple acoustic atmospheres were conjured up – no longer along the impressionistic lines of Duke Ellington's 'jungle', but with the precision of news reportage: the imitations of whale song on 'Song for the Whales' by Charlie Haden and the group Old and New Dreams; the atmosphere of the summer 1968 Democratic Party convention in 'Circus '68 '69' by the Liberation Music Orchestra; and the explosions of war, crowd noises and harbourside moods in the work of Weather Report. The modern sampling process was anticipated by the occasional use of pre-existing recordings: the historical revolutionary chants heard in the background of the Liberation Music Orchestra's latter-day versions of the same songs; the quartet of

LISTENING GUIDE
Michel Portal, *Dejarme Solo*, Dreyfus.
Albert Mangelsdorff, *Tromboneliness*, MPS.
Workshop de Lyon, *Tiens les Bourgeons Éclatent*, L'Oiseau Musicien.
Jan Garbarek and Bobo Stenson, *Wichi Tai To*, ECM.

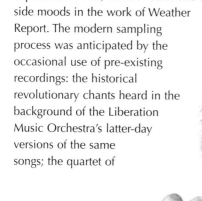

Michel Portal

LISTENING
GUIDE
Don Cherry, Dewey
Redman, Charlie Haden
and Ed Blackwell, *Old
and New Dreams*, ECM.
Charlie Haden,
*Liberation Music
Orchestra*, Impulse.
Marcello Melis, *The New
Village on the Left...*,
Black Saint.
Ornette Coleman,
Dancing in Your Head,
Horizon.
Gerry Mulligan and
Astor Piazzolla, *Summit*,
Accord.
Hozan Yamamoto, *Silver
World*, Philips.
Wayne Shorter, *Native
Dancer*, Columbia.
François Tusques, *Vers
une Musique Bretonne
Nouvelle*, Chant du
Monde.
Jan Garbarek, Egberto
Gismonti and Charlie
Haden, *Folk Songs*, ECM.
Henri Texier, *Amir*, JMS.
Oregon, *Out of the
Woods*, Elektra.
Masahiko Sato, *Spiritual
Nature*, East Wind.

the Italian double bassist Marcello Melis reacting to Sardinian singing; and Ornette Coleman interweaving Moroccan chants from the village of Jajouka with his saxophone playing.

There were many personal encounters with Indian or Brazilian musicians who enjoyed a good following in Europe or the United States. These encounters were sometimes passive, such as when Miles Davis gave scores of his music to the Indian sitar and tabla players that he invited to join his band. They could also be interactive, as they were in the group Shakti, or when Gerry Mulligan entered into a musical dialogue with Astor Piazzolla, or when the Japanese *shakuhachi* flute player Hozan Yamamoto recorded with a jazz trio, or when Wayne Shorter invited the Brazilian singer Milton Nascimento to sing on his album *Native Dancer*, or when François Tusques supplemented his Intercommunal Free Dance Music Orchestra with African and Breton musicians and a Catalan singer.

Imaginary folk music

In 1977, a number of Lyons-based groups associated with the Workshop de Lyon formed an association called L'Association pour la Recherche d'un Folklore Imaginaire (ARFI – Association for Research into an Imaginary Folklore). This 'imaginary folklore' borrowed many elements from real folk traditions, with musicians using these as models or as a form of compensation for the gradual disappearance of their own musical roots. Thus, Michel Portal combined acoustic memories of the Basque country with impressions of Africa; Jan Garbarek explored the Scandinavia of his imagination using a saxophone with the timbre and melismatic phrasing of a Middle-Eastern oboe; the Brazilian guitarist and pianist Egberto Gismonti collaborated with Garbarek; Henri Texier switched from the double bass to the lute and flute, revisiting his Breton roots as reflected in a kind of Mediterranean mirror; the Canadian guitarist and pianist Ralph Towner and his group Oregon conjured up an ideal America whose wild splendour was tamed to the sound of the Indian sitar and the ancient music of Europe; and Joe Zawinul drew up an inventory of the instruments, sounds and impressions he came across on his travels. Whether orchestrator, composer or improviser, the jazz musician became a sampler of acoustic information from all over the globe and from any period in time. It was less a case of musicians collecting folklore than feeding off it when constructing their own mental universes. Similarly, the Soviet avant-garde led by the Ganelin Trio was less remarkable for its ability to quote from the traditional musical forms of a multi-ethnic Soviet Union than for its quest for a Russian soul and its desire to reconnect with the astonishing creativity of the pre-Stalin artistic avant-garde. In Japan, beyond its ability to reproduce the American model to the very last detail and its use of quotations from folk music, the Japanese avant-garde – thanks to musicians such as the pianists Masahiko Satoh and Yosuke Yamashita and the drummer Masahiko Togashi – knew how to give voice to the deep roots of its imaginary heritage.

Back to the values of jazz

With its veteran artists passing away (Louis Armstrong in 1971, Duke Ellington in 1974), jazz seemed to be moving away from its original values. The time of the white jazz musician had definitely come – the Brecker brothers even made up the front line of the Horace Silver quintet. The black avant-garde had broken with the conventions that had prevailed since the 1920s. 'The spirit not the letter' was the order of the day. From the Art Ensemble of Chicago to popular music, black musicians handed over the blues form to white rock music, retaining only its essence.

Black musicians reposition themselves

Following Herbie Hancock's lead, many black musicians took a more radical approach than Horace Silver and the Adderley brothers, letting themselves be influenced by the styles of Miles Davis and James Brown. More or less electric, sometimes involving singing (George Benson owed his popular success to his voice rather than his guitar) and tending more towards popular Latin forms or disco (under the control of interventionist producers and arrangers), this soul-jazz-turned-funk-jazz provided an opportunity for labels such as Blue Note and Prestige to recycle their catalogues and artists. An extremely wide range of musicians were discovered, or rather rediscovered: the trumpeters Donald Byrd and Freddie Hubbard, the saxophonists Rusty Bryant and Grover Washington, the guitarist Grant Green, the pianists Ahmad Jamal and George Duke, the organist Jimmy Smith and his successors (such as Lonnie Smith), the vibraphone player Roy Ayers, the drummers Chico Hamilton and Idris Muhammad, a young generation of electric bassists and older, double-bass players who had been converted. As can be seen from Larry Carlton's work with the Crusaders and the Brecker brothers' contribution to the recording sessions of JB's Horns (made up of musicians from James Brown's band), white musicians were not totally absent from this predominantly black phenomenon.

The distinction between black musicians tempted by funk and those exploring more alternative positions on the fringes of the avant-garde while preserving the values of hard bop was hazy. Those who made a name for themselves in the area between free bop and free fusion included: Eddie Henderson, 'Hannibal' Marvin Peterson and Charles Tolliver (trumpet); Sonny Fortune, Gary Bartz, George Adams and Billy Harper (saxophone); Stanley Cowell, Kenny Barron and John Hicks (piano); Buster Williams and Clint Houston (double bass); and Billy Hart, Al Foster and Clifford Jarvis (drums). Also among them were musicians who had been active in the 1960s, such as the trumpeter Woody Shaw, the saxophonist Joe Henderson, the pianist McCoy Tyner, the bassists Ron Carter and Cecil McBee, and the drummer Jack DeJohnette.

Synthesis and classicism

In the second half of the 1970s, musicians who had come to maturity playing free jazz now reconnected with the phrasing and structure of bebop (for example, the saxophonists Arthur Blythe, John Stubblefield and Chico Freeman and the pianist Don Pullen). Archie Shepp recorded a collection of blues and spirituals with the pianist Horace Parlan.

His quintet as well as the quartet Old and New Dreams (Don Cherry, Dewey Redman, Charlie Haden and Ed Blackwell) came up with a calmer and wiser, more 'classic' version of free jazz. Pursuing a solo performing career, Cecil Taylor also recorded in a duo with the pianist Mary Lou Williams. Sun Ra and his orchestra, meanwhile, focused on the repertoire of Fletcher Henderson. Charles Mingus returned to prominence with a more structured format than before.

By contrast, the Europe-based Phil Woods, the most talented of Charlie Parker's white followers, performed a kind of free bop with his European Rhythm Machine, with a tendency to 'binary' phrasing. Bill Evans finally received the appreciation he deserved and Lee Konitz and Paul Desmond were rediscovered. While cool-jazz LPs were being reissued in Japan in their original sleeves, Chet Baker and Art Pepper both resurfaced, the former reconnecting with the most romantic aspects of West Coast jazz and the latter playing in a Coltrane-influenced style. From Archie Shepp to Martial Solal, jazz standards came back into fashion. Hard bop regained centre stage with a repertoire reinvigorated by the pianist Cedar Walton's group Eastern Rebellion, in which the white saxophonist Bob Berg made a name for himself. Berg was one of a number of musicians singled out by the critics as representative of a new generation of outstanding technicians whom they considered to be lacking in artistic sensibility. When former members of the Miles Davis Quintet got together with Freddie Hubbard to form the group VSOP, they were accused of trying to turn back the clock. The same accusation was levelled at the trumpeter Warren Vaché and the saxophonist Scott Hamilton, two young musicians who expressed themselves in the musical language of the 1930s. Jazz-rock and post-free jazz gradually gave way to neoclassicism and the art of reinterpreting earlier work. This could be seen in the solo performances of the guitarist Joe Pass, who dedicated himself to a synthesis of the stylistic inheritances of jazz guitar. Made up of West Coast veterans, the group Supersax performed arranged versions of Charlie Parker solos. In France, a new generation of musicians focused on the earliest jazz (the saxophonists Daniel Huck and Marc Richard and the pianist Philippe Baudoin, among others) while at the same time demonstrating their ability to break the rules of the genre and take account of post-Parker jazz. In a similar vein, the Anachronic Jazz Band took the bold step of reinterpreting the modern jazz repertoire in the style of the 1920s. Having become a classic genre, jazz began to feed off its own history.

Context

SOCIETY. America raised the stakes in the arms race, accelerating the economic collapse of the Soviet Union. Having started with the Russian revolution, the arrival of mechanized warfare, the telephone, Surrealism and the jazz band, the 20th century ended with the breaking up of the artistic avant-garde, the concept of 'clean' war, the development of the internet and the fall of the communist empire. The East–West split flipped over onto its side and became a North–South line dividing rich and poor countries. The collapse of communism left the field open for religious fanaticism and nationalist violence that transformed the geopolitical scene. Faced with economic crises, ultra-liberalism clashed with state interventionism (a legacy of the Great Depression) over the appropriate course of action. Traumatized in the 1980s by unemployment, AIDS, urban violence and terrorism, the protest movement re-organized itself at the end of the 1990s. The internet became the preferred forum for expression of counter-cultural groups, which mobilized opposition on the issues of ecological destruction, genetic engineering, globalization, xenophobia, social exclusion and the virtual economy. In the United States, the social sector was sorely neglected by politicians, both Republican and Democrat. In 2000, the World Health Organization ranked the world's greatest power 34th in an index of world health systems. The inequality gap widened and lack of job security made the US employment statistics look better than they were. Moreover, they did not take account of the nation's prison population of 1.6 million (1995) plus almost 4.4 million wards of court. While the black middle classes scored some successes on the road towards integration (Harold Washington became Mayor of Chicago in 1983; Colin Powell became Chairman of the Joint Chiefs of Staff in 1989; Toni Morrison won the Nobel Prize for Literature in 1993), the social group worst affected by the deterioration of the social landscape was the black community (12% of the total population and more than 50% of the prison population). The black ghettos developed self-contained parallel economies under the control of armed gangs.

Hip-hop dancers

THE MUSIC INDUSTRY. The music world was turned upside down by the arrival of computerized sound production and recording techniques. Digitalization turned previously analogue synthesizers into musical computers that could be linked using the MIDI (Musical Instrument Digital Interface) norm. They were operated via a keyboard, computer console, guitar or EWI (Electric Wind Instrument). The sampler allowed isolated sounds to be recorded and musical sequences to be borrowed from a pre-existing work and inserted into a new one. Studios also embraced musical robotics.

In 1983, the recording industry was given a new lease of life by the introduction of the compact disc. Jazz fans rebuilt their record collections on CD thanks to a policy of systematic reissuing by the major labels, who also scouted for safe bets discovered by the many independent labels. In 2000, the five multinationals that controlled the world market (BMG, Universal, Warner, Sony and EMI) marked time, faced with the prospect of online music distribution. The independents, whose position had long been threatened by a market saturated with both reissues and new releases, raised their heads above the parapet, betting on the capacity of the internet to absorb and distribute the mass of creativity they represented. At the same time they dreaded the moment when the multinationals would decide to apply the rules of maximum profit to the internet.

RELATED MUSICAL GENRES. The younger generations expressed their resentments and frustrations through hip-hop, a cultural movement that developed in the black ghettos and gave rise to new artistic forms based on virtuosic resourcefulness and appropriation: tag art, breakdancing and rap. On their turntables, DJs mixed and distorted 'breakbeats', rhythmic sequences picked out from commercial records. They manipulated these sequences, using a technique called 'scratching', in order to create new rhythms. This underground culture gradually invaded the clubs of the white neighbourhoods and cities across Europe. In the wake of the 'house' movement, which appropriated automated electronic instruments and gadgetry (synthesizers, drum machines, sequencers, home studios) and sampled existing recordings to provide raw material for the new artists, new genres (such as acid house, techno, jungle, and drum and bass) followed hard on each other's heels in a frantic rush to keep one step ahead of the recording industry.

Jazz had a place in this system of recycling (for example, the hip-hop of Gang Starr, the drum and bass of Photek, Carl Craig's techno and Galliano's acid jazz), but the young artists drew above all on rhythm and blues, which was a wellspring of soul-based and funk-based subgenres dominated by the unclassifiable Prince.

It was a white guitarist, Stevie Ray Vaughan, who launched a craze for the blues among rock audiences in the 1980s. The black guitarist and singer Robert Cray took up the baton. During the 1990s, a number of young black bluesmen well versed in the genre and possessing excellent technical skills looked at the entire tradition again, from its acoustic origins (Keb' Mo') to the frontiers of soul (Joe Louis Walker). The whole world over, gospel – often in a watered-down form – accompanied the religious revival embraced by the younger generations. In the United States, it remained the musical heart of black communities.

The musical traditions of Africa and the African diaspora occupied a central position in the vogue for world music.

LISTENING GUIDE
Rebirth of Cool (compilation, with Gang Starr and Galliano), 4th and Broadway.
Carl Craig, *More Songs about Food and Revolutionary Art*, Planet.
Photek, *Modus Operandi*, Source.
Prince, *Sign o' the Times*, Warner Bros.
Keb' Mo', *Keb' Mo'*, Epic.

Jazz in crisis?

The history of jazz seemed to have ground to a halt. Then, in the 1990s, it exploded. But this resumption of creativity was accompanied by an identity crisis. Never had so many festivals, venues, publications and schools been dedicated to jazz as in the period 1980 to 2000, but it was away from the cutting edge that things were happening and many of the musicians involved rejected the label 'jazz'.

Education and marketing

Having advanced at breakneck speed and opened up countless new fields of investigation, jazz now needed to pause and assimilate the new developments. Against a background of economic crisis, young musicians in search of models took their inspiration from a jazz whose essential identity was in no doubt, but they also aspired to a certain versatility so that they could meet the needs of a commercial scene with a strong demand for soul and 'jazzy' elements. From 'ternary' to 'binary', from bebop to jazz-rock, they absorbed all the great jazz styles of the past – as if jazz history had come to an end and all that remained to do was to manage what it had left behind. Others sought to recycle jazz, studying it less from personal taste than out of necessity, since this represented the best way to acquire the harmonic and rhythmic skills required by the studios. The innovators of the 1970s had often favoured musical poetics over the technical skills that would have matched their ambitions. The young jazzmen were reacting to the situation of their elders who not infrequently found themselves at a dead end. They preferred the accelerated apprenticeship offered by the jazz schools to the experience of real life and the joys and risks of experimentation. They played a hard bop that was more brilliant than the original or a jazz-rock more impressive than ever in terms of its power, rapidity and precision.

Cassandra Wilson

Sexy jazz and emancipated musicians

As in the Great Depression, the public wanted to be entertained. Modern jazz suffered from having a reputation as something hideous – a reputation perpetuated by a media in thrall to the automatic reflexes of the ratings. Unlike its music, however, the legend and image of jazz were much favoured by advertising executives. Its classic age was the inspiration behind their elegant black-and-white visuals, using a style borrowed from Blue Note record sleeves.

LISTENING
GUIDE
Dee Dee Bridgewater,
Dear Ella, Verve.
Cassandra Wilson,
Traveling Miles, Blue
Note.
Shirley Horn, *I
Remember Miles*, Verve.

Words like 'jazz', 'swing' and 'sax' were used in the creation of sexy, funny brand names. Singers of rock music or 'jazzy' pop such as Joe Jackson, Sade or Michel Jonasz were adept at exploiting this jazz image.

In the 1990s, authentic female jazz singers were used as loss leaders. Thanks to them, the jazz divisions of the multinationals were able to achieve the kind of turnover needed in order to keep their shareholders happy. The best of them, however, were real musicians, such as Dee Dee Bridgewater, Cassandra Wilson and Shirley Horn, a singer-pianist rediscovered relatively late on in life. By agreeing to a lavish production treatment featuring a string orchestra, the singer and pianist Diana Krall was able to sell a million copies of her album *When I Look in Your Eyes* in just a few months. John Coltrane's masterpiece *A Love Supreme*, by contrast, had sold only 500,000 copies after 35 years.

But female jazz musicians aspired to more than singing. The pianists Mary Lou Williams and Marian McPartland, the trombonist and arranger Melba Liston and the bandleader-composers Toshiko Akiyoshi and Carla Bley were already well known. Many other women could now be found on the jazz stage: Laurie Frink (first trumpet in the Maria Schneider band), the solo trumpeter Ingrid Jensen, the pianist Aki Takase and the drummer Cindy Blackman, as well as the many other names mentioned in this chapter.

From hard bop to acid jazz

The type of jazz that met with the approval of nearly all jazz fans had a precise iconography (Blue Note covers), good sound quality (from the early days of high fidelity and stereo) and a particular stylistic colour (hard bop). For those in their forties and below in the 1980s, hard bop and its derivatives (such as Coltrane's 'pre-free-jazz' quartet and Miles Davis's second quintet) embodied the reality of jazz more than any other style. The record companies reissued their hard-bop back lists and revived historic labels such as Blue Note and Verve for the benefit of this audience. At the same time, they also relaunched the careers of many veterans and found new, young heroes to replace the historical figures who had disappeared. The arrival of the young neo-boppers (see p.233) immortalized what was henceforth considered to be 'real jazz'.

At the end of the 1980s, the DJs in London clubs dug out forgotten recordings from the 1950s, 1960s and 1970s that emphasized the dance aspect of jazz (funky jazz, acoustic or electric soul jazz, Latin jazz). Under the name 'acid jazz', this phenomenon spread to continental Europe and America. The Riverside, Prestige and Blue Note catalogues enjoyed a second wind. The younger generations rediscovered Donald Byrd's trumpet playing, Lou Donaldson's sax, Grant Green's guitar, Herbie Hancock's keyboards, Roy Ayers's vibraphone and Herbie Mann's flute.

These were copied, remixed, sampled and scratched – not without inspiring some wonderful creations along the way (as revealed on the compilation *Rebirth of Cool*). The New York group Groove Collection was the perfect embodiment of this combination of brass, flute, vibraphone, electric piano and funk or Latin rhythms. Throughout the 1990s, artists such as John Medeski (organist with the trio Medeski, Martin & Wood), the pianist Rick Müller and Erik Truffaz's group reinterpreted and restyled the sounds of an earlier era of electromechanical instruments (Rhodes piano, Hammond organ) and analogue synthesizers.

Looking back

This retrospective approach gave rise to many themed works, ranging from the opportunistic to the inspired and including new versions of old pieces, tributes to great figures from the past and surveys of specific historical styles. They were often the result of a producer's desire to juxtapose different points of view or even different genres (for example, the anthologies compiled by the producer Hal Wilner). The veterans themselves were invited to revisit their earlier work. Ornette Coleman reformed his first quartet. Charles Mingus's former colleagues continued to play under his name after his death. The centenary of Duke Ellington's birth was celebrated with tributes and reunions, and the Duke's grandson, Paul Mercer Ellington, succeeded his father, Mercer Ellington, as leader of the Duke Ellington Orchestra. Taking their cue from the drummer T S Monk (the son of Thelonious), who formed the Monk Big Band, the sons of other former heroes also took to the stage. These included Joshua, the son of Dewey Redman; Ravi, the son of John Coltrane; and Graham, the son of Roy Haynes. While some members of this younger generation exceeded their fathers in terms of technical ability and had genuine creative talent, none of them was to find any kind of historical role worthy of their illustrious names.

One of the most striking developments of the 1980s was the second career embarked upon by Keith Jarrett in 1983 which led to two *Standards* albums. The trio formed for the purpose (Gary Peacock on double bass and Jack DeJohnette on drums) soon acquired the nickname 'The Standards Trio', becoming an institution comparable to Oscar Peterson's trio in the 1960s. It drew on the classic repertoire and employed the usual conventions and rituals of the jazz trio. This it did with an admirable combination of deference and familiarity, matched by interviews in which Jarrett expressed an amused condescension towards the adventurer he had previously been while displaying undisguised contempt for his contemporaries.

The reawakening of the 1990s

The 1990s witnessed a revival of creativity. The spectacle of social exclusion, ethnic wars and ecological disasters taking place against the background of an improving economic climate shook would-be campaigners out of their apathy. The approach of the 21st century with its new set of issues created a certain excited anticipation. While some musicians took refuge in a classicism disconnected from the real world, others moved with the times, adopting a positive outlook, celebrating the arrival of the global village and new technology, and overturning aesthetic and racial barriers in multi-ethnic performances featuring young, lively, big-hearted music ranging from the all-acoustic to the all-electric. Yet others turned their backs on the norms of 'academic' bebop and the commercial efficiency of fusion. Their music took on a certain rebelliousness again, showing a tendency to question aesthetic values. The 1990s revival is difficult to chart due to the dilution of the avant-garde and the dispersed nature of the different trends. Each artist was in effect the leader of his or her own avant-garde. In fact the word 'avant-garde' now served simply to refer to music of less immediate appeal, for nothing fundamentally innovative was produced during this period, nothing that had not already been created in the 1960s or 1970s. Musicians worked away on their own at developing and decompartmentalizing the styles of the past (before, in some cases, recompartmentalizing them differently). The successors to controlled freedom, the descendants of free jazz, the disciples of jazz-rock and the neo-boppers frequently exchanged the fruits of their research. This research, like their music, no longer followed a vertical, historical axis, but a horizontal, almost geographical one. Indeed, the real challenges now faced by jazzmen came from elsewhere: world music, rock derivatives, rhythm-and-blues derivatives, popular or serious electronic music and the Western classical tradition. The new composers and improvisers allowed themselves to be influenced by the visual arts, the cinema, the theatre, literature and philosophy. The subjects of the thematic or historical projects that flourished both on stage and in the catalogues of the record companies were often taken from beyond the boundaries of jazz or even beyond music of any kind.

This dual situation of dispersion and decompartmentalization brought about by continual aesthetic exchanges is all the more difficult to describe as the media hype around certain individuals and trends that were not necessarily seminal obscured a lively, flourishing scene. This situation becomes even less clear the further away one moves from New York, which was the focus of the recording industry's activities. Despite this, New York continued to produce a number of figures who were highly influential or typical of the period.

The legitimist branch

'Straight-ahead' jazz survived the questioning of jazz's rhythmic basis. This term, closely related to that of 'mainstream', describes a style of jazz based on a more or less clear *chabada* (ternary) beat, a walking bass and a theme–improvisation–theme structure. At the same time, the concept of

WYNTON MARSALIS: AN EXTRAORDINARY BUT CONTROVERSIAL TALENT

In 1980, when the 19-year-old Wynton Marsalis was discovered playing with Art Blakey's Jazz Messengers, and in 1981, when he was in Herbie Hancock's quartet, his exceptional classical technique masked a relative lack of experience. His playing was reminiscent of Clifford Brown's, more for its astounding precision than for its musicality. When he appeared in a quintet with his brother (the saxophonist Branford Marsalis) in 1982, his ostentatious stylistic effects and immoderate admiration for Miles Davis's second quintet annoyed his fellow musicians (none more so than Davis himself) as well as a large number of critics. Hardly more than an adolescent, he had attained a perfection of execution superior to that of the musicians he took as his models. As a result he came to be seen as a sort of clone, a machine that copied different musical styles.

However, on the album *Black Codes* (1985, recorded with the quintet) and even more so on *Live at Blues Alley* (1986, quartet) he revealed a maturity, a mastery and an irresistible power of conviction in his desire to pursue the aesthetic abandoned by Miles Davis in 1968. Some listeners may have missed that hint of uncertainty, the tension like an elastic band about to snap that sent a shiver up the spines of Miles Davis's audiences as he invented his own aesthetic on the spot; but were these impressions based on reality or were they the result of nostalgia or jaded ears?

Marsalis himself felt he had reached an impasse. No longer offering any technical resistance, the challenges thrown down by Miles Davis's quintet began to lose their interest. He needed a new creative direction. In his quest for identity, for the original expressivity of black music, he delved into history. This took him back to King Oliver and a preoccupation with form that led him into the intimate universe of Duke Ellington. Teaching and giving master-classes with exemplary commitment, Marsalis began to embody a form of musical fundamentalism. He pronounced a number of excommunications on musicians who strayed from the orthodoxy championed by Jazz at Lincoln Center (New York), of which he is artistic director. His rhythmic preoccupations within the context of the hard-bop quintet and his Ellington-inspired interest in form were not completely alien, however, to the research undertaken by more radical contemporaries such as Steve Coleman (see p.245) and Tim Berne (see p.248).

LISTENING GUIDE
Art Blakey , *Album of the Year*, Timeless.
Wynton Marsalis (with Branford Marsalis, Kenny Kirkland, Charnett Moffett and Jeff Watts), *Black Codes*, Columbia.
Wynton Marsalis (with Marcus Roberts and Jeff Watts), *Live at Blues Alley*, Columbia.
Wynton Marsalis (with Marcus Roberts and Herlin Riley), *The Majesty of the Blues*, Columbia.
Wynton Marsalis (with Eric Reed and Herlin Riley), *Citi Movement*, Columbia.

controlled freedom and the extended musical awareness of many musicians opened up other possibilities.

Neo-bop in search of respectability

In 1980, the success of Wynton Marsalis drew attention to the potential of the neo-boppers who were leaving jazz academies equipped with extraordinary technical skills. These young musicians looked likely to fill the places of the masters of earlier periods and bring their legacy to fruition without any radical upheavals. The big record companies recruited large numbers of them, gambled vast sums of money on them in terms of promotional expenditure and then disposed of the less successful ones in order to concentrate on the chosen few. How many genuinely creative artists were among the victims of this lottery and how many ill-deserved reputations were created by it? The public was unable to assimilate such a flood of talent, and as a result the credibility of those who were successful depended upon some exceptional and often overrated feature. In the main, attention focused on the black neo-boppers, the legitimate heirs to the jazz legacy. The neo-boppers took their cue not so much from bebop as from hard bop and its derivatives – from the Jazz Messengers (in which many members of this new generation got to know each other) to Miles Davis's second quintet (Wayne Shorter, Herbie Hancock, Ron Carter and Tony Williams). These styles corresponded better to the black community's desire for recognition. In the 1970s, this community had deserted jazz, relinquishing it to white audiences, and turned instead to rhythm-and-blues-derived music. At a time when the ghettos of Reagan's America were succumbing to gang warfare and ultra-violent 'gangsta rap', the neo-boppers offered young African Americans an alternative model of musical and social success. Their impeccable suits were symbols of a desire for respectability.

They demanded that 'black American classical music', with its canonical forms and orchestral conventions, be accorded the same respect as white classical music. And it was in the hard-bop quintet that these forms and conventions found their most up-to-date expression.

The neo-bop quintet

Black pianists such as Mulgrew Miller identified with McCoy Tyner and Herbie Hancock (although Kenny Kirkland also admired Keith Jarrett). Members of the next generation of pianists, such as Marcus Roberts and Eric Reed, pushed back these horizons towards the sources of the Afro-American legacy: the influences of Ahmad Jamal, Bud Powell, Thelonious Monk, Duke Ellington and even Jelly Roll Morton can all be discerned in their work. Similarly, regional influences that were thought to have died out are evident in the playing of the Memphis pianists (James Williams, Mulgrew Miller, Donald Brown). The black double bassists (Robert Leslie Hurst, Christian McBride, Charnett Moffett) were descended in a direct line from Ron Carter and Paul Chambers. In terms of power and rhythmic precision, the drummer Jeff 'Tain' Watts embodied the black ideal, combining Tony Williams's virtuoso

LISTENING
GUIDE
Wallace Roney (with
Antoine Roney), *The
Wallace Roney Quintet*,
Warner Bros.
Roy Hargrove (with
Antonio Hart), *The Vibe*,
Novus.
Terence Blanchard and
Donald Harrison (with
Mulgrew Miller, Lonnie
Plaxico and Marvin
Smith), *New York
Second Line*, Columbia.
Kenny Garrett (with
Charnett Moffett and
Brian Blade), *Trilogy*,
Warner Bros.
Branford Marsalis (with
Kenny Kirkland),
Random Abstract,
Columbia.
Ravi Coltrane, *From the
Round Box*, RCA/Victor.
Geri Allen, *The Nurturer*,
Blue Note.
Rodney Kendrick, *Dance
World Dance*, Verve.
James Hurt, *Dark
Grooves, Mystical
Rhythms*, Blue Note.
Leon Parker, *Above
Below*, Epicure/Sony.
Mark Turner *In This
World*, Warner Bros.

arithmetic with the fundamental values of swing. Brian Blade recaptured the economic elegance of the bebop drum-kit stylists, while Herlin Riley was steeped in the New Orleans tradition. The chosen instrument of Miles Davis and Clifford Brown had immense prestige in the eyes of black Americans. Although young trumpeters often made names for themselves in tandem with saxophonists (for example, Wynton Marsalis with his brother Branford, Wallace Roney with his brother Antoine, Roy Hargrove with Antonio Hart, and Terence Blanchard with Donald Harrison), it was they, the trumpeters, who were the real leaders of neo-bop. Indeed, the reputation of black American saxophonists was often eclipsed by that of their trumpet-playing colleagues. Notable exceptions were Branford Marsalis, Joshua Redman, Kenny Garrett and Gary Thomas, who freed themselves from the archetypes of the neo-bop quintet by playing in a quartet or trio.

Neo-bop opens up to outside influences

Over the years, the black neo-boppers relaxed their position (as well as their dress code). The cocktail of influences on their music grew more varied as they listened to alternative musicians such as Woody Shaw and Booker Little. Branford Marsalis's versatility was typical of this development. His interpretation of Ornette Coleman's masterpiece 'Lonely Woman' on his 1988 album *Random Abstract* was all the more surprising as it called to mind Keith Jarrett's European quartet with Jan Garbarek. When, in 1994, he adopted rap and turntables with his group Buckshot Lefonque, Branford Marsalis revealed the neo-boppers' ambitions to open up to outside influences.

There were many musical exchanges. The trumpeter Graham Haynes, the trombonist Robin Eubanks, the saxophonists Ravi Coltrane, Gary Thomas and Greg Osby, the pianist Geri Allen, the double bassist Lonnie Plaxico and the drummer Marvin 'Smitty' Smith all moved freely between the language of Steve Coleman (see p.245) and neo-bop. Neo-bop spread in all directions via younger artists (including the trumpeter Russell Gunn, the saxophonist David Sanchez, the pianists Rodney Kendrick and James Hurt and the drummer Leon Parker) who were more in touch with the music of the ghetto and the Caribbean, world music and the derivatives of free jazz. Even attitudes to jazz history changed: the trumpeter Kermit Ruffins followed hard on Wynton Marsalis's heels in going back to his New Orleans roots; the saxophonist James Carter started collecting period saxophones and pastiching styles from Johnny Hodges to Albert Ayler; the saxophonist Mark Turner confessed to being influenced by Lennie Tristano. Despite a continuing divide between the black and white scenes, there were also many bridges built between the two: for example, the Mel Lewis big band (in which Steve Coleman rubbed shoulders with Joe Lovano in 1980), the jam sessions at Smalls in New York at the beginning of the 1990s, and the catalogue of the Dutch label Criss Cross, which featured both black and white New York neo-boppers.

Joshua Redman's quartet was a model of easy-going relationships. The

Joshua Redman

LISTENING
GUIDE
Joshua Redman (with
Brad Mehldau, Christian
McBride and Brian
Blade), *Moodswing*,
Warner Bros.
Kenny Werner,
Uncovered Heart,
Sunnyside.
Tom Harrell, *Form*,
Contemporary.

drummer Brian Blade was paired with Brad Mehldau, a white pianist influenced by Bill Evans and Keith Jarrett, while the double-bass player Christian McBride was succeeded by the white bassist and member of the LaFaro school, Larry Grenadier. While there were many white musicians well versed in the standards who identified with the neo-boppers (including their dress sense), one thing they did not share with them was their preoccupation with identity, with the result that they often embraced a wider spectrum of aesthetic influences. Although he came to the fore playing funky jazz alongside Horace Silver, the white trumpeter Tom Harrell combined the influence of black trumpeters with that of Chet Baker. White pianists such as Fred Hersch and Kenny Werner were steeped in the work of Bill Evans. White jazzmen were more likely to regard jazz as a medium of exchange that could lend itself to a variety of styles, neo-bop being just one of them. The spirit of the first loft generation (see p.198 and p.201) found a particular resonance among these musicians. Two white saxophonists who had been active on the loft scene – Michael Brecker and David Liebman – extended their influence over the last 20 years of the century in contrasting yet complementary ways.

Michael Brecker

Such was the formal perfection of his playing, very much in keeping with the spirit of the day, that the saxophonist Michael Brecker was regarded as being in a league of his own. Sought after by commercial recording studios throughout the world, he was widely imitated by white saxophonists to the point of caricature. His manner of combining power with fluency, ease and precision, even in very fast passages, revealed the same degree of perfection. His detractors claimed he was a cold technician, thereby stigmatizing the white, sanitized style of sax playing of Bob Berg, Bob Mintzer and others in the Brecker mould. The careers of these saxophonists were divided between a straight-ahead jazz and a more or less radical fusion that was loathed by a section of the critics. The critics took a more relaxed view in the 1990s, however, when the young musicians turned to other models, selected less for their technical ability than for their musicality. In addition to alternative figures such as Jerry Bergonzi, Larry Schneider and George Garzone, the influence of Joe Lovano replaced that of Brecker in the world of the tenor sax. Through Lovano, the work of saxophonists who had been somewhat neglected found favour again (Joe Henderson, Charles Lloyd, Stan Getz, Ornette Coleman and Sam Rivers), as did rather more open-minded aesthetic approaches. The music of this freethinker also attracted interest from Europe, leading in particular to collaborations with the double bassist Henri Texier.

David Liebman

Although dedicated to the fundamental values of jazz, its repertoire and the expertise of his elders, David Liebman offered an alternative to the relatively tightly structured music of the Marsalis brothers and Michael Brecker. Experimenting with less clear-cut structures and not afraid to take risks, he anticipated the random aspects of interactive improvisation. Liebman impressed listeners with his range of timbre and expressive control on the soprano, which he played exclusively before taking up the tenor again towards the end of the 1990s, and he exerted a major influence on young musicians through his itinerant teaching work. His lucidity and the rigour of his musical approach meant that the impact of his teaching went beyond the strictly instrumental.

Having formed the group Quest with the pianist Richard Beirach, Liebman spent the 1980s exploring the combined legacy of Bill Evans, John Coltrane and Miles Davis, putting into practice his theories relating to chromatic harmony and the dramatic mechanisms of improvisation. In the group's final album (*Of One Mind*), he pushed the logic of controlled freedom and interactive improvisation to a stage where all thematic material and improvisational presuppositions disappeared. In the 1990s, while maintaining a fusion group in America, he frequently played with representatives of the most atypical of European styles – notably the French double bassist Jean-Paul Celea, whose roots were in the contemporary music scene, and the Austrian drummer Wolfgang Reisinger. It was as if he had come to the conclusion that he had to get away from a strictly American tradition.

On either side of straight-ahead jazz

The former leaders of the first loft generation, along with their peers and successors, thus split into two groups positioned on either side of straight-ahead jazz (of which they remained great players): fusion on the one side and free-jazz tendencies on the other. Distant descendants of White Elephant (see p.198), the big bands of Bob Moses and Jaco Pastorius were to jazz fusion what Dizzy Gillespie's big band was to bebop. Moses played in a more experimental style, while Pastorius was lusher.

Mike Mainieri and his group Steps favoured a more or less acoustic version of fusion featuring an ingenious interplay of 'binary' and 'ternary' phrasing, carefully planned sonorities and arrangements, something of the melodic quality of pop music and a precise, limpid musicality. From his experience of working with Chick Corea and Anthony Braxton, Dave Holland, by contrast, had acquired a taste for risk-taking and avant-garde experimentation that led him to hire the young Steve Coleman (see p.145). Chick Corea's dual career reflected the technical skill and aesthetic versatility of the lofts. Alongside Miroslav Vitous and Roy Haynes, Corea was able to maintain the tradition of the jazz trio and also practise a more adventurous form of free improvisation. In 1985, he teamed up with a lively rhythm section that was a perfect blend of precision, agility and power: the bassist John Patitucci and the drummer Dave Weckl, who were effective foils in both the Elektric Band and the Akoustic Band. At the end of the 1990s, Corea directed the sextet Origin, which had a very European flavour.

LISTENING GUIDE
Bob Moses, When Elephants Dream of Music, Gramavision.
Jaco Pastorius, Invitation, Warner Bros.
Steps, Steps Ahead, Elektra/Musician.
Chick Corea, Trio Music, ECM.
Mark Whitfield, 7th Ave Stroll, Verve
Peter Bernstein, Brain Dance, Criss Cross.
Pat Metheny Group, Offramp, ECM.
Pat Metheny and Ornette Coleman, Song X, Geffen.
John Scofield, Shinola, Enja.
Marc Johnson (with Bill Frisell, John Scofield and Peter Erskine), Bass Desires, ECM.
John Abercrombie (with Marc Johnson and Peter Erskine), Current Events, ECM.
John Abercrombie (with Joe Lovano and Kenny Wheeler), Open Land, ECM.
Peter Erskine, As It Is, ECM.

Unlike the neo-bop guitarists (such as the black guitarist Mark Whitfield or the white guitarist Peter Bernstein), whose style was based on the legacy of Wes Montgomery and Grant Green as developed by George Benson and dissected by Pat Martino, the new guitarists who had emerged in the 1970s (see p.199) showed great versatility. Pat Metheny alternated between solo free-jazz experimentation, sessions with Ornette Coleman, straight-ahead trio work and his own fusion group. John Scofield moved between a number of different styles, including a fairly radical controlled-freedom trio and a very muscular form of jazz-rock.

Having made a name for himself playing in Bill Evans's last trio, the double bassist Marc Johnson joined forces with John Scofield and Bill Frisell (see p.250) in a number of fairly raucous recording sessions, although he adopted more structured formats, similar to those defined by Steps, in his work with Peter Erskine and John Abercrombie. The latter tried his hand at the guitar synthesizer in this line-up, but was to make more adventurous music in the company of Joe Lovano and Kenny Wheeler. After experimenting with electric drums, Peter Erskine picked up the brushes again and returned to the art of the ballad. He also practised a form of interactive improvisation with the British pianist John Taylor and the Swedish double bassist Palle Danielsson.

Young musicians and veteran mentors

Trained by a dynasty of music-school students turned teachers (such as the pianists Fred Hersch and Kenny Werner), the white scene in America suffered from a certain academicism, particularly in New York, where fierce competition due to a high concentration of musicians from all over the world was combined with the instability inherent in the American social system. Compared to Europe, or even Chicago, where a jazz scene developed in the closing years of the century that was more focused on artistic ambitions, the creativity of the New Yorkers seemed to be held in check by the need to operate within a set of relatively narrow norms.

Maria Schneider

Under pressure from the constant injection of new blood, these norms were nevertheless subject to a process of continual transformation that seemed to gather pace towards the end of the century with the pianist Brad Mehldau, the saxophonists Chris Potter and David Binney, the guitarist Kurt Rosenwickel, the double bassist Scott Colley and the composer and bandleader Maria Schneider. The Sunnyside catalogue offers a detailed record of this constantly shifting New York scene, exemplified by the discovery of the pianist Armen Donelian, of Armenian parentage, and the young drummer Bill Stewart. A maverick like the pianist Bill Carrothers, however, felt it necessary to move away from New York in order to remain true to himself. This won him recognition in Europe and indifference in America.

The New York scene that developed out of neo-bop seemed to recycle the archetypes of jazz while keeping an eye on the avant-garde and undertaking a patient reform of the metric framework and the relationship between improvisation and composition. This led it down a route previously taken, with more radical consequences, by musicians such as Tim Berne and Steve Coleman (see p.245). A number of veterans encouraged these developments, becoming mentors to the young reformers. They included the saxophonist Lee Konitz, the guitarist Jim Hall, the pianist Andrew Hill and the drummers Paul Motian, Jack DeJohnette and Roy Haynes.

LISTENING GUIDE

Bill Carrothers, *Duets with Bill Stewart*, Birdology.

Brad Mehldau, *Back at the Vanguard*, Warner Bros.

David Binney (with Chris Potter and Scott Colley), *South*, Act.

Armen Donelian, *The Wayfarer*, Sunnyside.

Maria Schneider, *Evanescence*, Enja.

Wheeler–Konitz–Holland–Frisell, *Angel Song*, ECM.

Paul Motian (with Joe Lovano and Bill Frisell), *Monk in Motion*, JMT.

Greg Osby (with Jim Hall and Andrew Hill), *The Invisible Hand*, Blue Note.

Roy Haynes (with Donald Harrison, Pat Metheny and others), *Te-Vou!*, Dreyfus.

From the street to the electronic laboratory

The route taken by the neo-boppers, in particular the detours they made at the end of the 1990s and their many interactions with other musical forms, explored new byways on the edges of jazz's roadmap – in other words, on the margins of orthodoxy. It was mainly as a result of coming into contact with the new culture of the black ghettos that jazzmen became aware of the uses to which the new techniques of sound generation, storage and manipulation could be put.

The sounds of the studios

Electronic music was transformed at the beginning of the 1980s by the appearance of digital equipment (see p.226). This new technology allowed the creation of extraordinary sounds or simple special effects and the recycling of pre-existing sounds in creative or straightforward cloning processes. The exaggeration of the effects, the strengthening of the bass and the quality of the digital sound itself gave the music a high-tech feel. Concerts were often no more than a powerful, approximate reproduction of records made in the studio, instrument by instrument, with the help of musical robotics (see p.241).

This new environment was embraced to varying degrees by several generations of fusion groups (Weather Report, Chick Corea's Elektric Band, the saxophonist Bill Evans's group, the Didier Lockwood Group). It was transcended by the warmth of virtuoso performances (Uzeb, a group from Quebec), by the powerful, evocative use of timbres and rhythms (Weather Report, the Zawinul Syndicate) and by the harmonic and melodic charm of the compositions (Wayne Shorter, the Pat Metheny Group). Acoustic at the outset, the vibraphone player Mike Mainieri's group Steps Ahead became entirely electric, and on its album *Modern Times* succeeded in poeticizing the new technology surrounding Michael Brecker's saxophone. Brecker played the EWI (see p.226) for a while, and many guitarists adopted various versions of the guitar synthesizer.

From radio jazz to New Orleans groove

LISTENING
GUIDE
Chick Corea Elektric
Band, *Eye of the
Beholder*, GRP.
Uzeb, *Noisy Nights*,
Cream.
Joe Zawinul, *Black
Water*, Columbia.
Wayne Shorter, *Atlantis*,
Columbia.
Steps Ahead, *Modern
Times*, Elektra/Musician.
Michael Brecker, *Michael
Brecker*, Impulse.
David Sanborn, *Straight
to the Heart*, Warner
Bros.
Yellowjackets, *Politics*,
MCA.
John Scofield (with
Dennis Chambers), *Pick
Hits, Live*, Gramavision.
Guy Thomas (with Terri
Lyne Carrington), *Till We
Have Faces*, JMT.
The Dirty Dozen Brass
Band, *My Fee Can't Fail
Me Now*, Columbia.

The sophistication of recording techniques and the use of session musicians meant that music was a product that could be perfectly calibrated and precisely targeted at a specific audience. The right mix of ingredients borrowed from jazz, rhythm and blues, funk, pop and various commercial genres allowed the creation of a slick style that was 'jazzy' without being jazz in the true sense of the word – that is, music that would appeal to a wider audience. Back in the 1970s, a number of singer-songwriters (Donald Fagen and Walter Becker and their group Steely Dan, Michel Franks) were able to use this polished style to good effect and make a lasting impression on the world of jazz. A number of musicians familiar with these studio techniques – such as Steps, the Yellowjackets and the saxophonist David Sanborn – used them as aids to inspiration. In the hands of the majority, however, the end product was no more than an empty shell, soothing wallpaper music suitable for non-stop broadcast on FM radio.

These developments in sound production were accompanied by an exaggeration (inspired by the funk bands) of the syncopated beat. Dennis Chambers, the drummer with George Clinton's groups and the Sugarhill Gang, embodied the powerful, athletic technical skill that jazzmen from John Scofield to Gary Thomas looked for, often on a one-off basis, from black rhythm sections. A number of neo-bop drummers were

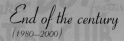
inspired by this style of drumming. Among them was Terri Lyne Carrington, who was occasionally tempted to adopt elements of the ghetto style. The key word in this jazz was no longer 'swing', but 'groove'.

Electric bassists such as Marcus Miller borrowed from funk a violent, virtuosic slap technique – a technique with which the first New Orleans bassists had experimented. The New Orleans brass band was making a comeback (in the form of the Dirty Dozen Brass Band, for example), and its tubas took their inspiration from the percussive style of the funk bassists. Conversely, these brass bands contributed to a revival of the taste for so-called 'second-line' drumming, a typical feature of New Orleans parades that had survived in some of the local funk bands.

The return of Miles Davis

LISTENING
GUIDE
Miles Davis, *We Want
Miles, Decoy*, Columbia.
*Live Around the World,
Doo Bop*, Warner Bros.

Returning to the scene after a retirement lasting five years, Miles Davis showed himself to be sensitive to this new environment. After the chaos of his 1970s sound, his music was now clearer, more clean-lined and more accessible. Attuned to the 1980s commercial scene, he used proper themes and a more structured harmonic framework. Turning to the songs of Cyndi Lauper ('Time after Time') or Scritti Politti ('Perfect Way'), he demonstrated that the repertoire of standards had to move with the times and that pop music was the ideal replacement for the musical theatre songs of years gone by. This point of view was shared by a growing number of musicians, both black and white, who opened up the repertoire to the songs of Sting or Suzanne Vega, indeed to the whole legacy of popular song from the Beatles to Edith Piaf (Davis had in his repertoire a bluesy version of the French lullaby 'Dodo l'enfant do', renamed 'Jean-Pierre'). But Davis's main preoccupation was the development of black music. He hoped to collaborate with Prince. His rhythm sections were inspired by modern funk. In 1981, the bass guitarist Marcus Miller began to play in his band. In 1987, Davis used the drummer Ricky Wellman, who came from the Washington 'go-go' funk scene. Hip-hop and rap provided the material for his posthumous album *Doo Bop*. One by one, jazz soloists such as the guitarist John Scofield and the saxophonists Bob Berg, Gary Thomas and Rick Margitza started to lose interest in a music in which the art of improvisation was becoming less and less important. Only the saxophonist Kenny Garrett continued to fit in. Nevertheless, the succession of groups under Davis's leadership during the 1980s had a significant influence on a large number of musicians, inspiring not only servile imitations but also music-making of great creativity.

The music of the ghetto

In parallel with the neo-bop phenomenon, a lot of black jazzmen shared Miles Davis's interest in the music of the ghetto. Many were inspired by hip-hop culture and incorporated DJs or rappers into their music. In doing so, they displayed their solidarity with the ghetto (sometimes for opportunistic reasons), while providing it with an opportunity to evolve

MILES DAVIS IN THE STUDIO

Afascinating figure on stage, Miles Davis was also adept throughout his entire career at making the most of the recording studio, technological developments and the tension that built up during sessions. In the studio with Charlie Parker, who liked to record take after take, Davis would tire quickly (see p.153); hence his enduring fondness for first takes (*Relaxin'*, 1956; *Miles Smiles*, 1967), a fondness he shared with many jazzmen who believed the initial attempt was when their inspiration was at its freshest. Towards the end of the 1960s, Davis changed his methods (*In a Silent Way*, 1969; *Jack Johnson*, 1970). His group started to improvise for extended periods guided only by minimal signals whose timing was worked out on the spot. The tapes would be played back and completed where necessary by means of overdubbing. They were then handed over to the producer Teo Macero in the same way that film directors pass their reels to an editor who is then responsible for selecting and joining sequences. Macero cut and pasted, turning one sequence into a thematic element that could be used at the beginning, in the middle or at the end of a piece, livening it up through a judicious use of the scissors or enhancing it with electronic effects. Multi-track recording meant that during the mixing process the sound of each instrument could be individually honed and its volume adjusted, the ensemble carefully distributed within the stereo image, and space added by means of artificial reverberation.

LISTENING GUIDE
Miles Davis, *Miles Smiles, In a Silent Way, Jack Johnson*, Columbia. *Tutu*, Warner.

In 1986, for his album *Tutu*, Davis brought in Marcus Miller, a bassist, multi-instrumentalist, composer and arranger. Miller had provided Davis with demos made on a computer using artificial trumpet, sampled from one of Davis's recordings. Miller recorded all the instrumental parts himself, one after the other, track by track, using real or virtual instruments. Davis then added his own (real) trumpet. During the mixing stage, various musicians came along to add the finishing touches with traditional instruments or to replace individual simulated parts.

In the 1980s, jazz musicians would record in one of three ways: one instrument after the other, collectively (in order to preserve a sense of interaction) but on separate tracks (which offered the opportunity to re-record individual parts as necessary), or the old way (in direct stereo and gambling on the freshness of the first attempt). This third technique is known as 'live recording', a term previously reserved for the recording of concerts.

towards a richer rhythmic language and open up horizons beyond the extremely violent language of gangsta rap. The saxophonists Branford Marsalis (under the pseudonym Buckshot Lefonque, borrowed from Cannonball Adderley) and Greg Osby were among those who tried this. With his group the Metrics, Steve Coleman even sought to apply the logic of his system (see p.245) to 'freestyle' (improvised rap). Conversely, in the 1990s, the rapper Guru invited jazzmen to contribute to his 'Jazzmatazz' projects.

More generally, what jazz musicians found particularly interesting about hip-hop and dance music were the new techniques of sound recycling (sampling, scratching, breakbeat) and rhythm generation (drum machines, electronic drums). As early as 1983, Herbie Hancock caused a stir with *Future Shock*, an album of dance music that used a DJ and turntables and had rhythms that were mostly machine-programmed. Produced by the white bassist Bill Laswell (see p.248), this record was merely the visible, provocative tip of a body of production work that went against the current of slick productions based on digital technology. In 1989, more diplomatically but with a more substantial project than Hancock's (the album *Back on the Block*), Quincy Jones introduced the jazz public to rap, DJs and their turntables, and drum machines.

LISTENING GUIDE
Branford Marsalis, *Buckshot Lefonque*, Columbia.
Greg Osby, *3-D Lifestyles*, Blue Note.
Steve Coleman and the Metrics, *A Tale of 3 Cities*, Novus.
Jazzmatazz, The New Reality Hosted by Guru, Cooltempo.
Herbie Hancock, *Future Shock*, Columbia.
Quincy Jones, *Back on the Block*, Warner Bros.
Jack DeJohnette, *Album Album* ('New Orleans Strut'), ECM.
Gary Peacock (with Peter Erskine), *Guamba* ('Thyme Time', 'Introending'), ECM.
Fred Frith, Kato Hideki and Ikue Mori, *Death Ambient*, Tzadik.

The advent of the drum machine

Jazzmen were intrigued by the drum machines that were beginning to be the norm in studios. Could electronic rhythms one day be made to swing? Two attempts were made to answer that question. The first took the form of electronic drums that kept the percussive gestures of the drummer but replaced the elements of the drum kit with sensors that allowed an infinite range of sounds to be produced. The second consisted in sampling a drummer's playing and then reconstructing it in the desired manner using special machinery. Both solutions were adopted by jazzmen – either in order to move closer to the music and popular culture associated with these techniques or in order to exploit the contrasts available from superimposing man-made music over robotic rhythms. The drum-machine experiments of the female drummer Ikue Mori, whose background was in experimental rock, opened up major opportunities for musical robotics on the New York avant-garde scene (see p.247). Following the acid-jazz wave, Detroit's techno scene and London's drum-and-bass scene also incorporated jazz into

LISTENING
GUIDE
Erik Truffaz, *Bending New Corners*, Blue Note.
Nils Petter Molvaer, *Khmer*, ECM.
Bugge Wesseltoft, *New Conception of Jazz*, Jazzland/Sonet.
Benoît Delbecq, *Pursuit*, Songlines.
Ambitronix, *We Da Man*, Plush.
Philipp Wachsmann and Paul Lytton, *Some Other Season*, ECM.
Evan Parker Electro-Acoustic Ensemble, *Drawn Inward*, ECM.
Graham Haynes, *Transition*, Verve.
Panthalassa: the Music of Miles Davis 1969–74 – Reconstruction & Mix Translation by Bill Laswell, Columbia.

their do-it-yourself sounds.
Many jazzmen paid close attention to the results – often 'dirtier', warmer sounds than could be achieved with the first digital synthesizers. Around 1997–8, the London club scene became the meeting place for many European jazzmen who came looking for inspiration, particularly from the black American drummer Marque Gilmore and his circle. They incorporated many ingredients of the new electronic music into their work: infra-bass, programmed beats, sonic atmospheres based on sampling and electronic sound generation, and turntables. In the work of the Norwegians Bugge Wesseltoft (keyboards) and Nils Petter Molvaer (trumpet), these techniques were used alongside full-scale flesh-and-blood rhythm sections. The Franco-Swiss group of the trumpeter Erik Truffaz did not use drum-and-bass-style programmed beats but they resonate in its work nonetheless, as the double-bass-and-drums team of Marcello Giuliani and Marc Erbetta seem to have taken their inspiration from them.

The programmers of the drum-and-bass-style drum machines were self-taught, practical rhythmists. They achieved a complex arithmetic and speed of flow that made drummers and bassists sit up and listen. These rhythms and sounds were reminiscent of the dexterity and virtuosity of the percussionists of the great non-European polyrhythmic traditions. Traces of Indian tabla, the Iranian zarb and African drums were present in both the rhythmic figures and the sounds sampled (particularly by Marque Gilmore).

Techno backgrounds

Another aspect of techno and its derivatives also attracted attention: the highly collective, highly organic sound produced by artists who often worked alone in their home studios under the cover of pseudonyms. Jazzmen, on the other hand, represented a type of music in which the ego constantly asserted itself through the solo. Some of them saw this ego as dysfunctional. Techno encouraged them to rethink their attitude to instrumental virtuosity. It showed them that this virtuosity could be intensified (no longer as an affirmation of the ego but because of the sound it produced) or reduced to a minimal gesture. Similar preoccupations were evident in the prepared piano of François Benoît Delbecq. The sound of his instrument was modified by adding foreign bodies to individual strings. This handicapped the piano in its traditional virtuoso role, thereby transforming the instrument and its presence within the collective sound of the band. Working alongside him, the British drummer Steve Argüelles practised a different anti-virtuoso minimalist technique by using an electronic device to filter and rework what his colleagues in the Benoît Delbecq 5 were playing. In Ambitronix, in which the pianist and drummer teamed up with a DJ and an electronics technician, the musicians sampled and remixed each other live.

This new relationship with rhythm, sound and the ensemble took a thousand different forms in the work of both the new jazzmen and the veterans of

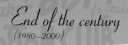

British 1970s experimentalism (Paul Lytton, Evan Parker, Derek Bailey). Although these new practices were rooted in the contemporary scene, Miles Davis had anticipated them in 1972, using not machines but three drummers and a tabla player on *On the Corner* – an album that was misunderstood in its day but which finally became relevant 25 years later. It became a cult album among the proponents of a rapprochement between jazz and techno. Its influence could be heard in the albums released by the black trumpeter Graham Haynes as well as in the work of the white bassist and producer Bill Laswell, who at the end of the 1990s made remixes of records by Davis that had originally been edited and mixed by Teo Macero (see p.241).

What is left of the avant-garde?

If there ever was an avant-garde that illustrated the difficulty of labelling the proliferation of styles at the end of the century, the M-Base collective, centred on the saxophonist Steve Coleman, was it. At least this movement had the advantage of having chosen its own name. However, no sooner had the collective been formed than it broke up, subsequently reuniting only partially and sporadically around its leader (see p.245). What, then, did the musicians who passed through the M-Base collective have in common? The answer is simply that they had crossed the path of Steve Coleman and, like him, were dissatisfied with the choice between neo-bop, which many of them had come from but which they now regarded as too inward-looking, and a free jazz that was no longer avant-garde except in name.

The free-jazz backwash and neo-free jazz

In the 1980s, the black American free-jazz scene seemed to have been abandoned not only by its public but also by many of its exponents. Archie Shepp was playing a kind of bebop, Anthony Braxton – now forgotten by the European audiences that had created his reputation in the 1970s – survived by teaching and George Lewis devoted himself to research into the use of computers in music. One of the most original concepts, developed by one of Anthony Braxton's students, was the series of pieces recorded by Anthony Davis between 1981 and 1983 that evoked European chamber music while displaying metric preoccupations not so far removed from those of Steve Coleman. By contrast, many protagonists of the 'second loft generation', such as Chico Freeman and Arthur Blythe, devoted themselves to music of a more or less predictable format. At the head of his festive Brass Fantasy, Lester Bowie adopted a repertoire of popular hits. Ornette Coleman's theory of harmolodics achieved a degree of success only in its most spectacular funk manifestations. In addition to his work with the group Decoding Society, which represented a continuation of the funk-harmolodics style of Coleman's Prime Time, the drummer Ronald Shannon Jackson collaborated on a one-off basis with two guitarists from opposite ends of the aesthetic spectrum: Bill Frisell, with the Power Tools trio, and

STEVE COLEMAN AND M-BASE

Born in 1956 and brought up in Chicago, Steve Coleman discovered the saxophone through the work of Charlie Parker and Maceo Parker (James Brown's saxophonist). On the Chicago scene he had two decisive encounters: the first with the tenor saxophonist Von Freeman and the second with the alto saxophonist Bunky Green, from whom he acquired a certain logic of phrasing and borrowed the ballad 'Little One I Miss You', which became a leitmotif in his work. After settling in New York, he worked with the Thad Jones–Mel Lewis and Sam Rivers big bands.

Steve Coleman's career

At the beginning of the 1980s, Coleman had another key encounter, this time with the drummer Doug Hammond, in whose band he experimented with uneven metres and the superimposition of polyrhythms. At that time, he was examining – with his friend the trumpeter Graham Haynes (son of the drummer Roy Haynes) – the interaction between singing and drums in the work of James Brown and between saxophone and drums in the music of Charlie Parker. They started to draw practical conclusions from this research together with an initial hardcore of musicians with whom they played on New York's streets. The rhythmic units devised by Steve Coleman were already so complex that two drummers were needed to produce them. He found the drummer capable of providing the necessary foil in Dave Holland's quintet: Marvin 'Smitty' Smith, who was also active on the neo-bop scene.

In 1985, Steve Coleman started to record at the head of Five Elements, a group with a variable line-up. Initially, its main figures were Graham Haynes, the alto saxophonist Greg Osby, the pianist Geri Allen, the double bassist Lonnie Plaxico, the electric bassist Kevin Bruce Harris, the drummers Mark Johnson and Marvin Smith, and the singer Cassandra Wilson. Over time, close relationships developed between Coleman and the guitarist David Gilmore, the pianist Andy Milne, the bassist Reggie Washington and the drummers Gene Lake and Sean Rickman. Coleman's early collaborators withdrew, a host of occasional guests joined in (in particular the trumpeter Ralph Alessi and the saxophonists Ravi Coltrane and Gary Thomas) and the result was a number of groups of various combinations (Five Elements, Metrics, Renegade Way, Mystic Rhythm Society, M-Base Collective and the Strata Institute).

The ideas behind Steve Coleman's work

Steve Coleman gave this ever-changing, disparate community the name M-Base (Macro-Basic Array of Structured Extemporizations), a term inspired by the language of information technology. It may not have referred to a clearly defined movement but it showed a clear conceptual intent. Steve Coleman's thinking was based on an architectural conception of rhythm, in which rhythmic units of different kinds fitted together one on top of the other. The resulting playful metrical instability was founded on highly complex logic and combined with an apparent sureness of rhythm inherited from the hammered-out 'binary' beat of funk. The remarkable sense of proportion that characterized this music involved a consideration of the uneven metres of central Europe, the music of Bartók, theories of the golden section, Greek and Egyptian mathematics and astronomy.

This was not the first manifestation of ancient Egypt in the African-American imagination, but Steve Coleman's interest in the arts and sciences of the Egypt of the pharaohs went beyond the usual type of imaginative references that, for example, dominated the work of Sun Ra. Egyptian civilization, taking root in black Africa, anchored modern Africa and its diaspora firmly within the history of humanity. It legitimized African thought as an alternative to Western thought with its ethnocentric view of humanity, civilization and progress. Coleman's study trips to Ghana, his collaboration with the Cuban group AfroCuba de Matanzas and his wider interest in non-European thought followed on from his knowledge of Egyptology. His remarkable polyrhythmic constructions formed a veritable cosmogony, in which it was possible to find a rejection of the Western dichotomy between logic and intuition and a refusal to see essentially African music as the mere trappings of local folk traditions.

Neither were the more spectacular aspects (funk accents and feats of technical prowess) allowed to overshadow the blend of logic and ease of delivery that characterize Steve Coleman's playing. The excitement comes not from the rhythmic element alone but from an ongoing interaction between the rhythm, the melodic movements (and the accompanying counterpoint derived from the skilful deployment of broken lines), the play of reflections and the proportional relationships. The fluency of his playing is reminiscent of the precision of martial arts and the inexorable nature of computer programs, and it should come as no surprise to learn that Coleman also experimented with artificial intelligence, designing a program for computerized improvisation at the IRCAM (the Institute for Music/Acoustic Research and Coordination) in Paris.

The influence exerted by Steve Coleman in many different areas of jazz in the 1990s did not lead to strict imitation of his style. He found significant support in France in the work of the saxophonist Guillaume Orti, the pianist Benoît Delbecq and the trombonist Geoffroy de Masure, but the most important lesson they learned from him was the need for each musician to follow his or her own path.

LISTENING GUIDE

Doug Hammond, *Spaces*, DIW.
Dave Holland, *Seeds of Time*, ECM.
Steve Coleman & the Five Elements, *On the Edge of Tomorrow*, JMT.
M-Base Collective, *Anatomy of a Groove*, DIW.
Strata Institute, *Cipher Syntax*, JMT.
Steve Coleman & the Five Elements, *Drop Kick*, Novus/RCA.
Steve Coleman & the Mystic Rhythm Society (with AfroCuba de Matanzas), *The Sign and the Seal*, BMG.
Steve Coleman, *The Ascension to Light*, BMG.

Sonny Sharrock, with his group Last Exit (alongside the bassist Bill Laswell and the saxophonist Peter Brötzmann, a radical member of the European free-jazz scene).

The bassist Jamaaladeen Tacuma developed a supremely elegant funk style with an eclectic outlook, which led to his close collaboration with the Austrian saxophonist Wolfgang Puschnig. The trombonist Joseph Bowie (of the group Defunkt), who had been active on the AACM/BAG scene, was interested like many young black musicians in the tumultuous funk of George Clinton. Following in the footsteps of James Blood Ulmer, the guitarist Jean-Paul Bourelly reinvigorated the Hendrix message, revealing a musical heritage that encompassed both rock and funk in their most fundamental aspects. The key element that these young black musicians took from free jazz was a militant approach to the sound they made, stemming from a desire to protect the common legacy of rock and funk from commercial dilution. Towards the end of the 1980s, these were also the clearly stated aims of Black Rock Coalition, whose leader, the guitarist Vernon Reid, played a combination of funk, rock and jazz. In the 1990s, the heroes of free jazz and the second loft generation experienced a slight increase in the prestige they enjoyed among the younger generation. Henry Threadgill and Butch Morris attracted attention as leaders of ambitious band projects. The trumpeter Olu Dara embarked on an astonishing second career as a bluesman. David Murray and Sam Rivers created large mixed groups made up of former members of the loft scene and musicians who had been active on the margins of free jazz and neo-bop, such as Ricky Ford, James Spaulding and John Stubblefield. This increased level of interest was not so much a chance to discover fresh talent (for example, the pianists Matthew Shipp and D D Jackson) as an opportunity to shed some light on a number of free-jazz figures who had long gone unnoticed, such as the tenor saxophonists Charles Gayle (a proponent of an extreme form of expressionism) and David S Ware. The latter's mastery of the free-jazz orthodoxy invited comparisons with the technicians of neo-bop – indeed to such an extent that the expression 'free-jazz revival' was used in connection with Ware. It was mainly from outside the black community, however, that free jazz experienced an influx of fresh blood: the drummer Susie Ibarra (the rhythm section partner of the black double bassist William Parker in David S Ware's quartet), the saxophonist Rob Brown (a member of William Parker's thunderous Little Huey Creative Orchestra), the pianist Marilyn Crispell (one of Anthony Braxton's regular collaborators) and the saxophonist Ken Vandermark (a key figure in the renaissance of Chicago's free-jazz scene at the end of the 1990s).

LISTENING
GUIDE
Anthony Davis, *Hemispheres*, Gramavision.
Lester Bowie, *Serious Fun*, DIW.
Ronald Shannon Jackson, *Barbecue Dog*, Antilles.
Power Tools, *Strange Meeting*, Antilles.
Last Exit, *The Noise of Trouble*, Enemy.
Jamaaladeen Tacuma, *Show Stopper*, Gramavision.
Defunkt, *Thermonuclear Sweat*, Hannibal.
Jean-Paul Bourelly, *Tribute to Jimi*, DIW.
Henry Threadgill, *Carry the Day*, Columbia.
Butch Morris, *Dust to Dust*, New World.
Sam Rivers, *Culmination*, RCA/Victor.
David S Ware, *Go See the World*, Columbia.
William Parker, *Sunrise in the Tone World*, AUM Fidelity.
Anthony Braxton (with Marilyn Crispell), *Quartet (Santa Cruz) 1993*, Hat Hut.
Ken Vandermark, *Design in Time*, Delmark.

The New York underground

The veterans of free jazz and their successors received a warm reception from Manhattan's so-called 'downtown' underground white scene, one of whose principal venues was the Knitting Factory. At the end of the 1980s, this club became the regular haunt of the New York avant-garde before it moved to the Tonic at the end of the 1990s. The black free-jazz tradition was carried on here in a variety of different ways by white artists such as the

LISTENING GUIDE

Tim Berne's *Caos Totale*, *Pace Yourself*, JMT.
Big Satan (with Tim Berne), *Big Satan*, Winter & Winter.
Material, *Memory Serves*, Celluloid.
Massacre, *Killing Time*, Celluloid.
Golden Palominos (with Arto Lindsay), *Golden Palominos*, Celluloid.
Lounge Lizards, *Lounge Lizards*, EG.
Eugene Chadbourne, *Strings*, Intakt.
Marc Ribot, *Requiem for What's-his-name*, Disques du Crépuscule.
Fred Frith, *Stone, Brick, Glass, Wood, Wire*, I Dischi di Angelica.
Ellery Eskelin, *The Secret Museum*, Hat Hut.
Tiny Bell Trio, *Tiny Bell Trio: Wandering Souls*, Winter & Winter.
Joey Baron, *Raised Pleasure Dot*, New World.

alto and baritone saxophonist Tim Berne, who was deeply influenced by Julius Hemphill (see p.210). With his rejection of the theme–variation–theme structure and stereotyped instrumental roles, with his ongoing renewal of the interaction between composition and improvisation and with his long suites with continual radical switches of metre, Tim Berne (whose influence was often combined with Steve Coleman's) was a major inspiration to the European avant-garde. One of the main founders of New York's white avant-garde (which was influenced by the various offshoots of the punk movement) was the bassist-producer Bill Laswell, whose aggressive approach brought him into contact with the most radical aspects of free jazz and heavy funk syncopation. A co-conspirator of Laswell in the bands Massacre, Material and Golden Palominos, Fred Frith brought to them his experience of free-jazz radicalism and the specifically British interplay between jazz and rock of the 1970s. Another key group on the 'downtown' scene was the saxophonist John Lurie's Lounge Lizards, who remained attached to 1930s swing, early bebop and early rhythm and blues, stressing the energy and rebelliousness of the latter, rather as the punk groups had done with rock and roll. The guitarists Arto Lindsay, Marc Ribot (who took over from Lindsay in the Lounge Lizards) and Eugene Chadbourne were other major figures active on the New York underground scene. They were split between the aggressive possibilities of the guitar and the instrument in its crudest manifestations (the home-made instruments of the spasm bands of the early part of the century, the sound of cheap rockabilly guitars, the electronic paraphernalia of rock and the clichés of jazz).

In the 1990s, an interest in jazz history became more pronounced on the Knitting Factory scene in the work of figures such as the drummer Joey Baron, the saxophonist Ellery Eskelin, the trumpeter Dave Douglas and the guitarist Bill Frisell. While Eskelin remained resolutely committed to free-jazz expressionism, Dave Douglas's musical language was relatively orthodox, whether he was paying a neoclassical tribute to the pianist Mary Lou Williams with his project *Soul on Soul* or leading his Tiny Bell Trio, which displayed more of a klezmer influence (see p.250), or his chamber-music-like quartet of violin, double bass and accordion. The trio Baron's Baron Down, brimming

Fred Frith

with energy and humour and with a style veering between rhythm and blues and jazzy brass band, was led by the drummer Joey Baron, playing opposite Jim Hall and subsequently John Zorn.

Irreverence and zapping

John Zorn was probably the key unifying and representative figure of the New York avant-garde scene. An alto sax player, Zorn first came to attention for his Parkeresque virtuosity, incredible sonic excursions and profound knowledge of jazz. He called on this knowledge to create musical tributes to some of the forgotten heroes of hard bop, such as Sonny Clark (with the Sonny Clark Memorial Quartet), Hank Mobley, Kenny Dorham and Freddie Redd (with the trio News For Lulu). Over the years, however, the tributes and musical, literary and film references grew exponentially, fighting for space and becoming mixed up, so that they resembled collage-making or channel-hopping – an impertinent, sarcastic end-of-the-century panorama. Due to the collapse of ideologies and the dead ends at which politically committed art found itself, the boundaries between different political positions became less distinct during the 1980s. The avant-garde movements nevertheless wanted to be seen as vigilant opponents of a society of off-the-peg ideas. They wanted to be seen as socially aware, anxious to avoid media stereotypes and keen to use new means of communication and new technologies to creative ends. The new improvisers had at their disposal a range of sounds and musical vocabularies that encouraged them to zap from one thing to another and to torpedo received ideas. Radical, acoustic, electric or based on sampling and sound synthesis, their initiatives amounted to a more or less conscious appraisal of the past century and of the state of the world as it entered the new century. At the same time they denounced the consumer society's need for aesthetic labels, academicism of all kinds and the negative effects on creativity of doctrinairism and the pursuit of profit. This basic attitude took a multitude of different forms not only in the United States but also in the rest of the world: the pianist Sergey Kuryokhin and the Ganelin Trio (see p.218) in Russia; the pianist Django Bates and the guitarist Billy Jenkins in Britain; the Clusone 3 (the saxophonist Michael Moore, the cellist Ernst Reijseger and the drummer Han Bennink) in the Netherlands; the guitarist René Lussier in Quebec; and Drame Musical Instantané, Compagnie Lubat and the short-lived Trash Corporation in France.

LISTENING GUIDE
John Zorn, George Lewis and Bill Frisell, *More News for Lulu*, Hat Hut.
John Zorn, *The Big Gundown*, Tzadik.
Sergey Kuryokhin, *Pop Mechanics No.17*, Leo.
Django Bates, *Summer Fruits*, JMT.
Clusone 3, *Rara Avis*, Hat Hut.
Drame Musical Instantané, *Machiavel*, GRRR.
Compagnie Lubat, *Scatrap Jazzcogne*, Labeluz

Jazz in an era of fusion

In parallel with his sound puzzles, John Zorn also led the quartet Masada (with Dave Douglas, Joey Baron and the double bassist Greg Cohen), the natural offspring of Ornette Coleman's quartets and the Jewish klezmer music of central Europe, which was well established in New York. Through this quartet, he demonstrated that he shared the interest of jazzmen all over the world in traditional musical forms.

Music of identity in the United States

LISTENING
GUIDE
John Zorn, *Masada*,
DIW.
Hassidic New Wave,
Jews and Abstract Truth,
Knitting Factory.
Bill Frisell, *Have a Little
Faith*, Elektra Nonesuch.
Danilo Pérez,
Panamonk, Impulse.
Omar Sosa, *Free Roots*,
Price Club.
Jerry Gonzalez (with
Steve Berrios), *Rumba
Para Monk*, Sunnyside.
Kip Hanrahan, *Conjure*,
American Clave.
Gonzalo Rubalcaba,
Inner Voyage, Blue
Note.

The economic situation forced New York musicians to accept all offers of work. For many, this included Jewish weddings, at which they turned their hand to klezmer music quite happily as many of them were Jewish. This also explains why New York jazz was particularly interested in the revival of Jewish identity in the 1980s. John Zorn's label Tzadik was at the vanguard of a movement that influenced numerous jazzmen (including the pianist Anthony Coleman, the guitarist Brad Shepik and the members of Hasidic New Wave). But Bill Frisell, playing alongside Zorn, produced quite different sounds. Born in the Midwest, Frisell stressed the 'country' aspects of the guitar, taking this far further than either Pat Metheny or John Scofield had dared to do. His electric guitar made constant reference to the sounds of the steel guitar (a glissando style typical of country music) and early rock guitars, which he blended with the sound of the local brass bands he had heard in his youth.

His mastery of the expressive range of the electric guitar and his independence from jazz-guitar orthodoxy had a considerable influence on

Omar Sosa

guitar playing over the last 15 years of the century. Less surprisingly, New York's Latin American community also played an important role. This was sustained by the constant arrival of new immigrants from Cuba (the saxophonist Paquito D'Rivera and the trumpeter Arturo Sandoval, who both left the group Irakere), Panama (the pianist Danilo Pérez), Puerto Rico (the saxophonist David Sanchez), Santo Domingo (the pianist Michel Camilo) and elsewhere. From the spontaneous musical dramas directed by the producer Kip Hanrahan to the interaction between the virtuoso Cuban pianist Omar Sosa and the world of hip-hop, from the repertoire of Thelonious Monk as reinterpreted by the Gonzalez brothers and Danilo Pérez to the classical and jazz-inspired Cuban piano of Gonzalo Rubalcaba, from the percussion of Anga Diaz (incorporating metres devised by Steve Coleman) to the versatile drumming of Steve Berrios, the cultural exchanges between the two Americas were one of the main focuses of jazz during the last two decades of the century.

Jazz uprooted

Even in America jazz could thus find itself severed from its historical roots. As the fashion for world music grew, this uprooting continued, particularly in South America, where the group Pau Brasil and Hermeto Pascoal's band re-examined the collective imagination of Brazil and the Chilean pianist Carlos Maza searched for an appropriate response to his exile among (at different times) Cuban and Brazilian musicians. On the west coast of the United States, Asian expatriates such as the Chinese pianist Jon Jang at the head of his Pan-Asian Orchestra and Miya Masaoka, who played Thelonious Monk on the koto (a kind of Japanese zither), maintained the delicate thread that still connected them to their homelands. In France, the guitarist Nguyên Lê (of Vietnamese origin) examined his roots in the show *Tales from Vietnam*. In Japan, as leader of the group Randooga (featuring the saxophonist Kohsuke Mine), the pianist Masahiko Satoh re-explored the Japanese tradition as affected by internationalist culture. The traditional Korean group Samul Nori collaborated on a regular basis with the Austrian saxophonist Wolfgang Puschnig's Red Sun group. The Siberian singer Sainkho Namchylak worked with members of the Russian, European and New York avant-gardes. The Moscow Art Trio (the pianist Mikhail Alperin, the French horn player Arkady Shilkloper and the clarinetist Sergey Starostin) achieved a synthesis of the various musics of the former USSR.

In Scandinavia, Jan Garbarek was influenced by regional traditions (*I Took Up the Runes*) but also explored new-age music together with the Hilliard Ensemble. In the United Kingdom, the pianist Huw Warren flirted with the folk scene, feeding his imagination with the British rural and urban folk tradition. The uilleann pipes (Irish bagpipes) made several appearances on the jazz scene – notably in Jacques Pellen's group Celtic Procession, in which the double bassist Riccardo Del Fra would often engage in a musical dialogue with the traditional Breton singer Annie Ebrel.

LISTENING
GUIDE
Jan Garbarek, *I Took Up the Runes*, ECM.
Huw Warren, *A Barrel Organ Far From Home*, Babel.
Jacques Pellen, *Celtic Procession*, Silex.
Annie Ebrel and Riccardo Del Fra, *Voulouz Loar*, Gwerz Pladenn.
Paris Musette, Vol 2, Swing et Manouche, Label La Lichère.
Richard Galliano, *French Touch*, Dreyfus.
Gianluigi Trovesi and Gianni Coscia, *Radici*, Egea.
Pino Minafra, *Sudori*, Victo.
Maria João and Mario Laginha, *Cor*, Verve.
Bojan Z Quartet, *Yopla!*, Label Bleu.
Jorge Pardo, *2332*, Nuevos Medios.
Chano Domínguez, *Hecho a Mano*, Nuba.
Renaud Garcia-Fons, *Oriental Bass*, Enja.
Alain Blesing, *3 Images du Désert*, Artalent.
Okay Temiz *Istanbul' da eylül*, Label La Lichère.
Rabih Abou-Khalil, *Yara*, Enja.
Anouar Brahem, *Khomsa*, ECM.
Mihaly Dresch, *Tul a vizen*, Fono.

Inspired by Astor Piazzolla's *nuevo tango*, the French accordionist Richard Galliano created the style *new musette*, and many French jazzmen rediscovered the folk music of their youth, contributing to the anthology albums entitled *Paris Musette*. Thanks to the world music phenomenon and new contemporary forms, the accordion made a highly visible comeback in jazz, whether in the form of the electronic accordion of Andrea Parkins or the new take on tarantellas by Gianni Coscia.

As represented by the clarinetist Gianluigi Trovesi and the trumpeter Pino Minafra, particularly in their work with the Italian Instabile Orchestra, the Italian jazz scene enjoyed a fruitful relationship with traditional music. The emerging Iberian scenes also took into account local traditions (the singer Maria João and the pianist Mario Laginha in Portugal, and the saxophonist Jorge Pardo and the pianist Chano Domínguez in Spain). In Hungary, the saxophonist Mihaly Dresch combined the verve of John Coltrane with Hungarian traditions. Bojan Zulfikarpasic, a Bosnian pianist living in France, rediscovered the music of his homeland thanks to the interest in it expressed by his French colleagues. More widely, the Mediterranean world inspired many projects which drew on the Moorish–Andalusian roots of flamenco, the gypsy diaspora and the rhythmic and modal similarities that united the Middle East, the Balkans, southern Europe and North Africa.

The virtues of fusion

Many more examples could be given. To some degree, all this activity simply extended practices begun in the 1970s. What was new, however, was the context. In an atmosphere of xenophobic tension following large waves of migration, jazz – on account of its history and open-mindedness – encouraged an examination of one's own roots while disapproving of any process of turning in on oneself. For young jazzmen keen to renew their musical language, 'otherness' was seen as a blessing rather than a threat. The multiracial fusion groups Sixun and Ultramarine provided the ideal soundtrack to the 'Keep your hands off my friend' campaign against the rise of the National Front in France. Going beyond a mere statement of intent, this openness towards the 'other' was no longer based on the easy use of exotic elements or on superficial encounters but on careful, patient sharing.

A major milestone was the percussionist Zakir Hussain's album *Makin' Music* (1986), which brought together the flautist Hariprasad Chaurasia, the guitarist John McLaughlin and the saxophonist Jan Garbarek. Never before had jazz musicians and traditional Indian musicians gone so far to meet each other.

The Indian percussionist Trilok Gurtu was discovered soon after. Gurtu combined elements of the drum kit

Randy Weston and Gnawa musicians

with the traditional tabla (which was taken up by many jazz drummers). In the second half of the 1990s, the music of the Belgian trio Aka Moon contributed to the dissection of Indian metres, thereby responding to the polyrhythmic challenges thrown down by Steve Coleman. In London, immigration provided an ideal window on the changing musical worlds of the Indian subcontinent and Jamaica. The studio practices of Jamaica and the rhythmic fluidity of reggae received enormous attention, and ska formed the object of a great deal of interaction with jazz. While Europe was discovering the Afro beat of the Nigerian saxophonist Fela Kuti in the early 1970s, French jazz festivals were embracing music from all over the world with a particular emphasis on the new African music. Joe Zawinul and Graham Haynes frequented the Parisian clubs, attracted by the bassists and drummers from the former French colonies and overseas territories who contributed so much to the richness of Eddy Louiss's groups in particular and French fusion in general. In the 1990s, the craze for rai (a mixture of North African and Western music) combined with the success of Randy Weston's collaboration with Morocco's Gnawa musicians served to focus attention on North Africa. Essaouira and Jajouk became places of pilgrimage for many jazzmen.

Of Algerian parentage, the drummer Karim Ziad (Orchestre National de

LISTENING
GUIDE
Sixun, *Nomads' Land,*
Emarcy.
Zakir Hussain, *Makin' Music,* ECM.
Trilok Gurtu, *Usfret,* CMP.
Aka Moon, *Elohim,* Carbon 7.
Jazz Jamaica, *Double Barrel,* Hannibal.
Graham Haynes, *The Griot's Footsteps,* Verve.
Randy Weston, *The Spirits of Our Ancestors,* Verve.
Graham Haynes, *Nocturne Parisian,* Muse.
Nguyên Lê, *Maghreb and Friends,* Act.

Barbès) succeeded the Ivory Coast drummer Paco Séry (Sixun) in Joe Zawinul's Syndicate and collaborated with Nguyên Lê (*Maghreb and Friends*) on a music based around the *gumbri* (Berber bass guitar) and *karkabous* (iron castanets). The latter underline the complexity of the rhythmic challenges inherent in the traditional music of Africa, eastern Europe and the Orient. Jazz no longer responded to these challenges with the bluff and dilettantism of the 1970s, but through a systematic process of assimilation and direct confrontation. However, there was a danger that in focusing too much on the teaching of the technical aspects of traditional cultures their essential character would be overlooked. In this respect, jazz fusion shared the unfortunate tendency of world music to relate the uniqueness of non-European traditions to Western norms.

The European exception

Away from New York and the United States, jazz inspired far too many disparate stylistic initiatives for them all to be described in just a few pages. At best we can attempt a survey of what was happening in Europe, where jazz was well established and most visible. The legacy of the major European movements of the 1970s could still be heard in the work of those of their representatives who were still active, including Jan Garbarek,

Joëlle Léandre

Michel Portal, Martial Solal, Fred Van Hove, Jean-François Jenny-Clark, Maarten Altena, Jon Christensen, Han Bennink, Mathias Rüegg and Barry Guy. This legacy was spread across a multitude of centres that can be best described in terms of their adherence or non-adherence to traditional jazz values.

The two Europes

This split dates from the emergence of free jazz in the United States. The first group placed an emphasis on clear rhythms, perfection of sound quality, elegant delivery and phrasing, and dependable reflexes. For them, the jazz stage was the setting for quasi-automatic reactions to more or less predictable situations (based on musical vocabularies and reflexes that adhered to the principle of controlled freedom). By contrast, whereas free-form jazz had achieved a certain maturity and high level of technical skill, the second group emphasized risk-taking, urgency, sudden changes of direction, torrents of notes, accident, random elements and the unprecedented – in terms of both a close physical relationship with the instrument and a more intellectual approach that condemned stylistic routine and acquired gestures, rhythmic and melodic comprehensibility, traditional instrumental roles and stereotyped sounds.

Paris was regarded as Europe's jazz capital, a direct competitor to New York, but it was also considered more conformist. The jazz scenes on the other side of the Rhine, the Alps and the Channel had the reputation of being more experimental than the French capital. This reputation was confirmed in different ways by the saxophonists Petras Vysniauskas (Lithuania), Mats Gustafsson (Sweden), Jon Lloyd (Britain), Ab Baars (Netherlands) and Carlo Actis Dato (Italy); the cellist Ernst Reijseger (Netherlands); the trumpeter Axel Dörner (Germany); and the pianist Sylvie Courvoisier (Switzerland). In France, an alternative club in the Paris suburbs called Les Instants Chavirés and the 'innovative' festivals produced many exceptions to the rule. They offered second careers to musicians who had remained loyal to the values of free jazz (such as the saxophonist Daunik Lazro and the Outlaws in Jazz) and provided a platform for younger musicians who found themselves at odds with the prevailing trends (many of whom were working in styles close to contemporary music or even experimental rock). These younger musicians included the trombonist Thierry Madiot, the saxophonist Michel Doneda, the clarinetist Denis Colin, the cellist Didier Petit, the pianist Sophie Agnel, the harpist Hélène Breschand, the tuba player Michel Godard, the double bassist Joëlle Léandre and the drummer Ramon Lopez. Neither did France have the monopoly on straight-ahead jazz (in which the dividing line between pure neo-boppers and free-thinkers was extremely thin). Musicians who made their names with straight-ahead jazz included the Sardinian Paolo Fresu, the Swiss Matthieu Michel and the Frenchman Stéphane Belmondo (trumpet); the France-based American Glenn Ferris and the Frenchman Denis Leloup (trombone); the German Christof Lauer, the Briton Andy Sheppard, the Frenchman Éric Barret, the Swiss Maurice Magnoni and the Italian Massimo Urbani (saxophones); the Belgians Nathalie Loriers and Diederik Wissels, the Italian Enrico Pieranunzi, the Frenchman Zool Fleischer, the Frenchwoman Sophia Domancich, the Norwegian Maria Kannegaard and the Swede Esbjörn Svenson (piano); the Frenchman Emmanuel Bex (organ); the Hungarian Gabor Gado and the Frenchman Serge Lazarévitch (guitar); the Italian Riccardo Del Fra and the Dutchman Hein Van de Geyn (double bass); and the Frenchman Simon Goubert and the Belgian Dré Pallemaerts (drums).

The French go-betweens

In actual fact, neither of these (not particularly uniform) musical movements had a monopoly on creativity and openness or on academicism and sectarianism. The boundary dividing them was visible only through the distorting prism of prejudice. Nevertheless, when it came to handing out the public subsidies for jazz introduced by the French socialists when they came to power in 1981, the decision-makers made a distinction between those musicians they considered to be merely cloning established forms and those they considered to be the heirs to a tradition of improvisation, describing them as creative or innovative artists. It was only reluctantly that

Marc Ducret

they took into account the large volume of jazz being played day in, day
out in Paris's private clubs. These decision-makers preferred to award
prestigious one-off commissions (and thereby increase their sense of self-
worth) rather than encourage established groups that had come together
independently in order to express themselves in their own way.

Around 1984, an important generation came to the fore in the clubs. Some
of its members (such as the pianists and composers Andy Emler and Antoine
Hervé) had studied at music college, while others (for example, the guitarist
Marc Ducret and the bandleader Laurent Cugny) were committed
autodidacts. This generation had come of age surrounded by rock music but
had found its first models among the pioneers of controlled freedom, jazz-
rock and the ECM catalogue. If they did not belong to the new Orchestre
National de Jazz (ONJ), where talent was immediately appreciated, they
were suspect in official eyes and remained so for a long time – even when,
at the end of the 1980s, many versatile figures (such as the guitarist Marc
Ducret, the violinist Dominique Pifarély and the double bassist Hélène
Labarrière) joined forces with the heirs to the improvised music of the
1970s, who had come of age in the network of cultural associations away
from the clubs (such as the trombonist Yves Robert, the saxophonist-
clarinetists Louis Sclavis and Sylvain Kassap, the guitarist Claude
Barthélémy and the double bassist Bruno Chevillon).

It was thanks to these 'go-betweens' that the following generations were
able to emerge: the generation which achieved recognition around 1990
with the saxophonists Julien Lourau, Guillaume Orti, Laurent Dehors and
François Corneloup, the guitarists Noël Akchoté and David Chevallier, the
pianist Benoît Delbecq, the cellist Vincent Courtois, the double bassists
Hubert Dupont and Claude Tchamitchian, and the drummers François
Merville, Christophe Marguet and Éric Échampard; the generation centred
on the jazz class of the Conservatoire National Supérieur in Paris in the
second half of the 1990s and whose prominent members included the
trombonist Gueorgi Kornazov, the saxophonists Mathieu Donarier and
Christophe Monniot, and the guitarist Manu Codjia; and the generation of

the saxophonist Alban Darche (from Nantes) and the double bassist Sébastien Boisseau (from the Tours region). The last-mentioned generation came to prominence in provincial France thanks to a network of exchanges established in order to benefit the regional scenes, which had up to then been overshadowed by Paris.

LISTENING GUIDE
Michel Petrucciani (with Wayne Shorter and Jim Hall), *The Power of Three*, Blue Note.
Jean-Michel Pilc, *Live at Sweet Basil*, A Records.
Laurent de Wilde, *Spoon-a-Rhythm*, Columbia.
Prysm, *Time*, Blue Note.
Sylvie Courvoisier and Mark Feldman, *Music for Violin and Piano*, Avant.
Han Bennink and Dave Douglas, *Serpentine*, Songlines.
Misha Mengelberg, *Two Days in Chicago*, Hat Hut.

To and fro across the Atlantic

During the 1990s, New York's straight-ahead scene attracted musicians from all over the world, such as the Argentinian Guillermo Klein, the Danish guitarist Thor Madsen and the Israeli double bassist Avishaï Cohen. In the wake of the pianist Michel Petrucciani's success in America, a large number of French musicians tried their luck in New York. While some maintained their unreserved loyalty to jazz's inviolable values, others were galvanized by a paradoxical climate of competition and solidarity between musicians, by a sense of urgency and of having one's back against the wall. Although their existence was precarious, at least they were not ignored, as they had been by the extremely protective and blindly selective French system. Their New York detour won belated recognition in France for the pianists Jean-Michel Pilc, Jacky Terrasson and Laurent de Wilde.

Conversely, Europe offered important opportunities to American artists, who benefited from ambitious cultural policies, a host of small labels and festivals, and much more respect than they received at home. The European subsidiaries of multinationals were remarkable for the high level of attention they paid to contemporary jazz. Many American jazz artists were signed up in the Paris offices of the multinationals, and this policy even extended to a number of young French signings (Laurent Cugny and his big band Lumière on the Emarcy label, Laurent de Wilde on Columbia, the trio Prysm on Blue Note).

Relatively cheap and accessible air travel encouraged musicians in different parts of the world to get together, in particular allowing the European and American avant-gardes to join forces: for example, duos between the French double bassist Joëlle Léandre and the double bassist William Parker, between the Swiss pianist Sylvie Courvoisier and the violinist Mark Feldman, between Han Bennink and Ellery Eskelin or Dave Douglas; the trio of the Portuguese violinist Carlos Zingaro, the cellist Tom Cora and the double bassist Mark Dresser; the contributions of Django Bates and Marc Ducret to Tim Berne's groups; and the involvement of the Swedish saxophonist Mats Gustafsson, the Dutch pianist Misha Mengelberg and the German saxophonist Peter Brötzmann in Chicago's free scene.

In its final issue of the twentieth century, the American magazine *Jazz Times* painted a picture of a European jazz that was eager for renewal and impatient to sever links with conservative American models. The interest of many American artists in Europe demonstrated above all that American artists had aspirations other than figuring in the jazz lists of the multinational record companies. It also demonstrated that jazz had become so diversified that it could no longer be restricted to a handful of capital cities or avant-garde or 'rearguard' centres identified by the media and cultural decision-makers. And, looking beyond the West, it seemed likely that the rest of the world had not had its final say either.

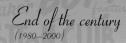

Jazz? Who cares?

In every age (hot jazz, swing, bebop, hard bop, free jazz or even jazz-rock), there have been jazz fans and musicians who have wanted to mummify the jazz of the day, to preserve it as a kind of desiccated folk music whose strains are endlessly repeated with only minor variations. Another, more positive point of view sees jazz as a living form of traditional music comparable to a team sport – as with rugby, say, it is all about creating pleasure and emotion within the framework of fixed rules. It is also possible, however, to share this pleasure and emotion but at the same time to see jazz as a constantly evolving music, one that regenerates itself from decade to decade while absorbing the energy peculiar to each new era. Those who are amazed that the label 'jazz' is still used in the 21st century to describe a range of music very different from the forms that originally bore the name almost a century ago should remember that 'classical music' was initially a specific term used to denote the short period between the Baroque and Pre-Romantic eras. This did not prevent the entire span of music from Hildegard of Bingen to John Adams from being added to either end of this 'golden age' and included under the term 'classical music' for the sake of convenience. Like classical music, jazz has its own genealogy. This leads in a direct, unbroken line from Buddy Bolden to Louis Armstrong, from Louis Armstrong to Coleman Hawkins, from Coleman Hawkins to Charlie Parker, from Charlie Parker to John Coltrane and from John Coltrane to Evan Parker. The trunk and main branches of this family tree can be easily identified, but this is not the case with its smaller branches, which extend so far that they risk becoming entangled with those of other, separate trees. It should also not be forgotten that at the outset jazz was fed by countless roots extending in all directions and that throughout its history it has received nourishment from a wide range of species.

Jazz was destined to extend beyond its folk-based boundaries and spread its influence to the four corners of the earth. It absorbed the different pulses of the 20th century and made them its own through swing, that graceful rhythmic force capable of transforming even the simplest tune into a masterpiece. The standards that make today's jazzmen swing continue in many cases to be drawn from a common repertoire of musical theatre songs. However, this repertoire has been supplemented by more recent songs and by rhythmic, melodic and harmonic archetypes borrowed from a multitude of musical genres, in the same way as jazzmen used to borrow from the musicals. These archetypes are often simple collective mental structures – acoustic, gestural, visual or intellectual reference points that make up the improvisers' musical fabric.

Just as the post-serialists extended serialism to parameters other than simply pitch, jazzmen have applied swing not only to the four-beat bar but also to a range of rhythmic languages with which they have come into contact, from the clave of Latin music to the emphatic beat of rock. Today's jazzmen apply the concept of swing even more widely, floating freely over their newly appropriated material just as their ancestors floated over the bar lines of the standards. What survives of swing now is a precision of gesture and a physical elation that transforms the beat into pure momentum. What also remains is the importance of the individual in spite of precision timing, the commonplaces of the standard and ensemble-based playing – an alertness that allows musicians to break free from conventional archetypes and transform them creatively, just as black America saved its soul by turning to its own advantage a culture that sought to crush it. More than simply a form of folk music, jazz is a lesson taught by the black American people and an opportunity for a world faced with a loss of cultural identity.

Will jazz become a much more widespread genre made up of short, ongoing exchanges between disciplines and continents? Jazz lovers of various persuasions continue to argue about the identity, reality and permanence of jazz (sometimes accusing each other of not being 'true' jazz lovers). But they are sufficiently aware of being different from other music lovers that they attend the same festivals and read the same magazines as one another. As for the musicians, often the only place those who reject the label 'jazz' can voice their rejection is in the jazz press. Nevertheless, there are enough bridges between this group and those most vehemently attached to jazz for the label 'jazz' to continue to be used (in the absence of anything better). In a large record store in January 2001, the author of this book bumped into one of the musicians who regularly cross these bridges in both directions. In answer to the author's question about the state of jazz, the musician gave an incredulous look and shrugged his shoulders: 'Jazz? Who cares?' Was it mere coincidence, however, that this exchange took place in the jazz section?

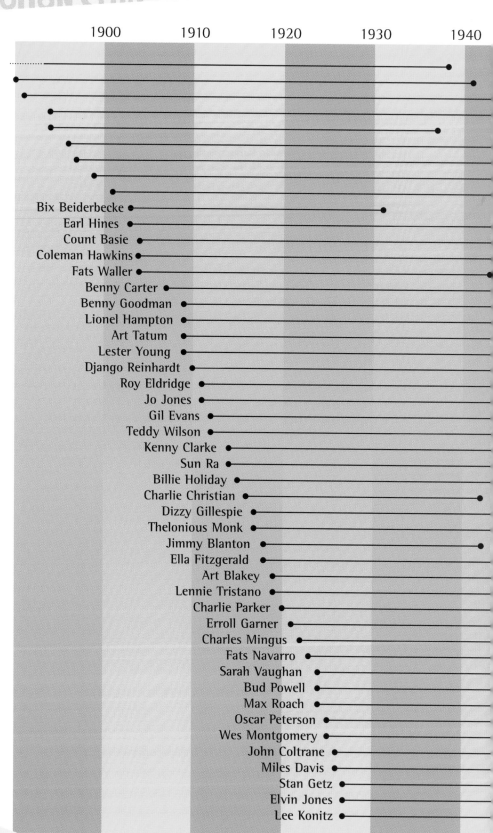

1900   1910   1920   1930   1940

Bix Beiderbecke
Earl Hines
Count Basie
Coleman Hawkins
Fats Waller
Benny Carter
Benny Goodman
Lionel Hampton
Art Tatum
Lester Young
Django Reinhardt
Roy Eldridge
Jo Jones
Gil Evans
Teddy Wilson
Kenny Clarke
Sun Ra
Billie Holiday
Charlie Christian
Dizzy Gillespie
Thelonious Monk
Jimmy Blanton
Ella Fitzgerald
Art Blakey
Lennie Tristano
Charlie Parker
Erroll Garner
Charles Mingus
Fats Navarro
Sarah Vaughan
Bud Powell
Max Roach
Oscar Peterson
Wes Montgomery
John Coltrane
Miles Davis
Stan Getz
Elvin Jones
Lee Konitz

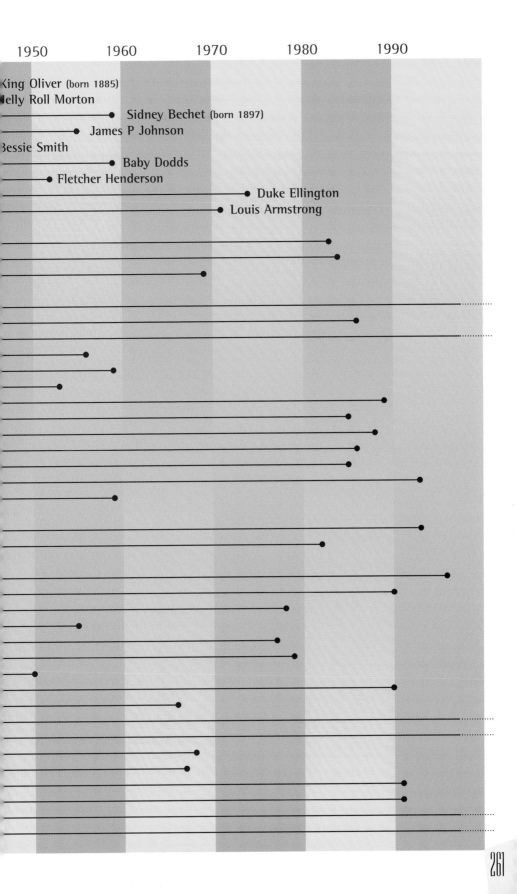

1950 1960 1970 1980 1990

King Oliver (born 1885)
Jelly Roll Morton
Sidney Bechet (born 1897)
James P Johnson
Bessie Smith
Baby Dodds
Fletcher Henderson
Duke Ellington
Louis Armstrong

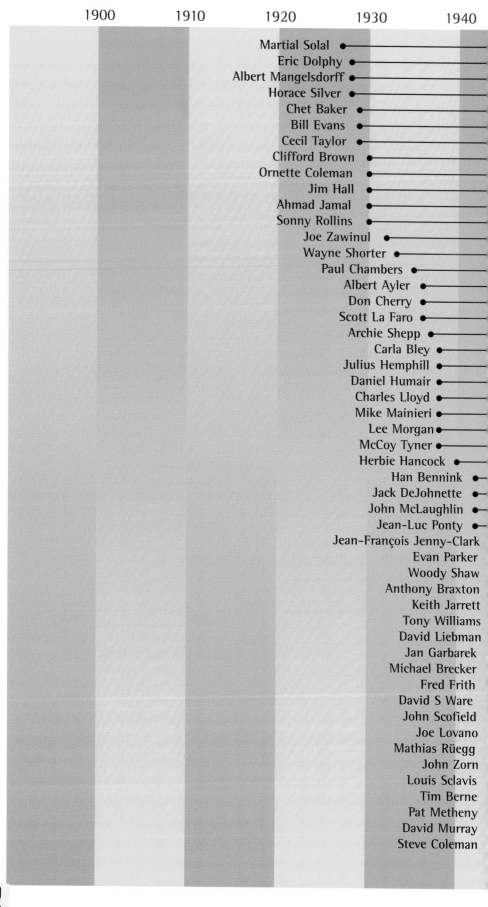

1900   1910   1920   1930   1940

Martial Solal
Eric Dolphy
Albert Mangelsdorff
Horace Silver
Chet Baker
Bill Evans
Cecil Taylor
Clifford Brown
Ornette Coleman
Jim Hall
Ahmad Jamal
Sonny Rollins
Joe Zawinul
Wayne Shorter
Paul Chambers
Albert Ayler
Don Cherry
Scott La Faro
Archie Shepp
Carla Bley
Julius Hemphill
Daniel Humair
Charles Lloyd
Mike Mainieri
Lee Morgan
McCoy Tyner
Herbie Hancock
Han Bennink
Jack DeJohnette
John McLaughlin
Jean-Luc Ponty
Jean-François Jenny-Clark
Evan Parker
Woody Shaw
Anthony Braxton
Keith Jarrett
Tony Williams
David Liebman
Jan Garbarek
Michael Brecker
Fred Frith
David S Ware
John Scofield
Joe Lovano
Mathias Rüegg
John Zorn
Louis Sclavis
Tim Berne
Pat Metheny
David Murray
Steve Coleman

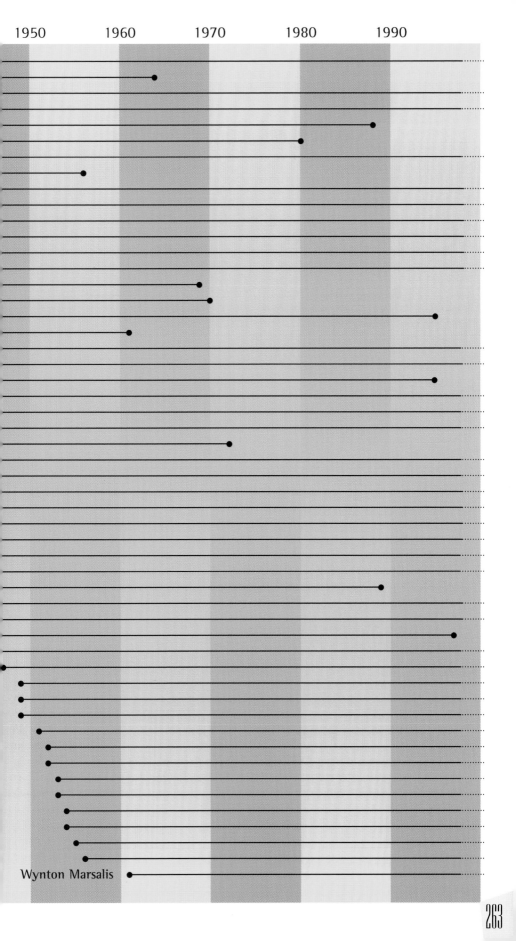

Wynton Marsalis

Film music and portrayals of jazz

C oming into existence at roughly the same time, jazz and cinema enjoyed an ambiguous relationship conditioned by the black community's lack of access to the means of production and the racism endemic in American society. As film music, the linear flow of straight-ahead improvisation did not fit in easily with the cutting process. Seen as exotic, jazz was often used for decorative purposes (providing an acoustic backdrop in nightclub scenes, for example). It was also used to accompany stereotypical situations such as nocturnal city scenes or chase sequences. The films listed below trace the history of the somewhat uneasy between jazz and cinema.

Alan Crosland, *The Jazz Singer*, 1927
The success of talking pictures opened studio doors cautiously to jazz. The blacked-up white entertainer Al Jolson was not from the jazz world, however, but was one of the first white minstrels.

Walt Disney, *The Jazz Fool, Jungle Rhythm*, 1929
Mickey Mouse (who began talking in 1928) and his rivals (Bosko, created by Hugh Harman and Rudolf Ising, and George Herriman's Krazy Kat) were descended from the heroes of the minstrel shows (Jim Crow and Zip Coon) but were already infected by jazz rhythms.

Dudley Murphy, *St Louis Blues*, 1929
A short based on Bessie Smith's 'St Louis Blues'. The same director made *Black and Tan* with Duke Ellington in the same year.

King Vidor, *Hallelujah*, 1929
Hollywood version of a cotton planter's story, featuring black actors and interspersed with spirituals.

Dave Fleischer, *Minnie the Moocher*, 1932
Betty Boop reveals her true personality to the music of Cab Calloway. Many jazzmen appeared with her over the years, including Louis Armstrong in *I'll Be Glad When You're Dead You Rascal You*.

Fred Waller, *Symphony in Black (Rhapsody of Negro Life)*, 1935
Duke Ellington composes a suite inspired by black American society on screen, with a guest appearance by Billie Holiday.

William Keighley and Marc Connelly, *The Green Pastures*, 1936
A black minister tells Bible stories to a group of children. The world of the Negro spiritual as idealized by white film-makers.

Spencer Williams, *The Blood of Jesus*, 1941
Drama set in a black Baptist community in the south. The world of Negro spirituals as seen by a black film-maker. The same year, in *Birth of the Blues*, Victor Schertzinger credits white Americans with the creation of the blues.

Vincente Minnelli, *Cabin in the Sky*, 1942
Parable featuring a gloomy paradise and a hell resembling a jazz club. With Duke
Ellington, Lena Horne, Ethel Waters and Louis Armstrong.

Andrew L Stone, *Stormy Weather*, 1943
The plot is an excuse to celebrate the black jazz of the 1930s revues. With Fats Waller,
Cab Calloway, Lena Horne and the dancer Bill Robinson.

Gjon Mili, *Jammin' the Blues*, 1944
Three pieces played by a combo led by Lester Young. The work of an Albanian
photographer, this is one of the most beautiful music films ever made.

Leonard Anderson, *Jivin' in Bebop*, 1947
A series of pieces performed by Dizzy Gillespie's big band with various guests. A rare
film record of the bebop revolution.

Arthur Lubin, *New Orleans*, 1947
With Louis Armstrong and Billie Holiday. Typical example of the jazz film in which black
jazzmen only appear in the background, the featured orchestra being a white band led by
Woody Herman.

George Pal, *Date with Duke*, 1947
The first animated film made with modelling clay – featuring music by Duke Ellington.

Michael Curtiz, *Young Man with a Horn*, 1950
In this adaptation of a Dorothy Baker novel, the main character Rick Martin (Kirk
Douglas, doubled by Harry James in the music scenes) is based on Bix Beiderbecke. One
in a long line of biographies of white jazzmen that started in 1930 with *King of Jazz*
(about Paul Whiteman) and continued in 1953 with *The Glenn Miller Story* (with James
Stewart in the lead role).

Lázló Benedek, *The Wild One*, 1953
With a soundtrack of arrangements by Shorty Rogers, played by his band. Teenagers and
their concerns were taking over the big screen, and West Coast jazzmen were taking
over the film studios.

Otto Preminger, *The Man with the Golden Arm*, 1955
The battle with drugs of an amateur drummer, played by Frank Sinatra. Music by Elmer
Bernstein, performed in part by Shorty Rogers & His Giants.

Louis Malle, *Lift to the Scaffold*, 1957
A film whose main point of interest is Miles Davis's soundtrack, which he improvised live
to a screening of the film. Following the example of Louis Malle and also Roger Vadim
(*Sait-on jamais...* with the Modern Jazz Quartet), many French directors have entrusted
their soundtracks to jazzmen.

Robert Wise, *I Want To Live*, 1958
Music by Johnny Mandel performed by Art Farmer, Frank Rosolino, Gerry Mulligan, Bud
Shank, Red Mitchell and Shelly Manne.

Jean-Luc Godard, *Breathless*, 1959
Martial Solal's score is in tune with the narrative innovations of the French New Wave.

Otto Preminger, *Anatomy of a Murder*, 1959
Thriller with a 100% jazz score by Duke Ellington and Billy Strayhorn.

John Cassavetes, *Shadows*, 1959
The storyline is improvised, jazz-style, by the actors to the accompaniment of a soundtrack improvised partly by Charles Mingus and partly by the saxophonist Curtis Porter. John Cassavetes gave jazz an important place in both his plots and his soundtracks (see *Too Late Blues*).

Bert Stern, *On a Summer's Day*, 1960
Film of the 1958 Newport Festival with Louis Armstrong, Gerry Mulligan, Thelonious Monk and Anita O'Day. Along with *The Sound of Jazz*, a CBS programme made in 1957, this film remained one of the best jazz documentaries for years to come.

Shirley Clarke, *The Connection*, 1962
Based on the play by Jack Gelber. Portrait of a group of musician drug addicts waiting for their dealer. Music by Freddie Redd, played by his quartet with Jackie McLean.

Shirley Clarke, *The Cool World*, 1964
Portrait of Harlem adolescence with a Mal Waldron score, performed by the Dizzy Gillespie quartet.

Michael Snow, *New York Eye and Ear Control*, 1964
Improvised by Albert Ayler, Don Cherry, John Tchicai, Roswell Rudd, Gary Peacock and Sonny Murray, the soundtrack came first and Michael Snow's images second. The following year, the music commissioned from Ornette Coleman by Conrad Rooks for his film *Chappaqua* was rejected as too experimental.

Norman Jewison, *In the Heat of the Night*, 1967
Drama about racism in the southern states. Quincy Jones injects a dose of rhythm and blues, anticipating the 'blaxploitation' genre (see below). The main theme is sung by Ray Charles.

Michelangelo Antonioni, *Blow Up*, 1967
The British rock band the Yardbirds and Herbie Hancock share the soundtrack of this film about swinging London.

Johan Van der Keuken, *Velocity*, 1967
The Dutch saxophonist and composer Willem Breuker provides the music for this experimental documentary. As jazz gradually freed itself from its original archetypes – particularly outside the United States – improvisers, arrangers and composers brought a new flexibility to the creation of film music.

Melvin Van Peebles, *Sweet Sweetback's Baadasssss Song*, 1971
A raw film rooted in black American culture and the violence of the ghetto, with a soundtrack by a funk group unknown at the time: Earth, Wind & Fire. The blaxploitation genre exemplified by Gordon Parks's *Shaft* (with music by Isaac Hayes) would tap into the triple vein of funk–sex–action while watering down the message of Van Peebles and black political cinema.

Stellan Olsson, *Sven Klangs Combo*, 1976
Retrospective look at young Swedish musicians' fascination with bebop, its music and its self-destructive tendencies. Inspired by the life of Lars Gullin.

Martin Scorsese, *New York, New York*, 1977
The interlocked destinies of a jazz saxophonist and a singer at the end of World War Two. Liza Minnelli sings for real, while Robert De Niro mimes to George Auld's saxophone. White heroes in the great Hollywood tradition, but there is an admirable subtlety of viewpoint.

John Landis, *The Blues Brothers*, 1980
The misadventures of two white rockers. The soundtrack provides a showcase for Aretha Franklin, Ray Charles, Cab Calloway, James Brown, John Lee Hooker and musicians from the Stax Studios in Memphis.

Bertrand Tavernier, *Around Midnight*, 1986
Inspired by the figures of Bud Powell and Lester Young, with the saxophonist Dexter Gordon playing the lead.

Clint Eastwood, *Bird*, 1988
Portrait of Charlie Parker, played by Forest Whitaker.

Charlotte Zwerin, *Straight, No Chaser*, 1989
Documentary portrait of Thelonious Monk.

Spike Lee, *Mo' Better Blues*, 1990
After the film *Do the Right Thing*, which depicted the violence of the ghettos in the 1980s, *Mo' Better Blues* is a tribute to the director's jazzman father. It features the young neo-bop generation: Branford Marsalis, Terence Blanchard, Kenny Kirkland, Robert Hurst and Jeff Watts.

Nicholas Humbert and Werner Penzel, *Step Across the Border*, 1990
Documentary about the work of Fred Frith.

Marc-Henri Wajnberg, *Just Friends*, 1993
This film could almost pass as a remake of *Sven Klangs Combo* transposed to Belgium. The main character is inspired by the life of the Flemish saxophonist Jack Sels. The music is composed by the pianist Michel Herr, and performed by Archie Shepp and others.

Robert Altman, *Jazz 34*, 1996
Reconstruction of a jam session held in Kansas in the 1930s (parts of the reconstruction were used in the film *Kansas City*). With Butch Morris, Olu Dara, Joshua Redman, James Carter, Geri Allen and Ron Carter.

Woody Allen, *Sweet and Lowdown*, 1999
Fantasy documentary about an imaginary guitarist from the 1930s, alternating interviews with fictitious scenes and music.

THE REPERTOIRE
AND EVOLUTION OF JAZZ

1920s
Jazz borrows from or is inspired by brass bands (marches), blues, spirituals, ragtime, salon music (polkas and quadrilles), traditional songs and popular Broadway songs.

'High Society', 'West End Blues', 'Tin Roof Blues', 'Royal Garden Blues', 'Tiger Rag', 'King Porter Stomp', 'Bugle Call Rag', 'Frankie and Johnny', 'The Stampede', 'Everybody Loves My Baby'

1930s
Having dropped all forms other than the twelve-bar blues and 32-bar structures, the jazz repertoire is now divided more clearly between Broadway songs occasionally written by jazzmen (standards) and pieces written specifically for instrumental performance (often adopting the same structure).

Jazz compositions: 'Caravan', 'In a Sentimental Mood', 'Jumpin' at the Woodside', 'Moten Swing', 'Stompin' at the Savoy', 'Topsy'

Songs of the day: 'All of Me', 'Honeysuckle Rose', 'Liza', 'Love for Sale', 'I Got Rhythm', 'Oh Lady Be Good', 'Stardust', 'Summertime', 'These Foolish Things', 'What Is This Thing Called Love'

1940–53
Bebop and cool jazz devise their own repertoires (often reworking Broadway and blues numbers) but the new harmonic practices also lead to the discovery of new standards and the rediscovery of old ones. The New Orleans revival provides an opportunity to resurrect forgotten pieces such as 'When the Saints'. The influence of Latin jazz and the experiments of cool jazz produce an increasingly diverse range of music.

Jazz compositions: 'Anthropology', 'Bernie's Tune', 'Billie's Bounce', 'Darn That Dream', 'Hot House', 'Lady Bird', 'Night in Tunisia', ''Round About Midnight', 'Salt Peanuts'

Songs of the day: 'All the Things You Are', 'Body and Soul', 'Cherokee', 'I'll Remember April', 'Lover Man', 'My Funny Valentine', 'Stella by Starlight'

1954–60
Hard bop invents a new harmonic ease and reinvents the values of spirituals and blues with a new repertoire. New standards continue to be taken from Broadway, however, and new tunes come from Jamaica ('Saint Thomas'), France ('Les Feuilles Mortes'), Sweden ('Dear Old Stockholm') and the Anglo-American tradition ('Billy Boy').

Jazz compositions: 'Doxy', 'Joy Spring', 'I Remember Clifford', 'Minority', 'Moment's Notice', 'Moanin'', 'Nardis', 'Oleo', 'The Preacher', 'Soul Eyes', 'Walkin'', 'Whisper Not'

Popular standards: 'Baubles', 'Bangles and Beads', 'Invitation', 'On Green Dolphin Street', 'Softly as in a Morning Sunrise'

From 1960 onwards
There is a tendency for the new forms of jazz to free themselves from the notion of repertoire, with each group developing its own musical material. The standard repertoire continues to be drawn upon, however, either in straight-ahead interpretations or reworkings. The emphasis is on the work of marginal composers (such as Thelonious Monk) or neglected composers (such as Herbie Nichols). The Broadway repertoire runs dry. While pop music exerts a certain influence on jazz composers, its numbers are only very tentatively borrowed by jazzmen. By contrast, jazz compositions – from Ornette Coleman's 'Lonely Woman' to Richard Beirach's 'ELM' – are assimilated into the repertoire and help to renew it on an ongoing basis.

Bibliography

Dictionaries

Kernfeld, B (ed), *The New Grove Dictionary of Jazz*, 2nd ed, (3 vols), Oxford University Press, Oxford, 2001

Komara, E (ed), *Encyclopedia of the Blues*, (2 vols), Routledge, New York, 2006

Mandel, H (ed), *Illustrated Encyclopedia of Jazz & Blues*, Flame Tree, London, 2005

McNeill, W K (ed), *Encyclopedia of American Gospel Music*, Routledge, New York, 2005

General works

Collier, J L, *The Making of Jazz: A Comprehensive History*, Houghton Mifflin, Boston, 1978

Collier, J L, *Jazz: The American Theme Song*, Oxford University Press, New York, 1995

Gioia, T, *The History of Jazz*, Oxford University Press, New York, 1999

Shipton, A, *A New History of Jazz*, Continuum, London, 2004

Tirro, F, *Jazz: A History*, 2nd ed, Norton, New York, 1993

Theory

Berliner, P, *Thinking In Jazz*, University of Chicago Press, Chicago, 1994

Kernfeld, B, *What to Listen For in Jazz*, Yale University Press, New Haven, 1995

By instrument

Alexander, C (ed), *Masters of Jazz Guitar*, Balafon, London, 1999

Friedwald, W, *Jazz Singing*, Quartet, London, 1990

Gelly, D, *Masters of Jazz Saxophone*, Balafon, London, 2000

Outside America

Atkins, T, *Blue Nippon: Authenticating Jazz in Japan*, Duke University Press, Durham, 2001

Ballantine, C, *Marabi Nights: Early South African Jazz and Vaudeville*, Ravan Press, Johannesburg, 1995

Feigin, L, *Russian Jazz: A New Identity*, Quartet, London, 1985

Godbolt, J, *A History of Jazz In Britain, 1919–50*, Quartet, London, 1984

Godbolt, J, *A History of Jazz in Britain, 1950–70*, Quartet, London, 1989

Kater, M H, *Different Drummers: Jazz in the Culture of Nazi Germany*, Oxford University Press, New York, 2003

Starr, S F, *Red & Hot: The Fate of Jazz in the Soviet Union*, Limelight Editions, New York, 1994

Whitehead, K, *New Dutch Swing*, Billboard, New York, 1999

Related music

Davis, F, *The History of the Blues*, Secker & Warburg, London, 1995

Work songs and spirituals

Hogan, M, *The Oxford Book of Spirituals*, Oxford University Press, Oxford, 2001

Johnson, J W and Johnson, J R, *The Books of American Negro Spirituals*, Da Capo Press, Cambridge, 2003

Gospel, blues and ragtime

Moore, A (ed), *The Cambridge Companion to Blues and Gospel Music*, Cambridge University Press, Cambridge, 2003

Morgan, T L and Barlow, W, *From Cakewalks to Concert Halls: An Illustrated History of African American Popular Music*, Elliott & Clark Publishing, Washington, 1992

Oliver, P, Harrison, M and Bolcom, W, *The New Grove Gospel, Blues and Jazz: With Spirituals and Ragtime*, Norton, New York, 1988

Hot jazz

Albertson, C, *Bessie*, revised and expanded ed, Yale University Press, New Haven, 2003

Ellington, E K (Duke Ellington), *Music Is My Mistress*, Da Capo Press, Cambridge, 1976

Giddens, G, *Satchmo*, Da Capo, New York, 1998

Schuller, G, *Early Jazz: Its Roots and Musical Development*, Oxford University Press, New York, 1986

Ward, G C and Burns, K, *Jazz: A History of America's Music*, Alfred A Knopf, New York, 2002

Swing

Basie, C and Murray, A, *Good Morning Blues: The Autobiography of Count Basie*, Da Capo Press, Cambridge, 2002

Hall, F, *Dialogues in Swing: Intimate Conversations with the Stars of the Big Band Era*, Pathfinder Publishing, Ventura, 1990

Schuller, G, *The Swing Era: The Development of Jazz, 1930–45*, Oxford University Press, New York, 2005

Bop

DeVeaux, S, *The Birth of Bebop*, University of California Press, Berkeley, 1997

Owens, T, *Bebop*, Oxford University Press, Oxford, 1995

Mathieson, K, *Giant Steps*, Payback Press, Edinburgh, 1999

Russell, R, *Bird Lives! The High Life and Hard Times of Charlie (Yardbird) Parker*, Da Capo Press, Cambridge, 1996

Shipton, A, *Groovin' High – The Life of Dizzy Gillespie*, Oxford University Press, Oxford, 1999

Woideck, C, *Charlie Parker – His Music and Life*, University of Michigan Press, Ann Arbor, 1996

Cool jazz

Gavin, J, *Deep In A Dream – The Long Night of Chet Baker*, Chatto & Windus, London, 2002
Goia, T, *West Coast Jazz*, Oxford University Press, Oxford, 1992
Klinkowitz, J, *Listen: Gerry Mulligan*, Schirmer, New York, 1991
Maggin, D L, *Stan Getz: A Life in Jazz*, William Morrow, New York, 1997

Hard bop

Gourse, L, *Straight, No Chaser: The Life and Genius of Thelonious Monk*, Schirmer Books, New York, 2000
Mathieson, K, *Cookin'*, Canongate, Edinburgh, 2002
Rosenthal, D, *Hard Bop*, Oxford University Press, Oxford, 1992

Free jazz

Kahn, A, *A Love Supreme: The Creation of John Coltrane's Classic Album*, Granta Books, New York, 2003
Litweiler, J, *The Freedom Principle: Jazz after 1958*, Da Capo Press, Cambridge, 1990

Litweiler, J, *Ornette Coleman: A Harmolodic Life*, Morrow, New York, 1992
Pettinger, P, *Bill Evans: How My Heart Sings*, Yale University Press, New Haven, 2002
Porter, L, *John Coltrane: His Life and Music*, University of Michigan Press, Ann Arbor, 2000
Santoro, G, *Myself When I am Real: The Life and Music of Charles Mingus*, Oxford University Press, Oxford, 2000
Szwed, J F, *Space is the Place: The Life and Times of Sun Ra*, Pantheon Books, New York, 1997

Fusion

Milkowski, B, *Jaco: The Extraordinary and Tragic Life of Jaco Pastorius*, Miller Freeman, San Francisco, 1995
Nicholson, S, *Jazz-Rock: A History*, Canongate, Edinburgh, 2001
Tingen, P, *Miles Beyond: The Electric Explorations of Miles Davis, 1967–1991*, Billboard, New York, 2003

End of the 20th century

Mandel, H, *Future Jazz*, Oxford University Press, Oxford, 1999

Index

Page numbers in italic refer to illustrations.

271

Photo credits

12-Rue des Archives *14*-DR *16*-Rue des Archives *19*-Rue des Archives *20*-Rue des Archives *21*-Rue des Archives *22*-Archives Larbor/DR *25*-Corbis Sygma *27*-DR *32*-DR *36*-Ph. Coll. Bisceglia/Mephisto *38*-Rue des Archives *39*-William Ransom Hogan Jazz Archive, Tulane University Library/Archives Larbor/DR *41*-William Ransom Hogan Jazz Archive, Tulane University Library/Archives Larbor/DR *42*-Rue des Archives *44*-Ph. Bettmann/Corbis Sygma *47*-Rue des Archives *50*-Rue des Archives *54*-Rue des Archives *60*-Rue des Archives *65*-Rue des Archives *66*-Rue des Archives *68*-Rue des Archives *72*-Rue des Archives/ADAGP, Paris 2001 *74*-The Granger Collection/Archives Larbor/DR *76*-Rue des Archives *79*-Rue des Archives *80*-Rue des Archives *85*-Rue des Archives *89*-Rue des Archives *90*-Rue des Archives *92*-Rue des Archives *95*-Ph. Stock/Magnum *96*-Franck Driggs Collection/Magnum *98*-Rue des Archives *101*-Rue des Archives *102*-Dessin Hugo Geliert/ DR *104*-Rue des Archives *106*-Ph. Bettman/Corbis Sygma *108*-Rue des Archives *110*-Rue des Archives *111*-Rue des Archives *113*-Savoy/DR *115*-Rue des Archives *117*-Rue des Archives *118*-Rue des Archives *119*-DR *120*-Palladium-Latin Jazz and Dance Records/DR *122*-Rue des Archives *124 top l*-Mephisto *124 top l*-Ph. Chenz/Mephisto **bottom** *l*-Rue des Archives *125 top l*-Rue des Archives *125 bottom r*-Rue des Archives *126*-Rue des Archives *129*-Cooper Square Press, New York/DR *131*-Rue des Archives *132*-Ph. G. Le Querrec/Magnum *136*-DR *138*-Fantasy Inc, 1987/DR *139*-Rue des Archives *140*-DR *143*-Rue des Archives *147*-Caney, 1995/DR *148*-Rue des Archives *150-* Ph. Sas/Mephisto *152*-Ph. Mosaôc Image/Corbis Sygma *154*-Ph. Chenz/Mephisto *155*-Ph. Chenz/Mephisto *156*-Rue des Archives *161*-Capitol Records Inc/DR *162*-Verve, 1959/DR *165*-Rue des Archives *166*-Rue des Archives *168*-Rue des Archives *171*-DR *172*-Rue des Archives *173*-Ph. Horace/Mephisto *174*-Ph. Coll. Bisceglia/Mephisto *177*-Rue des Archives *178*-Courtesy of Atlantic Records *180*-Ph. Francis Wolff, Sony Music/DR *181*-Ph. Jan Persson, Sony Music/DR *183*-DR *185*-Rue des Archives *188*-Ph. Chenz/Mephisto *190*-Rue des Archives *192*-Ph. Trombert/Mephisto *194*-Mephisto *195*-Ph. Horace/Mephisto *197*-Rue des Archives *199*-Ph. Dutihl/Mephisto *200*-Ph. Trombert/Mephisto *202 top l*-ECM Records GMBH, 1974/DR *202 bottom r*-ECM Records GMBH, 1975/DR *203*-ECM Records GMBH, 1978/DR *204*-Ph. Trombert/Mephisto *207*-Mephisto *208*-Arista Records Inc, 1978/DR *209*-Black Saint, 1986/DR *210*-Ph. Dutihl/Mephisto *213*-Ph. Horace/Mephisto *214*-Mephisto *215* G. Le Querrec/Magnum *217 top*-Ph. Dutihl/Mephisto *217 bottom r*-Mephisto *220*-Ph. G. Le Querrec/Magnum *221*-RCA Records/DR *222*-Ph. G. Le Querrec/Magnum *226*-Ph. Erling Mandelmann/Rapho *228*-Mephisto *230*-A&M Records Inc, 1984/DR *232*-Mephisto *235*-Ph. Marc Hom, Warner Bros Records Inc, 1994/DR *238*-Mephisto *241*-Mephisto *242*-Capitol Records Inc, 1993/DR *245*-Mephisto *248*-Mephisto *250*-Courtesy of Price Club Productions *252*-Omd/Jazzibao/DR *253*-Mephisto *254*-Mephisto *256*-Mephisto

We reserve the right to reproduce illustrations in cases where we have been unable to obtain contact details for the copyright holder despite research.